Browning Music

Browning Music

A Descriptive Catalog of the Music Related to Robert Browning and Elizabeth Barrett Browning in the Armstrong Browning Library: 1972

compiled by
Sally Keith Carroll East

Armstrong Browning Library   1973   Waco, Texas

International Standard Book Number: 0-914108-01-8

Library of Congress Catalog Card Number: 73-84533

Armstrong Browning Library, Baylor University, Waco, Texas 76706

Preface

This catalog is intended to be useful in three ways. The first way addresses itself to the Browning scholar who wants to learn how Browning poetry has been used by musicians. This is why the main entries of the catalog are arranged according to poem titles and why the lines of poetry the composer set to music are indicated. The second way the catalog can be useful is to the musicologist who wants to study the history and development of Browning music. It is hoped that this catalog will attract the young musician seeking a thesis or research topic to analyze and examine the music in depth. The third way this catalog can be useful is to the musician who is looking for music to perform. Most of the music in this catalog can serve the purposes of the young student musician of high school age. For this reason the performance medium index is included.

Finally, it is hoped that this catalog will create interest in Browning poetry among composers of a serious nature so that music such as that by Charles Ives, Ned Rorem, Egon Wellesz, and Norman Dello Joio, who represent only a small portion of the composers listed in this catalog, may be written and added to the collection of Browning music.

Acknowledgments

I wish to express my appreciation to those persons who helped me locate music which the Armstrong Browning Library needed to add to its collection. To William Lichtenwanger, Reference Librarian of the Music Division at the Library of Congress, I am grateful for his constant help and advice in securing the fifty-two pieces of music which the Library of Congress has that the Armstrong Browning Library needed. To Mabel Cortright I offer my thanks for the research she did to determine that the Library of Congress had these fifty-two pieces. To Maiva Dickson I am thankful for the help she gave in locating elusive music publishers and composers. To individuals, libraries, and publishers who gave music to the Armstrong Browning Library and who are acknowledged in the main entry sections of the catalog, I offer a special appreciation for their generosity and kindness. In addition to the Library of Congress, I wish to thank the staffs and librarians of other libraries who helped find music for our collection: Boston Public Library (Ruth Bleeker, Curator of Music), Wellesley College Library (Hannah D. French, Research Librarian), and Yale University (Isabel A. Clark, Assistant Librarian).

I wish to acknowledge the assistance I received from the staff of the Armstrong Browning Library; to Sharon Jarrard, former Acting Librarian, I am grateful for the help she provided toward solving the problems which occurred during the project. To Bessie Hess Smith, Music Librarian of Baylor Crouch Music Library, I offer my appreciation for the time and sound advice she gave me when cataloging the collection. I wish to thank Gladys Hudson of the Baylor English faculty for her help in locating lines of poetry for some of the Elizabeth Barrett Browning settings. I am particularly indebted to Jack William Herring, Director of the Armstrong Browning Library, who requested this project initially and provided the necessary resources for its completion.

The publication of this catalog was made possible through a gift by Mrs. John Leddy-Jones.

Illustrations

Original manuscript of "New Year's Hymn" by John Beach. RB350
See description on page xi

Original manuscript of "New Year's Hymn" by John Beach. RB350

John Beach was a composer from Boston living in Asolo, Italy in 1926 in the villa once owned by Robert Browning's son, Robert Wiedemann Barrett Browning. The villa (*La Torricella*) was referred to by Robert Browning as "Pippa's Tower." In 1926 when Andrew Joseph Armstrong led the first Browning Pilgrimage to Asolo, Mr. and Mrs. John Beach invited the Pilgrimage Party to this villa. Mr. Beach played for them the introduction to his opera *Pippa's Holiday,* and a guest of the Beaches, the concert singer Signorina Una Buenos, sang the "New Year's Hymn" which is herein illustrated.

The manuscript was given to the Armstrong Browning Library by Ola Jones Nisbet (d. 1929) who was a member of the 1926 Browning Pilgrimage and who was present during the event mentioned above. Mrs. Nisbet organized the Kansas City Browning Society and founded the Browning Memorial Gardens in Kansas City, Missouri and in Charlotte, North Carolina. She lectured on Browning before colleges and churches in several states. It is from her edition of *Browning's PIPPA PASSES* that these notes were compiled.

19, Warwick Crescent.
W. Aug. 3. '83.

Dear Miss Hickey,

First of all, I am very glad you are enjoying Shalstone, as I hope the weather — and above all the Lady there — help you to do.

Putting the "genius" on the pedestal usurped by the "germ" means — or tries to mean — substituting eventually the true notion of Strafford's endeavour and performance in the world, for what he conceives to be the ignoble and distorted conception of these by his contemporary judges.

Macready — nobody else, — played "Strafford": Vandenhoff — and afterwards, for a single night, Elton played "Pym".

I have no vanity about such a trifle as the "Lilt" — at all events, when you care

Letter from Robert Browning to Emily Henrietta Hickey. RB510, RB512
See description on page xiv

xii

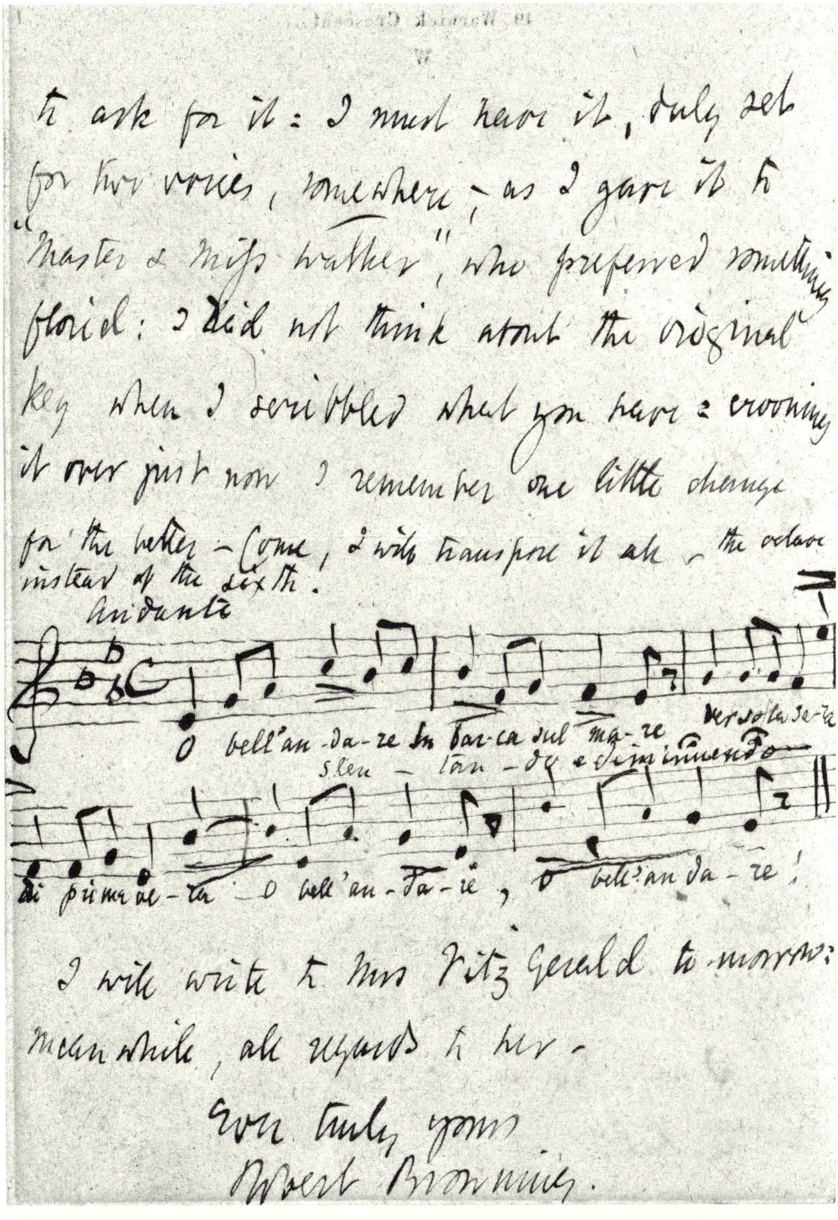

to ask for it: I must have it, duly set
for two voices, somewhere, — as I gave it to
"Master & Miss Walker", who preferred something
florid: I did not think about the original
key when I scribbled what you have — crooning
it over just now I remember one little change
for the better — Come, I will transpose it all — the octave
instead of the sixth.

Andante

O bell'an-da-re in bar-ca sul ma-re, Ver-so la se-ra
Stentando e diminuendo
di pri-ma-ve-ra — O bell'an-da-re, O bell'an-da-re!

I will write to Mrs FitzGerald to-morrow:
meanwhile, all regards to her —

Ever truly yours
Robert Browning.

Stentando e diminuendo.

Di pri-ma-ve-ra—O bell'an-da-re. O bell'an-da........re.

Letter from Robert Browning to Emily Henrietta Hickey hitherto unpublished. RB510, RB512

Aug. 3, '83.

Dear Miss Hickey,

First of all, I am very glad you are enjoying [Stratstone], as I hope the weather—and am sure the Lady there—help you to do.

"Putting the genius on the pedestal usurped by the [Term]" means—or tries to mean—substituting eventually the true notion of Strafford's endeavor and performance in the world, for what he conceives to be the ignoble and distorted conception of these by his contemporary judges.

Macready,—nobody else,—played "Strafford:" Vandenhoff—and afterwards, for a single night, Elton played Pym.

I have no vanity about such a trifle as the "Lilt"—at all events, when you care to ask for it: I must have it, only set for two voices, somewhere—as I gave it to "Master & Miss Walker," who preferred something florid: I did not think about the original key when I scribbled what you have: crooning it over just now I remember one little change for the better—(one, I will transpose it all—the octave instead of the sixth.

I will write to Mrs. Fitzgerald tomorrow: meanwhile, all regards to her.

Ever truly yours

Robert Browning.

Emily Henrietta Hickey (1845-1924) was the co-founder with Frederick James Furnivall of the London Browning Society. She became the first honorary secretary, a member of its committee, and one who tried to clarify Browning's works. She made an annotated edition of *Strafford* and it is with this that the above letter is concerned. (William Clyde DeVane and Kenneth Leslie Knickerbocker, editors, *New Letters of Robert Browning,* [New Haven: Yale University Press, 1950], p. 281, n.1, *2*).

This letter is accompanied by the music which appears below the signature (key of G major), and which is not written on the letter stationary but which is a separate piece of music on music staff paper which seems to have been included in the letter to Miss Hickey. Both the letter and the music insert (and a photograph of Browning) are framed together and were given to the Armstrong Browning Library as part of the Shields Collection.

The two musical examples are in Browning's handwriting and, I believe, are the only extant pieces of music which he wrote. *See* the biographical notes about Robert Browning's musical knowledge and training, p. 352.

For permission to print this letter, grateful acknowledgment is made to John Murray, London.

Contents

I

Introduction

This catalog is a description of the music collection in the Armstrong Browning Library (ABL) related to either Robert Browning (RB) or Elizabeth Barrett Browning (EBB). Chapter II contains the main or primary entries of the music related to RB; Chapter III contains the main entries for EBB; Chapter IV is an alphabetical listing by composer, arranger, or editor of the RB and EBB entries; Chapter V is an alphabetical listing by title of the RB and EBB entries; Chapter VI is a section arranged according to the performance medium of the setting; Chapter VII is the biographical section for the composers; Chapter VIII is a list of music the ABL wants to acquire.

The ABL Music Collection consists primarily of music, both published and unpublished, which is based on the poetry of RB or EBB; however, there are pieces such as entry number RB300 which is based on three letters in Robert *Browning*'s name, or entry RB487 which is an orchestral piece entitled *Robert Browning Overture,* or RB1 and RB530 whose composers are the subjects of poems by RB, or as EBB36 and EBB53 whose lyrics are mistakenly ascribed to EBB on the music. In such cases appropriate explanations are provided.

Main Entry

For the main entry, compositions were listed most often according to the poem to which they are related. The form of the poem title is taken from the following editions, the first four of which were seen through the press by either RB or EBB:

(1) *The Poetical Works of Robert Browning* (16 vols.; London: Smith, Elder, & Co., 1889);

(2) *Asolando: Fancies and Facts* by Robert Browning (London: Smith, Elder, & Co., 1894);

(3) *Poems* by Elizabeth Barrett Browning (3 vols., 4th ed.; London: Chapman & Hall, 1856);

(4) *Last Poems* by Elizabeth Barrett Browning (London: Chapman and Hall, 1862); and

(5) *New Poems by Robert Browning and Elizabeth Barrett Browning* edited by Sir Frederic G. Kenyon (London: Smith, Elder, & Co., 1914).

Where the poem title appears in the Contents of these editions in one form and above the poem in another form, the form over the poem is chosen. Where the poem as listed is actually composed of several short poems, each of which is subtitled, the individual parts of the poem are given by subtitle in the order in which they appear in the volume of poetry, not in alphabetical order. For example, "Cavalier Tunes" is composed of three short poems, each of which is subtitled as follows: I. Marching Along, II. Give a Rouse, and III. Boot and Saddle. In this catalog these three short poems appear under the poem, "Cavalier Tunes" in the same order in which they appear in the volume of poetry, that is, the first subtitle to appear is "Marching Along," the second is "Give a Rouse," and the third is "Boot and Saddle." Where a composition could not be listed according to a poem title, the title of the composition is used; it is accompanied with an appropriate explanation.

There are 594 entries related to RB and 290 to EBB. Entries are first listed according to poem titles or composition titles and then alphabetized by the name of the composer. Complete names of the composers are provided when possible. If research produces the full name of the composer, when only a partial name is given on the music, the additions are placed in brackets. Anonymous entries are alphabetized according to the title of the composition. Where a composer wrote several settings related to the same poem and bound them together, the settings are listed as a single entry; however, where a composer wrote several settings about a poem and bound them separately, each setting is listed and assigned an entry number. For purposes of this compilation, a setting is considered to be a unique and specific musical composition which may be considered complete in itself. For an example of a composer's several settings related to the same poem and bound together see RB167; for an example of a composer's settings related to the same poem and bound separately see items RB134-RB141. Where the same poem is arranged in several settings which differ only in key, or where settings by the same composer are published in different editions or bear different imprints, such settings are numbered individually in the present catalog, that is, a change of key, a different edition, or a different imprint is sufficient reason for the composition to be treated as unique and specific.

The information given for each entry is intended to identify the entry positively so that a reader can determine if a copy located elsewhere is an exact copy of the one located in the ABL. The information given is in the following order:

(1)   composer;

(2)   title of setting as written on the music;

(3)   key or key signature found at the beginning of setting; when possible, opus numbers and/or the number of a setting when it appears as part of a group of settings is included; this information appears after item three or four;

(4)   group of compositions from which setting comes as written on the music;

(5) imprint, including the plate number, as written on the music; punctuation and spacing are not changed; and

(6) Broughton number that refers to the setting listed in the Broughton *Bibliography* which corresponds *strictly* to the setting found in the ABL; the Broughton number, for example, E3, refers to item 3, section E ("Musical Settings to Browning's Poems"), pp. 389-402 from *Robert Browning: A Bibliography, 1830-1950* compiled by Leslie Nathan Broughton, Clark Sutherland Northup, and Robert Pearsall (Ithaca: Cornell University Press, 1953).

Where there seemed to be an error of wording or otherwise in the Broughton *Bibliography* and therefore only a probability exists that the Broughton setting is the same as that in the ABL, the Broughton number is not given. In addition to the aforementioned six items, the following information is also given:

(1) where the lines of poetry set to music are located in the poem, the line numbers based on the previously listed editions from which the poem title is taken; the following abbreviated references used are: volume number only indicates either a volume of *The Poetical Works of Robert Browning* or a volume of *Poems* by EBB, *Asolando* indicates *Asolando: Fancies and Facts, New Poems* indicates *New Poems by Robert Browning and Elizabeth Barrett Browning,* and *Letters* indicates *The Letters of Robert Browning and Elizabeth Barrett Barrett* (2 vols.; London: John Murray, 1899);

(2) form of setting; and

(3) performance medium of setting.

All titles of music, that is, entry title and group title, follow standard capitalization. The spelling is not changed except that *&* is written as *and,* and numbers are spelled out. Punctuation is not changed except that it is added where necessary for clarification. No title of music is given in italics. A title is placed in quotation marks only if the quotation marks appear on the music.

For solo songs where the composer has specified the type of voice, only the range is given; but in songs where no specific voice has been indicated the *tessitura* is also given. The tessitura is the general compass of the song, that is, where most of the notes lie. The letter *r* indicates range and the letter *t* indicates tessitura. In songs where I determined the type of voice, it is placed in brackets. The types of voices referred to are: low (female r: $a - c^2$, male r: $A - c^1$), medium low (female r: $b - d^2$, male r: $B - d^1$), medium (female r: $c^1 - e^2$, male r: $c - e^1$), medium high (female r: $d^1 - f^2$, male r: $D - f^1$), high (female r: $e^1 - g^2$, male r: $E - g^1$). (Music for low voice corresponds to music for bass and contralto; medium voice corresponds to music for baritone and mezzo soprano; and high voice corresponds to tenor and soprano.) The indication of notes is based on Middle C being written lower case, superior one, i.e., c^1. The octave below Middle C is written with lower case letters, i.e., c, d, e, f, etc. The second octave below Middle C is indicated by upper case letters, i.e., C, D, etc. The third octave below Middle C is indicated by upper case letters, subscript one, i.e., C_1, D_1, etc. The octave above Middle C is indicated with lower case letters, superior two, i.e., c^2, d^2, etc. The second octave above Middle C is indicated with lower case letters, superior three, i.e., c^3, d^3, etc.

Where the composer did not specify the kind of keyboard instrument to be used, the term *keyboard* is used.

Other information which aids in the specific identification of the entry is also given, but not necessarily in this order:

(a)   editor;

(b)   edition;

(c)   arranger;

(d)   librettist;

(e)   translator;

(f)   descriptions of the entry written on the music;

(g)   facts about the group of which the entry is a part, such as form (e.g., song cycle), series number, kind and number (e.g., The Orpheus, a Collection of Glees and Part-Songs for Male Voices, no. 320); and

(h)   the copyright holder if other than the publisher (the copyright holder precedes the copyright date and is *not* followed by a comma).

Information which is written on the music or which is kept with the music in the ABL Collection and which I deemed valuable or significant is given in the note at the end of the entry. Also found in this note are explanations of misleading or confusing information in the main entry. The reader may assume that each item is not bound with other music or materials unless stated otherwise in the note. The number of copies of each entry is not indicated except when information is given about a particular copy.

Entry Number Alterations

There are 594 entries related to RB and 290 to EBB. Music which the ABL received after entry numbers had been assigned are included in the main entry section, but with certain alterations in the numbering sequence. RB entries begin with RB1 and end with RB592. Additional entry numbers are as follows: RB7.1, RB57.1, and RB291.1. The entry number RB27 is omitted. EBB entries begin with EBB1 and end with EBB289. Additional entry numbers are as follows: EBB11.1 and EBB164.1. The entry number EBB244 is omitted.

Composer, Arranger, and Editor Entry

The composer, arranger, and editor entry (Chapter IV) is a combination of the RB and EBB main entries and is arranged alphabetically by composer, arranger, or editor. The information given is in the following order:

(1) composer, arranger, or editor of the entry;
(2) title of setting;
(3) form and/or performance medium of setting; for solo songs the type of voice and accompaniment is given; where I determined the type of voice, the type of voice is placed in brackets; where the composer did not specifiy the kind of keyboard instrument to be used, the term *keyboard* is used; for larger works, such as operas, cantatas, and orchestral pieces, only the form is given; and
(4) main entry number.

Also included are the names of editors and compilers of the group of settings of which the main entry is a part and of transcribers, librettists and lyricists (when other than RB or EBB), and any other persons listed on the setting. The only information given for these names is the main entry number(s).

Title Entry

The title entry is an alphabetical listing by the title as it is written in the main entry. RB and EBB entries are combined. The information appears in the following order: (1) title of setting; (2) composer; (3) form and/or performance medium of setting, the same as in the composer, arranger, and editor entry; and (4) main entry number.

For the title of the group of settings from which the main entry is taken (except for titles of song cycles, which are followed by the information listed in the above paragraph), only the main entry number is given except where additional information is necessary to distinguish the group title from another title. For example, there are many individual settings which are from a group of settings entitled *Songs*. In such cases, the name of the composer who wrote the individual setting is added to distinguish among the many collections named *Songs*.

Performance Medium Entry

The performance medium entry is an arrangement of the RB and EBB entries according to the kinds of performers the entry requires. There are three main divisions: vocal music, instrumental music, and recitations. The vocal music division contains five kinds of music: solo voice music, duets, quartets, choral music, and dramatic forms. The music under solo voice is composed of entries which employ but are not limited to the solo voice, so that not only songs and song cycles can be found, but also any music which employs the solo voice can be found, such as chamber music using solo voice or choral works using solo voice. All titles are listed so that a song cycle as well as the songs within the cycle can be found. There are six kinds of solo voice music listed:

    (1)   solo high voice (high voice, soprano, and tenor);

    (2)   solo medium high voice (medium high voice, high or medium voice, and tenor or baritone);

    (3)   solo medium voice (medium voice, mezzo soprano, and baritone);

    (4)   solo medium low voice (medium low voice, low or medium voice, low or middle voice, baritone or bass, baritone or contralto, and mezzo soprano or contralto); and

    (5)   solo low voice (low voice, bass, and contralto).

The music for chorus is composed of entries which employ but are not limited to a chorus, as is the case with the solo voice music. The five kinds of choruses which are listed are (1) women's chorus, (2) male chorus, (3) mixed chorus, (4) children's chorus, and (5) unison chorus. Except for dramatic forms such as cantatas and operas, all music requiring a chorus is listed under one of these choruses.

The four kinds of dramatic forms are (1) cantatas, (2) oratorios, (3) operas and operettas, and (4) other dramatic forms (musical plays, dances, and incidental music).

The instrumental music contains three categories: music using solo instruments, chamber music, and orchestral music. The music under solo instruments is composed of entries which employ but are not limited to a single solo instrument. There are eleven headings of solo instruments:

    (1)   piano;

    (2)   piano (four hands);

    (3)   harpsichord and clavichord;

    (4)   organ;

    (5)   flute;

    (6)   oboe;

    (7)   clarinet;

    (8)   violin;

    (9)   cello;

   (10)   harp; and

   (11)   other solo instruments (piccolo, flageolet, bassoon, guitar, harmonium, cymbal, and double bass).

Songs and other vocal music with piano accompaniment are not included in the piano entries unless other instruments are also part of the accompaniment or if an instrument other than piano is given as an alternative to the piano. Also listed under the piano heading is instrumental music and recitations which require a piano accompaniment. The term *keyboard* is used when the composer did not specify the kind of keyboard instrument to be used.

The remaining ten headings of solo instruments include all entries which require the specified instrument as a solo instrument.

There are two kinds of chamber music listed. The first is music using string quartet. The second is music for chamber music instruments other than string quartet. In this second kind the term *chamber music* is used in a broad sense to include music written for three to nine solo performers. Included is dance music, incidental music, recitatives, songs which call for more than two performers, and duets which call for more than three performers.

The orchestral music section includes entries which originally call for orchestra even though the ABL only has the piano-vocal score. In such cases, this fact is given.

The final division is composed of entries which employ a reader, reciter, or speaker.

Within each group of specific kind of performer the entries are arranged alphabetically by composer.

Biographical Data

The biographical section provides a biographical sketch arranged alphabetically of the composers found in the RB and EBB main entries.

Desiderata

The desiderata is a list of music believed related to either RB or EBB which is desired for addition to the ABL Collection. The list is arranged alphabetically by composer. The performance medium and imprint are given when known. The reference(s) in which the music was mentioned is also given. Any help the reader can offer to verify and/or correct the information in the Desiderata will be appreciated.

II

Musical Settings Related to Robert Browning

Key to Abbreviations and Symbol

ABL Armstrong Browning Library

EBB Elizabeth Barrett Browning

n.d. no date

op. opus

pl. no. plate number

r range

RB Robert Browning

t tessistura, i.e., the general compass of a song or where most of the notes lie

unacc. unaccompanied

+ this symbol is used for easy location of the settings which are listed in Broughton, *Bibliography*

For the complete description and explanation of this chapter, read pages 1-4 of Chapter I.

ABT VOGLER
(After He Has Been Extemporizing upon the
Musical Instrument of His Invention)

RB1. True, Latham. Abt Vogler, key of C major. From Accompanied Readings by Latham True. Portland, Maine: Cressey and Allen, Latham True c1932. No pl. no.

VII, 101-108: 1-96
Recitation for reader with piano.

RB2. Vogler, [George Joseph]. (L'Abe Vogler). The Request,[1] key of C major. Manuscript, [Boston: G. Granpues], n.d. No pl. no.

---

[1]*The Request* is herein listed because the composer is that Vogler of whom RB writes in his poem *Abt Vogler*; the lyricist is unknown (I found no evidence suggesting the lyrics to be by RB).

Song for [high] voice with keyboard.
r: e^1 - g^2 t: c^2 - g^2

Note: On the front cover is written "Boston, published and sold by G. Granpues, at his Music Store No 6 Franklin St."

RB3. —————. The Request,[2] key of C major. Manuscript, no place: no publisher, n.d. No pl. no.

Song for [high] voice with keyboard.
r: e^1 - g^2 t: c^2 - g^2

Note: RB3 appears to be a copy of RB2 except that there is no indication of the publisher.

AFTER

RB4. +Somervell, Arthur. After, key of D major, no. 7. From the song cycle, A Broken Arc. London: Boosey & Co., c1923. H. 10770. E2

VI, 186: 1-18
Song for [medium] voice with piano.
r: b - e^2 t: b - b^1

Note: RB4 is bound in A Broken Arc.

THE AGAMEMNON OF AESCHYLUS

RB5. +Bantock, Granville. O Zeus the King, from the "Agamemnon" of Aeschylus, key of A minor. From The Oxford Choral Songs, Three Choruses for Male Voices, no. 615. London: Oxford University Press, c1930. No pl. no. E3

XII, 285-286: 375-388
Part-song for male chorus (tenor I and II, bass I and II) with short score for keyboard.

AMONG THE ROCKS. *See* JAMES LEE'S WIFE VII

AMPHIBIAN. *See* FIFINE AT THE FAIR

APPEARANCES

RB6. +Rogers, Clara Kathleen. Appearances, key of E-flat major, no. 2. From Browning Songs, Second Series, op. 32. Edition Schmidt, no. 24. Boston: Arthur P. Schmidt, c1900. A.P.S. 5037b. E4

XIV, 70: 1-12
Song for [high] voice with keyboard.
r: c^1 - a^2 t: a^1 - a^2

Note: RB6 is bound in Browning Songs, Second Series.

---

[2]*Ibid.*

ASOLANDO. *See* titles of individual poems

ASOLANDO, "EPILOGUE" FROM. *See* EPILOGUE

AT THE "MERMAID"

RB7. +Bickford, Zahr Myron. I Find Earth Not Gray but Rosy, key of D-flat major. New York: Wm. A. Pond & Co., c1917. No pl. no. E5

XIV, 36: 93-96
Song for soprano or tenor with keyboard.
r: a^1 - a^2

AVENGE THE GOOD SHIP MAINE[3]

RB7.1. Browning, [Robert and Elizabeth Barrett]. Avenge the Good Ship Maine, key of C major. Written and composed by "The Brownings." Arranged by R. M. Stults. Xerox copy, Philadelphia: M. D. Swisher, c1898. No pl. no.

Song for [medium high] voice with keyboard.
r: e^1 - f^2 t: g^1 - e^2

Note: The Spanish-American War began with the sinking of the ship Maine on Feb. 15, 1898. The lyrics of the song are explicitly about this event and neither RB or EBB were alive at this time.

BAD DREAMS I

RB8. +Bateman, Alice. In My Sleep, "Last Night I Saw You in My Sleep," key of G-flat major. London: Joseph Williams, n.d. N. 10422. E6

Asolando, 16: 1-8
Song for [low] voice with keyboard.
r: b - $f\#^2$ t: d^1 - gb^1

Note: RB8 is autographed "Alice Bateman."

A BEAN-STRIPE: ALSO APPLE-EATING.
See FERISHTAH'S FANCIES

A BLOT IN THE 'SCUTCHEON

RB9. +Branscombe, Gena. There's a Woman Like a Dew-drop, key of E-flat major. Boston: Arthur P. Schmidt, c1911. A.P.S. 9138-5. E8

IV, 21-22: 81-92
Song for high voice with piano.
r: d^1 - a^2

---

[3]This is not the title of an RB poem; it is herein listed because the words are attributed to "The Brownings" on the music. The Library of Congress lists it with the music related to RB and EBB.

RB10.   +Bullard, Frederic Field. There's a Woman Like a Dewdrop,
         key of A-flat major. Boston: The Boston Music Company,
         G. Schirmer, Jr. c1901. B.M.C.617 and 617a. E9

         IV, 21-22: 81-92
         Song for high voice, violin, and piano. With violin part.
         r: c^1 - ab^2

RB11.   Chanter, Arthur. There's a Woman Like a Dewdrop, key of
         C-sharp major. Melbourne: Allan & Co. Ltd., n.d. Pl. no. 59.

         IV, 21-22: 81-92
         Song for bass or contralto with piano.
         r: a - $d\#^2$

RB12.   De Koven, Reginald. There's a Woman Like a Dewdrop, key
         of G major, op. 61. New-York: G. Schirmer, c1890. Pl. no.
         8920.

         IV, 21-22: 81-92
         Song for soprano or tenor with piano.
         r: $d\#^1$ - a^2

RB13.   Hadley, Henry K[imball]. There's a Woman Like a Dew-drop,
         key of C major, op. 12, no. 8 [only]. From Songs by Henry
         K. Hadley. Boston: Arthur P. Schmidt, c1903. A.P.S.6242-4.

         IV, 21-22: 81-92
         Song for [medium] voice with keyboard.
         r: b - f^2 (optional g^2)   t: c^1 - d^2

RB14.   +Lewis, Leo Rich. Symphonic Prelude to Robert Browning's
         Tragedy, a Blot in the 'Scutcheon, key of D major, op. 7. From
         The Music of Tufts College . . . Serial Number Sixty-Seven.
         Tufts College: Tufts Music, L. R. Lewis c1928. No pl. no.
         E12

         IV, 3-70
         Symphonic prelude for orchestra. Full score. No parts.

2 flutes	horns I-IV (in F)	violins I and II
piccolo	trumpets I and II	viola
oboe	(in F)	cello
English horn	trombones I-III	double bass
clarinets I and II	tuba	
(in A)	timpani	
2 bassoons	harp	
contrabassoon		

RB15.   +Mackenzie, A[lexander] C[ampbell]. There's a Woman Like
         a Dew-drop, key of D major. London: Novello and Company,
         Limited, n.d. Pl. no. 7032. E14

IV, 21-22: 81-92
Song for [high] voice with harp or piano.
r: f#^{1} - a^2 t: a^1 - f#^{2}

Note: Broughton, *Bibliography* gives 1885 as the date of publication.

BOOT AND SADDLE. *See* CAVALIER TUNES III

THE BOY AND THE ANGEL

RB16.   Beringer, Marjorie. The Boy and the Angel, key of F major. Manuscript, no place: no publisher, n.d. No pl. no.

V, 19: 1-5
Chant for [unison] voice[s] with unspecified keyboard (?) instrument.

BY THE FIRESIDE. *See also* JAMES LEE'S WIFE II

BY THE FIRE-SIDE

RB17.   +Bantock, Granville. By the Fireside, key of C major. Swan Edition, no. 15. London: Swan & Co., c1921. S.&Co.W.&W. Ltd.2777. E15

VI, 136-137: 186-200
Song for high voice with piano.
r: c^1 - g^2

RB18.   +—————. By the Fireside, key of E-flat major. Swan Edition, no. 15. London: Swan & Co., c1921. S.&Co.W.&W.Ltd. 2778. E15

VI, 136-137: 186-200
Song for low voice with piano.
r: a - e^2

CALIBAN UPON SETEBOS; OR,
NATURAL THEOLOGY IN THE ISLAND

RB19.   +Bantock, Granville. Caliban upon Setebos, key of C major. Berners Edition. London: Joseph Williams Limited, c1935. W.14. E17

VII, 149: 1, 2
Solo for piano.

A CAMEL-DRIVER. *See* FERISHTAH'S FANCIES

CAVALIER TUNES

I.　Marching Along

RB20.　+Bantock, Granville. Marching Along, key of F major. From The Orpheus, a Collection of Glees and Part-Songs for Male Voices, no. 320. London: Novello and Company, Limited, c1898. No pl. no. E18.1

VI, 3-4: 1-24
Part-song for male chorus (tenor I and II, bass I and II) with piano (for rehearsal only).

RB21.　+Boyle, George F[rederick]. Marching Along, key of G major From Two Songs with Piano Accompaniment. New York: G. Schirmer, c1911. Pl. no. 22322. E19

VI, 3-4: 1-24
Song for bass with piano.
r: B - d^1 (optional e^1)

RB22.　+Branscombe, Gena. Marching Along! key of A major. New York: G. Schirmer, c1907. Pl. no. 19593. E20

VI, 3-4: 1-24
Song for medium voice with piano.
r: b - d^2

RB23.　+Dansie, Redgewell. Marching Along, key of E-flat major, no. 1. From Cavalier Tunes by Robert Browning. London: Stainer & Bell, Ltd., Redgewell Dansie c1914. St.&B.1731. E21

VI, 3-4: 1-24
Song for [medium] voice with piano.
r: c^1 - f^2　　t: d^1 - d^2

Note: RB23 is bound in the above mentioned Cavalier Tunes.

RB24.　+Drakeford, Louis. Marching Along, key of E-flat major. From Three Cavalier Tunes by Robert Browning. London: Winthrop Rogers, Ltd., Hawkes & Son c1929. W.R.4512. E22

VI, 3-4: 1-24
Song for [medium] voice with piano.
r: c^1 - e^2　　t: e^1 - c^2

RB25.　+Harrison, Julius. Marching Along, key of D minor. From Four Cavalier Tunes. London: Winthrop Rogers Edition, Hawkes & Son c1930. W.R.4616. E23

VI, 3-4: 1-24
Song for tenor or baritone with piano.
r: c#^{1} - f^2

RB26.   +McLeod, Robert. *March Them Along*, key of F major, no. 26.
From A Heritage of Song, a Song Book for Adolescent Boys,
edited and arranged by Robert McLeod. Curwen Edition, no.
6351. London: J. Curwen & Sons Ltd., Robert McLeod
c1932. Pl. no. 6351. E24

VI, 3-4: 1-24
Song for unison boys' chorus with piano.

Note: RB26 is bound in A Heritage of Song. Broughton,
Bibliography gives the title as "Marching Along."

RB28.   +Stanford, C[harles] Villiers. *Marching Along*, key of A-flat
major, no. 1 [only]. From Three Cavalier Songs, op. 17.
London: Boosey & Co, n.d. No pl. no. E25

VI, 3-4: 1-24
Song for baritone solo, male chorus (tenor I and II, bass I
and II) with piano.

Note: Broughton, *Bibliography* gives [1882] as the possible
publication date.

RB29.   Sykes, Harold H. *Marching Along*, key of A-flat major. Curwen
Edition 72635. London: J. Curwen & Sons Ltd., c1967. Pl.
no. 72635.

VI, 3-4: 1-6, 19-24
Song for unison choir (with optional descant) with keyboard.

Note: RB29 was the gift of Roberton Publications March 27,
1972.

RB30.   +White, Maude Valèrie. *Marching Along*, key of A major.
London: Chappell & Co. Ltd., c1897. Pl. no. 20445. E26

VI, 3-4: 1-24
Song for [medium] voice wth piano.
r: d^1 - d^2 t: d^1 - b^1

RB31.   +————————. *Marching Along*, key of G major. London: Chappell & Co Ltd., c1897. Pl. no. 20445. E26

VI, 3-4: 1-24
Song for [high] voice with piano.
r: e^1 - e^2 t: e^1 - c^2

II. Give a Rouse

RB32. +Arnott, A. Davidson. Give a Rouse, key of D major. London:
Novello & Company, Limited, c1893. Pl. no. 9736. E27

VI, 5: 1-20
Song for baritone or bass with keyboard.
r: a - e^2

RB33. +Bantock, Granville. Give a Rouse, key of F major. From The
Orpheus, a Collection of Glees and Part-Songs for Male Voices,
no. 321. London: Novello and Company, Limited, c1898. No
pl. no. E28

VI, 5: 1-20
Part-song for male chorus (tenor I and II, bass I and II)
with piano (for rehearsal only).

RB34. +Dansie, Redgewell. Give a Rouse, key of E-flat major, no. 2.
From Cavalier Tunes by Robert Browning. London: Stainer
& Bell, Ltd., Redgewell Dansie c1914. St.&B.1731. E29

VI, 5: 1-20
Song for [medium high] voice with piano.
r: bb - gb^2 t: g^1 - eb^2

Note: RB34 is bound in the above mentioned Cavalier Tunes.

RB35. +de Sousa, Leon. Give a Rouse! key of E-flat major. London:
Elkin & Co., Ltd., c1908. E.&Co.465. E30

VI, 5: 1-20
Song for [medium] voice with piano.
r: bb - f^2 t: eb^1 - c^2

RB36. +Drakeford, Louis. Give a Rouse, key of E-flat major. From
Three Cavalier Tunes by Robert Browning. London: Winthrop Rogers, Ltd., Hawkes & Son c1929. W.R.4513. E31

VI, 5: 1-20
Song for [medium high] voice with piano.
r: c^1 - e^2 t: e^1 - c^2

RB37. +Harrison, Julius. King Charles, key of A minor. From Four
Cavalier Tunes. London: Winthrop Rogers, Ltd., Hawkes &
Son c1930. W.R.4617. E32

VI, 5: 1-20
Song for baritone with piano.
r: c^1 - e^2

RB38. +Kernochan, Marshall. Give a Rouse! key of A-flat major. From Two Poems by Robert Browning. New York: G. Schirmer, c1908. Pl. no. 20615. E34

VI, 5: 1-20
Song for medium voice with piano.
r: c^1 - f^2

RB39. ————. King Charles, key of A-flat major. New York: Galaxy Music Corporation, c1936. G.M.705.

VI, 5: 1-20
Chorus for male chorus (tenor I and II, bass I and II) with piano.

RB40. +Liddle, Samuel. King Charles, key of B-flat major, no. 9. From Nine Songs by Samuel Liddle. London: Boosey & Co., c1897. H.1795. E35

VI, 5: 1-20
Song for [high] voice with piano.
r: b^b - f^2 t: f^1 - eb^2

Note: RB40 is bound in Nine Songs. Broughton, *Bibliography* gives the title as "Give a Rouse."

RB41. +Stanford, C[harles] Villiers. King Charles, key of D-flat major, no. 2 [only]. From Three Cavalier Songs, op. 17. London: Boosey & Co., n.d. No pl. no. E36

VI, 5: 1-20
Song for baritone solo, male chorus (tenor I and II, bass I and II) with piano.

Note: The ABL has 3 copies; in the bottom right corner of p. 7 in copies 2 and 3 are the numbers "10. 06." instead of "4. 24" as in copy 1. Broughton, *Bibliography* gives the title as "Give a Rouse."

RB42. +White, Maude Valérie. King Charles, Cavalier Song, key of G major. London: Boosey & Co., c1898. H.2201. E37

VI, 5: 1-20
Song for [medium] voice with piano.
r: d^1 - d^2 t: f^1 - d^2

Note: Broughton, *Bibliography* gives the title as "Give a Rouse."

III. Boot and Saddle

RB43. Bantock, Granville. Boot and Saddle, key of G major. From The Orpheus, a Collection of Glees and Part-Songs for Male Voices, no. 322. London: Novello and Company, Limited, c1899. No pl. no.

VI, 6: 1-16
Part-song for male chorus (tenor I and II, bass I and II) with
piano (for rehearsal only).

RB44.   +Branscombe, Gena. Boot and Saddle, key of D major. Boston:
Oliver Ditson Company, c1907. Pl. no. 5-32-66368-4. E39

VI, 6: 1-16
Song for medium voice with piano.
r: a - e^2

RB45.   +Dansie, Redgewell. Boot and Saddle, key of A minor, no. 3.
From Cavalier Tunes by Robert Browning. London: Stainer
& Bell, Ltd., Redgewell Dansie c1914. St.&B.1731. E40

VI, 6: 1-16
Song for [medium high] voice with piano.
r: c^1 - e^2 t: e^1 - c^2

Note: RB45 is bound in the above mentioned Cavalier Tunes.

RB46.   +Demuth, Norman. Boot and Saddle, key of G minor. From
The Oxford Choral Songs, no. 1044. London: Oxford University Press, c1930. No pl. no. E41

VI, 6: 1-16
Song for unison chorus with piano.

RB47.   +Drakeford, Louis. Boot and Saddle, key of B-flat major. From
Three Cavalier Tunes by Robert Browning. London: Winthrop Rogers, Ltd., Hawkes & Son c1929. W.R.4514. E42

VI, 6: 1-16
Song for [medium high] voice with piano.
r: c^1 - d^2 t: f^1 - d^2

RB48.   +Dyson, George. Boot, Saddle, to Horse, and Away! key of D
major. From The Year Book Press Series of Unison and Part-
Songs, edited by Martin Akerman, no. 209. London: H. F. W.
Deane & Sons The Year Book Press, Ltd., c1922. Pl. no. 209.
E43

VI, 6: 1-16
Song for unison chorus with piano.

RB49.   Easson, James. Boot, Saddle, to Horse and Away, key of B-flat
major. Curwen Edition, no. 72183. London: J. Curwen &
Sons Ltd., James Easson c1949. Pl. no. 72183.

VI, 6: 1-16
Song for unison chorus with piano.

RB50. +Harrison, Julius. Boot, Saddle, to Horse and Away, key of A major. From Four Cavalier Tunes. London: Winthrop Rogers, Ltd., Hawkes & Son c1930. W.R.4627. E44

VI, 6: 1-16
Song for tenor or baritone with piano.
r: e^1 - g^2 (optional a^2)

RB51. ——————. Boot, Saddle, to Horse and Away, key of G major. From Four Cavalier Tunes. London: Winthrop Rogers, Ltd., Hawkes & Son c1930. W.R.4619.

VI, 6: 1-16
Song for baritone with piano.
r: d^1 - f^2 (optional g^2)

RB52. +Hollins, Dorothea. Boot and Saddle, key of E-flat major. Photostat copy, Cincinnati: The John Church Company, c1903. Pl. no. 14431-5. E45

VI, 6: 1-16
Song for [medium] voice with keyboard.
r: g - eb^2 t: bb - bb^1

RB53. +Kobbé, Gustav. To Horse! key of C major. New York: C. H. Ditson & Co., O. Ditson & Co. c1887. Pl. no. 52339. E46

VI, 6: 1-16
Song for [medium] voice with keyboard.
r: g - d^2 (optional g^2)   t: e^1 - b^1

Note: Broughton, *Bibliography* gives the title as "Boot and Saddle."

RB54. +Peel, Graham. Boot, Saddle, to Horse, key of D major. London: Chappell & Co. Ltd., c1911. Pl. no. 24692. E47

VI, 6: 1-16
Song for [high] voice with piano.
r: d^1 - $f\#^2$ t: $f\#^1$ - e^2

RB55. Reed, C. H. Cavalier Song, key of D major, no. [? only]. From Twelve Songs. Photostat copy, London: Weekes & Co., printed for private circulation, n.d. W.7098.

VI, 6: 1-16
Song for [high] voice with piano.
r: d^1 - e^2 t: f^1 - c^2

Note: The ABL received RB55 Sept. 18, 1940.

RB56.   +Rogers, James H[otchkiss]. Boot and Saddle—Cavalier Song
by Robert Browning, key of G minor. New York: G. Schirmer,
Rogers & Eastman c1900. Ten.4. E48

VI, 6: 1-16
Song for tenor with piano.
r: c^1 - g^2

RB57.   +—————. Boot and Saddle—Cavalier Song, key of G minor.
New York: G. Schirmer, c1900. Pl. no. 19056. E48

VI, 6: 1-16
Song for high voice with piano.
r: c^1 - g^2

RB57.1.   Sarson, May. Cavalier Song, key of B-flat major. From
Novello's School Songs, no. 1642. Xerox copy, London:
Novello and Company, Limited, c1933. No pl. no.

VI, 6: 1-12, 1-4
Song for unison voices with keyboard.

RB58.   +Stanford, Charles Villiers. Boot, Saddle, to Horse and Away,
key of E-flat major, no. 3 [only]. From Three Cavalier Songs,
op. 17. London: Boosey & Co, Ltd., n.d. No pl. no. E49

VI, 6: 1-16
Song for baritone solo, male chorus (tenor I and II, bass I
and II) with piano.

Note: The ABL has 3 copies; copy 3 has as the publisher
"Boosey & Co;" also, on p. 5 bottom right corner the numbers
"4.23" appear instead of "8. 27" as in copies 1 and 2. Broughton, *Bibliography* gives [1882] as the possible date of publication.

RB59.   Stratton, G[eorge] R[obert]. Boot, Saddle, to Horse, and Away,
key of E-flat major. London: Murdoch, Murdoch & Co.,
c1929. M.M.&Co.513.

VI, 6: 1-16
Song for [high] voice with piano.
r: d^1 - f^2 t: a^1 - e^2

RB60.   —————. Boot, Saddle, to Horse, and Away, key of F major.
London: Murdoch, Murdoch & Co., c1929. M.M.&Co.501.

VI, 6: 1-16
Song for [medium high] voice with piano.
r: c^1 - eb^2 t: g^1 - d^2

CHERRIES. *See* FERISHTAH'S FANCIES

"CHILDE ROLAND TO THE DARK TOWER CAME"

RB61.　+Bantock, Granville. Ballade (Childe Roland to the Dark Tower Came), key of C major. Berners Edition. London: Joseph Williams Limited, c1934. J.W.16942. E52

V, 205: 203
Solo for piano.

COLOMBE'S BIRTHDAY

RB62.　+Gow, George Coleman. Intermezzo Music to "Colombe's Birthday," key of C major, no. 1. "Colombe," key of A-flat major, no. 4. "Valence," key of B major, no. 5. Wedding March, key of C major, no. 8. From "Colombe's Birthday," Intermezzo Music, op. 4. Boston: The Boston Music Co., G. Schirmer, Jr. c1892. B.M.Co. 213, 216, 217, 220. E54

IV, 75-169
Intermezzo solos for piano.

Note: RB62 is bound in "Colombe's Birthday," Intermezzo Music. The ABL has 6 copies; copies 2 and 6 are signed "Boston Browning Society." Copy 4 contains a program of an 1897 production of "Colombe's Birthday" (RB's play).

A DEATH IN THE DESERT

RB63.　+Slater, Gordon. For Life, with All It Yields, key of F major. From The Oxford Series of Modern Anthems, edited by E. Stanley Roper. London: Oxford University Press, c1928. No pl. no. E55

VII, 130: 244-250
Short anthem for mixed chorus (soprano, alto, tenor, bass) with organ.

THE EAGLE. *See* FERISHTAH'S FANCIES

EARTH'S IMMORTALITIES

Love

RB64.　+Bryson, Ernest. So, the Year's Done With! key of A major. London: Oxford University Press, c1927. No pl. no. E59

VI, 45: 1-9
Song for high voice with piano.
r: $f\#^1$ - $f\#^2$

RB65.　————. So, the Year's Done With! key of G major. London: Oxford University Press, c1927. No pl. no.

VI, 45: 1-9
Song for medium voice with piano.
r: $e^1 - e^2$

RB66.   Gelrud, Paul. Love, key of C major, no. 42 [only]. From Two
        Leaves of Green—Fifty Unaccompanied Love Songs for Solo
        Voice. Manuscript, no place: no publisher, Nov. 12, 1940.
        No pl. no.

        VI, 45: 1-9
        Song for [medium] voice, unacc.
        r: $c^1 - e^2$ t: $e^1 - a^1$

        Note: On the front cover is written "To Dr. A. J. Armstrong
        [signed] Paul Gelrud."

RB67.   +Renaud, Emiliano. Love Me Forever, key of E-flat major.
        From Four Songs by Robert Browning. Boston: White-Smith
        Music Publishing Co., c1914. Pl. no. 14669. E60

        VI, 45: 1-9
        Song for [high] voice with piano.
        r: $c^1 - ab^2$ t: $f^1 - c^2$

RB68.   +Rogers, Clara Kathleen. Love, key of E major, no. 6. From
        Browning Songs, Second Series, op. 32. Edition Schmidt, no.
        24. Boston: Arthur P. Schmidt, c1900. A.P.S.5037f. E61

        VI, 45: 1-9
        Song for [high] voice with piano.
        r: $e^1 - a^2$ t: $g^1 - g^2$

        Note: RB68 is bound in Browning Songs, Second Series.

RB69.   Weems, Mrs. J. Eddie. Love, key of E minor, no. 1 [only].
        From The Browning Cycle of Love Lyrics. Manuscript, no
        place: no publisher, n.d. No pl. no.

        VI, 45: 1-9
        Song for [medium high] voice with keyboard.
        r: $e^1 - e^2$ t: $g^1 - c^2$

        Note: The ABL received RB69 in 1938. On the front cover
        is written "Mrs. J. Eddie Weems, 1121 West 79th Street, Los
        Angeles, California."

EASTER-DAY

RB70.   +Somervell, Arthur. From "Easter Day," key of B-flat minor,
        no. 7. From the song cycle, A Broken Arc. London: Boosey
        & Co., c1923. H. 10770. E53

V, 305-306: 991-1003
Song for [medium] voice with piano.
r: bb - d^2 t: db^1 - db^2

Note: RB70 is bound in A Broken Arc.

RB71. Vaille, Clara Hinman. Death Is a Door, key of B-flat major. Words by Nancy Byrd Turner, based on the poem by RB. Manuscript, no place: no publisher, March 26, 1934. No pl. no.

V, 264-307
Song for [high] voice with keyboard.
r: f^1 - gb^2 t: g^1 - f^2

Note: On the front cover is written "Poem furnished and set to music for Mrs. Katherine Cole to illuminate her interpretation of Browning's 'Easter Day' for the Browning Club of St. Petersburg, Florida March 26."

EPILOGUE[4]

RB72. +Aldrich, Leslie. Paean, "One Who Never Turn'd His Back," key of D-flat major. London: Novello and Company, Limited, Leslie Aldrich c1918. Pl. no. 14512. E62

Asolando, 131: 11-14
Song for [medium] voice with keyboard.
r: c^1 - d^2 t: f^1 - b^1

RB73. +Bantock, Granville. Midnight, key of B minor. From Festival Music, no. 35659. Ashdown Edition. London: Edwin Ashdown, Ltd., c1926. (E.A. 35659). E63

Asolando, 130-131: 1-20
Part-song for male chorus (tenor I and II, baritone I and II, bass I and II) with keyboard (for rehearsal only).

RB74. +Farmer, John. Epilogue, "At the Midnight in the Silence of the Sleeptime," key of E-flat major. From (Balliol College Song Book). London: Joseph Williams, n.d. No pl. no. E64

Asolando, 130-131: 1-20
Song for unison chorus with piano.

RB75. +————————. Epilogue, key of E-flat major, no. 52. From Gaudeamus: Songs for Colleges and Schools, edited by John Farmer. London: Cassell & Company, Limited, c1890. No pl. no. E64

Asolando, 130-131: 1-20
Song for unison chorus with piano.

Note: RB75 is bound in Gaudeamus. On the fly-leaf is the autograph "Sarianna Browning—March 27th, 1891—."

---

[4]from *Asolando.*

RB76.   Krull, F[ritz]. Epilogue, key of E major. Manuscript, no place:
no publisher, 1903. No pl. no.

Asolando, 130-131: 1-20
Song for [medium high] voice with keyboard.
r: b - e²   t: f#¹ - e²

Note: RB76 appears to be the original manuscript, cf., RB77.

RB77.   ——————. Epilogue, key of E major. Original manuscript,
[Indianapolis]: no publisher, 1903. No pl. no.

Asolando, 130-131: 1-20
Song for [medium high] voice with piano.
r: b - e²   t: f#¹ - e²

Note: On the front cover is written "To Miss Charity Dye by
whose ever fresh enthusiasm this composition was inspired and
fostered, the music is devotedly inscribed. F. Krull, Indian-
apolis, 1903. Copied by Mrs. B. M. Price." Cf., RB76.

RB78.   +Mackenzie, Alexander C[ampbell]. "One Who Never Turned
His Back," key of D major. From *King Albert's Book.*
[London]: The Daily Telegraph, n.d. No pl. no. E65

Asolando, 131: 11-14
Song for [medium] voice with piano.
r: b - e²   t: f#¹ - b¹

Note: RB78 is bound in the complete book, *King Albert's
Book.* Broughton, *Bibliography* gives 1914 as the publication
date.

RB79.   +——————. "One Who Never Turned His Back," key of D
major. From *King Albert's Book,* pp. 34-35 [only]. New
York: Hearst's International Library Co, n.d. No pl. no. E65

Asolando, 131: 11-14
Song for [medium] voice with piano.
r: b - e²   t: f#¹ - b¹

Note: Broughton, *Bibliography* gives [1914] as the possible
date of publication.

EPILOGUE TO FERISHTAH'S FANCIES.
See FERISHTAH'S FANCIES

AN EPISTLE
Containing the Strange Medical Experience
Of Karshish, the Arab Physician

RB80.   England, Nick. The All-Loving, key of C major. Manuscript, no place: no publisher, n.d. No pl. no.
IV, 198: 306-311
Song for baritone, reader, and piano.
r: G - d¹

RB81.   +Harwood, Basil. Love Incarnate, key of D major, op. 37. A Setting of Lines by Robert Browning, with a Verse of the Hymn "Jesu, Dulcis Memoria" by St. Bernard of Clairvaux, translated by the Rev. J. M. Neale. Novello's Original Octavo Edition. London: Novello and Company, Limited, c1925. Pl. no. 15141. E68
IV, 198: 304-311
Choral setting for mixed chorus (soprano I and II, alto I and II, tenor I and II, bass I and II), boy sopranos, and organ.

EVELYN HOPE

RB82.   Ayres, Harold. I Loved You, key of D major. Xerox copy, manuscript, no place: no publisher, Harold Ayres cJan. 27, 1936. No pl. no.
VI, 53: 49-56
Song for [medium] voice with keyboard.
r: c#¹ - d#²   t: e¹ - c#²

RB83.   Ellingham, Harry. Evelyn, key of F major. Manuscript, [London]: Boosey & Hawkes Ltd., n.d. No pl. no.
VI, 53: 49-56
Song for [medium high] voice with keyboard.
r: c¹ - f²   t: f¹ - c²

RB84.   Worth, John W. Evelyn Hope, key of C major, no. 9. From Twelve Songs by Browning by John W. Worth. Manuscript, no place: no publisher, n.d. No pl. no.
VI, 51-52: 1-5, 9-24
Song for [high] voice with keyboard.
r: d¹ - g²   t: g¹ - e²
Note: RB84 is bound in Twelve Songs by Browning.

THE FAMILY. *See* FERISHTAH'S FANCIES

FERISHTAH'S FANCIES
The Eagle

RB85.   +Bantock, Granville. The Eagle, "Round Us the Wild Creatures" (Der Adler, „Um uns des Waldes Tiere"), key of F major, no. 1. From Lyrics from Ferishtah's Fancies (Lyrische Gedichte aus Ferishtah's Fantasien). Deutsche Uebersetzung von Joh. Bernhoff-Leipzig. Leipzig: Breitkopf & Härtel, c1905. V. A.2031. E56

XVI, 7-8: 36-47
Song for [high] voice with piano.
r: d^1 - g#^{2} t: a^1 - e^2

Note: RB85 is bound in Lyrics from Ferishtah's Fancies.

RB86.   Clarke, Helen A[rchibald]. Round Us the Wild Creatures, key
of E major. Manuscript, no place: no publisher, n.d. No pl. no.

XVI, 7-8: 36-47
Song for [high] voice with keyboard.
r: d^1 - a^2 t: a^1 - f^2

RB87.   +Kernochan, Marshall. Round Us the Wild Creatures, key of
A-flat major. From Two Songs. New York: G. Schirmer,
c1913. Pl. no. 23860. E58

XVI, 7-8: 36-47
Song for medium voice with piano.
r: c^1 - f#^{2}

Note: Broughton, *Bibliography* gives [1913] as the possible
publication date.

RB88.   Krull, Fritz. Round Us the Wild Creatures, key of C major, no.
3. From Three Songs by Fritz Krull. Manuscript, no place:
no publisher, 1908. No pl. no.

XVI, 7-8: 36-47
Song for [high] voice with keyboard.
r: d^1 - f^2 t: a^1 - d^2

Note: RB88 is bound in Three Songs.

The Melon-Seller

RB89.   +Bantock, Granville. The Melon-Seller, "Wish No Word Un-
spoken" (Der Melonenhändler, „Ach, dem Wort, dem Blicke"),
key of B-flat major, no. 2. From Lyrics for Ferishtah's Fancies
(Lyrische Gedichte aus Ferishtah's Fantasien). Deutsche
Uebersetzung von Joh. Bernhoff-Leipzig. Leipzig: Breitkopf
& Härtel, c1905. V. A.2031. E161

XVI, 11: 43-48
Song for [high] voice with piano.
r: c^1 - g#^{2} t: g^1 - e^2

Note: RB89 is bound in Lyrics from Ferishtah's Fancies.

Shah Abbas

RB90.   +Bantock, Granville. Shah Abbas, "You Groped Your Way"
(Schach Abbas, „Du tastetest den Weg"), key of C minor, no.
3. From Lyrics from Ferishtah's Fancies (Lyrische Gedichte
aus Ferishtah's Fantasien). Deutsche Uebersetzung von Joh.
Bernhoff-Leipzig. Leipzig: Breitkopf & Härtel, c1905. V. A.
2031. E347

XVI, 18: 141-149
Song for [high] voice with piano.
r: eb^1 - g^2 t: a^1 - f^2

Note: RB90 is bound in Lyrics from Ferishtah's Fancies.

The Family

RB91.   +Bantock, Granville. The Family, "Man I Am and Man Would Be" (Die Familie, „Ich bin Mann und bleib' auch Mann"), key of A-flat major, no. 4. From Lyrics from Ferishtah's Fancies (Lyrische Gedichte aus Ferishtah's Fantasien). Deutsche Uebersetzung von Joh. Bernhoff-Leipzig. Leipzig: Breitkopf & Härtel, c1905. V. A.2031. E70

XVI, 7-8: 36-47
Song for [high] voice with piano.
r: d^1 - g#^{2} t: a^1 - e^2

Note: RB91 is bound in Lyrics from Ferishtah's Fancies.

The Sun

RB92.   +Bantock, Granville. The Sun, "Fire Is the Flint" (Die Sonne, „Feuer berget der Stein"), key of A-flat major, no. 5. From Lyrics from Ferishtah's Fancies (Lyrische Gedichte aus Ferish-tah's Fantasien). Deutsche Uebersetzung von Joh. Bernhoff-Leipzig. Leipzig: Breitkopf & Härtel, c1905. V. A.2031. E374

XVI, 31: 177-182
Song for [high] voice with piano.
r: db^1 - g^2 t: f^1 - d^2

Note: RB92 is bound in Lyrics from Ferishtah's Fancies.

Mihrab Shah

RB93.   +Bantock, Granville. Mihrab Shah, "So, the Head Aches" (Mihrab Schach, „So das Haupt schmerzt"), key of F-sharp minor, no. 6. From Lyrics from Ferishtah's Fancies (Lyrische Gedichte aus Ferishtah's Fantasien). Deutsche Uebersetzung von Joh. Bernhoff-Leipzig. Leipzig: Breitkopf & Härtel, c1905. V. A.2031. E162

XVI, 38-39: 137-156
Song for [high] voice with piano.
r: c^1 - g^2 t: a^1 - eb^2

Note: RB93 is bound in Lyrics from Ferishtah's Fancies.

A Camel-Driver

RB94.　+Bantock, Granville. A Camel-Driver, "When I Vexed You"
(Ein Kamel-treiber, „Ich erzurnt' dich"), key of E major, no.
7. From Lyrics from Ferishtah's Fancies (Lyrische Gedichte
aus Ferishtah's Fantasien). Deutsche Uebersetzung von Joh.
Bernhoff-Leipzig. Leipzig: Brietkopf & Härtel, c1905. V. A.
2031. E18

XVI, 45-46: 112-123
Song for [medium] voice with piano.
r: b - e^2　　t: f#^{1} - b^1

Note: RB94 is bound in Lyrics from Ferishtah's Fancies.

Two Camels

RB95.　+Bantock, Granville. Two Camels, "Once I Saw a Chemist"
(Zwei Kamels, „War beim Apotheker: Pulverkörnchen Kraut'
er"), key of F-sharp major, no. 8. From Lyrics from Ferish-
tah's Fancies (Lyrische Gedichte aus Ferishtah's Fantasien).
Deutsche Uebersetzung von Joh. Bernhoff-Leipzig. Leipzig:
Brietkopf & Härtel, c1905. V. A.2031. E377

XVI, 51-52: 109-120
Song for [high] voice with piano.
r: c#^{1} - g#^{2} (optional a#^{2})　　t: g#^{1} - e^2

Note: RB95 is bound in Lyrics from Ferishtah's Fancies.

Cherries

RB96.　+Bantock, Granville. Cherries, "Verse-Making—Love-Making"
(Kirschen „Dichten-Minnen"), key of G major, no. 9. From
Lyrics from Ferishtah's Fancies (Lyrische Gedichte aus Ferish-
tah's Fantasien). Deutsche Uebersetzung von Joh. Bernhoff-
Leipzig. Leipzig: Breitkopf & Härtel, c1905. V. A.2031. E51

XVI, 57-58: 102-109
Song for [high] voice with piano.
r: b - a^2 (optional b^2)　　t: f#^{1} - d^2

Note: RB96 is bound in Lyrics from Ferishtah's Fancies.

Plot-Culture

RB97.　+Bantock, Granville. Plot-Culture, "Not with My Soul, Love!"
(Landbau, „Nicht meiner Seele, Lieb!"), key of D-flat major,
no. 10. From Lyrics from Ferishtah's Fancies (Lyrische
Gedichte aus Ferishtah's Fantasien). Deutsche Uebersetzung
von Joh. Bernhoff-Leipzig. Leipzig: Breitkopf & Härtel,
c1905. V. A.2031. E325

XVI, 60-61: 61-76
Song for [high] voice with piano.
r: c^1 - bb^2 t: f^1 - db^2

Note: RB97 is bound in Lyrics from Ferishtah's Fancies.

A Pillar at Sebzevah

RB98.   +Bantock, Granville. A Pillar at Sebzevah, "Ask Not One Least Word of Praise!" (Eine Säule in Sebzevar, „Heische nicht das Lob der Welt!"), key of G major, no. 11. From Lyrics from Ferishtah's Fancies (Lyrische Gedichte aus Ferishtah's Fantasien). Deutsche Uebersetzung von Joh. Bernhoff-Leipzig. Leipzig: Brietkopf & Härtel, c1905. V. A.2031. E236

XVI, 68: 152-161
Song for [high] voice with piano.
r: d^1 - g^2 t: f^1 - $d\#^2$

Note: RB98 is bound in Lyrics from Ferishtah's Fancies.

RB99.   Clarke, Helen Archibald. Song: Ask Not One Least Word of Praise, key of E-flat major. From *Poet-Lore*, III, 5, edited by Charlotte Porter and Helen A. Clarke. Xerox copy, Philadelphia: Poet-Lore Company, 1891. No pl. no.

XVI, 68: 152-161
Song for [medium] voice with keyboard.
r: b - g^2 t: e^1 - eb^2

RB100.   +Mana-Zucca. A Query, key of G major, no. 2 [only]. From Two Poems by Robert Browning, op. 42. New York: G. Schirmer, c1921. Pl. no. 30211. E238

XVI, 68: 152-161
Song for high voice with piano.
r: d^1 - e^2 (optional g^2)

A Bean-Stripe: Also, Apple-Eating

RB101.   +Bantock, Granville. A Bean-Stripe: Also, Apple Eating, "Why from the World" (Ein Bohnenstreifen: auch Apfelessen, Ferishtah sprach: „Wieso verdient"), key of C major, no. 12. From Lyrics from Ferishtah's Fancies (Lyrische Gedichte aus Ferishtah's Fantasien). Deutsche Uebersetzung von Joh. Bernhoff-Leipzig. Leipzig: Breitkopf & Härtel, c1905. V. A.2031. E7

XVI, 89: 479-492
Song for [high] voice with piano.
r: $d\#^1$ - g^2 (optional bb^2)   t: a^1 - $f\#^2$

Note: RB101 is bound in Lyrics from Ferishtah's Fancies.

Epilogue[5]

RB102.   +Bantock, Granville. Epilogue, "Oh, Love—No, Love!" (Epilog, „Mein Lieb—nein, Lieb!"), key of C major, no. 13. From Lyrics from Ferishtah's Fancies (Lyrische Gedichte aus Ferishtah's Fantasien). Deutsche Uebersetzung von Joh. Bernhoff-Leipzig. Leipzig: Breitkopf & Härtel, c1905. V.A.2031. E66

XVI, 90-92: 1-28
Song for [high] voice with piano.
r: c^1 - a^2 (optional bb^2)   t: a^1 - f^2

Note: RB102 is bound in Lyrics from Ferishtah's Fancies.

RB103.   +Farmer, John. Heroes, key of E-flat major. (From the Balliol Song Book). London: Joseph Williams, Limited, n.d. No pl. no. E67

XVI, 90-92: 8-24
Song for unison male chorus with piano.

RB104.   +————. Heroes, key of E-flat major, no. 29. From Gaudeamus: Songs for Colleges and Schools, edited by John Farmer. London: Cassell & Company, Limited, 1890. No pl. no. E67

XVI, 90-92: 9-12
Song for unison male chorus with piano.

Note: RB104 is bound in Gaudeamus. On the fly-leaf is the autograph "Sarianna Browning—March 27th, 1891—".

FIFINE AT THE FAIR

RB105.   Bantock, Granville. Fifine at the Fair, key of D major. London: Novello and Company Limited, c1912. Pl. no. 13678.

XI, 213-343
Orchestral drama with a prologue for orchestra. Miniature score. No parts.

piccolo	3 timpani
3 flutes	
oboe	tambourine, triangle, small
English horn	tambourine, glockenspiel,
3 clarinets (in A)	bass drum, and cymbals
bass clarinet (in A)	(3 percussion players)
3 bassoons	
contrabassoon	2 harps (2^a ad libitum)
6 horns (in F)	
3 trumpets (or cornets)	12 violin I
(in A)	10 violin II
3 trombones	8 viola
tuba	8 cello
	8 double bass

---

[5]to Ferishtah's Fancies.

Prologue

Amphibian

RB106. +Bantock, Granville. Amphibian, key of F-sharp major.
Berners Edition. London: Joseph Williams Limited, c1935.
W.21. E71

XI, 215: 9-12
Solo for piano.

GARDEN FANCIES

I. The Flower's Name

RB107. +del Riego, Teresa. June, and My Lady, key of E-flat major.
London: Chappell & Co. Ltd., c1909. Pl. no. 24185. E73

VI, 21: 41-44
Song for [medium] voice with piano.
r: d^1 - eb^2 t: f^1 - c^2

RB108. +——————. June, and My Lady, key of F major. London:
Chappell & Co. Ltd., c1909. Pl. no. 24170. E73

VI, 21: 41-44
Song for [high] voice with piano.
r: e^1 - f^2 t: g^1 - d^2

GIVE A ROUSE. *See* **CAVALIER TUNES II**

GOLD HAIR:

A Story of Pornic

RB109. +Bantock, Granville. Gold Hair, key of E-flat major. Berners
Edition. London: Joseph Williams Limited, c1935. W.18. E74

VII, 69: 1-3
Solo for piano.

THE GUARDIAN-ANGEL

A Picture at Fano

RB110. Bantock, Granville. The Guardian Angel, key of C major. From
Dramatic Lyrics by Robert Browning. Swan Edition, no. 2.
London: Swan & Co. (Music Publishers) Limited, c1920.
S&Co.W&W.Ltd.2720.

VI, 187-188: 1-14, 29-35
Song for low voice with piano.
r: b - f^2

RB111.   —————————. The Guardian Angel, key of E-flat major. From
          Dramatic Lyrics by Robert Browning. Swan Edition, no. 2.
          London: Swan & Co. (Music Publishers) Limited, c1920.
          S&Co.W&W.Ltd.2707.

          VI, 187-188: 1-14, 29-35
          Song for high voice with piano.
          r: d^1 - ab^2

HERVE RIEL

RB112.   +Davies, H[enry] Walford. Hervé Riel, key of D major. No-
          vello's Original Edition. London: Novello Ewer & Co, c1895.
          Pl. no. 8223. E77

          XIV, 77-83: 1-30, 33-86, 94-99
          Choral setting for baritone solo, mixed chorus (soprano I and
          II, alto I and II, tenor I and II, bass I and II), and orchestra.
          Piano-vocal score. No parts.

HOME-THOUGHTS, FROM ABROAD

RB113.   +Austin, Frederic. Home-Thoughts from Abroad, key of A
          major. London: Novello & Co., Ltd., c1909. Pl. no. 13058. E79

          VI, 95-96: 1-20
          Song for [high] voice with keyboard.
          r: e^1 - a^2 t: a^1 - e^2

RB114.   Bantock, Granville. Home Thoughts, key of A-flat major. From
          Dramatic Lyrics by Robert Browning. Swan Edition, no. 5.
          London: Swan & Co. (Music Publishers) Limited, c1920.
          S.&Co.,W.&W.Ltd.2710.

          VI, 95-96: 1-20
          Song for high voice with piano.
          r: c^1 - a^2

RB115.   —————————. Home Thoughts, key of B-flat major. From Dra-
          matic Lyrics by Robert Browning. Swan Edition, no. 5. Lon-
          don: Swan & Co. (Music Publishers) Limited, c1920. S.&Co.
          W.&W.Ltd.2719.

          VI, 95-96: 1-20
          Song for low voice with piano.
          r: a - $f\#^2$

RB116.   +Brahe, May H. Oh, to Be in England! key of A major, no. 1
          [only]. From Two Songs. London: Enoch & Sons Ld, c1915.
          E.&S.4784. E81

          VI, 95: 1-8
          Song for medium voice with piano.
          r: $c\#^1$ - $f\#^2$

RB117.   +Clarke, Reginald. Home Thoughts from Abroad, key of F
          major. London: Weekes & Co., n.d. W. 4833. E82

          VI, 95: 1-16
          Song for [high] voice with piano.
          r: c^1 - bb^2 (optional c^3)   t: a^1 - f^2

          Note: The ABL received RB117 June 7, 1940. Broughton,
          Bibliography gives [1903] as the possible publication date.

RB118.   +Cooke, Greville. Oh, to Be in England, key of E-flat major.
          From The Winthrop Rogers Edition of Choral Music for
          Festivals, Series II, edited by Julius Harrison. London:
          Boosey & Hawkes, Ltd., c1928. W.R.4503. E83

          VI, 95-96: 1-20
          Part-song for mixed chorus (soprano I and II, alto I and II,
          tenor I and II, bass I and II) with piano (for rehearsal only).

RB119.   +Goatley, Alma. Now That April's There, key of D major, no.
          1 [only]. From Two Songs. Boston: The Arthur P. Schmidt
          Co., c1917. A.P.S. 11201. E84

          VI, 95-96: 1-20
          Song for soprano or tenor with piano.
          r: b - f#^{2}

RB120.   Hinkle, Daisy. Home Thoughts from Abroad, key of E-flat
          major. Manuscript, no place: no publisher, Jan. 5, 1928. No
          pl. no.

          VI, 95: 1-8
          Song for mezzo soprano with piano.
          r: bb - eb^2

          Note: With RB120 is Catherine Parmentes' "The Crossroads."
          It is not clear if she is the composer and/or the lyricist.

RB121.   ——————. "Home Thoughts from Abroad," key of E-flat
          major. Manuscript, no place: no publisher, n.d. No pl. no.

          VI, 95: 1-8
          Song for mezzo soprano with piano.
          r: bb - eb^2

RB122.   Rowley, Alec. Oh to Be in England, key of D major. Manu-
          script, no place: no publisher, n.d. No pl. no.

          VI, 95: 1-8
          Duet for [high] voice and [medium low] voice with keyboard.

RB123.   Shapleigh, Bertram. O to Be in England, key of D-flat major,
          no. 2. From Three English Songs, op. 49. London: Breitkopf
          & Härtel, c1906. L.118.

VI, 95: 1-16
Song for contralto with piano.
r: ab - eb²

Note: RB123 is bound in Three English Songs.

RB124. White, Grace. Three Descriptions from Browning, no. 2, key of
D major. From Three Descriptions from Browning. New
York: G. Schirmer, c1917. Pl. no. 26881.

VI, 95: 11-13
Solo for violin with piano.

Note: RB124 is bound in the above mentioned Three Descriptions from Browning.

RB125. +White, Maude Valérie. Home Thoughts from Abroad, key of
G minor. London: Stanley Lucas, Weber & Co., n.d. S.L.
W.&Co.2296. E88

VI, 95: 1-8
Song for [medium high] voice with piano.
r: d¹ - d²   t: a¹ - d²

Note: Broughton, *Bibliography* gives 1885 as the publication
date.

RB126. +Wickins, Florence. Oh, to Be in England, key of D major.
London: Wickins & Co., c1903. Wickins & Co.3194. E89

VI, 95-96: 1-20
Duet for mezzo soprano and baritone with piano.

RB127. Wilson, Alec. Oh! To Be in England, key of C major. Manuscript, London: J. B. Cramer & Co. Ltd., n.d. No pl. no.

VI, 95: 1-16
Song for [high] voice with piano.
r: c#¹ - g²   t: a¹ - d²

Note: The ABL received RB127 Jan. 24, 1938.

"HOW THEY BROUGHT THE GOOD NEWS
FROM GHENT TO AIX"

RB128. +Duncan, Edmondstoune. Good News to Aix, key of B-flat
major, no. 6. From English Songs, Book III. Glasgow: Aird
& Coghill, Ltd., Edmondstoune Duncan c1919. No pl. no. E91

VI, 9-12: 1-60
Song for [high] voice with piano.
r: c¹ - g²   t: f¹ - c²

Note: RB128 is bound in English Songs, Book III.

RB129. +Hattersley, F. Kilvington. Good News from Ghent, key of D minor. Novello's Original Octavo Edition. London: Novello & Co. Ltd., c1904. Pl. no. 12016. E92

VI, 9-12: 1-60
Ballad for mixed chorus (soprano, alto, tenor, bass) with keyboard.

RB130. +Ormerod, H[elen] J. How They Brought the Good News from Ghent to Aix, key of F minor. London: Forsyth Brothers, n.d. No pl. no. E93

VI, 9-12: 1-6, 13-18, 31-60
Song for baritone with piano.
r: c^1 - f^2

Note: On the front cover is written "W. G. Kingsland." Broughton, *Bibliography* gives [188-] as the possible publication date.

IN A BALCONY

RB131. +Cowley, Elsie M. But Love, key of C major. Johannesburg: Mackay Bros: Pianoforte & Music Saloons, n.d. S.O.&Co.25. E94

VII, 18: 374-377
Song for [low] voice with piano.
r: b^b - e^{b2} t: c^1 - g^1

Note: On the front cover is written "Madame Clara Butt with the composer's compliments   Elsie M. Cowley."

IN A GONDOLA

RB132. Ayres, Harold. I Send My Heart, key of B-flat major. Xerox copy, manuscript, Eugene, Oregon: no publisher, Harold Ayres cJan. 27, 1936. No pl. no.

V, 66: 1-7
Song for [high] voice with keyboard.
r: c^1 - a^{b2} t: f^1 - g^2

RB133. +Bantock, Granville. In a Gondola, key of E major. Berners Edition. London: Joseph Williams Limited, c1935. W.13. E95

V, 66-77
Solo for piano.

RB134. +Barnett, Alice. Boat-Song, key of E major, no. 2 [only]. From the song cycle, In a Gondola. New York: G. Schirmer, c1920. Pl. no. 29147. E96

V, 67-68: 37-48
Song for high voice with piano.
r: eb^1 - $g\#^2$

Note: On the front cover is written "Yours sincerely, [signed] Alice Barnett. 1932—"

RB135. +————. Dip Your Arm o'er the Boatside, key of E major, no. 6 [only]. From the song cycle, In a Gondola. New York: G. Schirmer, c1920. Pl. no. 29151. E96

V, 72: 116-124
Song for high voice with piano.
r: $f\#^1$ - g^2

RB136. +————. He Muses—Drifting, key of C major, no. 5 [only]. From the song cycle, In a Gondola. New York: G. Schirmer, c1920. Pl. no. 29150. E96

V, 70: 79-86
Song for high voice with piano.
r: $f\#^1$ - $f\#^2$

RB137. +————. It Was Ordained to Be So, Sweet, key of C major, no. 8 [only]. From the song cycle, In a Gondola. New York: G. Schirmer, c1920. Pl. no. 29153. E96

V, 76-77: 225-231
Song for high voice with piano.
r: $f\#^1$ - $g\#^2$

RB138. +————. The Moth's Kiss, First, key of E major, no. 3 [only]. From the song cycle, In a Gondola. New York: G. Schirmer, c1920. Pl. no. 29148. E96

V, 68-69: 49-62
Song for high voice with piano.
r: e^1 - $g\#^2$

RB139. +————. Serenade, key of E major, no. 1 [only]. From the song cycle, In a Gondola. New York: G. Schirmer, c1920. Pl. no. 29146. E96

V, 66: 1-7
Song for high voice with piano.
r: e^1 - $g\#^2$

RB140. +————. To-morrow, If a Harp-String, Say, key of A-flat major, no. 7 [only]. From the song cycle, In a Gondola. New York: G. Schirmer, c1920. Pl. no. 29152. E96

V, 75-76: 203-224
Song for high voice with piano.
r: d^1 - ab^2

RB141. +————. What Are We Two, key of C major, no. 4 [only]. From the song cycle, In a Gondola. New York: G. Schirmer, c1920. Pl. no. 29149. E96

V, 69-70: 63-88
Song for high voice with piano.
r: e^1 - g^2

RB142. Beach, Mrs. H[enry] H[arris] A[ubrey]. I Send My Heart Up to Thee! key of B-flat major, no. 3 [only]. From Three Browning Songs, op. 44. Boston: Arthur P. Schmidt, c1900. A.P.S. 5156.

V, 66: 1-7
Song for low voice with keyboard.
r: b^b - g^2

RB143. +————. I Send My Heart Up to Thee! key of D-flat major, no. 3 [only]. From Three Browning Songs, op. 44. Boston: Arthur P. Schmidt, c1900. A.P.S. 5140. E97

V, 66: 1-7
Song for soprano or tenor with keyboard.
r: eb^1 - ab^2

RB144. +Beach, John. In a Gondola, key of C major. From the Wa-Wan Series of American Compositions, IV, 25. Newton Center, Mass.: The Wa-Wan Press, c1905. No pl. no. E98

V, 66-68: 1-7, 37-48; 70-72: 79-99, 104-119; 76-77: 223, 225-231
Dramatic monologue for baritone with keyboard.
r: b^b - $f\#^2$

RB145. +Bending, Edwin. In a Gondola, key of F major. Photostat copy, London: Purcell & Co., n.d. No pl. no. E99

V, 66-67: 1-19
Duet for soprano and tenor with cello or violin obbligato and piano. With parts.

Note: Broughton, *Bibliography* gives 1886 and 1890 as publication dates.

RB146. Branscombe, Gena. I Send My Heart Up to Thee (Serenade), key of A-flat major. Boston: The Arthur P. Schmidt Co., c1905. A.P.S.9363.

V, 66: 1-7
Song for soprano or tenor with keyboard.
r: eb^1 - a^2

RB147. ——————. Serenade (I Send My Heart Up to Thee), key of A-flat major. From Songs by Gena Branscombe. Boston: Arthur P. Schmidt, c1905. A.P.S.9363.

V, 66: 1-7
Song for soprano or tenor with keyboard.
r: $eb^1 - a^2$

RB148. ——————. Serenade (I Send My Heart Up to Thee), key of F major. From Songs by Gena Branscombe. Boston: Arthur P. Schmidt, c1905. A.P.S.9364.

V, 66: 1-7
Song for mezzo soprano or baritone with keyboard.
r: $c^1 - f\#^2$

RB149. ——————. What Are We Two? key of B-flat major. Newton Center, Mass: The Wa-Wan Press, c1905. No pl. no.

V, 69-70: 63-78
Song for [medium] voice with keyboard.
r: $d^1 - eb^2$ t: $f^1 - bb^1$

Note: The ABL has 2 copies. Inside copy 1 is written "To Dr: [*sic*] A. J. Armstrong with all the good wishes of Gena Branscombe." Inside copy 2 is written "To Mr. Besph[as?] with the best wishes of Gena Branscombe."

RB150. +Elman, Mischa. In a Gondola, key of F major. New York: G. Schirmer, c1916. Pl. no. 26303. E102

V, 66-77
Impromptu for violin with piano.

RB151. Fergus, Phyllis. Thoughts, key of B-flat major. From Readings with Musical Settings by Phyllis Fergus. Chicago: Clayton F. Summy Co., c1919. C.F.S.Co.1896.

V, 66: 1-7; 69-70: 71, 63, 78, 79; 72-73: 125, 137-140
Recitation for reader with violin and piano. With violin part.

RB152. +Hartmann, Arthur. In a Gondola, key of A major. From Songs. Chicago: Gamble Hinged Music Co., c1911. No pl. no. E104

V, 68-69: 49-62
Song for [medium low] voice with keyboard.
r: $a - e^2$ t: $e^1 - b^1$

RB153. +Hughes, Rupert. A Gondolier's Song, key of A major. From Songs by Rupert Hughes. Cleveland: J. H. Rogers, c1892. No pl. no. E105

V, 66: 1-7
Song for [high] voice with keyboard.
r: e^1 - a^2 t: a^1 - e^2

RB154. Komter, Jan Maarten. In a Gondola, key of E major. Amsterdam: Donemus, c1963. No pl. no.

V, 68-69: 49-62
Song for [medium] voice with guitar.
r: e^1 - e^2 t: e^1 - e^2

RB155. +Protheroe, Daniel. I Send My Heart Up to Thee, key of G major, no. 2. From Three Lyrics by Robert Browning. Chicago: Gamble Hinged Music Co., c1910. No pl. no. E106

V, 66: 1-7
Song for high voice with keyboard.
r: f^1 - ab^2

Note: RB155 is bound in Three Lyrics by Robert Browning.

RB156. Rorem, Ned. In a Gondola, key of E major. New York: C. F. Peters Corporation, Henmar Press Inc. c1963. Edition Peters 6373 E.

V, 68-69: 49-62
Song for high voice with piano.
r: $f\#^1$ - c^3

RB157. +Saminsky, Lazare. Venezia, key of E major, no. 2. From Ausonia (Italian Pages), op. 39. Paris: Editions Maurice Sénart, c1931. E-M-S 8380. E107

V, 66: 1-7
[Symphonic poem] for orchestra. Conductor's score. No parts.

2 flutes	piano, celesta
2 clarinets (in A)	harp
bass clarinet (in B)	violin I and II
bassoon	viola
4 horns (in F)	cello
triangle, grand rattle, cymbals, xylophone	double bass

Note: RB157 is bound in Ausonia (Italian Pages).

RB158. +Schuyler, Georgina. In a Gondola, key of E-flat, no. 4. From Album of Songs by Georgina Schuyler. New York: G. Schirmer, c1894. Pl. no. 3122b. E108

V, 66: 1-7
Song for mezzo soprano or contralto with piano.
r: bb - bb^1

Note: RB158 is bound in Album of Songs. On the inside is written "For /[Mrs. Fish?] in memory of ['Mr. Lamar'?] and his playing the Chopin Impromptu! G. Schuyler March 1899." Broughton, *Bibliography* gives "I Send My Heart up to Thee" as the title.

RB159. +————————. In a Gondola, key of F major, no. 4. From Songs from English and American Poets by Georgina Schuyler. New York: G. Schirmer, c1882. Pl. no. 3122. E108

V, 66: 1-7
Song for mezzo soprano with piano.
r: c^1 - c^2

Note: The music for RB159 is the same as RB160 except for the key. Broughton, *Bibliography* gives "I Send My Heart up to Thee" as the title.

RB160. ————————. Venetian Serenade, key of E-flat major. Photostat copy, no place: no publisher, printed for private circulation, 1875. No pl. no.

V, 66: 1-7
Song for contralto or baritone with piano.
r: bb - bb^1

Note: The music for RB160 is the same as RB159 except for the key.

RB161. Smith, Lewis Worthington. In a Gondola, key of B-flat major. Manuscript, no place: no publisher, 1895. No pl. no.

V, 66-70: 1-7, 37-78
Duet for tenor and alto with keyboard.

Note: On the bottom margin is written "This music written in 1895! The harmony needs some further work before any presentation. L. W. Smith."

RB162. +Treharne, Bryceson. In a Gondola, key of D major. From Lyrical Songs by Bryceson Treharne. New York City: Composers' Music Corporation, c1921. C.M.C.233. E109

V, 68-69: 49-62
Song for [high] voice with piano.
r: eb^1 - ab^2 t: a^1 - e^2

RB163. +True, Latham. I Send My Heart Up to Thee, key of D-flat major. From Browning Songs by Latham True. Portland, Maine: Cressey & Allen, Latham True c1932. No pl. no. E110

V, 66: 1-7
Song for [high] voice with keyboard.
r: eb^1 - ab^2 t: a^1 - e^2

RB164.   +——————. The Moth's Kiss and the Bee's Kiss, key of G
major. From Browning Songs by Latham True. Portland,
Maine: Cressey & Allen, Latham True c1932. No pl. no. E111

V, 68-69: 49-62
Song for [high] voice with keyboard.
r: f#^{1} - g^2 t: a^1 - e^2

RB165.   +Wodell, Frederick W[illiam]. A Venetian Night, key of F
major. Libretto compiled by F. W. Wodell, based on the poem
by RB. New York: J. Fischer & Bro., c1923. J.F.&B.5297.
E112

V, 66-69: 1-7, 37-62; 76-77: 215-217, 223-231
Cantata for soloists (tenor, soprano), women's chorus (soprano
I and II, alto I and II) with piano.

Note: On the front cover is written "For Baylor College Library Compliments of F. W. Wodell."

RB166.   +Worth, John W. In a Gondola, [a song cycle]. 1. Prelude,
key of F major. 2. He Sings: I Send My Heart Up to Thee,
key of A-flat major. 3. Barcarola, key of E major. 4. She
Speaks: Say after Me, and Try to Say My Very Words, key
of A-flat. 5. He Sings: Past We Glide, key of C major. 6.
She Sings: The Moth's Kiss, First, key of G major. 7. He
Sings: What Are We Two, key of F major. 8. He Muses:
Oh, Which Were Best to Roam or Rest, key of G major. 9.
Still He Muses: What If the Three, key of G major. 10. She
Replies, Musing: Dip Your Arm o'er the Boatside, key of A
major. 11. He Speaks: Row Home? Must We Row Home,
key of A major. 12. Gondoliera in Lontanza, key of A major.
13. She Speaks: To-morrow, If a Harp-String, Say, key of
A-flat major. 14. He Is Surprised and Stabbed: It Was
Ordained to Be So, key of A major. New York: The H. W.
Gray Co., John W. Worth c1912. No pl. no. E113

[Song cycle] for soprano, tenor, reader, and piano [to be
performed successively, not as solos].

1. Solo for piano.

2. V, 66: 1-7
    Song for tenor with piano.
    r: eb^1 - ab^2

3. Solo for piano.

4. V, 66-67: 8-36
    Recitation for reader with piano.

5. V, 67-68: 37-48
    Song for tenor with piano.
    r: g^1 - g^2

6. V, 68-69: 49-62
    Song for soprano with piano.
    r: $c\#^1$ - g^2

7. V, 69-70: 63-78
    Song for tenor with piano.
    r: d^1 - ab^2

8. V, 70-71: 79-103
    Recitation for reader with piano.

9. V, 71: 104-115
    Recitation for reader with piano.

10. V, 72: 116-124
    Song for soprano with piano.
    r: $c\#^1$ - e^2

11. V, 72-75: 125-164, 168-175, 199-202
    Recitation for reader with piano.

12. Solo for piano.

13. V, 75-76: 203-224
    Song for soprano with piano.
    r: db^1 - a^2

14. V, 76-77: 225-231
    Song for tenor with piano.
    r: db^1 - f^2

RB167. +Young, Dal[housie]. In a Gondola, a song cycle, op. 8. 1. I
        Send My Heart Up to Thee, key of D minor. 2. Say after Me,
        key of E-flat major. 3. Past We Glide, key of E minor. 4. The
        Moth's Kiss, key of D major. 5. What Are We Two? key of
        F minor. 6. Dip Your Arm o'er the Boatside, key of F major.
        7. What If the Three, key of C major. 8. There's Zanse's
        Vigilant Taper, key of F major. London: Weekes & Co.,
        [1896]. W.3656. E114

Song cycle for tenor, soprano, and piano. Songs may be sung
separately also.

1. V, 66: 1-7
    Song for tenor with piano.
    r: d^1 - $f\#^2$

2. V, 66-67: 8-19
    Duet for soprano and tenor with piano.

3. V, 67-68: 37-48
Song for tenor with piano.
r: g^1 - g^2

4. V, 68-69: 49-62
Song for soprano with piano.
r: e^1 - g^2

5. V, 69-70: 63-78
Song for tenor with piano.
r: f^1 - g^2

6. V, 72: 116-124
Song for soprano with piano.
r: f^1 - f^2

7. V, 71: 104-115
Song for tenor with piano.
r: eb^1 - a^2

8. V, 76-77: 215-231
Duet for soprano and tenor with piano.

Note: Broughton, *Bibliography* gives [1896] as the possible publication date.

RB168. ———————. The Moth's Kiss, key of D major, no. 4 [only]. From the song cycle, In a Gondola, op. 8. London: Weekes & Co., n.d. W.3656.

V, 68-69: 49-62
Song for soprano with piano.
r: e^1 - g^2

Note: Broughton, *Bibliography* gives [1896] as the possible date of publication.

IN A YEAR

RB169. Bantock, Granville. In a Year, key of B-flat major. From Dramatic Lyrics by Robert Browning. Swan Edition, no. 1. London: Swan & Co., c1920. S.&Co.W.&W.Ltd.2706.

VI, 175-179: 1-32, 41-64, 73-80
Song for high voice with piano.
r: d^1 - ab^2

RB170. ———————. In a Year, key of G major. From Dramatic Lyrics by Robert Browning. Swan Edition, no. 1. London: Swan & Co., c1920. S.&Co.W.&W.Ltd.2725.

VI, 175-179: 1-32, 41-64, 73-80
Song for low voice with piano.
r: b - f^2

RB171. +Reinagle, Caroline. In a Year, key of D-flat major, no. 1 [only]. From Three Songs by Caroline Reinagle. London: Augener & Co., n.d. A&Co.2006. E116

VI, 175: 1-8; 178-179: 57-64, 73-80
Song for [medium] voice with piano.
r: f^1 - db^2 t: f^1 - bb^1

Note: Broughton, *Bibliography* gives [188-] as the possible publication date.

INCIDENT OF THE FRENCH CAMP

RB172. +Lehmann, Liza. Incident of the French Camp, key of F major. London: Chappell & Co. Ltd., c1910. Pl. no. 24419. E120

V, 3-5: 1-40
Song for [low] voice with piano.
r: a - f#^{1} t: d^1 - a^1

THE ISLE'S ENCHANTRESS

RB173. +Hopkins, Franklin. The Isle Enchantress, key of B major. Photostat copy, no place: Cecil Mackie, Inc., c1913. No pl. no. E121

New Poems, 60: 1-5
Song for [high] voice with piano.
r: c#^{1} - g#^{2} t: b^1 - f#^{2}

JAMES LEE'S WIFE

I.—James Lee's Wife Speaks at the Window

RB174. Beach, Mrs. H[enry] H[arris] A[ubrey]. Ah, Love, but a Day! key of A-flat major, no. 2 [only]. From Three Browning Songs, op. 44. Boston: Arthur P. Schmidt, c1900. A.P.S.5139.

VII, 45: 1-14
Song for soprano or tenor with keyboard.
r: eb^1 - ab^2

RB175. —————. Ah, Love, but a Day, key of A-flat major, op. 44, no. 2 [only]. From Vocal Duets by Mrs. H. H. A. Beach. Boston: The Arthur P. Schmidt Co., Mrs. H. H. A. Beach c1928. A.P.S.11295.

VII, 45: 1-14
Duet for soprano and tenor with keyboard.

RB176. —————. Ah, Love, but a Day! key of F major, no. 2 [only]. From Three Browning Songs, op. 44. Boston: The Arthur P. Schmidt Co., Mrs. H. H. A. Beach c1928. A.P.S.5155.

VII, 45: 1-14
Song for mezzo soprano or baritone with piano.
r: c^1 - $f\#^2$

RB177. —————. Ah, Love, but a Day! key of F major, op. 44, no. 2 [only]. From Selected Songs by Mrs. H. H. A. Beach. Boston: The Arthur P. Schmidt Co., Mrs. H. H. A. Beach c1928. A.P.S.5155.

VII, 45: 1-14
Song for mezzo soprano or baritone with piano.
r: c^1 - $f\#^2$

RB178. —————. Ah, Love, but a Day, key of G major. Edited and arranged by William Creston. Belwin Choral Series, no. 1948. Rockville Centre, L. I., New York: Belwin, Inc., c1962. Oct 1948.

VII, 45: 1-14
Part-song for women's chorus (soprano I and II, alto) with piano.

RB179. +Borton, Alice. Ah, Love, but a Day, key of E minor. Cincinnati: The John Church Company, c1911. Pl. no. 16494. E123

VII, 45-46: 1-21
Song for high voice with keyboard.
r: e^1 - g^2

RB180. +Cain, Noble. Ah, Love, but a Day, key of E-flat major. From Harold Flammer Choral Series, Secular Three-Part Choruses for Women's Voices, no. 83142. New York: Harold Flammer Publisher Incorporated, c1941. Pl. no. 2167. E124

VII, 45-46: 1-13
Three-part chorus for women's voices (soprano I and II, alto) with piano.

RB181. +De Francesco, Louis E. Ah, Love but a Day, key of C minor. New York: Movietone Music Corporation, c1934. No pl. no. E125

VII, 45: 1-14
Ballad for high voice with keyboard.
r: e^1 - a^2

RB182. +—————. Ah, Love but a Day, key of A minor. Xerox copy, New York: Movietone Music Corporation, c1934. No pl. no. E125

VII, 45: 1-14
Ballad for medium voice with keyboard.
r: $c\#^1$ - $f\#^2$

RB183.   —————————. Ah, Love but a Day, key of A minor. Xerox copy,
            manuscript, New York: Movietone Music Corporation, c1934.
            No pl. no.

            VII, 45: 1-7
            Song for [medium] voice with keyboard.
            r: d^1 - bb^1 t: d^1 - a^1

            Note: Written below the title is "(D minor) (Original Ver-
            sion)," but the key signature is C major.

RB184.   +Fuller, Caroline M. The Changing Year, key of D major, no.
            1. From Three Songs from Robert Browning. [New York:
            J. H. Schroeder], Caroline M. Fuller c1898. E 2559 8. E126

            VII, 45: 1-14
            Song for contralto or bass with keyboard.
            r: a - f^1

            Note: RB184 is bound in Three Songs. The ABL has 2
            copies; on the front cover of copy 1 is written "Florence Wier
            Gibson—from the Composer—." Miss Gibson presented this
            copy to the ABL July 16, 1945. Stamped at the bottom of the
            front cover of copy 1 is "J. H. Schroeder, 10 East 16th St.,
            New York."

RB185.   +Gabriel, Virginia. At the Window, key of B minor. London:
            Addison & Lucas, n.d. (A.&L.6117). E127

            VII, 45-46: 1-21
            Song for [high] voice with piano.
            r: b - g^2 t: a^1 - e^2

            Note: Broughton, *Bibliography* gives 1864 as the publication
            date.

RB186.   +—————————. At the Window, key of G minor. London:
            Addison & Lucas, n.d. (A.&L.6117a). E127

            VII, 45-46: 1-21
            Song for [medium low] voice with piano.
            r: g - eb^2 t: f^1 - c^2

            Note: Broughton, *Bibliography* gives 1864 as the date of
            publication.

RB187.   +Gilberté, Hallett. Ah! Love but a Day, key of E minor. From
            Songs. Boston: Carl Fischer, c1914. Pl. no. 17656. E129

            VII, 45-46: 1-21
            Song for low voice with piano.
            r: b - g^2

            Note: Broughton, *Bibliography* gives [1912] as the possible
            date of publication.

RB188.   +————————. Ah! Love but a Day, key of G minor. From
Songs. Boston: Carl Fischer, c1912. Pl. no. 15349. E129

VII, 45-46: 1-21
Song for high voice with piano.
r: d^1 - bb^2

RB189.   +Gregory, E[leanor] C. James Lee's Wife, key of E minor,
no. 5. From Six Songs. London: Novello Ewer & Co, n.d.
Pl. no. 7519. E130

VII, 45-46: 1-21
Song for [high] voice with keyboard.
r: e^1 - g^2 t: $f\#^1$ - $f\#^2$

Note: RB189 is bound in Six Songs.

RB190.   +Harraden, Ethel. Wilt Thou Change Too? key of A major.
London: C. Jefferys, n.d. J.3188. E131

VII, 45: 1-14
Song for [medium] voice with piano.
r: a - e^2 t: d^1 - b^1

Note: Broughton, *Bibliography* gives [1884] and 1885 as
possible dates of publication.

RB191.   Kernochan, Marshall. At the Window, key of E major. From
Songs by Marshall Kernochan. Revised edition. New York:
Galaxy Music Corporation, c1933. G.M.612.

VII, 45: 1-14
Song for medium voice with keyboard.
r: b - $f\#^2$

Note: RB191 was the gift of Joseph Boonin, Inc. May 11,
1972.

RB192.   +————————. At the Window, key of E major. From Two
Poems by Robert Browning. New York: G. Schirmer, c1908.
Pl. no. 20616. E132

VII, 45: 1-14
Song for medium voice with piano.
r: b - $f\#^2$

RB193.   +Metcalf, C. S. Ah Love, but a Day, key of F major. New
York: The William Maxwell Music Co., c1908. Pl. no. 1-86.
E133

VII, 45: 1-14
Song for [medium] voice with piano.
r: c^1 - e^2 (optional f^2)   t: f^1 - c^2

RB194.   +Pascal, Julian. Ah, Love, but a Day, key of B minor. Boston:
          Oliver Ditson Company, c1900. Pl. no. 4-67-62763. E134

          VII, 45-46: 1-21
          Song for medium voice with piano.
          r: b - g^2

RB195.   Protheroe, Daniel. Ah, Love, but a Day, key of G minor.
          Arranged by Wayne Howorth. Radio Choral Series, no. 1290.
          Chicago: Gamble Hinged Music Co., c1937. Pl. no. 1290.

          VII, 45: 1-14
          Part-song for male chorus (tenor I and II, bass I and II) with
          keyboard.

RB196.   +——————. Ah, Love, but a Day, key of G-sharp minor, no.
          1. From Three Lyrics by Robert Browning. Chicago: Gamble
          Hinged Music Co., c1910. No pl. no. E135

          VII, 45: 1-14
          Song for high voice with keyboard.
          r: f^1 - ab^2

          Note: RB196 is bound in Three Lyrics by Robert Browning.

RB197.   +Rogers, Clara Kathleen. Ah, Love, but a Day, key of G major,
          no. 4. From Browning Songs, First Series, op. 27. Edition
          Schmidt, no. 24a. Boston: Arthur P. Schmidt, c1893. A.P.S.
          2910d. E136

          VII, 45-46: 1-21
          Song for [medium] voice with piano.
          r: d^1 - g^2 t: e^1 - e^2

          Note: RB197 is bound in Browning Songs, First Series.

RB198.   +Somervell, Arthur. James Lee's Wife Speaks at the Window,
          key of A-flat major, no. 1. From the song cycle, James Lee's
          Wife. London: Boosey & Co., c1907. H.5425. E137

          VII, 45-46: 1-21
          Song for contralto solo and orchestra. Piano-vocal score [only].
          r: a - f^2

          Note: RB198 is bound in the song cycle, James Lee's Wife.

RB199.   +Whitmer, T[homas] Carl. "Ah! Love, but a Day," key of
          G-flat major, no. 3 [only]. From Three Songs, op. 3. No place:
          no publisher, T. Carl Whitmer c1903. Pl. no. III__5. E139

          VII, 45-46: 1-21
          Song for mezzo soprano with piano.
          r: db^1 - a^2

RB200. Worth, John W. Ah Love, but a Day, key of B major, no. 5. From Twelve Songs by Browning by John W. Worth. Manuscript, no place: no publisher, n.d. No pl. no.

VII, 45-46: 1-21
Song for [medium] voice with keyboard.
r: b# - f#^{2} t: d#^{1} - d#^{2}

Note: RB200 is bound in Twelve Songs by Browning.

II.—By the Fireside

RB201. +Somervell, Arthur. By the Fireside, key of E-flat major, no. 2. From the song cycle, James Lee's Wife. London: Boosey & Co, c1907. H.5425. E137

VII, 47-48: 1-24
Song for contralto solo and orchestra. Piano-vocal score [only].
r: g - g^2

Note: RB201 is bound in the song cycle, James Lee's Wife.

III.—In the Doorway

RB202. Galsworthy, Ada. In the Doorway, key of G minor, no. 2. From Two Songs by Mrs. John Galsworthy. London: Weekes & Co., n.d. W.5333.

VII, 49-50: 1-7, 15-21
Song for [medium] voice with piano.
r: c#^{1} - g^2 t: f^1 - f^2

Note: RB202 is bound in Two Songs. Broughton, *Bibliography* gives [1907] as the possible date of publication.

RB203. +Somervell, Arthur. In the Doorway, key of F major, no. 3. From the song cycle, James Lee's Wife. London: Boosey & Co, c1907. H.5425. E137

VII, 49-50: 1-7, 22-28
Song for contralto solo and orchestra. Piano-vocal score [only].
r: d^1 - f^2

Note: RB203 is bound in the song cycle, James Lee's Wife.

V.—On the Cliff

RB204. +Somervell, Arthur. On the Cliff, key of D major, no. 4. From the song cycle, James Lee's Wife. London: Boosey & Co, c1907. H.5425. E137

VII, 54-55: 1-30
Song for contralto solo and orchestra. Piano-vocal score [only].
r: b - f^2

Note: RB204 is bound in the song cycle, James Lee's Wife.

VII.—Among the Rocks

RB205.　　+Somervell, Arthur. Among the Rocks, key of A-flat major, no. 5. From the song cycle, James Lee's Wife. London: Boosey & Co, c1907. H.5425. E137

VII, 61: 1-12
Song for contralto solo and orchestra. Piano-vocal score [only].
r: bb - f²

Note: RB205 is bound in the song cycle, James Lee's Wife.

RB206.　　+True, Latham. Among the Rocks, key of E-flat major. From Browning Songs by Latham True. Portland, Maine: Cressey & Allen, Latham True c1932. No pl. no. E138

VII, 61: 1-12
Song for [medium] voice with keyboard.
r: c¹ - f²　　t: eb¹ - bb¹

JOCOSERIA[6]

RB207.　　+Bantock, Granville. Wanting Is—What? key of B-flat major. Swan Edition, no. 21. London: Swan & Co. (Music Publishers) Limited, c1922. Swan 2804. E399

XV, 167: 1-15
Song for low voice with piano.
r: g - f²

RB208.　　+————————. Wanting Is—What? key of E-flat major. Swan Edition, no. 21. London: Swan & Co. (Music Publishers) Limited, c1922. Swan 2803. E399

XV, 167: 1-15
Song for high voice with piano.
r: c¹ - bb²

RB209.　　+Forster, Beatrice. Wanting Is—What? key of C major. London: Forsyth Brothers, Ltd., n.d. No pl. no. E400

XV, 167: 1-15
Song for [high] voice with piano.
r: e¹ - g²　　t: a¹ - e²

Note: On the front cover is written "Beatrice Forster Sep. 2nd, 1902." Broughton, *Bibliography* gives [c1902?] as the possible copyright date.

RB210.　　Halley, M[argaret] A. To Perfect the Summer, key of D-flat major. Manuscript, no place: no publisher, n.d. No pl. no.

XV, 167: 1-15

---

[6]There is no title immediately above the poem beginning "Wanting is—what;" the title appears on the preceding page.

Song for [medium] voice with keyboard.
r: b♭ - f^2 t: f^1 - c^2

Note: The ABL received RB210 April 16, 1941.

RB211.   Halley, Margaret A. To Perfect the Summer, key of D-flat major. Photostat copy, Dundee: Paterson, Sons & Co, n.d. No pl. no.

XV, 167: 1-15
Song for [high] voice with piano.
r: b♭ - f^2 t: f^1 - c^2

Note: The ABL received RB211 Nov. 1, 1940.

RB212.   +Kernochan, Marshall. Wanting Is—What? key of E major. From Songs. Boston: C. W. Thompson & Co., c1908. T.&Co. 1368. E402

XV, 167: 1-15
Song for [high] voice with piano.
r: b - f^2 t: g#^{1} - e^2

JOHANNES AGRICOLA IN MEDITATION

RB213.   Brahms, Johannes. There's Heaven Above, and Night by Night, key of G major, no. 667. From Songs of Praise, edited by Percy Dearmer, Ralph Vaughan Williams, and Martin Shaw. Enlarged edition. London: Oxford University Press, Humphrey Milford, [1931]. No pl. no.

IV, 199: 1-15; 201: 56-60
Hymn for soprano, alto, tenor, bass (unacc.).

Note: RB213 is bound in Songs of Praise.

RB214.   +Homer, Sidney. There's Heaven Above, key of E-flat minor, op. 21, no. 2 [only]. New York: G. Schirmer, c1910. Pl. no. 21582. E140

IV, 199: 1-15
Song for high voice with piano.
r: d^1 - gb^2

RB215.   +Huhn, Bruno [Siegfried]. A Meditation, key of E-flat major. From Part-Songs for Mens Voices, no. 12,705. Boston: Oliver Ditson Company, c1914. Pl. no. 5-199-70627. E141

IV, 199: 1-15
Part-song for male chorus (tenor I and II, bass I and II) with organ or piano.

LA SAISIAZ[7]

RB216.   +Robyn, Alfred G. "Good to Forgive," key of A major. New York: G. Schirmer, c1895. Pl. no. 11870. E142

XIV, 155-156: 1-24
Song for mezzo soprano or baritone with piano.
r: $c\#^1$ - $f\#^2$

RB217.   +Rogers, Clara Kathleen. Good to Forgive, key of D major, no. 4. From Browning Songs, Second Series, op. 32. Edition Schmidt, no. 24. Boston: Arthur P. Schmidt, c1900. A.P.S. 5037d. E143

XIV, 155-156: 1-24
Song for [high] voice with keyboard.
r: b - $f\#^2$ t: g - e^2

Note: RB217 is bound in Browning Songs, Second Series.

RB218.   Worth, John W. Good to Forgive, key of E-flat major, no. 8. From Twelve Songs by Browning by John W. Worth. Manuscript, no place: no publisher, n.d. No pl. no.

XIV, 155-156: 1-24
Song for [high] voice with keyboard.
r: eb^1 - a^2 t: g^1 - $f\#^2$

Note: RB218 is bound in Twelve Songs by Browning.

LETTERS FROM ROBERT BROWNING TO ELIZABETH BARRETT BROWNING[8]

RB219.   Saar, Louis Victor. Browning Song Cycle from Letters of R. B. to E. B. B., op. 74. 1. Thou Shalt Know Me, key of F major. 2. Some Happy Day, key of F major. 3. Thou Wilt Know, key of E-flat major. 4. The Rose Tree, key of C major. 5. This Little Flower, key of E-flat major. Words by Jessie Andrews, based on letters of RB. Boston: Carl Fischer, c1914. Pl. no. 17506.

Song cycle for high voice with piano.
1.   *Letters*, I, 102: 9-10
     r: d^1 - g^2
2.   *Letters*, II, 2: 30
     r: db^1 - a^2
3.   *Letters*, II, 7: 5-8
     r: e^1 - g^2
4.   *Letters*, II, 10: 4
     r: $d\#^1$ - g^2

---

[7]There is no title immediately above the poem beginning "Good, to forgive;" the title appears on the preceding and succeeding pages so that this poem may be acting somewhat like a prologue.

[8]This is not the title of an RB poem; it is herein listed because the lyrics are based on the letters by RB.

5. *Letters,* II, 147: 1-4
r: eb^1 - bb^2

LIFE IN A LOVE

RB220. +Bantock, Granville. Life in a Love, key of B-flat major. Swan Edition, no. 20. London: Swan & Co. (Music Publishers) Limited, c1922. Swan2805. E144

VI, 171: 1-22
Song for high voice with piano.
r: cb^1 - g^2

RB221. +————. Life in a Love, key of G major. Swan Edition, no. 20. London: Swan & Co. (Music Publishers) Limited, c1922. Swan2806. E144

VI, 171: 1-22
Song for low voice with piano.
r: a^b - e^2

RB222. +Bruguiere, E. A. Life in a Love (Liebesringen), key of G major. German words by F. H. Schneider. From Songs by E. A. Bruguiere. New York: Breitkopf & Härtel, c1901. No pl. no. E145

VI, 171: 1-22
Song for [medium] voice with piano.
r: b - f^2 t: e^1 - c^2

RB223. +Mc. Hardy, James M. P. Life in a Love, key of F major, no. 5 [only]. Photostat copy, London: Alphonse Bertini, Seymour & Co., n.d. No pl. no. E146

VI, 171: 1-22
Song for [high] voice with piano.
r: c^1 - f^2 (optional a^2)   t: g^1 - e^2

Note: The ABL received RB223 Nov. 1, 1940. Broughton, *Bibliography* gives [1876] as the possible date of publication.

THE LOST LEADER

RB224. +Bantock, Granville. The Lost Leader, key of A major. From Breitkopf and Härtel's Choruses for Mens Voices, no. 73. London: Breitkopf & Härtel, c1910. Pl. no. 26468. E147

VI, 7-8: 1-12, 17-32
Part-song for male chorus (tenor I and II, bass I and II) with keyboard (for rehearsal only).

RB225. +Hullah, John [Pyke]. The Lost Leader, "Just for a Handful of Silver He Left Us," key of A major. Photostat copy, London: Lamborn Cock, n.d. (L.C.624). E148

VI, 7-8: 1-32
Song for [medium low] voice with piano.
r: a - e² t: f¹ - c²

Note: The ABL received RB225 Nov. 1, 1940. Broughton, *Bibliography* gives [1877] as the possible date of publication.

RB226.   —————. The Lost Leader, key of A major. Manuscript, no place: no publisher, n.d. No pl. no.

VI, 7-8: 1-32
Song for [medium low] voice with piano.
r: a - e² t: f¹ - c²

Note: The ABL received RB226 April 16, 1941.

LOVE. *See* EARTH'S IMMORTALITIES

LOVE AMONG THE RUINS

RB227.   +Kramer, A[rthur] Walter. At Evening, key of A major, no. 1. From Three Preludes, op. 33. Boston: Oliver Ditson Company, c1912. Pl. no. 5-86-69071-6. E149

VI, 54: 1-2
Prelude for piano.

Note: RB227 is bound in Three Preludes.

LOVE HAS COME[9]

RB228.   Graham, A. Cyril. Love Has Come, key of F major. From Songs by A. Cyril Graham. Chicago: Clayton F. Summy Co., c1911. C.F.S.Co.1307.

Song for [high] voice with keyboard.
r: f¹ - a² t: a¹ - f²

A LOVERS' QUARREL

RB229.   +Gregory, E[leanor] C. A Lover's Quarrel, key of A major, no. 6. From Six Songs. London: Novello Ewer & Co, n.d. Pl. no. 7519. E150

VI, 58: 1-14; 63: 113-119
Song for [medium high] voice with keyboard.
r: e¹ - f#² t: e¹ - e²

Note: RB229 is bound in Six Songs.

RB230.   +Lehmann, Liza. Love, If You Knew the Light, key of G major. From Three Songs. New York: G. Schirmer, Inc., c1922. Pl. no. 30696. E153

---

[9]This is not the title of an RB poem; it is herein listed because the lyrics are mistakenly attributed to him on the music; actually the lyrics are those of Alfred, Lord Tennyson, *Harold* (Act I, scene ii, lines 7-12).

VI, 63: 99-103
Song for low voice with piano.
r: a^1 - e^2

RB231. Stoker, Richard. Here's the Spring Back, [no. 2]. From Songs of Spring [by] Richard Stoker. L.C.S.5. London: Leeds Music Limited, c1969. No pl. no.

VI, 64: 120-124
Part-song for women's chorus (soprano I and II, alto) with piano (for rehearsal only).

Note: RB231 is bound in Songs of Spring.

MARCHING ALONG. *See* CAVALIER TUNES I

MASTER HUGHES OF SAXE-GOTHA

RB232. +Bantock, Granville. Master Hughes of Saxe-Gotha, key of A-flat major. Berners Edition. London: Joseph Williams Limited, c1935. W.16. E154

VI, 196: 2-4
Solo for piano.

RB233. +Hathaway, Joseph W. G. Master Hughes of Saxe-Gotha, key of B-flat major, op. 35. London: Weekes & Co., c1910. W.4881. E155

VI, 196-197: 1-5, 11-15; 199-200: 56-65, 71-75, 81-85; 204: 136-140, 142-149
Choral rhapsody for mixed chorus (soprano I and II, alto I and II, tenor I and II, bass I and II) with piano.

MEETING AT NIGHT

RB234. [Armes, Nancy.] Meeting at Night, key of F major. Manuscript, no place: no publisher, n.d. No pl. no.

VI, 46: 1-12
Song for [medium] voice with keyboard.
r: c^1 - d^2 t: f^1 - c^2

Note: "Nancy Armes" is written on the front cover only, i.e., not above the first line of music on the right side where the composer's name is usually found.

RB235. Dello Joio, Norman. Meeting at Night, key of C major. From Songs by Norman Dello Joio. New York: Carl Fischer Inc., c1954. Pl. no. 31063.

VI, 46: 1-12
Song for high voice with keyboard.
r: f^1 - g^2

RB236.   +Fisher, Charles R. Meeting at Night, key of G major. London: Weekes & Co., n.d. W.4929. E156

VI, 46: 1-12
Song for [medium high] voice with piano.
r: d^1 - $f\#^2$ t: f^1 - c^2

Note: Broughton, *Bibliography* gives [1904] as the possible date of publication.

RB237.   Reed, C. H. Meeting at Night, key of D-flat major, no. 7(a) [only]. From Twelve Songs. Photostat copy, London: Weekes & Co., printed for private circulation, n.d. W.7098.

VI, 46: 1-12
Song for [high] voice with piano.
r: d^1 - gb^2 t: a^1 - f^2

Note: A transition to 7(b), Parting at Morning, is provided if the two are sung successively; *see* RB297. The ABL received RB237 Sept. 18, 1940.

RB238.   +Ryan, Margaret. Meeting at Night, key of F major. From Two Songs by Margaret Ryan. New York: G. Schirmer (Inc.), c1932. Pl. no. 35906. E157

VI, 46: 1-12
Song for high voice with piano.
r: eb^1 - a^2

RB239.   +Somervell, Arthur. Meeting at Night, key of C major, no. 2. From the song cycle, A Broken Arc. London: Boosey & Co., c1923. H. 10770. E158

VI, 46: 1-12
Song for [medium high] voice with piano.
r: d^1 - e^2 t: g^1 - e^2

Note: RB239 is bound in A Broken Arc.

RB240.   +Stebbins, G. Waring. Meeting, key of C major. New York: G. Schirmer, c1909. Pl. no. 20673. E159

VI, 46: 1-12
Song for high voice with piano.
r: d^1 - g^2

RB241.   White, Grace. Three Descriptions from Browning, no. 1, key of F major. From Three Descriptions from Browning. New York: G. Schirmer, c1917. Pl. no. 26881.

VI, 46: 1-4
Solo for violin with piano.

Note: RB241 is bound in the above mentioned Three Descriptions from Browning.

RB242. Whitney, Maurice C. Meeting at Night, key of F major.
W 7 -1006. [New York:] W7 choral library, W-7 Music
Corp. c1960. Pl. no. 209.

VI, 46: 1-12
Part-song for mixed chorus (soprano, alto, tenor, bass) with
piano.

RB243. ——————. Meeting at Night, key of F major. W 7 -1007.
New York: Warner Bros. Music, W-7 Music Corp. c1968.
Pl. no. 210.

VI, 46: 1-12
Part-song for women's chorus (soprano I and II, alto) with
piano.

RB244. Worth, John W. Meeting at Night, key of E major, no. 6.
From Twelve Songs by Browning by John W. Worth. Manuscript, no place: no publisher, n.d. No pl. no.

VI, 46: 1-12
Song for [medium] voice with keyboard.
r: $c\#^1$ - $f\#^2$ t: $f\#^1$ - $d\#^2$

Note: RB244 is bound in Twelve Songs by Browning.

THE MELON-SELLER. *See* FERISHTAH'S FANCIES

MIHRAB SHAH. *See* FERISHTAH'S FANCIES

MISCONCEPTIONS

RB245. +Gow, George Coleman. Misconceptions, key of B major, no.
7. From "Colombe's Birthday," Intermezzo Music, op. 4.
Boston: The Boston Music Co., c1892. B.M.Co.219. E54

VI, 154: 1-14
Part-song for women's voices (soprano I and II, alto I and II),
unacc.

Note: RB245 is bound in "Colombe's Birthday," Intermezzo
Music.

RB246. +Gregory, E[leanor] C. Misconceptions, key of D major, no.
2. From Six Songs. London: Novello Ewer & Co, n.d. Pl.
no. 7519. E163

VI, 154: 1-14
Song for [medium] voice with keyboard.
r: b - $f\#^2$ t: $f\#^1$ - d^2

Note: RB246 is bound in Six Songs.

RB247.   +Reinagle, Caroline. This Is a Spray the Bird Clung To, key
of B major, no. 3 [only]. From Three Songs by Caroline
Reinagle. London: Augener & Co., n.d. A&Co.2007. E164

VI, 154: 1-14
Song for [medium] voice with piano.
r: d^1 - d^2 t: $f\#^1$ - b^1

Note: Broughton, *Bibliography* gives [188-] as the possible
date of publication.

RB248.   +Schuyler, Georgina. This Is a Spray the Bird Clung To, key
of A major, no. 7. From Album of Songs by Georgina
Schuyler. New York: G. Schirmer, c1894. Pl. no. 3125. E165

VI, 154: 1-14
Song for mezzo soprano or contralto with piano.
r: $c\#^1$ - e^2

Note: RB248 is bound in Album of Songs.

RB249.   Worth, John W. Misconceptions, key of D major, no. 11.
From Twelve Songs by Browning by John W. Worth. Manuscript, no place: no publisher, n.d. No pl. no.

VI, 154: 1-14
Song for [high] voice with keyboard.
r: e^1 - a^2 t: b^1 - $f\#^2$

Note: RB249 is bound in Twelve Songs by Browning.

MY STAR

RB250.   Atkins, Evelyn Harper. My Star, key of C major. Manuscript,
no place: no publisher, n.d. No pl. no.

VI, 125: 1-13
Song for [high] voice with violin. No violin part.

RB251.   Bantock, Granville. My Star, key of A major. From Dramatic
Lyrics by Robert Browning. Swan Edition, no. 3. London:
Swan & Co. (Music Publishers) Limited, c1920. S.&Co.
W.&W.Ltd.2722.

VI, 125: 1-13
Song for low voice with piano.
r: $c\#^1$ - e^2

RB252.   —————. My Star, key of C major. From Dramatic Lyrics
by Robert Browning. Swan Edition, no. 3. London: Swan &
Co. (Music Publishers) Limited, c1920. S.&Co.W.&W.Ltd.
2708.

VI, 125: 1-13
Song for high voice with piano.
r: e^1 - g^2

RB253. +Clarke, Helen A[rchibald]. My Star, key of E-flat major.
From *Poet-Lore,* I, 349-353, edited by Charlotte Porter and
Helen A. Clarke. Philadelphia: The Poet-Lore Co., 1889.
No pl. no. E167

VI, 125: 1-13
Song for [high] voice with piano.
r: b^b - g^2 t: g^1 - e^2

Note: RB253 is bound in *Poet-Lore.*

RB254. ——————. My Star, key of E-flat major. [Philadelphia]:
Poet-Lore Co., H. A. Clarke c1889. No pl. no.

VI, 125: 1-13
Song for [high] voice with piano.
r: b^b - g^2 t: g^1 - e^2

RB255. Freer, Eleanor Everest. All That I Know of a Certain Star,
key of C major. From the opera, The Brownings Go to Italy,
(or) (A Love Story), op. 43. Libretto by G. A. Hawkins-
Ambler. Chicago: The Music Library of Chicago, c1936.
Pl. no. 38977.

VI, 125: 1-13
Song for baritone with keyboard.
r: c^1 - e^2

Note: RB255 is bound in The Brownings Go to Italy (piano-
vocal score).

RB256. +——————. My Star, key of C major, op. 4, no. 2 [only].
Chicago: The Music Library of Chicago, Eleanor Everest
Freer c1929. Pl. no. 31083. E169

VI, 125: 1-13
Song for baritone with keyboard.
r: c^1 - e^2

Note: On the front cover is written "Latest edition (in Opera)
1938 May" in what looks like the handwriting of the composer.

RB257. ——————. "My Star," key of C major, op. 4, no. 2 [only].
Revised edition, Vol. II. Manuscript, [Milwaukee: Wm. A.
Kaun Music Co.], n.d. No pl. no.

VI, 125: 1-13
Song for [medium] voice with keyboard.
r: c^1 - e^2 t: d^1 - d^2

Note: At the bottom of the first page of music is written "Revised Edition, Volume II. Wm. A. Kaun Music Co. Milwaukee, Wis."

RB258.   +Hill, Mildred J. My Star, key of E major. From Songs by Mildred J. Hill. Boston: Arthur P. Schmidt, P. L. Jung c1898. P.L.J.452. E170

VI, 125: 1-13
Song for [medium] voice with piano.
r: d^1 - $f\#^2$ t: f^1 - c^2

RB259.   +Homer, Sidney. My Star, key of A-flat major, op. 12, no. 1 [only]. From Three Songs. New York: G. Schirmer, c1903. Pl. no. 16339. E171

VI, 125: 1-13
Song for high voice with piano.
r: eb^1 - f^2

RB260.   +————. My Star, key of F-sharp major, op. 12, no. 1 [only]. From Three Songs. New York: G. Schirmer, c1903. Pl. no. 16338. E171

VI, 125: 1-13
Song for low voice with piano.
r: $c\#^1$ - $d\#^2$

RB261.   +Millar, A. F. My Star, key of C major. London: West & Co, c1915. W.&Co.926. E172

VI, 125: 1-13
Song for [low] voice with piano.
r: g - e^2 t: c^1 - a^1

RB262.   +Neidlinger, W[illiam] H[arold]. My Star: "All That I Know of a Certain Star," key of F major. From Songs and Ballads by W. H. Neidlinger. New York: G. Schirmer, c1895. Pl. no. 12108. E173

VI, 125: 1-13
Song for soprano or tenor with piano.
r: f^1 - a^2

RB263.   +Renaud, Emiliano. My Star, key of D-flat major. From Four Songs by Robert Browning. Boston: White-Smith Music Publishing Co., c1914. Pl. no. 14668. E174

VI, 125: 1-13
Song for [high] voice with piano.
r: eb^1 - f t: g^1 - d^2

RB264.   +Rogers, Clara Kathleen. My Star, key of E major, no. 1.
From Browning Songs, Second Series, op. 32. Edition
Schmidt, no. 24. Boston: Arthur P. Schmidt, c1900. A.P.S.
5037a. E175

VI, 125: 1-13
Song for [high] voice with keyboard.
r: e^1 - $g\#^2$ t: g^1 - e^2

Note: RB264 is bound in Browning Songs, Second Series.

RB265.   +Smith, Leo. My Star, key of E-flat major. From Five Songs
by Leo Smith. New York: G. Schirmer, Leo Smith c1912.
Pl. no. 24599. E176

VI, 125: 1-13
Song for [high] voice with piano.
r: eb^1 - ab^2 (optional bb^2)   t: g^1 - g^2

RB266.   +Somervell, Arthur. My Star, key of E-flat major, no. 3. From
the song cycle, A Broken Arc. London: Boosey & Co., c1923.
H. 10770. E177

VI, 125: 1-13
Song for [medium high] voice with piano.
r: db^1 - eb^2 t: eb^1 - c^2

Note: RB266 is bound in A Broken Arc.

RB267.   +True, Latham. My Star, key of E major. From Browning
Songs by Latham True. Portland, Maine: Cressey & Allen,
Latham True c1932. No pl. no. E178

VI, 125: 1-13
Song for [medium] voice with keyboard.
r: $d\#^1$ - $g\#^2$ t: $f\#^1$ - e^2

RB268.   Weems, Mrs. J. Eddie. My Star, key of D major. From "The
Browning Cycle of Love Lyrics." Manuscript, no place: no
publisher, n.d. No pl. no.

VI, 125: 1-13
Song for [medium] voice with keyboard.
r: d^1 - e^2 (optional $f\#^2$)   t: $f\#^1$ - $c\#^2$

RB269.   +Whitmer, T[homas] Carl. "My Star," key of G major, no. 2
[only]. From Three Songs, op. 3. No place: T. Carl Whitmer
c1903. Pl. no. II—4. E179

VI, 125: 1-13
Song for mezzo soprano with piano.
r: db^1 - e^2

RB270. Worth, John W. My Star, key of A major, no. 10. From Twelve Songs by Browning by John W. Worth. Manuscript, no place: no publisher, n.d. No pl. no.

VI, 125: 1-13
Song for [high] voice with keyboard.
r: e^1 - $f\#^2$ t: f^1 - e^2

Note: RB270 is bound in Twelve Songs by Browning.

NEVER THE TIME AND THE PLACE

RB271. +Bantock, Granville. Never the Time and the Place, key of A major. Swan Edition, no. 22. London: Swan & Co. (Music Publishers) Limited, c1922. Swan 2800. E180

XV, 256-257: 1-22
Song for low voice with piano.
r: a - f^2

RB272. +————. Never the Time and the Place, key of C major. Swan Edition, no. 22. London: Swan & Co. (Music Publishers) Limited, c1922. Swan 2799. E180

XV, 256-257: 1-22
Song for high voice with piano.
r: c^1 - ab^2

NOW

RB273. Bantock, Granville. Now, key of A major. From Dramatic Lyrics by Robert Browning. Swan Edition, no. 7. London: Swan & Co. (Music Publishers) Limited, c1921. S.&Co. W.&W.Ltd.2745.

Asolando, 8: 1-14
Song for low voice with piano.
r: a - e^2

RB274. ————. Now, key of C major. From Dramatic Lyrics by Robert Browning. Swan Edition, no. 7. London: Swan & Co. (Music Publishers) Limited, c1921. S.&Co.W.&W.Ltd. 2743.

Asolando, 8: 1-14
Song for high voice with piano.
r: c^1 - g^2

O GOD OUR HELP[10]

RB275. Croft, William. O God, Our Help, key of C major. Words by Isaac Watts. Manuscript, no place: no publisher, n.d. No pl. no.

Hymn for soprano, alto, tenor, bass (unacc.).

---

[10]This is not the title of an RB poem; it is herein listed because it is the hymn sung at RB's funeral in Westminster Abbey, Dec. 31, 1889; the ABL has a book autographed "Robert Browning" which contains this hymn by Watts; Isaac Watts, *Hymns and Spiritual Songs* (London: A. Wilson, 1813) is bound in *The Psalms of David* (London: A. Wilson, n.d.).

AN OLD STORY. *See* THE PATRIOT

ONE WAY OF LOVE

RB276. +Clarke, Helen A[rchibald]. One Way of Love, key of A major. [Philadelphia: Poet-Lore, 1892.] E.305. E182

VI, 159-160: 1-18
Song for [high] voice with cello obbligato and keyboard. No parts.
r: $c\#^1$ - g^2 t: e^1 - e^2

Note: The ABL received RB276 Sept. 18, 1940.

RB277. +Gregory, E[leanor] C. One Way of Loving, key of G major, no. 1. From Six Songs. London: Novello Ewer & Co, n.d. Pl. no. 7519. E183

VI, 159-160: 1-18
Song for [medium] voice with keyboard.
r: d^1 - $g\#^2$ t: $f\#^1$ - c^2

Note: RB277 is bound in Six Songs.

RB278. +Rogers, Clara Kathleen. One Way of Love, key of E minor, no. 5. From Browning Songs, Second Series, op. 32. Edition Schmidt, no. 24. Boston: Arthur P. Schmidt, c1900. A.P.S. 5037e. E184

VI, 159-160: 1-18
Song for [high] voice with keyboard.
r: c^1 - a^2 t: $f\#^1$ - $f\#^2$

Note: RB278 is bound in Browning Songs, Second Series.

RB279. +Thayer, Arthur W. One Way of Love, key of D major, no. 3 [only]. From Three Songs by Arthur W. Thayer. Boston: H. B. Stevens Company, c1892. H.B.S.Co.435. E185

VI, 159-160: 1-18
Song for high voice with piano.
r: e^1 - g^2

PAN AND LUNA

RB280. +Bantock, Granville. Pan and Luna, key of E-flat major. Berners Edition. London: Joseph Williams Limited, c1935. W.20. E186

XV, 163: 1-4
Solo for piano.

PARACELSUS

RB281.   +Bantock, Granville. I Go to Prove My Soul, key of B-flat major. Swan Edition, no. 50. London: Swan & Co. (Music Publishers) Limited, c1925. Swan. 2920. E187

II, 27-28: 559-565
Song for [low] voice with piano.
r: bb - d²   t: d¹ - a¹

RB282.   +————. I Go to Prove My Soul, key of D-flat major. Swan Edition, no. 50. London: Swan & Co. (Music Publishers) Limited, c1925. Swan. 2919. E187

II, 27-28: 559-565
Song for [high] voice with piano.
r: db¹ - f²   t: ab¹ - eb²

RB283.   +————. Paracelsus, key of C major, no. 3 [only]. From Three Choruses for Male Voices, The Oxford Choral Songs, no. 617. London: Oxford University Press, c1930. No pl. no. E188

II, 167-168: 653-681
Part-song for male chorus (tenor I and II, baritone I and II, bass I and II) with keyboard (for rehearsal only).

RB284.   +————. Song of the Galleys from "Paracelsus," key of D-flat major. London: W. Paxton & Co., Ltd., c1938. Paxton 80245. E189

II, 129-131: 450-499
Part-song for male chorus (tenor I and II, bass I and II) with keyboard (for rehearsal only).

RB285.   de Lacey, Robert. I Stoop into a Dark Tremendous Sea of Cloud, key of F major. Manuscript, no place: no publisher, n.d. No pl. no.

II, 176-177: 899-903
Anthem for bass and alto soloists, mixed chorus (soprano, alto, tenor, bass) and organ.

Note: On the front cover is written "Set to music by Robert de Lacy [sic], Organist and Choir Master of the Smith Place Religious Society, [. . .] Square, London."

RB286.   +Harraden, Ethel. I Go to Prove My Soul, key of F major. Edited by Emma L. Taussig. From Selected Octavo Publications, Solos, no. 6004. St. Louis: Thiebes-Stierlin Music Co., c1901. No pl. no. E190

II, 27-28: 559-565
Song for soprano or tenor with keyboard.
r: c¹ - g²

RB287. +—————. I Go to Prove My Soul, key of G major. London: C. Jefferys, n.d. J.3194. E190

II, 27-28: 559-565
Song for [high] voice with piano.
r: d^1 - a^2 t: g^1 - e^2

Note: Broughton, *Bibliography* gives 1885 as the date of publication.

RB288. +—————. "Over the Sea Our Galleys Went," (Paracelsus), key of A-flat major. London: C. Jeffreys, n.d. No pl. no. E191

II, 129-131: 450-486
Part-song for male chorus (tenor I and II, bass I and II) with piano.

Note: On the front cover is written "Lily E. Kingsland." Broughton, *Bibliography* gives 1885 as the date of publication.

RB289. +Huhn, Bruno. Faith, key of E-flat major. Manuscript, Boston: The Boston Music Co., c1934. B.M.Co.9016. E194

II, 142-143: 51, 54, 55, 71-73; 176-177: 901-904
Song for [high] voice with keyboard.
r: eb^1 - f^2 t: g^1 - e^2

Note: On the front cover is printed in pencil "To Helen and Minot Simons."

RB290. Ives, Charles. From "Paracelsus," key of C major, [no. 14]. From Nineteen Songs by Charles Ives. Bryn Mawr, Pennsylvania: Merion Music, Inc., c1935. Pl. no. 441-41007-50.

II, 173-175: 804-807, 846, 847, 854, 856-858
Song for [medium] voice with keyboard.
r: cb^1 - $f\#^2$ t: eb^1 - e^2

Note: RB290 is bound in Nineteen Songs.

RB291. Krull, Fritz. I Go to Prove My Soul, key of D major, no. 2. From Three Songs by Fritz Krull. Manuscript, no place: no publisher, 1908. No pl. no.

II, 27-28: 559-565
Song for [high] voice with keyboard.
r: d^1 - e^2 t: g^1 - e^2

Note: RB291 is bound in Three Songs.

RB291.1. Robbins, Reginald C. The Wanderers, key of G major. Xerox copy, Paris: Editions Maurice Senart, c1922. E.M.S.4912.

II, 129-132: 450-453, 462-481, 491-522
Song for [medium low] voice with keyboard.
r: A - d^1 t: e - b

RB292.   Rogers, James H[otchkiss]. I Go to Prove My Soul, key of
          E-flat major. New York: G. Schirmer, Inc., c1945. Pl. no.
          41096.

          II, *27-28*: 559-565
          Song for medium voice with piano.
          r: d^1 - f^2

RB293.   ——————. I Go to Prove My Soul, key of E-flat major.
          Xerox manuscript, no place: no publisher, n.d. No pl. no.

          II, *27-28*: 559-565
          Song for [medium high] voice with keyboard.
          r: d^1 - f^2 t: g^1 - eb^2

          Note: The ABL received RB293 Oct. 22, 1941.

PARLEYINGS WITH CERTAIN PEOPLE

With Charles Avison

RB294.   Avison, Charles. "Grand March,"[11] key of C major. Photostat
          copy, no place: no publisher, n.d. No pl. no.

          XVI, 221-240, especially 240
          March for unspecified keyboard (?) instrument.

          Note: The photostat appears as p. 9 in Willa Lee Clements
          Moore, "The Baylor University Collection of the Musical
          Settings of the Poetry of Robert Browning" (unpublished
          M.M. thesis, Baylor University, Waco, Texas, 1951).

RB295.   ——————. [March],[12] key of C major. From *The Poetical
          Works of Robert Browning* (London: Smith Elder, & Co.,
          1889), XVI, 240. No pl. no.

          XVI, 221-240, especially 240
          March for unspecified keyboard (?) instrument.

PARTING AT MORNING

RB296.   +Miller, Anne Stratton. Parting at Morning, key of E-flat
          major. New York: Harold Flammer Inc. Publisher of Amer-
          ican Works, c1920. Pl. no. 270. E195

          VI, 46: 1-4
          Song for [medium] voice with piano.
          r: d^1 - g^2 t: eb^1 - c^2

---

[11]Moore labels her photostat copy as follows: Charles Avison's "Grand March,"
cf. W. Hall Griffin, *The Life of Robert Browning*, edited by Harry Christopher
Minchin (London: Methuen & Co. Ltd., 1910), p. 16; in the poem *With Charles
Avison*, RB refers to the music as *March*.

[12]There is no title above the music, but in the poem RB refers to the music as
March.

RB297. Reed, C. H. Parting at Morning, key of A major, no. 7(b) [only]. From Twelve Songs. Photostat copy, no place: no publisher, n.d. W.7098.

VI, 46: 1-4
Song for [high] voice with piano.
r: e^1 - f$^{\#2}$ t: a^1 - e^2

Note: A transition from Meeting at Night, 7(a), is provided with RB237. The ABL received RB297 Sept. 18, 1940.

RB298. White, Grace. Three Descriptions from Browning, no. 3, key of E major. From Three Descriptions from Browning. New York: G. Schirmer, c1917. Pl. no. 26881.

VI, 46: 1-4
Solo for violin with piano.

Note: RB298 is bound in the above mentioned Three Descriptions from Browning.

RB299. Worth, John W. Parting at Morning, key of D-flat major, no. 7. From Twelve Songs by Browning by John W. Worth. Manuscript, no place: no publisher, n.d. No pl. no.

VI, 46: 1-4
Song for [high] voice with keyboard.
r: db^1 - ab^2 t: f^1 - f^2

Note: RB299 is bound in Twelve Songs by Browning.

PASSACAGLIA[13]

RB300. Church, Frank M. A Passacaglia, key of G major. Manuscript, no place: no publisher, Jan., 1951. No pl. no.

Based on the italicized letters in Ro*b*ert *B*rownin*g*.
Solo for unspecified keyboard (?) instrument.

Note: Above the first line of music is written "Written in January 1951 at Boaz, Alabama Dedicated to Dr. A. J. Armstrong, Ph.D. Litt.D. Baylor University, Waco, Texas by Frank M. Church, Dir. of Music. Baylor Univ. 1921-22."

THE PATRIOT
An Old Story

RB301. +Kramer, A[rthur] Walter. The Patriot, key of C major and C minor. Cincinnati: The John Church Company, c1925. Pl. no. 18961. E197

V, 6-7: 1-30
Song for low voice with piano.
r: bb - e^2

---

[13]This is not the title of an RB poem; it is herein listed because the music is based on the poet's name.

RB302.   +——————. The Patriot, key of E major and E minor. Cincinnati: The John Church Company, c1925. Pl. no. 18960.
E197

V, 6-7: 1-30
Song for high voice with piano.
r: d^1 - $g\#^2$

RB303.   Worth, John W. The Patriot, key of G major, no. 2. From
Twelve Songs by Browning by John W. Worth. Manuscript,
no place: no publisher, n.d. No pl. no.

V, 6-7: 1-30
Song for [high] voice with keyboard.
r: d^1 - g^2 t: f^1 - f^2

Note: RB303 is bound in Twelve Songs by Browning.

A PEARL, A GIRL

RB304.   +Bantock, Granville. A Pearl, a Girl, key of B-flat major.
Swan Edition, no. 9. London: Swan & Co., c1921. S.&Co.
W.&W.Ltd.2764. E197.1

Asolando, 12: 1-14
Song for low voice with piano.
r: c^1 - f^2

RB305.   +——————. A Pearl, a Girl, key of D-flat major. Swan
Edition, no. 9. London: Swan & Co., c1921. S.&Co.W.&W.
Ltd.2763. E197.1

Asolando, 12: 1-14
Song for high voice with piano.
r: eb^1 - ab^2

THE PIED PIPER OF HAMELIN;

A Child's Story

(Written for, and Inscribed to, W. M. the Younger)

RB306.   +Aiken, Walter H. The Pied Piper of Hamelin. Words by
C. J. Brooks, based on the poem by RB. Cincinnati: The
Willis Music Company, c1917. Pl. no. 3070. E198
V, 102-115
Operetta for [high school or upper elementary] treble voices:
8 soloists, three-part chorus (soprano I and II, alto) with
chimes and violin. Piano-vocal score. No parts.

Characters

Pied Piper
Father, Mother, Boy

Children, including Hansel and Gretel
Villagers, men, women, cook, etc.
Mayor
Corporation (4 or more)
Seer
Villagers, flower girls, toy man, song vendor
Lame Boy
Rats (6 or more)

RB307. +Aylwin, Josephine Crew. The Pied Piper of Hamelin. Boston: C. W. Thompson & Co., c1912. T.&Co.58-48. E200

V, 102-114: 1-14, 17-27, 35-42, 52-62, 65, 66, 71-79, 94-96, 98-101, 106-114, 116-120, 146-152, 154-156, 164-173, 175, 183-185, 189-193, 197-207, 226-231, 256, 261-268, 284-287
Cantata for women's chorus (soprano I and II, alto), soloists (soprano, contralto) with piano.

RB308. +Bergh, Arthur. The Pied Piper of Hamelin, key of E major, op. 23. New York: G. Schirmer, Inc., c1914. Pl. no. 25001. E203

V, 102-114: 1-288
Recitation for reader with piano.

RB309. Boyle, George F[rederick]. The Pied Piper of Hamelin. Chappell's Choral Library. London: Chappell & Co. Ltd., c1911. Pl. no. 24470.

V, 102-114: 1-27, 30-36, 38-45, 52-66, 70-81, 83-88, 94-122, 146-156, 161-175, 182-184, 189-256, 261-268, 276-287
Cantata for soloists (contralto, tenor, baritone), mixed chorus (soprano I and II, alto I and II, tenor I and II, bass I and II) with orchestra. Piano-vocal score. No parts.

RB310. +Brumleu, Ernest. The Pied Piper. Written and adapted by E. Elliot Stock, based on the poem by RB. London: Heath Cranton & Ousley Ltd., n.d. No pl. no. E207

V, 102-115
One-act musical play for children: two-part children's chorus, soloist (Mayor) with keyboard.

Characters

The Mayor	Hans, a crippled boy
First Alderman	Gretschen, Brenda, Freda (3 housewives)
Second Alderman	Martha, a little girl
Notary	Captain of the Guard
The Piper	Chorus of women and children

Note: Broughton, *Bibliography* gives [1913] as the possible publication date.

RB311.   Brydson, John C. The Pied Piper of Hamelin, a piano suite.
          1. The River Weser, key of D major. 2. The Rats, key of
          B-flat major. 3. The Mayor and Corporation, key of E-flat
          major. 4. The Pied Piper, key of G major. 5. The Bells of
          Hamelin, key of E-flat major. 6. The Children, key of G
          major. London: Francis Day & Hunter Limited, c1949.
          A.&D.Ltd.21950.

          1. V, 102: 1, 3, 4
          2. V, 102-103: 10, 19, 20
          3. V, 104: 35
          4. V, 106: 98-101
          5. V, 108: 146, 147
          6. V, 111: 203, 204, 206, 207
          Suite for piano.

RB312.   Christopher, Carol. The Magic Piper. Libretto by N. Mitchell
          Hubrich, based on the poem by RB. An operetta in three acts.
          Wichita, [Kansas]: The Raymond A. Hoffman Co., c1959.
          R.A.H. Co. 86.

          V, 102-112: 1-27, 30-45, 52-58, 70-79, 88-110, 119-122,
          146-156, 161-196, 202-205, 208-231
          Operetta in three acts for children (unspecified voice parts).
          Piano-vocal score. No parts.

                              Characters

          Reader of Poem   Mayor of Hamelin
          Town Crier   First Councilman
          Gretchen   Second Councilman
          Katrina   Third Councilman
          Hans   First, Second, Third, Fourth, and
          Peter   Fifth Woman
          Clown Rat   First, Second, Third, Fourth, and
          Mutter Katzenheimer   Fifth Man
          Yacob   Piper
          Frieda   Chorus of Men and Women of
          Fido   Hamelin, Children and Rats

RB313.   +Clokey, Joseph W[addell]. The Pied Piper of Hamelin. Li-
          bretto by Anna J. Beiswenger, based on the poem by RB.
          Boston: C. C. Birchard & Co., c1923. Pl. no. 1040. E202

          V, 102-115
          Opera in three acts. Piano-vocal score. No parts.

                              Characters

          Prologue (baritone or mezzo soprano)
          The Mayor (bass)
          The Corporation (male voices)
          The Piper (baritone)

A Townsman (baritone)
The Lame Boy (soprano)
The Dreamlady (mezzo soprano)
Chorus of Citizens, Chorus of Priests, Chorus of Children,
Ballet of Tops, Jumping Jacks, Dolls, Soldiers, and Night
Wind Sprites

Note: The original instrumentation is not given on the music.

RB314. +Davies, [Henry] Walford. The Pied Piper. Novello's Original Octavo Edition. London: Novello and Company, Limited, c1939. Pl. no. 16687. E209

V, 102-115: 1-27, 30-45, 53-60, 63, 65, 66, 70-79, 84-86, 93-104, 106-122, 146-156, 161-175, 183-185, 187-211, 213, 214, 217-244, 256-260, 277, 278, 283-289, 300-303
Chamber cantata for mixed chorus (soprano, alto, tenor, bass), soloists (narrator, pianist, clarinetist), Mayor (bass), Piper (tenor), Lame Child (treble), with piano. Piano-vocal score. No parts.

RB315. +Dittenhaver, Sarah Louise. Pied Piper's Tune, key of G major. From Advanced Piano Compositions for Small Hands. Boston: Boston Music Company, c1942. B.M.Co.9998. E210

V, 110-111: 191-197
Solo for piano.

RB316. +Dunhill, Thomas F[rederick]. The Pied Piper. 1. Hamelin Town's in Brunswick, key of C major. 2. Rats! key of B-flat major. 3. Into the Street, key of D major. 4. Ringing the Bells, key of G major. 5. The Mayor Expostulates, key of C major. 6. The Children Follow, key of D major. Paxton's Edition, no. 15,293. London: W. Paxton & Co. Ltd., c1927. Pl. no. 15293. E211

V, 102-115
[Suite] for piano.

RB317. +Farmer, John. The Pied Piper; or The Rat-Catcher of Hamelin. Libretto by A. O'D. Bartholeyns, based on the poem by RB. London: Joseph Williams, Limited, c1896. N.10415. E201

V, 102-115
Opera for children (unspecified voice parts). Piano-vocal score. No parts.

Characters

Children's chorus (unison voices)
Gretchen [soprano]

Piper [alto]
Townspeople (unison chorus)
Elsa [soprano]
Hans [soprano or tenor]
4 soloists (unspecified voices)

RB318.   +Farrington, Frederick W. The Piper of Hamelin. Words by
Marmaduke E. Browne, based on the poem by RB. London:
Weekes & Co., c1891. W.2658. E206

V, 102-115
Cantata for school children: soloists (boy, narrator), two-part
chorus, with flageolet or flute, piano, and harmonium. Piano-
vocal score. No parts.

Characters

Piper (boy)
Reciter
Chorus of boys and girls (two parts)

RB319.   Freer, Eleanor Everest. The Legend of the Piper, op. 28. Libretto by Josephine Preston Peabody, based on the poem by
RB. Boston: C. C. Birchard & Co., c1922. No pl. no.

V, 102-115
[Opera]. Piano-vocal score. No parts.

Characters

The Piper (tenor)
Michael-the-Sword-Eater
Cheat-the-Devil (bass)

Jacobus the Burgomeister (baritone)
Kurt the Syndic (tenor)
Peter the Cobbler (baritone)
Hans the Butcher (baritone)
Axel the Smith (tenor)
Martin the Watch (baritone)
Peter the Sacristan (tenor)
Anselm, a Young Priest (baritone)
Old Claus, a Miser (tenor)
Town Crier (tenor)

Jan, Hansel, Ilse, Trude, Rudi (children sopranos)

Veronika, Wife of Kurt (mezzo soprano)
Barbara, Daughter of Jacobus (soprano)
Wife of Hans the Butcher (mezzo soprano)
Wife of Axel the Smith (mezzo soprano)
Wife of Martin the Watch (mezzo soprano)
Old Ursula (soprano)

Burghers, Nuns, Priests, and Children

RB320. +Geisler, Paul. Der Rattenfänger von Hameln, key of B-flat major. Symphonische Dichtung. Arrangement für Pianoforte zu vier Händen. Berlin: Ed. Bote & G. Bock, n.d. Pl. no. 13400. E215

V, 102-115
Piano solo for 4 hands.

RB321. Graham, A. Cyril. The Piper of Hamelin. New York: The H. W. Gray Company, c1916. No pl. no.

V, 102-115
Cantata for women's chorus (soprano I and II, alto), tenor solo, with orchestra. Piano-vocal score. No parts.

Note: The original instrumentation is not given on the music.

RB322. +Hirsch, Carl. Der Rattenfänger von Hameln, op. 11. Dramatisches Gedicht von Walter Bloem. Berlin: Verlag von Ries & Erler, c1895. R.6108E. E218

V, 102-115
[Cantata] for mixed chorus (soprano, alto, tenor, bass), children's chorus (soprano, alto), 3 or 4 soloists [baritone or tenor, soprano, baritone, baritone], piano, and organ.

Characters

Rattenfänger [baritone or tenor]
Gerlind [soprano]
Bürgermeister [baritone]
Bürgerm [baritone]

RB323. +Hudson, Henry. The Pied Piper of Hamelin. London: Joseph Williams, Limited, c1912. J.W.15268. E219

V, 102-115: 1-24, 30-45, 53-64, 70-79, 88-122, 146-160, 163-211, 213, 216-231, 261-268, 276-278, 283-287
Cantata for women's voices (two parts), soloists (mezzo soprano, contralto), and piano. Piano-vocal score.

RB324. Hurless, Don. The Pied Piper of Hamelin. For Chorus—S.A.T.B. and Orchestra, Soloists, Sop.—"Narrator," Tenor—"Piper," Bass—"Mayor." Photocopy, manuscript, Lima, Ohio: no publisher, Don Hurless c1967. No pl. no.

V, 102-115: 1-27, 30-38, 43, 44, 55, 56, 70-75, 80, 81, 76-79, 84, 94-96, 98-122, 146-152, 154-156, 161-166, 170-173, 175, 183-186, 189-199, 203, 213, 226-231, 256, 277-280, 300-303
Cantata for 3 soloists, mixed chorus (soprano, alto, tenor, bass) and orchestra. Piano-vocal score [only].

Characters

Narrator (soprano), Piper (tenor), Mayor (bass)

RB325. +Klein, Manuel. The Pied Piper. Lyrics by R. H. Burnside, book by Austin Strong and R. H. Burnside, based on the poem by RB. New York: M. Witmark & Sons, c1909. M.W.&Sons 8613/8635. E208

V, 102-115
Operatic fantasy for mixed chorus (soprano, alto, tenor, bass) and 8 soloists (unspecified voice parts). Piano-vocal score. No parts.

Characters

The Pied Piper [bass]	Lizzie Dizzy [soprano]
His Official Advisor [baritone]	The Housekeeper
His Official Reminder	[mezzo soprano]
[baritone]	The Model Couple (2)
The Board of Aldermen	Romance
The Bad Boy	Poetry
Willie Van Cortlandt [baritone]	Song
Sammy Struggles	Father Time
[tenor or baritone]	Elvira [soprano]

RB326. +Krug, Arnold. The Pied Piper of Hamelin Pipes and Disappears with the Children in the Mountain (Der Rattenfänger von Hameln bläst und verschwindet mit den Kindern im Berge), key of G major, [no. 5]. From Scenes from Fairy-Land, Book II. London: Novello & Co., Ltd., c1903. Pl. no. 11581. E222

V, 111-115
Solo for piano.

RB327. +Martin, Margaret R. The Children's Skipping Dance, key of F major, no. 3 [only]. From The Pied Piper of Hamelin. Chicago: Clayton F. Summy Co., c1922. C.F.S.Co.2064C. E223

V, 102-115: (especially) 194-196, 230, 231
Dance for children with flute and keyboard. No parts.

RB328. +——————. The Dance of the Rats, key of G major, no. 2 [only]. From The Pied Piper of Hamelin. Chicago: Clayton F. Summy Co., c1922. C.F.S.Co.2064B. E223

V, 102-115: (especially) 194-196, 230, 231
Dance for children with flute or piccolo and keyboard. No parts.

RB329. +——————. The Story, key of C major, no. 1 [only]. From The Pied Piper of Hamelin. Chicago: Clayton F. Summy Co., c1922. C.F.S.Co.2064A. E223

V, 102-115
Recitation for reader, children, and keyboard.

RB330.   Miller, Lewis. Suite for Pied Piper. 1. Chorale, key of G major.
2. Limp Waltz, key of F major. 3. Rondette, key of G major.
Manuscript, no place: no publisher, n.d. No pl. no.

V, 102-115
Trio for flute, piano, and double bass. Piano-conductor's score.
No parts.

RB331.   +Neuendorff, Adolf. The Rat-Charmer of Hamelin (Der Rattenfänger von Hameln). Libretto by H. Italiener. English
words by Fred. Williams, based on the poem by RB. New
York: Edward Schuberth & Co., c1881. E.S.&Co.1084. E220

V, 102-115
Comic opera in four acts. Piano-vocal score [only]. Unspecified voice parts.

Characters

von Wahren, Burgomaster of Hamelin
Elfriede, his daughter
Veronika, housekeeper
Reichling, city treasurer
Olga, his daughter
von Boch, Pilsner, Budweiss, Croton, Schnelle (members of
   Council)
Qualm, town clerk
Schnubb, messenger of Council
Hans, the Rat Charmer
Oscar, a merchant from Bremen, Elfriede's betrothed
Rattat, cobbler
Mrs. Rattat
Breitzel, baker
Schneider, tailor
Mrs. Schneider
Rhor, butcher
Hooffe, blacksmith
Hans Gras, beadle
Hostess of the "Stag"
Drummer
A Citizen

Councilmen, Patricians, Citizens, Ladies, Citizens' Wives and
   Children, Guards, Millers, Choir Boys, etc. [*sic*]

RB332.   +Parry, C[harles] Hubert H[astings]. The Pied Piper of
Hamelin. Novello's Original Octavo Edition. London: Novello & Co. Ltd., c1905. Pl. no. 12155. E224

V, 102-115: 1-45, 53-64, 70-82, 84-122, 146-160, 163-211, 214-231, 256-268, 276-278, 283-288
[Cantata] for soloists (tenor and bass), mixed chorus (soprano, alto, tenor, bass), and orchestra. Piano-vocal score. No parts.

Note: The original instrumentation is not given on the music.

RB333. +Paulsen, P. Marinus. The Tale of the Pied Piper. Chicago: Gamble Hinged Music Co., P. Marinus Paulsen c1927. No pl. no. E225

V, 102-115
Operetta-pageant for unspecified voice parts with keyboard.

Characters

The Piper	Children	Couriers
The Mayor	Townsmen	Dancers
The Miller	Council Members	Rats
The Lame Boy	Citizens	

RB334. +Rathbone, George. The Pied Piper of Hamelin. Novello's School Music. London: Novello & Co., Ltd., c1923. Pl. no. 15034. E228

V, 102-115: 1-27, 30-45, 53-64, 70-81, 83-88, 94-122, 146-156, 161-175, 182-211, 214-256, 261-268, 276-278, 283-288
[Cantata] for soprano soloist and chorus (soprano I and II) with piano. Piano-vocal score [only].

RB335. +Truman, Ernest. The Pied Piper, op. 50. Sydney: W. H. Paling & Co., Ltd., c1911. W.H.P.1008. E229

V, 102-115: 1-45, 52-268, 284-288
Cantata Grotesque for 4 soloists, mixed chorus (soprano, alto, tenor, bass), male chorus (tenor I and II, bass I and II), and orchestra. Piano-vocal score. No parts.

Characters

The Pied Piper (dramatic tenor)
The Mayor (baritone)
The Rat (bass)
The Lame Boy (mezzo soprano)

Orchestra

1 piccolo	3 horns	violins I
2 flutes	2 trumpets	violins II
2 oboes	3 trombones	viola
2 clarinets	triangle	cello
2 bassoons	cymbals	double bass
	timpani	

RB336. +Urban, Heinrich. Der Rattenfänger von Hameln, key of F major, op. 25. Fantasiestück nach Julius Wolff's Adventiure für Orchester. Clavier-Auszug zu zwei Händen von Oscar Raif. Berlin: C. A. Challier & Co., n.d. C.&Co.2869-2870. E227

V, 102-115
Fantasy for piano.

RB337. Walthew, Richard H[enry]. The Pied Piper of Hamelin. Novello's Original Octavo Edition. London: Novello & Co. Ltd., c1893. Pl. no. 9515.

V, 102-115: 1-27, 30-45, 52-66, 70-122, 146-231, 256-268, 284-288
[Cantata] for tenor and bass soloists, mixed chorus (soprano, alto, tenor, bass) and orchestra. Piano-vocal score. No parts.

Note: The original instrumentation is not given on the music.

RB338. +Weigl, Karl. Der Rattenfänger von Hameln, op. 24. Märchenspiel in 4 Bildern. Text nach einer Dichtung von Helen Scheu-Riez. Für die Vertonung bearbeitet von Rud. [St.?] Hoffman. Engl. Uebersetzung von Sylvia Spencer-Welch. Klavierauszug von E. Simon. Mimeograph copy, manuscript, Vienna: Universal Edition, c1932. U.E.10.425. E232

V, 102-115
[Operetta] with chamber orchestra. Piano-vocal score. No parts.

Characters

Der Rattenfänger (tenor or mezzo soprano)
Bürger, Bürgerinnen und Kinder von Hameln (children's chorus)

Speaking Parts

Der Burgermeister von Hameln	Haustock der Tischler
Kunz der Schuster (alderman)	Frau Haustock
Hinz der Schneider (alderman)	Klara, beider Tachter
Kauz der [H]utmacher (alderman)	Frau Kunz
Schnauz der Lehrer (alderman)	Frau Riebeisen
Riebeisen der Steinmetz (alderman)	Anna, Johanna
Schlafsack, Nachwächter und	(children)
Gemeindedeiner	Peter, Otto, Karl, Hans, Fritz (children)

Chamber Orchestra

1 flute (also piccolo)	2 violins
1 oboe	1 viola
1 clarinet	1 cello
1 bassoon	piano (and harmonium)
1 horn	

on stage: children trumpeters and children drummers

RB339.   +Woyrsch, Felix von. Rattenfänger Lieder, op. 16. 1. Wo ich mich zeige, key of G major. 2. Nun stellt euch auf, ihr Kinderlein, key of C major. 3. Wenn du kein Spielmann wärst! key of A major. 4. Waldesruh, key of A major. 5. Röslein, wann blühst du auf? key of F major. 6. Stelldichein, key of B-flat major. 7. Eine Rose gepflückt! key of D major. 8. Die Nächste, key of E minor. 9. Erinnerung, key of G major. 10. Nach Hameln! key of E minor. Aus Jul. Wolff's „Singuf" für mittlere Singstimme mit Pianoforte-Begleitung. Leipzig: Carl Ruhle's Music-Verlag, n.d. C.10343R. E233

V, 102-115
Songs for medium voice with piano.
  1. r: b - e²
  2. r: c¹ - f²
  3. r: e¹ - e²
  4. r: d#¹ - e²
  5. r: b - f²
  6. r: c¹ - d²
  7. r: d¹ - eb²
  8. r: b - e²
  9. r: c#¹ - e²
10. r: b - e²

A PILLAR AT SEBZEVAH. *See* FERISHTAH'S FANCIES

PIPPA PASSES

RB340.   +Alsop, Marion. The Year's at the Spring, key of C major, no. 2. From Two Short Songs. London: Leonard & Co., n.d. No pl. no. E239

III, 24: 221-228
Song for soprano with piano.
r: c¹ - f²

Note: RB340 is bound in Two Short Songs.

RB341.   +Atkins, Ivor. The Year's at the Spring, key of C major. London: Novello & Co., Ltd., c1924. Pl. no. 15106. E241

III, 24: 221-228
Song for [high] voice with keyboard.
r: d¹ - f²   t: a¹ - e²

RB342.   +Bantock, Granville. Pippa Passes, key of C major. Swan Edition, no. 23. London: Swan & Co. (Music Publishers) Limited, c1922. Swan 2802. E242

III, 24: 221-228
Song for medium voice with piano.
r: d¹ - g²

Note: Contrary to the copyright date which appears on the front cover, at the bottom of the first page of music the copyright is given as "MCMXIXII."

RB343. +————————. Pippa Passes, key of E-flat major. Swan Edition,
no. 23. London: Swan && Co. (Music Publishers) Limited,
c1922. Swan 2801. E242

III, 24: 221-228
Song for high voice with piano.
r: f¹ - bb²

Note: Contrary to the copyright date which appears on the
front cover, at the bottom of the first page of music the copyright is given as "MCMXIXII."

RB344. Beach, Mrs. H[enry] H[arris] A[ubrey]. The Year's at the
Spring, key of A-flat major, op. 44, no. 1 [only]. London:
Boosey & Co, Arthur P. Schmidt c1904. H.4554.

III, 24: 221-228
Song for [medium] voice with piano.
r: eb¹ - eb²   t: eb¹ - c²

RB345. ————————. The Year's at the Spring, key of B-flat major, no.
1 [only]. From Three Browning Songs, op. 44. Boston:
Arthur P. Schmidt, c1900. A.P.S.5138-4.

III, 24: 221-228
Song for low voice with keyboard.
r: f¹ - f²

RB346. ————————. The Year's at the Spring, key of C major, op. 44,
no. 1 [only]. Octavo Series (Women's Voices), no. 460.
Boston: Arthur P. Schmidt, c1909. A.P.S.8450-2.

III, 24: 221-228
Part-song for women's chorus (soprano I and II, alto I and
II) with keyboard.

RB347. ————————. The Year's at the Spring, key of D-flat major, no.
1 [only]. From Three Browning Songs, op. 44. Boston: The
Arthur P. Schmidt Co., c1900. A.P.S.5137.

III, 24: 221-228
Song for soprano or tenor with piano.
r: ab¹ - ab²

RB348. ————————. The Year's at the Spring, key of D-flat major, op.
44, no. 1 [only]. Arranged by Francis Moore. From Octavo
Series (Men's Voices) No. 539. Xerox copy, Boston: The
Arthur P. Schmidt Co., c1933. A.P.S.14659-2.

III, 24: 221-224, 221, 222, 225-228
Part-song for male chorus (tenor I and II, bass I and II)
with piano.

RB349.   ——————. The Year's at the Spring, key of D-flat major, op. 44, no. 1 [only]. From Octavo Series (Mixed Voices, Secular) No. 244. Xerox copy, [Boston]: The Arthur P. Schmidt Co., c1927. A.P.S.13792-3.

III, 24: 221-224, 221, 222, 225-228
Part-song for mixed chorus (soprano, alto, tenor, bass) with keyboard.

Note: On the music the composer's name is written "Mrs. H. H. Beach."

RB350.   Beach, John [Parsons]. New Year's Hymn, key of G major. From Pippa's Holiday. Original manuscript, no place: no publisher, n.d. No pl. no.

III, 13: 190-201
Song for [medium] voice with keyboard.
r: e^1 - e^2 t: e^1 - c^2

Note: Pippa's Holiday was written by July 26, 1926, cf., Ola Jones Nisbet, *Browning's Pippa Passes* (Charlotte, N. C.: Presbyterian Standard Publishing Co.), pp. 22, 27, 28. At the bottom of the manuscript is written "This is the original manuscript. Presented to the Baylor University Browning Collection by Mrs. Charles R. Nisbet." *See* illustration, pp. x-xi.

RB351.   +Behrend, A. H. All's Right, "The Year's at the Spring," key of G major, no. 2. From The School Music Review, no. 228. London: Novello and Company, Limited, c1908. No pl. no. E244

III, 24: 221-228
Song for soprano with keyboard.
r: e^1 - g^2 (optional a^2)

Note: RB351 is bound with the song, "Sons of the Isles" by W. McNaught.

RB352.   +Black, Kate Gilmore. Pippa's Song, key of E major. From Three Songs with Piano Accompaniment by Kate Gilmore Black. New York: G. Schirmer, Inc., c1922. Pl. no. 30656. E245

III, 24: 221-228
Song for high voice with piano.
r: $g\#^1$ - a^2 (optional b^2)

Note: The ABL has 2 copies. On the front cover of copy 1 is written "For Dr. A. Joseph Armstrong Baylor University Waco, Texas—with the best wishes of Evaline Hartley Kansas City Mo March 23, 1933."

RB353. +————————. The Year's at the Spring, key of E major. From *Browning's Pippa Passes,* p. 163, edited by Ola Jones Nisbet. [New York]: G. Schirmer, Inc., Publisher, c1922. No pl. no. E296

III, 24: 221-228
Song for [high] voice, unacc.
r: $g\#^1$ - a^2 (optional b^2)   t: b^1 - $g\#^2$

Note: Also contained in *Browning's Pippa Passes* are items RB418, RB447, and RB449. The melody of RB353 is the same as RB352. *Browning's Pippa Passes* was published in 1929.

RB354. +Blair, William. The Year's at the Spring, key of A major. Cincinnati: The John Church Company, c1915. Pl. no. 17490. E246

III, 24: 221-228
Song for [medium] voice with piano.
r: e^1 - $f\#^2$ t: $f\#^1$ - e^2

RB355. +Bode, Alice M. The Year's at the Spring, key of F major. Photostat copy, London: Houghton & Co., c1908. No pl. no. E247

III, 24: 221-228
Song for [high] voice with piano.
r: f^1 - f^2 t: a^1 - f^2

RB356. Brahe, May H. The Year's at the Spring, key of C major. New York: Enoch & Sons, c1915. No pl. no.

III, 24: 221-228
Song for [medium] voice with piano.
r: e^1 - g^2 t: g^1 - e^2

RB357. +————————. The Year's at the Spring, key of C major, no. 2. From Two Songs. London: Enoch & Sons Ld, c1915. E.&S.4784. E248

III, 24: 221-228
Song for medium voice with piano.
r: e^1 - g^2

Note: RB357 is bound in Two Songs.

RB358. ————————. The Year's at the Spring, key of E-flat major. New York: Enoch & Sons, c1915. No pl. no.

III, 24: 221-228
Song for [high] voice with piano.
r: g^1 - bb^2 (optional g^2)   t: bb^1 - g^2

RB359.   +Cain, Noble. The Year's at the Spring, key of F major. From
          Harold Flammer Choral Series, Secular, Three-Part Choruses
          for Women's Voices, no. 83131. New York: Harold Flammer
          Publishing Incorporated, c1940. Pl. no. 1983. E249

          III, 24: 221-228
          Chorus for women's voices (soprano, soprano-alto, alto) with
          piano.

RB360.   Caldwell, Mary E. Year's at the Spring, key of F major. Code
          4557-08. JF 008. Nashville: Broadman Press, c1964.

          III, 24: 221-228
          Song for unison chorus with organ or piano.

RB361.   —————. Year's at the Spring, key of F major. Code 455-
          046. JF 046. Nashville: Broadman Press, c1968.

          III, 24: 221-228
          Part-song for mixed chorus (soprano, alto, baritone) with
          keyboard.

RB362.   Carter, Esther May. The Year's at the Spring, key of D-flat
          major. Xerox copy, [Oneida, Ky.]: no publisher, Esther
          May Carter c1928. No pl. no.

          III, 24: 221-228
          Song for [medium] voice with piano.
          r: b♭ - a♭²   t: f¹ - f²

RB363.   Caruthers, Julia Lois. Pippa's Spring Song, key of A-flat major.
          From Music, a Monthly Magazine, [p. 181], edited by W. S.
          B. Mathews. Chicago: W. S. B. Mathews, c1891. No pl. no.

          III, 24: 221-228
          Song for [high] voice with keyboard.
          r: e♭¹ - f²   t: a♭¹ - e♭²

RB364.   Clark, Ruth Kinney. The Year's at the Spring, key of E-flat
          major. Hollywood: Cloister Press, Ruth Kinney Clark c1968.
          No pl. no.

          III, 24: 221-228
          Song for [medium high] voice with keyboard.
          r: e♭¹ - e♭²   t: f¹ - e♭²

RB365.   Clarke, Helen A[rchibald]. You'll Love Me Yet, key of F
          major. Manuscript, no place: no publisher, n.d. No pl. no.

          III, 64-65: 304-315
          Song for [high] voice with cello and piano. No parts.
          r: e¹ - a²   t: a♭¹ - g♭²

RB366.   Clarke, Henry Leland. The Year's at the Spring, key of B-flat major. Photostat copy, manuscript, no place: no publisher, Oct. 1, 1930. No pl. no.

III, 24: 221-228
Song for [medium] voice with keyboard.
r: bb - f²   t: c¹ - c²

RB367.   Clarke, H[ugh] A[rchibald]. Give Her but a Least Excuse, key of G major. Manuscript, no place: no publisher, Jan. 9, 1899. No pl. no.

III, 44-45: 253-270
Song for [high] voice with keyboard.
r: d¹ - e²   t: f#¹ - d²

Note: On the front cover is written "Give her but a least excuse By H. A. Clarke, Mus. D. Philadelphia, January 9, 1899. Hugh A. Clarke was the father of Helen Archibald Clarke."

RB368.   Clarke, Hugh A[rchibald]. Overhead the Treetops Meet, key of D-flat major. Manuscript, no place: no publisher, March 20, 1899. No pl. no.

III, 74: 196-211
Song for [high] voice with keyboard.
r: db¹ - eb²   t: f¹ - db²

Note: On the front cover is written "Overhead the treetops meet. Music by Hugh A. Clarke, Mus. D. Philadelphia, March 20, 1899. Written for the Boston Browning Society."

RB369.   +Coleridge-Taylor, S[amuel]. You'll Love Me Yet, key of G minor, op. 37, no. 1 [only]. London: Novello & Co., Ltd., c1899. Pl. no. 10818a. E252

III, 64-65: 304-315
Song for contralto or baritone with keyboard.
r: d¹ - d²

RB370.   Cripps, A. Redgrave. The Year's at the Spring, key of F major. London: Novello and Company, Limited, A. Redgrave Cripps c1909. Pl. no. 13097.

III, 24: 221-228
Song for [medium] voice with keyboard.
r: d¹ - g²   t: g¹ - d²

RB371.   Crumpler, Mary Frances. You'll Love Me Yet! Pippa's Song, key of D-flat major. Manuscript, no place: no publisher, n.d. No pl. no.

III, 64-65: 304-315
Song for [medium high] voice with piano.
r: d^1 - gb^2 t: f^1 - f^2

RB372.   +Curtis, Natalie. Song from Pippa Passes, key of G major. New York: Edward Schuberth & Co., c1899. E.S.&Co.738. E254

III, 24: 221-228
Song for [medium] voice with piano.
r: d^1 - g^2 t: d^1 - d^2

RB373.   David, Elizabeth Harbison. Pippa's Song, key of E-flat major. Manuscript, no place: no publisher, Jan. 28, 1927. No pl. no.

III, 13: 190-195
Song for [medium high] voice with flute, violin, and keyboard. No parts.
r: g^1 - f^2 t: g^1 - eb^2

Note: On the front cover is written "written for, and affectionately inscribed to Jessie Voigt In the evening of January 28*th* 1927 For Prof. Armstrong from Jessie Voigt—copied from original by Lorraine Voigt and autographed (with original dedication) by Elizabeth Harbison David."

RB374.   +Davis, Carlyle. Pippa Passes, Four Moods from Browning, op. 35. 1. Morning at Asolo, key of E major. 2. Ottima's Regret, key of D major. 3. The King's Dancer, key of C major. 4. Heart's-Ease, key of E major. Cincinnati: The John Church Company, c1924. Pl. no. 18739. E256

1.   III, 5: 1-4
2.   III, 26-27: 271, 282
3.   III, 60: 216-218
4.   III, 78: 302; 77: 275
Suite for piano.

RB375.   del Riego, Teresa. All's Right with the World, key of C major, no. 5. From Teresa del Riego Album. The Portrait Series. London: Chappell & Co. Ltd., c1906. Pl. no. 23822.

III, 24: 221-228
Song for [medium] voice with piano.
r: c^1 - a^2 t: e^1 - e^2

Note: RB375 is bound in Teresa del Riego Album.

RB376. +Duncan, Edmondstoune. The Year's at the Spring, key of D-flat major, no. 10. From English Songs, Book II. Glasgow: Aird & Coghill, Ltd., Edmondstoune Duncan c1919. No pl. no. E258

III, 24: 221-228
Song for [medium high] voice with piano.
r: c^1 - f^2 t: f^1 - eb^2

Note: RB376 is bound in English Songs, Book II.

RB377. Easson, James. God's in His Heaven, key of F major, no. 22. From Troubadour Song Book, Part I, edited and arranged by James Easson and W. Prentice Torrance. Curwen Edition 6366. London: J. Curwen & Sons Ltd., n.d. No pl. no.

III, 24: 227, 228
Two-part round, unacc.

Note: RB377 is bound in Troubadour Song Book. The ABL received RB377 April 16, 1941.

RB378. —————. God's in His Heaven, key of F major, no. 22. From Troubadour Song Book, Part I, Vocal Edition, edited and arranged by James Easson and W. Prentice Torrance. Curwen Edition 6366. London: J. Curwen & Sons Ltd., n.d. Pl. no. 6366.

III, 24: 227-228
Two-part round, unacc.

Note: RB378 is bound in Troubadour Song Book, Vocal Edition. The ABL received RB378 April 16, 1941.

RB379. +Ehrmann, Mary B[artholomew]. Pippa's Song, key of D major, [no. 5]. From Little Songs for Little Folks by Mary B. Ehrmann. Cincinnati: The Willis Music Co., c1911. Pl. no. 1495. E259

III, 24: 221-228
Chorus for unison children's voices with keyboard.

Note: RB379 is bound in Little Songs for Little Folks.

RB380. +Floyd, A. E. The Year's at the Spring, key of A major. Manuscript, [London], J. Curwen & Sons, Ltd., n.d. No pl. no. E260

III, 24: 221-228
Part-song for women's chorus (soprano I and II, alto) with piano (for rehearsal only).

Note: The ABL received RB380 Oct. 1, 1942.

RB381. Freer, Eleanor Everest. The Year's at the Spring, key of E major, op. 43. Chicago: The Music Library of Chicago, Eleanor Everest Freer c1936. No pl. no.

III, 24: 221-228
Song for low voice with keyboard.
r: b - c#^{2} (optional e#^{2})

RB382. ——————. The Year's at the Spring, key of G major. From the opera, The Brownings Go to Italy, (or) (A Love Story), op. 43. Libretto by G. A. Hawkins-Ambler. Chicago: The Music Library of Chicago, c1936. Pl. no. 38977.

III, 24: 221-228
Song for baritone with keyboard.
r: d^1 - g#^{2}

Note: RB382 is bound in The Brownings Go to Italy (piano-vocal score).

RB383. ——————. The Year's at the Spring, key of G major, op. 43. Chicago: The Music Library of Chicago, Eleanor Everest Freer c1936. No pl. no.

III, 24: 221-228
Song for medium voice with keyboard.
r: d^1 - e^2 (optional g#^{2})

RB384. +Fuller, Caroline M. The Year's at the Spring, key of F major, no. 2. Over-head the Tree-tops Meet, key of C major, no. 3. From Three Songs from Robert Browning. [New York: J. H. Schroeder], Caroline M. Fuller c1898. E 2559 8. E263 E262

 2. III, 24: 221-228
  Song for soprano with keyboard.
  r: a - g^2

 3. III, 74: 196-211
  Song for mezzo soprano with keyboard.
  r: b - e^2

Note: RB384 is bound in Three Songs from Robert Browning. The ABL has 2 copies. On the front cover of copy 1 is written "Florence Wier Gibson—from the Composer—." Miss Gibson presented this copy to the ABL July 16, 1945. Stamped at the bottom of the front cover of copy 1 is "J. H. Schroeder, 10 East 16th St., New York."

RB385. [Galsworthy, Ada.] (Anglia). Pippa's Song, key of C major, op. 1, no. 1. London: [The Montague Fordham Gallery], n.d. No pl. no.

III, 24: 221-228
Song for [high] voice with keyboard.
r: c^1 - a^2 t: g^1 - e^2

Note: On the second page of music is written "Greetings for Xmas & New Year 1902-1903."

RB386.   +Galsworthy, Ada. Pippa's Song, key of C major, no. 1. From Two Songs by Mrs. John Galsworthy. London: Weekes & Co., n.d. W.5333. E264

III, 24: 221-228
Song for [high] voice with keyboard.
r: c^1 - a^2 t: g^1 - e^2

Note: RB386 is bound in Two Songs. Broughton, *Bibliography* gives [1907] as the possible publication date.

RB387.   Gilchrist, W. W. All Service Ranks the Same with God, key of B-flat major. Manuscript, no place: no publisher, n.d. No pl. no.

III, 13: 190-214; 79: 327-331
Song for [medium] voice with keyboard.
r: b^b - f^2 t: d^1 - d^2

RB388.   +————. Pippa's Song, key of D major, no. 1. From The Laurel Music-Reader, edited by W. L. Tomlins. The Laurel Music Series. Teachers Edition. Boston: C. C. Birchard & Company, c1914. No pl. no. E265

III, 24: 221-228
Chorus for unison voices with piano.

Note: RB388 is bound in The Laurel Music-Reader.

RB389.   +Gow, George Coleman. "Give Her but a Least Excuse to Love Me," key of C major, no. 2. "The Year's at the Spring," key of G major, no. 3. "You'll Love Me Yet," key of B major, no. 6. From "Colombe's Birthday," Intermezzo Music, op. 4. Boston: The Boston Music Co., c1892. B.M.Co. 214, 215, 218. E54

    2.   III, 44-45: 253-270
       Part-song for women's voices (soprano I and II, alto I and II), unacc.

    3.   III, 24: 221-228
       Song for [medium high] voice with piano.
       r: e^1 - e^2 t: g^1 - d^2

    6.   III, 64-65: 304-315
       Part-song for women's voices (soprano I and II, alto I and II) with piano.

Note: RB389 is bound in "Colombe's Birthday," Intermezzo Music.

RB390.   Grace, Harvey. The Year's at the Spring, key of C major, op. 8, no. 1 [only]. Manuscript, London: Leonard, Gould & Bolttler (L. J. Saville) Music Publishers, n.d. No pl. no.

III, 24: 221-228
Song for mezzo soprano with piano.
r: f#¹ - f²

RB391.   +Hadley, Henry [Kimball]. The Year's at the Spring, key of
         B-flat major, no. 4. From Five Songs, op. 44. Cincinnati:
         The John Church Company, c1909. Pl. no. 16080. E268

         III, 24: 221-228
         Song for [medium] voice with keyboard.
         r: (optional bb) c¹ - f²   t: f¹ - d²

RB392.   +Hadley, Henry K[imball]. You'll Love Me Yet, key of A-flat
         major, no. 1 [only]. From Five Songs, op. 20. Boston: Oliver
         Ditson Company, c1900. Pl. no. 4-54-62191. E269

         III, 64-65: 304-315
         Song for high voice with keyboard.
         r: eb¹ - ab²

RB393.   Halley, Margaret A. The Year's at the Spring, key of F major,
         no. 2. Edinburgh: Paterson and Sons, c1910. No pl. no.

         III, 24: 221-228
         Song for [medium] voice with piano.
         r: c¹ - f²   t: d¹ - d²

         Note: RB393 is bound with "As Flowers in Rain," music by
         Halley, words by [Ralph Waldo] Emerson.

RB394.   +—————. The Year's at the Spring, key of G-flat major,
         no. 2. Dundee: Paterson, Sons & Co., n.d. No pl. no. E270

         III, 24: 221-228
         Song for [high] voice with piano.
         r: db¹ - gb²   t: eb¹ - eb²

         Note: RB394 is bound with "As Flowers in Rain," music by
         Halley, words by [Ralph Waldo] Emerson. The ABL has 3
         copies. On the front cover of copy 3, the key of "As Flowers
         in Rain" is given, i.e., C major; the lyricist of "As Flowers in
         Rain" is given as Frances Mary Butt instead of Emerson as
         is stated in copies 1 and 2; also, the place of publication on copy
         3 is given as Edinburgh and a copyright date (c1910) is given.
         The music is the same for all 3 copies.

RB395.   Hammond, William G. Pippa's Song, key of C major. From
         The Progressive Music Series, Book Three, by Horatio Parker,
         Osbourne Mc Conathy, Edward Bailey Birge, W. Otto
         Miessner. Enlarged Edition. Boston: Silver Burdett and
         Company, c1920. No pl. no.

         III, 24: 221-228
         Two-part song for children's chorus, unacc.

         Note: RB395 is bound in The Progressive Music Series, Book
         Three.

RB396.   +Hartog, Cécile S. The Year's at the Spring, key of A-flat major. London: Boosey & Co., n.d. No pl. no. E272

III, 24: 221-228
Song for [high] voice with piano.
r: eb¹ - ab²   t: f¹ - eb²

Note: The ABL has 2 copies. On the front cover of copy 2 is written "Mary T. Hedley R. B. L." Broughton, *Bibliography* gives 1885 as the date of publication.

RB397.   ————————. The Year's at the Spring, key of G major. From English Songs, Second Series. Boston: Oliver Ditson Company, n.d. Pl. no. 4-110-64897-6.

III, 24: 221-228
Song for high voice with piano.
r: d¹ - g²

RB398.   ————————. The Year's at the Spring, key of G major. London: Boosey & Co., n.d. No pl. no.

III, 24: 221-228
Song for [high] voice with piano.
r: d¹ - g²   t: e¹ - d²

RB399.   +Herz, Maria. Pippa Passes (Pippa's Lied), key of D major, no. 1. From Two Songs by Maria Herz. Stainer & Bell's Modern Songs, no. 27. London: Stainer & Bell, Ltd., c1910. St. & B. Ltd. 561. E275

III, 24: 221-228
Song for [medium] voice with piano.
r: d¹ - e²   t: g¹ - e²

Note: RB399 is bound in Two Songs.

RB400.   +Hollins, Dorothea. The Year's at the Spring, key of B major. London: Novello and Company, Limited, n.d. Pl. no. 9882. E277

III, 24: 221-228
Song for mezzo soprano with keyboard.
r: f#¹ - g²

Note: The ABL has 4 copies. Copies 3 and 4 were received in 1940. Broughton, *Bibliography* gives [1894] as the possible publication date.

RB401.   Johnson, F. Arthur. Song from Pippa Passes, key of G major. Manuscript, no place: no publisher, Sept. 25, 1931. No pl. no.

III, 24: 221-228
Song for [high] voice with keyboard.
r: d¹ - f#² (optional g²)   t: e¹ - e²

Note: At the bottom of the first page is written "For Dr. A. J. Armstrong's Browning Room, Baylor University, Waco, Texas."

RB402.	————————. Song from Pippa Passes, key of G major, no. 2. From Six Compositions [by] F. Arthur Johnson. San Francisco: Groené Music Publishing Company, F. Arthur Johnson c1966. No pl. no.

III, 24: 221-228
Song for [high] voice with piano.
r: d^1 - g^2 t: e^1 - e^2

Note: RB402 is bound in Six Compositions.

RB403.	————————. Song from Pippa Passes, key of G major, no. 7. From Nine Compositions [by] F. Arthur Johnson. London: Edward Schuberth & Co., Inc., F. Arthur Johnson c1946. E.S.&Co. 7473.

III, 24: 221-228
Song for [high] voice with piano.
r: d^1 - g^2 t: e^1 - e^2

RB404.	+Johnstone, Harry. Pippa's Song, key of E-flat major. From The Stock Exchange Christmas Annual, 1905-6, compiled by W. A. Morgan. Enfield, England: F. Wetherman & Co., Ltd., 1905-06. No pl. no. E278

III, 24: 221-228
Song for [medium high] voice with keyboard.
r: e^1 - f^2 t: f^1 - eb^2

RB405.	+Jordan, Jules. Love's Confidence, key of D major, no. 2. From Two Songs by Jules Jordan. Boston: H. B. Stevens, c1887. H.B.S.49. E279

III, 64-65: 304-315
Song for soprano or tenor with piano.
r: $d\#^1$ - g^2

RB406.	+Kernochan, Marshall. You'll Love Me Yet, key of D major. From Songs by Marshall Kernochan. Boston: C. W. Thompson & Co., c1908. T.&Co.1376. E280

III, 64-65: 304-315
Song for [medium high] voice with piano.
r: d^1 - $f\#^2$ t: $f\#^1$ - d^2

RB407.	+————————. You'll Love Me Yet, key of D major. New York: G. Ricordi & Co., Inc. [Galaxy Music Corp.], c1929. N.Y.798. E280

III, 64-65: 304-315
Song for [medium high] voice with piano.
r: d^1 - $f\#^2$ t: $f\#^1$ - d^2

Note: "Galaxy Music Corp." is pasted over "G. Ricordi & Co., Inc."

RB408. +Lee, E[rnest] Markham. The Year's at the Spring, key of F major. From The Anglo French Unison and Part Songs, no. 1016. London: The Anglo-French Music Co. Ltd., c1924. A.F.M.Co.1016. E283

III, 24: 221-228
Part-song for women's chorus (soprano, alto) with piano.

RB409. +Lewis, Ella V. The Year's at the Spring, key of C major, no. 1. London: Grove-Patterson Ltd., c1933. No pl. no. E284

III, 24: 221-228
Song for [medium] voice with piano.
r: c^1 - f^2 t: e^1 - e^2

Note: RB409 is bound with "A Garden Is a Lovesome Thing," music by Lewis, words by T. E. Brown.

RB410. +Lewis, Leo Rich. A King Lived Long Ago, key of D major, [no. 1]. From Three Songs. The Music of Tufts College . . . Serial Numbers 270, 271, 272. Tufts College: Tufts Music, L. R. Lewis c1936. TM270. E285

III, 58-60: 164-177, 179-203, 205-222
Song for medium voice with piano. Piano-conductor's score [only].
r: a - g^2

Note: RB410 is bound in Three Songs.

RB411. Loomis, Harvey Worthington. Morning Song, key of E major. Newton Center: The Wa-Wan Press, c1907. No pl. no.

III, 24: 221-228
Song for [high] voice with keyboard.
r: $d\#^1$ - $f\#^2$ t: g^1 - e^2

RB412. Loughridge, Jean [M.] Pippa's Song, key of B-flat major. From Fifty Rote-Songs for Little Singers by Jean Loughridge. Manuscript, no place: no publisher, n.d. No pl. no.

III, 24: 221-228
Song for unison children's chorus with keyboard.

Note: The ABL received RB412 Sept. 13, 1940.

RB413. +Loughridge, Jean M. Pippa's Song, key of B-flat major, no. 49. From Fifty Rote-Songs for Little Singers by Jean M. Loughridge. Boston: Oliver Ditson Company, c1922. Pl. no. 74246. E287

III, 24: 221-228
Song for unison children's chorus with piano.

Note: RB413 is bound in Fifty Rote-Songs for Little Singers.

RB414.   +Macmillen, Francis. The Year's at the Spring, key of G major.
          New York: Carl Fischer, c1917. Pl. no. 19937. E288

          III, 24: 221-228
          Song for high voice with piano.
          r: db^1 - g^2

RB415.   +Mason, Mrs. Alexander O. The Year's at the Spring (Song
          from Pippa Passes), key of A-flat major. Chicago: F. Summy
          Co., c1895. C.F.S.Co.306. E290

          III, 24: 221-228
          Song for soprano with keyboard.
          r: eb^1 - ab^2

RB416.   +Mayer, Max. Pippa's Song, key of D-flat major, no. 2 [only].
          From Eight Songs, op. 24. [Manchester: Hime & Addison];
          London: Goodwin & Tabb, Ltd., c1924. No pl. no. E291

          III, 24: 221-228
          Song for [medium] voice with piano.
          r: a - fb^2 t: f^1 - eb^2

          Note: "Manchester: Hime & Addison" is pasted over "Lon-
          don: Goodwin & Tabb, Ltd."

RB417.   +Mokrejs, John. You'll Love Me Yet (Song from Pippa
          Passes), key of E-flat major, no. 1. Revised edition. From
          Compositions by John Mokrejs. Cedar Rapids: Odowan Pub-
          lishing Co., John Mokrejs c1920. No pl. no. E292

          III, 64-65: 304-315
          Song for [medium] voice with keyboard.
          r: c^1 - g^2 t: f^1 - e^2

          Note: RB417 is bound in Compositions.

RB418.   +Mozart, W[olfgang] A[madeus]. You'll Love Me Yet, key
          of E-flat major. From *Browning's Pippa Passes,* p. 199, edited
          by Ola Jones Nisbet. Charlotte, N.C.: Presbyterian Standard
          Publishing Co., c1929. No pl. no. E296

          III, 64-65: 304-315
          Song for [medium] voice, unacc.
          r: eb^1 - eb^2 t: eb^1 - bb^1

          Note: Also contained in *Browning's Pippa Passes* are items
          RB353, RB447, and RB449. The person responsible for
          placing RB's words to Mozart's music is not given.

RB419.   +Neidlinger, W[illiam] H[arold]. The Year's at the Spring,
          key of F major. From Songs and Ballads by W. H. Neidlinger.
          New York: G. Schirmer, c1895. Pl. no. 12110. E294

          III, 24: 221-228
          Song for soprano or tenor with piano.
          r: c^1 - c^3

RB420.   Nevin, Ethelbert [Woodbridge]. The Lark Is on the Wing, key of D major, [no. 4]. From "O'er Hill and Dale," by Ethelbert Nevin. [Cincinnati]: The John Church Company, c1902. Pl. no. 14174.

III, 24: 221-228
Solo for piano.

Note: RB420 is bound in "O'er Hill and Dale."

RB421.   —————. The Wedding Morning, key of G-flat major. No place: Anne Paul Nevin, c1909. Pl. no. 21667.

III, 24: 221-228
Song for high voice with piano.
r: db^1 - gb^2

Note: RB421 is sold by G. Schirmer, New York.

RB422.   +Norén, Helmer. The Year's at the Spring, key of D major, no. 2. Curwen Edition 2361. London: J. Curwen & Sons Ltd., Helmer Norén c1925. Pl. no. 2361. E297

III, 24: 221-228
Song for [high] voice with piano.
r: b - $f\#^2$ t: $f\#^1$ - $f\#^2$

Note: Bound with RB422 is "Alone," music by Norén, words by Robert Nichols.

RB423.   Olds, W. B. A King Lived Long Ago, key of A-flat major. Manuscript, no place: no publisher, n.d. No pl. no.

III, 58-60: 164-222
Song for [high] voice with piano.
r: c^1 - f^2

RB424.   —————. The Page's Song, key of D minor. Manuscript, no place: no publisher, n.d. No pl. no.

III, 44-45: 253-270
Song for [medium] voice with keyboard.
r: c^1 - e^2 t: f^1 - c^2

RB425.   +Parker, Willetta. Pippa's Song, key of G major. From Three Songs by Willetta Parker. Boston: C. W. Thompson & Co., Miles & Thompson c1896. M.&T.648. E298

III, 24: 221-228
Song for [medium] voice with piano.
r: b - d^2 t: c^1 - c^2

RB426.   +Protheroe, Daniel. The Year's at the Spring, key of C major, no. 3. From Three Lyrics by Robert Browning. Chicago: Gamble Hinged Music Co., c1910. No pl. no. E299

III, 24: 222-228
Song for high voice with keyboard.
r: g^1 - a^2

Note: RB426 is bound in Three Lyrics by Robert Browning.

RB427.   +Renaud, Emiliano. All's Right with the World, key of D major. From Four Songs by Robert Browning. Boston: White-Smith Music Publishing Co., c1914. Pl. no. 14666. E300

III, 24: 221-228
Song for [high] voice with piano.
r: d^1 - a^2 t: a^1 - e^2

RB428.   +————. You'll Love Me Yet, key of A-flat major. From Four Songs by Robert Browning. Boston: White-Smith Music Publishing Co., c1914. Pl. no. 14667. E301

III, 64-65: 304-315
Song for [high] voice with piano.
r: f^1 - a^2 t: a^1 - a^2

RB429.   +Rogers, Clara Kathleen. "Overhead the Tree-tops Meet," key of D major, op. 36. Boston: Arthur P. Schmidt, c1903. A.P.S.5987. E303

III, 74: 196-211
Song for [medium] voice with keyboard.
r: $c\#^1$ - $f\#^2$ t: e^1 - e^2

RB430.   +————. The Year's at the Spring, key of A major, no. 6. From Browning Songs, First Series, op. 27. Edition Schmidt, no. 24a. Boston: Arthur P. Schmidt, c1893. A.P.S. 2910f. E304

III, 24: 221-228
Song for [medium high] voice with piano.
r: d^1 - a^2 t: e^1 - e^2

Note: RB430 is bound in Browning Songs, First Series.

RB431.   Rohrer, Mildred. Pippa Passes, key of C major. Xerox copy, manuscript, Gilman, Ill.: no publisher, Mildred Rohrer cJune 25, 1934. No pl. no.

III, 24: 221-228
Song for [low] voice with keyboard.
r: g - c^2 t: g - a^1

RB432.   Rorem, Ned. Pippa's Song, key of G major. New York: C. F. Peters Corporation, Henmar Press Inc. c1963. Edition Peters 6373 a.

III, 24: 221-228
Song for high voice with piano.
r: d¹ - d³

RB433.   +Rossman, Floy Adele. The Year's at the Spring, key of B-flat major. From Song-Time for Women's Voices, harmonized and edited by Floy Adele Rossman. Two-and Three-Part Choruses with Piano Accompaniment. New York: Paull-Pioneer Music Corp., c1933. No pl. no. E305

III, 24: 221-228
Part-song for women's chorus (soprano I and II, alto I and II) **with piano.**

RB434.   +Sarson, H. M. The Year's at the Spring, key of F major. From Kent County Song Book. London: Novello and Company, Limited, n.d. Pl. no. 16086. E306

III, 24: 221-228
Two-part song for children's chorus (soprano I and II), unacc.

Note: RB434 is bound in Kent County Song Book. The ABL received RB434 April 16, 1941. Broughton, *Bibliography* gives 1935 as the publication date.

RB435.   Schmidt, Louis. All's Right with the World, key of B-flat major. New York: The William Maxwell Music Co., c1907. Pl. no. 948.

III, 24: 221-228
Song for [medium] voice with piano.
r: c¹ - g² (optional bb²)   t: f¹ - d¹

RB436.   +Schuyler, Georgina. The Page Sings to the Queen, key of F major, no. 6. From Album of Songs by Georgina Schuyler. New York: G. Schirmer, c1894. Pl. no. 3124. E308

III, 44-45: 223-270
Song for mezzo soprano or contralto with piano.
r: c¹ - d²

Note: RB436 is bound in Album of Songs.

RB437.   +Sharpe, Cedric. The Year's at the Spring, key of B-flat major. Modern Songs [edition]. London: Joseph Williams Limited, c1927. J.W.16392. E309

III, 24: 221-228
Song for [medium high] voice with piano.
r: c¹ - f²   t: f¹ - eb²

RB438.   +Somervell, Arthur. The Year's at the Spring, key of F major, no. 8. From the song cycle, A Broken Arc. London: Boosey & Co., c1923. H. 10770. E310

III, 24: 221-228
Song for [medium high] voice with piano.
r: c¹ - f²   t: g¹ - d²

Note: RB438 is bound in A Broken Arc.

RB439.   Spier, La Salle. A Cycle of Six Songs from Pippa Passes. 1. Day! key of F-sharp major. 2. And You Are Ever by Me, key of E-flat major. 3. Overhead the Tree-tops Meet, key of D minor. 4. But Winter Hastens at Summer's End, key of G major. 5. Oh, What a Drear, Dark Close to My Poor Day! key of E-flat major. 6. New-Year's Hymn, key of C major. Photostat copy, manuscript, no place: no publisher, Sept. 22, 1940. No pl. no.

Song cycle for [medium high] voice with string quartet and piano. Piano-conductor's score. No parts.

1.   III, 5: 1-12
      r: d¹ - f#²   t: d¹ - e²

2.   III, 47: 320-327
      r: c¹ - a² (optional g¹)   t: e¹ - d#²

3.   III, 74: 196-211
      r: d¹ - g²   t: e¹ - e²

4.   III, 75: 217-222, 225-229
      r: d¹ - f#²   t: a¹ - e²

5.   III, 78: 298-302
      r: eb¹ - f¹   t: e¹ - c²

6.   III, 13: 190-201
      r: g¹ - g²   t: g¹ - f#²

Note: On the first page is written "With friendly greetings To Dr. A. J. Armstrong and the Baylor Browning Collection LaSalle Spier   Washington, D.C.   September 22, 1940."

RB440.   +Stephens, Ward. You'll Love Me Yet, key of G-flat major. New York: The William Maxwell Music Co., c1908. Pl. no. 1092. E312

III, 64-65: 304-315
Song for [high] voice with piano.
r: f¹ - bb²   t: gb¹ - gb²

RB441.   Sternberg, Daniel Arie. Pippa's Song, key of B major. Photostat copy, manuscript, no place: no publisher, 1945. No pl. no.

III, 24: 221-228
Song for high voice with keyboard.
r: d^1 - $a\#^2$

Note: On the front cover is written "With the best compliments of the composer to Dr. A. J. Armstrong. Waco, 2/7, 1945."

RB442.   True, Latham. Give Her but the Least Excuse to Love Me, key of E-flat major. From Browning Songs by Latham True. Portland, Maine: Cressey & Allen, Latham True c1940. No pl. no.

III, 44-45: 253-270
Song for [medium] voice with keyboard.
r: b - eb^2 t: d^1 - eb^2

Note: RB442 was the gift of the composer March 22, 1943.

RB443.   +—————. Overhead the Treetops Meet, key of D major. From Browning Songs by Latham True. Portland, Maine: Cressey & Allen, Latham True c1940. No pl. no. E314

III, 74: 196-202, 204-211
Song for [medium] voice with keyboard.
r: b - eb^2 t: d^1 - eb^2

Note: RB443 was the gift of the composer March 22, 1943.

RB444.   Vaughan Williams, Ralph. Spring, key of C major, no. 6. From Songs of Praise, edited by Percy Dearmer, Ralph Vaughan Williams, and Martin Shaw. Enlarged edition. London: Oxford University Press, Humphrey Milford, [1931]. No pl. no.

III, 24: 221-228
Hymn for soprano, alto, tenor, bass (unacc.).

Note: RB444 is bound in the hymn collection, Songs of Praise.

RB445.   +Warren, Jeanne. Pippa's Holiday (Danse Grotesque), key of F major. From Modern Piano Solos, Series II. Cincinnati: The Willis Music Company, c1918. Pl. no. 3379-4W. E315

III, 5-79
Solo for piano.

RB446.   Watson, Mary E. Give Her but a Least Excuse to Love Me, key of D major. From *Browning's Pippa Passes,* edited by Ola Jones Nisbet. Manuscript, no place: no publisher, n.d. No pl. no.

III, 44-45: 253-270
Song for [high] voice, unacc.
r: d^1 - g^2 t: e^1 - $f\#^2$

RB447.   +————————. [1.] Incidental Music to *Pippa's Soliloquy,* key of A major, pp. 118-144: [(a)] Day! key of D major, pp. 118-130. [(b)] I Am Queen of Thee, Floweret! key of D major, pp. 130-131. [(c)] Worship Whom Else? key of D major, pp. 132-139. [(d)] All Service Ranks the Same with God, key of A major, pp. 139-141. [(e)] And More of It, key of E-flat major, pp. 142-144. [2.] Let the Watching Lids Wink, key of G major, p. 154. [3.] Give Her but a Least Excuse to Love Me, key of D major, pp. 178-180. [4.] Overhead the Tree Tops Meet, key of A major, pp. 208-209. [5.] All Service Ranks the Same with God, key of A major, p. 213, adapted by Ola Jones Nisbet. From *Browning's Pippa Passes,* edited by Ola Jones Nisbet. Charlotte, N.C.: Presbyterian Standard Publishing Co., c1929. No pl. no. E296

[1.]   Incidental music for speaker, voice, violin, and harp. Piano-conductor's score [only]. No parts. [To be performed successively, although can be performed separately.]

[(a)]   III, 5-9: [1-94]
        Recitation for speaker, violin, and harp.
[(b)]   III, 9: 95-103
        Song for [high] voice, unacc.
        r: g^1 - a^2 t: a^1 - f^2
[(c)]   III, 9-12: [104-189]
        Recitation for speaker, violin, and harp.
[(d)]   III, 13: 190-201
        Hymn for [medium] voice, unacc.
[(e)]   III, 13: [202-214]
        Recitation for speaker, violin, and harp.

Note: For the recitations, it appears that only the lines of poetry necessary for timing are indicated to the musicians.

[2.]   III, 14: 1-3
       Song for [medium] voice, unacc.
       r: g^1 - g^2 t: g^1 - g^2

Note: The composer is not indicated above the music, but in the preface Nisbet states that most of the music was written by Watson, *see* p. 12.

[3.]   III, 44-45: 253-270
       Song for [high] voice, unacc.
       r: d^1 - g^2 t: e^1 - $f\#^2$

[4.]   III, 24: 221-228
       Song for [high] voice, unacc.
       r: d^1 - a^2 t: f^1 - $f\#^2$

[5.]   III, 13: 190, 194, 195
       Song for [medium] voice, unacc.
       r: $c\#^1$ - $f\#^2$ t: e^1 - e^2

Note: Also contained in *Browning's Pippa Passes* are items
RB353, RB418, and RB449.

RB448.   Watson, Mary E. and Nisbet, Ola Jones. A King Lived Long
Ago, key of B-flat major. From *Browning's Pippa Passes,*
edited by Ola Jones Nisbet. Manuscript, no place: no publisher, n.d. No pl. no.

III, 58-60: 164-166, 175-178, 180-186, 189-191, 202-204,
209, 210, 219, 220, 222
Song for [high] voice, unacc.
r: d^1 - g^2 t: g^1 - g^2

RB449.   +———————. A King Lived Long Ago, key of B-flat major.
From *Browning's Pippa Passes,* pp. 193-195, edited by Ola
Jones Nisbet. Charlotte, N.C.: Presbyterian Standard Pub-
lishing Co., c1929. No pl. no. E296

III, 58-60: 164-166, 175-178, 180-186, 189-191, 202-204, 209,
210, 219, 220, 222
Song for [high] voice, unacc.
r: d^1 - g^2 t: g^1 - g^2

Note: Also contained in *Browning's Pippa Passes* are items
RB353, RB418, and RB447.

RB450.   Welch, Jay. Music for Robert Browning's Pippa Passes. 1.
Prelude, key of E-flat major. 2. All Service Ranks the Same
with God, key of F major. 3. The Year's at the Spring, key of
F major. 4. Give Her the Least Excuse to Love Me, key of
F major. 5. Play IV from A to end (Clarinet playing vocal
line). 6. Prelude to Act Two—same as III, The Year's at the
Spring. 7. Prelude to Act Three—The Night Wind, key of F
major. 8. Night Wind—same as VII. 9. A King Lived Long
Ago, key of F major. 10. You'll Love Me Yet, key of C major.
11. Overhead the Treetops Meet, key of E-flat major. No
place: no publisher, Jay Welch c1958. No pl. no.

Incidental music for oboe, clarinet, harp, soprano, [medium]
voice, and [low] voice. Conductor's score. No parts.

1. Prelude for oboe, clarinet, and harp.

2. III, 13: 190-195; 14: 1-3
Song for soprano, oboe, harp, and clarinet.
r: d^1 - f^2

3. and 6. III, 24: 221-228
Song for soprano with harp.
r: f^1 - f^2

4. III, 44-45: 253, 255-260, 262-269
Song for soprano, oboe, clarinet, and harp.
r: c^1 - f^2

5. Solo for clarinet with oboe and harp.

7. and 8. Prelude for harp.

9. III, 58: 164, 165, 167, 168, 171, 175-177; 60: 209-214, 219, 221, 222
Song for soprano, oboe, and harp.
r: d^1 - $f\#^2$

10. III, 64-65: 304-315
Song for [medium] voice, unacc.
r: c^1 - d^2 t: d^1 - b^1

11. III, 74: 196-199, 204, 205, 209-211
Song for soprano with harp.
r: d^1 - eb^2

RB451. +Whitmer, T[homas] Carl. Song from Pippa Passes, key of G major, no. 1 [only]. From Three Songs, op. 3. No place: no publisher, T. Carl Whitmer c1903. Pl. no. I-3. E318

III, 24: 221-228
Song for mezzo soprano with piano.
r: d^1 - e^2

RB452. Wilson, Harry Robert. All's Right with the World, key of E-flat major. From the Harry Robert Wilson Series. Octavo No. R3-107. Photocopy, Winona, Minn.: Hal Leonard Music Inc., c1967. R3-107.

III, 24: 221-228
Part-song for mixed chorus (soprano, alto, tenor, bass) with piano.

Note: RB452 was the gift of Hal Leonard Music/Pointer Publications May 25, 1972.

RB453. Worth, John W. Four Songs from Pippa Passes. 1. The Year's at the Spring, key of D major. 2. Give Her but a Least Excuse to Love Me, key of E-flat major. 3. A King Lived Long Ago, key of C major. 4. Overhead the Tree-tops Meet, key of A major. From Twelve Songs by Browning by John W. Worth. Manuscript, no place: no publisher, n.d. No pl. no.

Songs for [high] voice with keyboard.

1. III, 24: 221-228
r: e^1 - g^2 t: a^1 - $f\#^2$

2. III, 44-45: 253-270
r: f^1 - f^2 t: g^1 - eb^2

3. III, 58-60: 164-177, 179-189, 202, 203, 205-214, 219-222
r: d^1 - g^2 t: e^1 - e^2

4. III, 74: 196-211
r: c^1 - $f\#^2$ t: g^1 - $f\#^2$

Note: RB453 is bound in Twelve Songs by Browning.

RB454. +Young, Dalhousie. Pippa's Song ("The Year's at the Spring"), key of G major. London: Boosey & Co, c1904. (H.4432). E319

III, 24: 221-228
Song for [high] voice with piano.
r: f#^{1} - g^2 t: g^1 - g^2

PLOT-CULTURE. *See* FERISHTAH'S FANCIES

PORPHYRIA'S LOVER

RB455. Dillon, Fannie Charles. Porphyria, key of E major. Manuscript, no place: no publisher, n.d. No pl. no.

V, 191-193: 1-60
Song for [high] voice with keyboard.
r: d^1 - a#^{2} t: a^1 - f#^{2}

PROLOGUE. *See* FIFINE AT THE FAIR

PROSPICE

RB456. +Boughton, Rutland. Prospice, key of C major. London: J. Curwen & Sons Ltd., c1924. Pl. no. 50604. E326

VII, 168-169: 1-13, 15-28
Part-song for male chorus (tenor I and II, bass I and II) with piano (for rehearsal only).

RB457. +Davies, H[enry] Walford. Prospice, key of C major, op. 6. London: Novello & Co., Ltd., n.d. No pl. no. E327

VII, 168-169: 1-28
Song for baritone with string quartet. Conductor's score. With parts.
r: B - e^1

Note: Broughton, *Bibliography* gives [1900] as the possible date of publication.

RB458. +Duncan, Edmondstoune. Prospice, key of C major, no. 1. From Six Declamatory Songs, op. 115. London: The Walter Scott Publishing Co. Ltd., n.d. No pl. no. E328

VII, 168-169: 1-28
Song for [low] voice with keyboard.
r: b - e^2 t: c^1 - d^2

Note: RB458 is bound in Six Declamatory Songs.

RB459. +Hadley, Henry. Prospice, key of C major, op. 105, no. 1 [only]. From Songs by Henry Hadley. Sheet Music Edition V. 923. New York: Carl Fischer, Inc., c1926. Pl. no. 23785. E329

VII, 168-169: 1-28
Song for medium voice with piano.
r: c^1 - g^2

RB460. +Homer, Sidney. Prospice, key of B-flat major, op. 12, no. 3
[only]. From Three Songs by Sidney Homer. New York:
G. Schirmer, c1903. Pl. no. 16445. E330

VII, 168-169: 1-28
Song for high voice with piano.
r: e^1 - g^2

RB461. ————————. Prospice, key of G major, op. 12, no. 3 [only].
From Three Songs by Sidney Homer. New York: G.
Schirmer, c1903. Pl. no. 16446.

VII, 168-169: 1-28
Song for low voice with piano.
r: c^1 - e^2

RB462. +Lehmann, Liza. Prospice, key of E-flat major. From Three
Songs by Liza Lehmann. New York: G. Schirmer, Inc.,
c1922. Pl. no. 30697. E331

VII, 168-169: 1-28
Song for low voice with piano.
r: g - f^1

RB463. +Stanford, C[harles] Villiers. Prospice, key of B-flat major.
London: Stanley Lucas, Weber & Co., n.d. S.L.W.&Co.2220.
E332

VII, 168-169: 1-28
Song for [medium high] voice with piano.
r: c^1 - f^2 t: $f\#^1$ - d^2

Note: On the front cover is written "Lily E. Kingsland." The
music is the same as RB464; the differences are the publisher
and pl. no. Broughton, *Bibliography* gives [1884] as the possible date of publication.

RB464. ————————. Prospice, key of B-flat major. London: Stanley
Lucas, Weber, Pitt & Hatzfeld Ltd; Boston: H. B. Stevens
Company, c1893. S.L.W.P.&H. 3250.3255.

VII, 168-169: 1-28
Song for [medium high] voice with piano.
r: c^1 - f^2 t: $f\#^1$ - d^2

Note: The ABL has 2 copies. Copy 2 lists as the London
publisher, Augener & Co., does not give a pl. no., and begins
pagination with 24. The music for copy 2 is the same as copy
1 and also the same as RB463.

RB465.   Thomas, Adelaida. Prospice, key of A-flat major. Photostat
copy, Sussex: Brighton, Adelaida Thomas c1909. No pl. no.

VII, 168-169: 1-5, 8-28
Song for [medium] voice with piano.
r: c^1 - eb^2 t: c^1 - c^2

RB466.   +Thomas, D[avid] Vaughan. Prospice, key of F major. Wrex-
ham: Hughes & Sons, Publishers, c1936. No pl. no. E334

VII, 168-169: 1-28
Part-song for male chorus (tenor I and II, bass I and II)
with piano (for rehearsal only).

RB467.   True, Latham. Prospice, key of F major. From Browning Songs
by Latham True. Portland, Maine: Cressey & Allen, Latham
True c1932.

VII, 168-169: 1-21, 23-28
Song for [medium] voice with keyboard.
r: a - g^2 t: d^1 - d^2

Note: RB467 is a gift from the composer.

RB468.   +————. Prospice, key of G major. From Browning Songs
by Latham True. Portland, Maine: Cressey & Allen, Latham
True revised c1943. No pl. no. E335

VII, 168-169: 1-21, 23-28
Song for [high] voice with keyboard.
r: d^1 - g^2 t: $f\#^1$ - $f\#^2$

Note: RB468 is a gift from the composer.

RABBI BEN EZRA

RB469.   Ackert, Bernard G. Rabbi Ben Ezra, key of E-flat major. Manuscript, no place: no publisher, n.d. No pl. no.

VII, 109: 1-6
Song for [medium] voice with keyboard.
r: c^1 - g^2 t: f^1 - c^2

Note: At the bottom of the first page is written "Autographed
copy, Bernard G. Ackert Testified by A. J. Armstrong."

RB470.   +Branscombe, Gena. The Best Is Yet to Be, key of C major.
Boston: The Arthur P. Schmidt Co., c1921. A.P.S.12139.
E337

VII, 109: 1-6; 111: 31-36
Song for soprano or tenor with keyboard.
r: d^1 - g^2

RB471.   Hadley, Henry K[imball]. Rabbi Ben Ezra, key of F major, no.
          1. From The Laurel Song Book, edited by W. L. Tomlins.
          The Laurel Music Series. Boston: C. C. Birchard & Company,
          c1901. No pl. no.

          VII, 109: 1-6
          Part-song for mixed chorus (soprano, alto, tenor, bass), unacc.

          Note: RB471 is bound in The Laurel Song Book.

RB472.   Madsen, Dora L. Rabbi Ben Ezra, key of D major. Manuscript,
          no place: no publisher, n.d. No pl. no.

          VII, 109: 1-6
          [Song for medium voice] with keyboard.
          r: d^1 - f#^{2} t: f#^{1} - d^2

          Note: The vocal line appears to have been omitted, unless the
          singer is expected to sing the top note of the keyboard line.
          At the top of the first page is written "The music of this song
          is dedicated to Mrs. Ella H. Canover." At the bottom of the
          first page is written "Mrs. J. Chester Madsen, 1267 Crystal
          Ave., Salt Lake City, Ut." RB472 was the gift of the com-
          poser June 23, 1943.

RB473.   Mueller, Carl F. Grow Old Along with Me! key of A major.
          From G. S. 8vo Choruses, no. 7744. Xerox copy, [New
          York]: G. Schirmer (Inc.), c1934. Pl. no. 36141.

          VII, 109: 1-6
          Part-song for mixed chorus (soprano, alto, tenor, bass I and
          II) with piano (for rehearsal only).

          Note: RB473 is the gift of the Library of Congress.

RB474.   Ralston, Frances Marion. Now Who Shall Arbitrate, key of
          B-flat major, [no. 9]. From Rabbi Ben Ezra. Manuscript,
          no place: no publisher, n.d. No pl. no.

          VII, 116: 127-150
          Song for [medium high] voice with keyboard.
          r: bb - g^2 t: f^1 - f^2

          Note: On the front cover is written "Copied from original
          manuscript."

RB475.   +————————. Rabbi Ben Ezra. 1. Grow Old Along with Me,
          key of C major. 2. Not That, Amassing Flowers, key of C
          major. 3. Then Welcome Each Rebuff, key of A-flat major.
          4. Yet Gifts Should Prove Their Use, key of C major. 5. For
          Pleasant Is This Flesh, key of E-flat major. 6. Youth Ended,
          key of E-flat major. [7.] For Note When Evening Shuts, key
          of E-flat major. [8.] So Still within This Life, key of D-flat
          major. 9. Now Who Shall Arbitrate? key of C major. 10. Ay!
          Note That Potter's Wheel, key of E-flat major. 11. But I
          Need Now As Then, key of F major. 12. So Take and Use

Thy Work, key of F major. Pasadena: no publisher, Frances Marion Ralston c1922. No pl. no. E339

[Cantata] for women's chorus (soprano I and II, alto I and II), soloists (alto, soprano, mezzo soprano), vocal quartet (soprano, alto, tenor, bass), and piano. To be sung successively, although the parts can be sung separately.

1. VII, 109: 1-6
   Part-song for women's chorus (soprano I and II, alto I and II) with piano.

2. VII, 109-110: 7-30
   Part-song for women's chorus (soprano I and II, alto I and II) with piano.

3. VII, 111: 31-36
   Song for alto with piano.
   r: b^b - e^2

4. VII, 112: 49-60
   Part-song for women's chorus (soprano I and II, alto I and II) with piano.

5. VII, 112: 61-66
   Song for soprano with piano.
   r: g^1 - g^2

6. VII, 113: 85-90
   Song for mezzo soprano with piano.
   r: c^1 - f^2

7. VII, 114: 91-96
   Part-song for women's chorus (soprano I and II, alto I and II) with piano.

8. VII, 114-115: 97-120
   Vocal quartet for 2 treble voices and 2 bass voices, unacc.

9. VII, 116-117: 127-150
   Song for soprano with piano.
   r: c^1 - a^2

10. VII, 117-118: 151-162
    Piano solo with choral monotone accompaniment (soprano I and II, alto I and II) and soprano solo.

11. VII, 119: 181-186
    Song for alto with piano.
    r: b - d^2

12. VII, 119: 187-192
    Part-song for two women's choruses (soprano I and II, alto I and II) (soprano I and II, alto I and II) with piano.

RB476. +Schuyler, Georgina. Grow Old Along with Me, key of D major, no. 5. From Album of Songs by Georgina Schuyler. New York: G. Schirmer, c1894. Pl. no. 3123. E340

VII, 109: 1-6
Song for mezzo soprano or contralto with piano.
r: b - b^1

Note: RB476 is bound in Album of Songs.

RB477. +————. Grow Old Along with Me, key of D major, no. 5 [only]. From Songs from English and American Poets by Georgina Schuyler. New York: G. Schirmer, c1882. Pl. no. 3123. E340

VII, 109: 1-6
Song for mezzo soprano with piano.
r: b - b^1

RB478. True, Latham. Grow Old Along with Me, key of D-flat major. No place: no publisher, Latham True c1942. No pl. no.

VII, 109: 1-6
Song for [medium] voice with keyboard.
r: db^1 - f^2 t: eb^1 - c^2

Note: RB478 is the gift of the composer.

RB479. Vaughan Williams, Ralph. Then Welcome Each Rebuff, key of E-flat major, no. 662. From Songs of Praise, edited by Percy Dearmer, Ralph Vaughan Williams, and Martin Shaw. Enlarged edition. London: Oxford University Press, Humphrey Milford, [1931]. No pl. no.

VII, 111-112: 31-36, 49-60; 119: 187-192
Hymn for soprano, alto, tenor, bass (unacc.).

Note: RB479 is bound in the hymn collection, Songs of Praise.

RB480. Wiant, Bliss, editor. Then Welcome Each Rebuff, key of E-flat major. Chinese translation of the poem by RB [only]. From *Christian Fellowship Hymns* by T. C. Chao, translator and editor of the text, and Bliss Wiant, editor of the music. (2nd edition. Peiping, China: Yenching University, 1933.) Manuscript, no place: no publisher, n.d. No pl. no.

VII, 111-112: 31-36, 49-60; 119: 187-192
Hymn for soprano, alto, tenor, bass (unacc.).

Note: RB480 was the gift of Dryden Linsley Phelps in 1959. It is written on ancient rice paper.

RB481.   +————————. Then Welcome Each Rebuff, key of E-flat major, no. 128. Chinese translation of the poem by RB [only]. From *Christian Fellowship Hymns* by T. C. Chao, translator and editor of the text, and Bliss Wiant, editor of the music. 2nd edition. Peiping, China: Yenching University, 1933. No pl. no. E336

VII, 111-112: 31-36, 49-60; 119: 187-192
Hymn for soprano, alto, tenor, bass (unacc.).

Note: RB481 is bound in *Christian Fellowship Hymns*.

RED COTTON NIGHT-CAP COUNTRY, OR TURF AND TOWERS

RB482.   +Bantock, Granville. Red Cotton Night-Cap Country, key of D-flat major. Berners Edition. London: Joseph Williams Limited, c1935. W.15. E342

XII, 11: 147-150
Solo for piano.

THE RING AND THE BOOK

RB483.   Bollinger, Sam[ue]l. Pompilia e Caponsacchi, key of G major, op. 3. Manuscript, [Leipzig]: no publisher, n.d. No pl. no.

IX-X
Dramatic overture for orchestra. Conductor's score [only]. No parts.

flutes	horns I-IV (in F)	timpani
oboes	trumpets I and II (in B♭)	(in G, D)
English horn	alto trombone I	violins I
clarinets	tenor trombone II	and II
(in B♭)	bass trombone III	viola
bassoons	bass tuba	cello
		double bass

Note: Inside the music is an explanatory note apparently written by the composer and also an explanatory note by the composer's nephew, E. E. Briscoe.

RB484.   ————————. Pompilia e Caponsacchi, key of G major, op. 3. Manuscript, [Leipzig]: no publisher, n.d. No pl. no.

IX-X
Overture for large orchestra. Conductor's score. With parts.

flutes I and II	tenor trombone II
oboes I and II	bass trombone III
English horn	bass tuba
clarinets I and II (in B♭)	timpani (in G, D)
bassoons I and II	violins I and II
horns I-IV (in F)	viola
trumpets I and II (in B♭)	cello
alto trombone I	double bass

RB485.   Cooley, Carlton. "Caponsacchi," key of C major. Photostat copy, manuscript, no place: no publisher, 1933. No pl. no.

IX-X
Epic poem for orchestra. Conductor's score [only]. No parts.

2 flutes	tuba
piccolo (and 3rd flute)	timpani, side drum, bass drum,
2 oboes	cymbals, tambourine, triangle,
English horn	tam-tam, tubular bells (chimes),
2 clarinets (in Bb)	xylophone
bass clarinet (in Bb)	celesta
2 bassoons	harp
contrabassoon	violins I and II
4 horns (in F)	viola
3 trumpets (in C)	cello
3 trombones	double bass

RB486.   +Hageman, Richard. Tragödie in Arezzo (Caponsacchi). Libretto by Arthur Goodrich. Berlin: Edition Adler G.M.B.H., c1931. E.A. 12. E343

IX-X
Opera in 3 acts, prologue and epilogue. Piano-vocal score [only]. No parts.

Characters

Caponsacchi (tenor)
Guido Franceschini (baritone)
Pope Innocent XII (bass)
Tommati, Judge of the Papal Court (bass)
Venturini, Judge of the Papal Court (baritone)
Scalchi, Judge of the Papal Court (tenor)
Montini, Captain of the Papal Guard (baritone)
Giotto, Soldier of the Papal Guard (bass)
Melchior, Soldier of the Papal Guard (baritone)
Andrea, Soldier of the Papal Guard (tenor)
Canon Conti (baritone)
Pietro, Pompilia's father (bass)
Gherardi (tenor)
Governor of Arezzo (bass)
Archbishop of Arezzo (baritone)
Innkeeper at Castelnuovo (bass)
His Servant (tenor)
Guard (tenor)
Messenger (tenor)
Pompilia, Wife of Guido (soprano)
Violante, her mother (mezzo soprano)
Margherita, her servant (mezzo soprano)
Marinetta (mezzo soprano)
Citizens, Peasants, Guards, etc.

Orchestra

2 flutes	timpani
piccolo (and 3rd flute)	battery
2 oboes	chimes
English horn	guitars
2 clarinets (in B♭ and A)	harp
bass clarinet (in B♭)	celesta
contrabassoon	organ
4 horns	violins I and II
3 trumpets	viola
3 trombones	cello
tuba	double bass

Note: With the music are newspaper articles about the opera, composer, and singers.

ROBERT BROWNING OVERTURE[14]

RB487. Ives, Charles E. Robert Browning Overture, key of C major. New York: Peer International Corporation, c1959. Pl. no. 351.

Orchestral overture. Study score. No parts.

piccolo	2 trumpets (in C)
2 flutes	3 trombones
2 oboes	tuba
English horn	timpani, snare drum, bass drum,
2 clarinets (in B♭)	cymbals
2 bassoons	violins I and II
contrabassoon	viola
4 horns (in F)	cello
	double bass

SAUL

RB488. Dillon, Fannie Charles. Saul, key of D major, op. 14. Mimeograph copy, manuscript, no place: no publisher, n.d. No pl. no.

VI, 98: 1; 100-106: 22-28, 35-70, 96, 97; 111: 160, 161; 113-117: 190, 206, 225-232, 237; 120-124: 282, 287, 288, 294, 299, 305, 312, 313, 321-327, 329-335
Recitation for reader with keyboard.

RB489. Moore, Mary Carr. Saul, key of F major, op. 30. Manuscript, no place: no publisher, July, 1916. No pl. no.

VI, 98-124
Setting for reader, violin, cello, and piano. Full score. With parts.

---

[14]This is not the title of an RB poem; it is herein listed because the music is based on RB in general, although not on one particular poem.

RB490. —————————. Suite for Strings and Piano, key of F major. Manuscript, no place: no publisher, July, 1916. No pl. no.

VI, 98-124
Suite for string quartet and piano. Full score. With parts.

RB491. Ralston, Frances Marion. Saul, key of E-flat major. Words arranged by Bertha Lovewell Dickinson, dramatic presentation by Andrew Joseph Armstrong. Manuscript, no place: no publisher, n.d. No pl. no.

VI, 98-124
Oratorio for chorus (soprano, alto, tenor, bass), soloists (tenor, baritone, mezzo soprano), pipe organ or piano, and reader. Full score.

A SERENADE AT THE VILLA

RB492. +Bantock, Granville. A Serenade at the Villa, key of D major. Berners Edition. London: Joseph Williams Limited, c1935. W.17. E344

VI, 156: 18-20
Solo for piano.

RB493. +Kernochan, Marshall. A Serenade at the Villa, key of E-flat major. From Two Songs by Marshall Kernochan. New York: G. Schirmer, c1913. Pl. no. 23861. E345

VI, 155-156: 1-10, 16-25
Song for medium voice with piano.
r: d^1 - f^2

RB494. +Mana-Zucca. That Was I, key of A-flat major, op. 42. From Two Poems by Mana-Zucca. New York: G. Schirmer, c1921. Pl. no. 30209. E346

VI, 155: 1-10
Song for high voice with piano.
r: f^1 - f^2

SHAH ABBAS. *See* FERISHTAH'S FANCIES

SINCE WE PARTED[15]

RB495. Versel, Louis. Since We Parted, key of D major. New York: G. Schirmer, c1917. Pl. no. 27968.

Song for high voice with piano.
r: e^1 - a^2

---

[15]This is not the title of a poem by RB; it is herein listed because the words are mistakenly attributed to him on the music; actually the words are by Owen Meredith.

SOLILOQUY OF THE SPANISH CLOISTER

RB496. +Bantock, Granville. Soliloquy of the Spanish Cloister, key of D major. Berners Edition. London: Joseph Williams Limited, c1935. W.19. E348

VI, 26: 1, 3, 4
Solo for piano.

SONG

RB497. +Beach, John [Parsons]. Is She Not Pure Gold, key of G-flat major. Newton Center: The Wa-Wan Press, c1907. No pl. no. E349

VI, 47: 1-12
Song for [medium] voice with piano.
r: $c\#^1$ - e^2 t: eb^1 - $c\#^2$

RB498. Ellingham, Harry. Her Tresses, key of G major. Manuscript, [London]: Boosey & Hawkes Ltd., n.d. No pl. no.

VI, 47: 1-12
Song for [medium] voice with keyboard.
r: d^1 - e^2 t: e^1 - d^2

RB499. Forrester, J. Cliffe. Devotion, key of F major. London: The London Music Publishing and General Agency Company, (Lim.), n.d. Pl. no. 11.

VI, 47: 1-12
Song for [high] voice with piano.
r: e^1 - g^2 t: f^1 - f^2

RB500. +Freer, Eleanor Everest. Nay! But You Do Not Love Her, key of C major, op. 18, no. 4 [only]. From Songs by Eleanor Everest Freer. New York: Church, Paxton and Company, c1912. No pl. no. E352

VI, 47: 1-12
Song for low voice with piano.
r: d^1 - d^2

RB501. ——————. Nay, but You, Who Do Not Love Her, key of C major. From the opera, The Brownings Go to Italy, (or) (A Love Story), op. 43. Libretto by G. A. Hawkins-Ambler. Chicago: The Music Library of Chicago, Eleanor Everest Freer c1936. Pl. no. 38977.

VI, 47: 1-12
Song for baritone with keyboard.
r: d^1 - d^2

Note: RB501 is bound in the opera, The Brownings Go to Italy. (Piano-vocal score [only].) The ABL has 2 copies. Inside the front cover of copy 2 is written "For the Browning Library of Baylor University Compliments of Eleanor Everest Freer 1936."

RB502.   +Gregory, E[leanor] C. Song, key of E major, no. 3. From Six Songs by E. C. Gregory. London: Novello Ewer & Co, n.d. Pl. no. 7519. E352.5

VI, 47: 1-12
Song for [medium high] voice with keyboard.
r: b# - e²   t: e¹ - e²

Note: RB502 is bound in Six Songs.

RB503.   +Iles, Edward. Nay but Do You Not Love Her, key of D-flat major, no. 2. From Three Songs by Edward Iles. London: Stainer & Bell, Ltd., c1920. S&B.2202. E353

VI, 47: 1-12
Song for [medium] voice with piano.
r: ab - eb²   t: f¹ - db²

Note: RB503 is bound in Three Songs.

RB504.   Jervis-Read, H[arold] V[incent]. My Mistress, key of F major, no. 1. From Two Ecstasies by H. V. Jervis-Read, op. 18. London: Edwin Ashdown (Limited), c1910. (E.A.33488).

VI, 47: 1-12
Song for [medium] voice with piano.
r: c¹ - e²   t: e¹ - e²

Note: RB504 is bound in Two Ecstasies.

RB505.   +Oldroyd, George. Tresses, key of A-flat major. London: Elkin & Co., Ltd., c1924. E.&Co.1409. E355

VI, 47: 1-12
Song for [high] voice with piano.
r: eb¹ - ab² (optional bb²)   t: ab¹ - f²

RB506.   +Pickard-Cambridge, W. A. Nay, but You Who Do Not Love Her, key of G major, no. 1. From Six Songs by W. A. Pickard-Cambridge, op. 2. London: Novello and Company, Limited, c1928. Pl. no. 15408. E350

VI, 47: 1-12
Song for low or middle voice with keyboard.
r: g - e²

Note: RB506 is bound in Six Songs.

RB507.   +Somervell, Arthur. Nay, but You, Who Do Not Love Her, key of A-flat major, no. 4. From the song cycle, A Broken Arc. London: Boosey & Co., c1923. H. 10770. E356

VI, 47: 1-12
Song for [medium high] voice with piano.
r: eb¹ - gb²   t: f¹ - db²

Note: RB507 is bound in A Broken Arc.

RB508. +Thayer, Arthur W. Nay but You, key of B-flat major, no. 2 [only]. From Three Songs by Arthur W. Thayer. Boston: H. B. Stevens Company, c1892. H.B.S.Co.433. E357

VI, 47: 1-12
Song for high voice with piano.
r: e^1 - g^2

Note: Contrary to what is on the front cover, the copyright is given as c1893 on the first page of music.

RB509. Toye, Francis. Nay but You Who Do Not Love Her, key of F major. From Songs by Francis Toye. London: Elkin & Co. Ltd., c1938. E.&Co.1998.

VI, 47: 1-12
Song for [medium] voice with piano.
r: c^1 - f^2 t: e^1 - d^2

STRAFFORD

RB510. Browning, Robert. O Bell' Andare, key of E-flat major. From RB's letter to Emily H. Hickey dated August 3, 1882. Manuscript. No pl. no.

II, 290: 1-4
Two-part children's chorus [soprano, alto], unacc.

Note: RB510 is contained in the letter. *See also* RB512 *and* illustration, pp. xii-xv.

RB511. +————. O Bell' Andare, key of G major. From *Poet-Lore,* I, 236, edited by Charlotte Porter and Helen A. Clarke. Philadelphia: The Poet-Lore Co., 1889. No pl. no. E360

II, 290: 1-4
Two-part children's chorus [soprano, alto], unacc.

Note: RB511 is bound in *Poet-Lore.*

RB512. ————. O Bell' Andare, key of G major. From RB's letter to Emily H. Hickey dated August 3, 1883. Manuscript. No pl. no.

II, 290: 1-4
Two-part children's chorus [soprano, alto], unacc.

Note: RB512 is contained in the letter. *See also* RB510 *and* illustration, pp. xii-xv.

RB513. +Coleridge-Taylor, S[amuel]. Earth Fades! Heaven Breaks on Me, key of B-flat major, no. 1. From In Memoriam, Three Rhapsodies, op. 24. Augener's Edition, no. 8868. London: Augener Limited, n.d. Pl. no. 11278. E359

II, 300: 205-210
Song for low voice with piano.
r: d^1 - eb^2

Note: RB513 is bound in In Memoriam.

RB514.   +————. Earth Fades! Heaven Breaks on Me, key of B-flat major, no. 1 [only]. From In Memoriam, Three Rhapsodies, op. 24. London: Augener Ltd., n.d. Pl. no. 11278a. E359

II, 300: 205-210
Song for low voice with piano.
r: d^1 - eb^2

SUMMUM BONUM

RB515.   +Bantock, Granville. Summum Bonum, key of A-flat major. Swan Edition, no. 8. London: Swan & Co., c1921. S.&Co. W.&W.Ltd.2765. E363

Asolando, 11: 1-8
Song for high voice with piano.
r: c^1 - ab^2

RB516.   +————. Summum Bonum, key of F major. Swan Edition, no. 8. London: Swan & Co., c1921. S.&Co.W.&W.Ltd. 2766. E363

Asolando, 11: 1-8
Song for low voice with piano.
r: a - f^2

RB517.   +Davidson, Frank. Summum Bonum, key of C major. London: Augener Limited, n.d. Pl. no. 12884. E364

Asolando, 11: 1-8
Song for tenor with piano.
r: b - g^2

Note: Broughton, *Bibliography* gives [1905] as the possible date of publication.

RB518.   +Dickinson, Clarence. Summum Bonum, key of B-flat major. From Duets by Clarence Dickinson. Chicago: Clayton F. Summy Co., c1909. C.F.S.Co.1142. E365

Asolando, 11: 1-8
Duet for [medium] voices with keyboard.

RB519.   +Hollander, Benoit. Summum Bonum, key of E minor, no. 1. From Two Songs by Benoit Hollander. Photostat copy, London: Phillips & Page, c1897. No pl. no. E366

Asolando, 11: 1-8
Song for [medium] voice with piano.
r: b - e^2 t: e^1 - $c\#^2$

Note: RB519 is bound in Two Songs.

RB520. +Inches, Charles. Summum Bonum, key of E major, no. 1. From Two Songs by Charles Inches. Edinburgh: R. W. Pentland, n.d. No pl. no. E367

Asolando, 11: 1-8
Song for [medium] voice with piano.
r: a - f#^{2} t: e^1 - e^2

Note: RB520 is bound in Two Songs. Broughton, *Bibliography* gives 1909 as the publication date.

RB521. +Johnson, Noel. All the Bloom of the Year (Summum Bonum), key of A-flat major. London: Houghton & Co., c1898. H.&Co. 228. E368

Asolando, 11: 1-8
Song for [high] voice with piano.
r: eb^1 - ab^2 t: ab^1 - eb^2

RB522. +Löhr, Harvey. Summum Bonum, key of E major, no. 10. From Album of Ten Songs by Harvey Löhr. London: Chappell & Co., n.d. Pl. no. 19479. E369

Asolando, 11: 1-8
Song for [high] voice with piano.
r: e^1 - g#^{2} t: g#^{1} - e^2

Note: RB522 is bound in Album of Ten Songs. Broughton, *Bibliography* gives [1893] as the possible date of publication.

RB523. +Mallinson, Albert. All the Breath and the Bloom of the Year, key of B-flat. From Songs by Albert Mallinson. London: J. B. Cramer & Co Ltd, c1925. J.B.C&Co.13156. E370

Asolando, 11: 1-8
Song for [high] voice with piano.
r: db^1 - a^2 t: f^1 - g^2

RB524. +Rogers, Clara Kathleen. Summum Bonum, key of C major, no. 2. From Browning Songs, First Series, op. 27. Edition Schmidt, no. 24a. Boston: Arthur P. Schmidt, c1893. A.P.S. 2910b. E371

Asolando, 11: 1-8
Song for [medium] voice with piano.
r: b - g^2 (optional a^2)   t: d^1 - d^2

Note: RB524 is bound in Browning Songs, First Series.

RB525. +Royle, Popplewell. Summum Bonum, key of A-flat major. London: J. B. Cramer & Co., c1891. (J.B.C&Co.10,437.) E372

Asolando, 11: 1-8
Song for [high] voice with piano.
r: eb^1 - f^2 t: g^1 - eb^2

RB526. +Stewart, Humphrey J[ohn]. Best of All, key of G major.
From Songs. First Series. Fischer's Edition. New York: J.
Fischer & Bro., c1911. J.F.&B.3486. E373

Asolando, 11: 1-8
Song for [high] voice with piano.
r: d^1 - a^2

THE SUN. *See* FERISHTAH'S FANCIES

THROUGH THE METIDJA TO ABD-EL-KADR

RB527. +Bantock, Granville. As I Ride ("Through the Metidja to
Abd-el-Kadr"), key of C major. London: Boosey & Co, c1912.
H. 7381. E375

VI, 13-15: 1-40
Song for [medium] voice with piano.
r: c^1 - e^2 t: e^1 - b^1

A TOCCATA OF GALUPPI'S

RB528. +Bantock, Granville. A Toccata of Galuppi's, key of C major,
no. 1. From Music for the Examinations of Trinity College
of Music, London. Junior Division. G. Group 7. London:
Joseph Williams Limited, c1934. J.W.16932. E376

VI, 74: 18
Solo for piano.

Note: Bound with RB528 is a Mazurka in D minor by P. I.
Tchaikovsky.

RB529. Forbes, J. Winchell. Toccata, key of E-flat major. No place:
no publisher, n.d. Pl. no. 2722-1.

VI, 72-76
Solo for unspecified keyboard instrument.

Note: The ABL has 2 copies. Copy 2 is a photostat of copy 1.
Copy 2 was made Oct. 16, 1946.

RB530. Galuppi, Baldassare. Sei Sonate.[16] 1. Sonata, key of C major.
2. Sonata, key of B-flat major. 3. Sonata, key of G major. 4.
Sonata, key of B-flat major. 5. Toccata, key of D minor. 6.
Toccata, key of F major. Transcribed by Iris Caruana. Padova,
Italy: Gugliemo Zanibon, c1968. G. 5052 Z.

VI, 72-76
4 sonatas and 2 toccatas for harpsichord.

Note: Galuppi entitles the entire volume *Six Sonatas,* so he
probably used the terms *sonata* and *toccata* interchangeably.

---

[16]This is not based on the poetry of RB; it is herein listed because the composer is
that Galuppi of whom RB speaks in his poem.

RB531. ——————. Sonata, key of A major.[17] Edited and revised by Joseph Henius. From The Early Sonata Forms and Other Pieces by the French, Italian and German Composers of the Seventeenth and Eighteenth Centuries. Superior Ed. 1925. New York: Carl Fischer, c1909. Pl. no. 15713.

VI, 72-76
Sonata for piano.

RB532. ——————. Sonata, key of D major. Edited and revised by Joseph Henius. From The Early Sonata Forms and Other Pieces by the French, Italian and German Composers of the Seventeenth and Eighteenth Centuries. Superior Ed. 1915. New York: Carl Fischer, c1909. Pl. no. 15712.

VI, 72-76
Sonata for piano.

Note: Above the first line of music is a note from the editor or publisher: "This is that Galuppi of whom Robert Browning speaks in his poem 'A Toccata of Galuppi.' We have vainly tried, however, to find the toccata in question."

RB533. [——————. Toccata],[18] key of G major. From RB's letter to Euphrasia Fanny Haworth dated [April, 1839], reprinted in William Clyde DeVane and Kenneth Leslie Knickerbocker, editors, *New Letters of Robert Browning* (New Haven: Yale University Press, 1950), pp. 15-18.

[Toccata for clavichord.]

Note: Betty Miller claims that the music RB wrote in the letter to Haworth is a toccata of Galuppi's "which on summer evenings he heard whistled or sung at every street corner in Venice. ('It is all to the tune of the Toccata of Galuppi,' wrote Florence Nightingale, who . . . had arrived in Italy three or four months before Robert Browning)."[19] In n. 1 Miller invites the musical expert to identify specifically the music in the letter.[20] I have not been able to determine how Miller concludes that the music in the letter is, in fact, a toccata of Galuppi's. The music appears at the end of the letter following RB's signature. The only explanation offered by RB is in the one sentence following the music: "What the children were singing last year in Venice, arm over neck."

The term "toccata" is an Italian word meaning "to be touched" and is therefore ordinarily indicative of keyboard music. Originally (ca. 1500) the keyboard toccata referred to an improvisational introduction or prelude. At the end of the

---

[17]*Ibid.*
[18]This is not based on the poetry of RB; it is herein listed because it may be the toccata to which RB refers in his poem.
[19]*Robert Browning, a Portrait* (New York: Charles Scribner's Sons, 1953), p. 71.
[20]*Ibid.*

eighteenth century the toccata had reached its present-day definition, i.e., it is a keyboard (organ or harpsichord usually) composition in free, idiomatic keyboard style, having full chords and running passages, with or without the inclusions of sections in imitative styles (such as fugues).[21] The music in RB's letter to Haworth does not meet this definition, but the terms sonata and toccata were probably used interchangeably by Galuppi, *see* RB530.

It is doubtful to me if RB had a particular toccata in mind when he wrote the poem. Although the poem title is "A Toccata of Galuppi's," in the poem itself he refers to more than one toccata, i.e., "While you sat and played Toccatas, stately at the clavichord?" It is also unrealistic of RB to have Galuppi playing the clavichord, whose sound has the least carrying power of the keyboard instruments, particularly when the toccatas were supposedly heard in the midst of balls and social gatherings. RB probably had heard some of Galuppi's music, but it is unlikely that he based his poem on one specific toccata, the music of which he had actually seen and examined. "Lesser thirds" or minor ones may well sound plaintive and sevenths "commiserating" and the dominant may be persistent, but its answer in music such as Galuppi's is certainly the tonic and not, as RB says, the octave. Diminished sixths are dubious at best. *See* W. Wright Roberts, "Music in Browning" (*Music & Letters,* XVII, 243).

TWO CAMELS. *See* FERISHTAH'S FANCIES

TWO IN THE CAMPAGNA

RB534.   Molineux, Marie Ada. In the Campagna, key of A-flat major. Arranged by Harry Lawson Harts. Manuscript, no place: no publisher, 1935.

VI, 150-152: 1-5, 21-25, 36-40
Song for [medium] voice with keyboard.
r: bb - ab^2 t: eb^1 - eb^2

Note: On the front cover is written "Final form. Music by Marie Ada Molineux. 1906: Arrangement by Harry Lawson Harts. 1935."

RB535.   ——————. In the Campagna, key of A-flat major. Arranged by Harry Lawson Harts. Manuscript, no place: no publisher, n.d. No pl. no.

VI, 150-152: 1-5, 21-25, 36-40
Song for [medium] voice with keyboard.
r: bb - ab^2 t: eb^1 - eb^2

---

[21]Willi Apel, *Harvard Dictionary of Music* (2nd ed., rev. & enl.; Cambridge: The Bellknap Press of Harvard University Press, 1969), pp. 853-54.

RB536. ——————————. In the Campagna, key of E-flat major. Manuscript, no place: no publisher, 1905. No pl. no.

VI, 150-152: 1-5, 21-25, 36-40
Song for [medium] voice, unacc.
r: b^b - a^{b2} t: e^{b1} - e^{b2}

Note: On the front cover is written "First ideas for In the Campagna April 1905   Later I Had Harry Lawson Harts (Heartz Härtz) of [71 Warmick Road, West Boston] put it into shape for me."

RB537. +Reinagle, Caroline. I Would That You Were All to Me, key of E major, no. 2 [only]. From Three Songs by Caroline Reinagle. London: Augener & Co., n.d. A&Co.2008. E378

VI, 152: 36-45
Song for [medium] voice with piano.
r: d^1 - e^{b2} t: e^{b1} - d^2

Note: Broughton, *Bibliography* gives [188–] as the possible date of publication.

THE TWO POETS OF CROISIC[22]

RB538. +Bates, Anna Craig. Apparitions, key of D major. From Songs and Ballads by Anna Craig Bates. New York: Schroeder & Gunther, c1922. S.&G.1013. E379

VI, 207-208: 1-12
Song for [high] voice with keyboard.
r: c$^{\#1}$ - f$^{\#2}$ t: a^1 - d^2

RB539. Berdahl, Arthur C. Epithalamium, key of C major. Photostat copy, manuscript, Fresno, Calif.: no publisher, June 30, 1952. No pl. no.

VI, 207-208: 1-12
Song for [high] voice with keyboard.
r: d^1 - f$^{\#2}$ t: f$^{\#1}$ - d^2

Note: At the end of the music is written "Fresno, Calif. June 21-25, 1952."

RB540. +Bliss, Paul. Thy Face, key of B major. From Songs by Paul Bliss. Cincinnati: Paul Bliss, c1905. No pl. no. E380

VI, 207-208: 1-12
Song for [medium low] voice with keyboard.
r: b - e^2 t: b - b^1

---

[22]There is no title immediately above the poem beginning "Such a starved bank of moss;" the title appears on the preceding and succeeding pages, so that this poem serves somewhat like a prologue.

RB541.   +Clarke, Helen A[rchibald]. Apparitions, key of E-flat major.
Philadelphia: Poet-Lore Company, 1892. No pl. no. E381

VI, 207-208: 1-12
Song for [medium high] voice with keyboard.
r: d^1 - f^2 t: f^1 - f^2

RB542.   +Coombs, C[harles] Whitney. Thy Face, key of D-flat major.
New York: G. Schirmer, c1913. Pl. no. 24363. E382

VI, 207-208: 1-12
Song for medium voice with piano.
r: db^1 - f^2

RB543.   +Craddock, Reginald W. Apparitions, key of G major, no. 1.
From Three Songs. London: Robert Cocks & Co., n.d. Pl.
no. 1619A. E383

VI, 207-208: 1-12
Song for medium voice with piano.
r: d^1 - f#^{2}

Note: RB543 is bound in Three Songs. Broughton, *Bibliography* gives 1898 as the date of publication.

RB544.   Dougherty, Celius. Portrait, key of E-flat major. New York:
G. Schirmer, Inc., c1948. Pl. no. 41800.

VI, 207-208: 1-12
Song for medium voice with piano.
r: b^b - g^2

Note: On the front cover is written "For the Baylor University
Browning Collection Sincerely—Celius Dougherty."

RB545.   +Downing, Lulu Jones. Apparitions, key of E major. From
Songs by Lulu Jones Downing. Edition Bryant. New York:
Bryant Music Co., Lulu Jones Downing c1909. No pl. no. E384

VI, 207-208: 1-12
Song for medium voice with keyboard.
r: a^1 - f#^{2}

RB546.   +Farley, Roland. God's Own Smile, key of A major. New
York: G. Schirmer, Inc., c1923. Pl. no. 31232. E385

VI, 207-208: 1-12
Song for high voice with piano.
r: e^1 - a^2

RB547.   +Freer, Eleanor Everest. Apparitions, key of F major, no. 2
[only]. From Four Songs, op. 9. Milwaukee: Wm. A. Kaun
Music Co., Eleanor Everest Freer c1906. No pl. no. E386

VI, 207-208: 1-12
Song for [high] voice with keyboard.
r: d^1 - f^2 (optional a^2)   t: f#^{1} - eb^2

RB548. +————————. Apparitions, key of F major, op. 9, no. 2 [only]. Chicago: The Music Library of Chicago, Eleanor Everest Freer c1929. Pl. no. 31083. E386

VI, 207-208: 1-12
Song for tenor with keyboard.
r: d^1 - f^2 (optional a^2)

RB549. ————————. Such a Starved Bank of Moss, key of F major. From the opera, The Brownings Go to Italy, (or) (A Love Story), op. 43. Libretto by G. A. Hawkins-Ambler. Chicago: The Music Library of Chicago, c1936. Pl. no. 38977.

VI, 207-208: 1-12
Song for baritone with keyboard.
r: (optional c^1) d^1 - eb^2 (optional a^2)

Note: RB549 is bound in The Brownings Go to Italy (piano-vocal score).

RB550. +Frey, Adolf. Apparitions, key of F major, no. 3 [only]. From Four Songs by Adolf Frey. Boston: Arthur P. Schmidt, c1904. A.P.S.6556. E387

VI, 207-208: 1-12
Song for [high] voice with keyboard.
r: e^1 - f^2 t: g^1 - e^2

RB551. +Gregory, E[leanor] C. Apparitions, key of B-flat major, no. 4. From Six Songs by E. C. Gregory. London: Novello Ewer & Co, n.d. Pl. no. 7519. E388

VI, 207-208: 1-12
Song for [medium] voice with keyboard.
r: bb - $f\#^2$ t: $f\#^1$ - d^2

Note: RB551 is bound in Six Songs.

RB552. +Hoberg, Margaret. Such a Starved Bank of Moss, (Apparitions), key of G major. From Songs by Margaret Hoberg. Boston: The Arthur P. Schmidt Co., c1917. A.P.S. 11239. E389

VI, 207-208: 1-12
Song for soprano or tenor with keyboard.
r: eb^1 - g^2

RB553. Krull, Fritz. Such a Starved Bank of Moss, key of C major, no. 1. From Three Songs by Fritz Krull. Manuscript, no place: no publisher, 1908. No pl. no.

VI, 207-208: 1-12
Song for [high] voice with keyboard.
r: f^1 - f^2 t: a^1 - d^2

Note: RB553 is bound in Three Songs.

RB554. +Lynes, Frank. Apparitions, key of B-flat major, no. 1 [only].
From Songs, op. 43. Boston: Arthur P. Schmidt, c1903.
A.P.S. 6071. E390

VI, 207-208: 1-12
Song for high voice with keyboard.
r: f^1 - gb^2

RB555. +Manney, Charles Fonteyn. Transformations ("Such a Starved
Bank of Moss"), key of A minor, no. 4 [only]. From Four
Songs, op. 18. Boston: Arthur P. Schmidt, c1906. A.P.S.
7312. E391

VI, 207-208: 1-12
Song for mezzo soprano or baritone with keyboard.
r: c^1 - f^2

RB556. Molineux, Marie Ada. Thy Face, key of E-flat major. Arranged
by Harry Lawson Harts. Final form. Manuscript, no place:
no publisher, 1935. No pl. no.

VI, 207-208: 1-12
Song for [high] voice with keyboard.
r: b - b^2 t: bb^1 - g^2

Note: On the front cover is written "Final form. Sung by
Miss Helen True May 7, 1921 before the Boston Browning
Society." Above the first line of music is written "Music by
Marie Ada Molineux 1905. Assisted by Harry Lawson Harts
1935." Below the last line of music is the signature "Marie
Ada Molineux."

RB557. ——————. Thy Face, key of E-flat major. First form. Manuscript, no place: no publisher, 1905. No pl. no.

VI, 207-208: 1-12
Song for [high] voice with keyboard.
r: b - b^2 t: bb^1 - g^2

Note: On the front cover is written "First form. As sung May
7, 1921 before the Boston Browning Society by Miss Helen
True. Composed about 1905 but never offered for publication."
At the end of the last line of music is the signature "Marie Ada
Molineux."

RB558. ——————. Thy Face, key of E-flat major. Second form.
Arranged by Harry Lawson Harts. Manuscript, no place: no
publisher, 1935. No pl. no.

VI, 207-208: 1-12
Song for [high] voice with keyboard.
r: b - bb^2 t: bb^1 - g^2

Note: On the front cover is written "Second form. Sung by
Miss Helen True May 7, 1921 before The Boston Browning
Society. Rearranged by Harry Lawson Harts in 1935."

RB559. +Neidlinger, W[illiam] H[arold]. Thy Face, key of F minor, no. 1 [only]. From Two Songs by W. H. Neidlinger. New York: G. Schirmer, c1900. Pl. no. 12577. E392

VI, 207-208: 1-12
Song for baritone or mezzo soprano with piano.
r: c^1 - f^2

RB560. +Nicholson, Mary E. That May Morn, key of F major. London: Duff & Stewart, n.d. No pl. no. E395

VI, 207-208: 1-12
Song for [medium] voice with piano.
r: d^1 - f^2 (optional a^2)   t: f^1 - d^2

RB561. +Rogers, Clara Kathleen. Apparitions, key of E-flat major, no. 2. From Browning Songs, First Series, op. 27. Edition Schmidt, no. 24a. Boston: Arthur P. Schmidt, c1893. A.P.S. 2910c. E396

VI, 207-208: 1-12
Song for [medium] voice with piano.
r: eb^1 - g^2 t: eb^1 - eb^2

Note: RB561 is bound in Browning Songs, First Series.

RB562. +Shillington, Mary. Apparitions, key of E minor. London: J. B. Cramer & Co. Ltd., c1902. J.B.C&Co. 619a. E397

VI, 207-208: 1-12
Song for [medium] voice with piano.
r: b - $g\#^2$ t: e^1 - e^2

RB563. +Somervell, Arthur. Such a Starved Bank of Moss, key of E major, no. 1. From the song cycle, A Broken Arc. London: Boosey & Co., c1923. H. 10770. E398

VI, 207-208: 1-12
Song for [medium high] voice with piano.
r: $f\#^1$ - e^2 t: $g\#^1$ - $d\#^2$

Note: RB563 is bound in A Broken Arc.

RB564. Tedaldi, F. Apparitions, key of G major. No place: no publisher, n.d. No pl. no.

VI, 207-208: 1-12
Song for [medium] voice with keyboard.
r: d^1 - e^2 t: e^1 - e^2

WANTING IS—WHAT? *See* JOCOSERIA
A WOMAN'S LAST WORD

RB565. Bantock, Granville. A Woman's Last Word, key of C major. Swan Edition, no. 4. London: Swan & Co. (Music Publishers) Limited, c1920. S.&Co., W.&W.Ltd. 2721.

VI, 48-50: 1-40
Song for low voice with piano.
r: bb - f#²

RB566.   ——————. A Woman's Last Word, key of E-flat major. Swan Edition, no. 4. London: Swan & Co. (Music Publishers) Limited, c1920. S.&Co.W.&W.Ltd.2709.

VI, 48-50: 1-40
Song for high voice with piano.
r: c#¹ - a²

RB567.   Barlow, Emily. Entreaty, key of A-flat major. London: J. B. Cramer & Co. Ltd., c1907. (J.B.C&Co.11520.)

VI, 48-50: 1-4, 13-28, 37-40
Song for [medium] voice with piano.
r: c¹ - f²   t: c¹ - d²

RB568.   +Beach, John Parsons. A Woman's Last Word, key of E-flat major. Newton Center: The Wa-Wan Press, c1903. No pl. no. E404

VI, 48: 1-8; 50: 35-40
Song for [medium high] voice with piano.
r: db¹ - f²   t: db¹ - db²

RB569.   +Beckett, Bessie D. Submission, key of A-flat major. London: Weekes & Co., n.d. W. 4813. E405

VI, 49-50: 21-40
Song for [medium] voice with piano.
r: eb¹ - f²   t: eb¹ - eb²

RB570.   +Boys, Reginald S. Devotion, key of E major, op. 6, no. 1 [only]. Sydney: W. H. Paling & Co Ltd., n.d. No pl. no. E406

VI, 48-50: 1-40
Song for [medium] voice with keyboard.
r: c#¹ - e²   t: f#¹ - d#²

RB571.   +Cantor, Otto. Lov'd by Thee, key of D-flat major, no. 2 [only]. From Two Songs by Otto Cantor. New York: G. Schirmer, c1894. Pl. no. 11926. E407

VI, 49-50: 21-40
Song for alto or baritone with piano.
r: ab - f²

Note: The lyricist is mistakenly given as Elizabeth Barrett Browning instead of RB; subsequent editions are correct.

RB572.   +——————. Lov'd by Thee, key of E-flat major, no. 2 [only]. From Two Songs by Otto Cantor. New York: G. Schirmer, c1894. Pl. no. 11925. E407

VI, 49-50: 21-40
Song for soprano or tenor with piano.
r: b♭ - g²

RB573. +————————. Loved by Thee, key of E-flat major. London: Leonard & Co., G. Schirmer c1894. Pl. no. 2228. E407

VI, 49-50: 21-40
Song for [high] voice with piano.
r: b♭ - g²   t: g¹ - eb²

RB574. +————————. Loved by Thee, key of E-flat major. London: Stanley Lucas, Weber, Pitt & Hatzfeld Ltd., G. Schirmer c1894. S.L.W.P.&H. 3534. E407

VI, 49-50: 21-40
Song for [high] voice with piano.
r: b♭ - g²   t: g¹ - eb²

RB575. +Dichmont, William. A Woman's Last Word, op. 50. 1. Let's Contend No More, key of C-sharp minor. 2. What So Wild, key of E major. 3. Be a God and Hold Me, key of D-flat major. Boston: Oliver Ditson Company, c1915. Pl. no. 5-119-70634. E408

Songs for high voice with piano.

1. VI, 48: 1-5
    r: c#¹ - e²

2. VI, 48-49: 5-20
    r: c#¹ - a²

3. VI, 49-50: 21-40
    r: e¹ - g² (optional ab²)

RB576. Foote, David. A Woman's Last Word, key of G major. Manuscript, London: Ascherberg, Hopwood & Crew Ltd., n.d. No pl. no.

VI, 49-50: 21-40
Song for [medium high] voice with keyboard.
r: d#¹ - e²   t: e¹ - e²

RB577. +Ganz, Rudolph. A Woman's Last Word, key of E-flat major. New York: The H. W. Gray Co., c1916. No pl. no. E409

VI: 48-50: 1-40
Song for [medium] voice with piano.
r: b♭ - f#²   t: b♭ - c²

RB578. ————————. A Woman's Last Word, key of G-flat major. New York: The H. W. Gray Co., c1916. No pl. no.

VI, 48-50: 1-40
Song for [high] voice with piano.
r: db^1 - a^2 t: db^1 - eb^2

RB579.   +Homer, Sidney. A Woman's Last Word, key of G major, no. 2 [only]. From Three Songs, op. 12. New York: G. Schirmer, c1903. Pl. no. 16340. E410

VI, 48-50: 1-40
Song for high voice with piano.
r: d#^{1} - e^2

RB580.   Johnson, Leslie. "Only Sleep," a Slumber Song, key of E-flat major. Xerox copy, no place: no publisher, Nov., 1884. No pl. no.

VI, 48-50: 1-4, 21-40
Song for [medium high] voice with keyboard.
r: c^1 - eb^2 t: f^1 - db^2

Note: RB580 is the gift of Boston Wellesley College.

RB581.   —————. A Woman's Last Word, key of C major. No place: no publisher, n.d. No pl. no.

VI, 48-50: 1-4, 21-40
Song for [medium low] voice with piano.
r: a - d^2 t: c^1 - c^2

Note: On the front cover is written "Kingsland."

RB582.   Jowett, Albert. Love's Surrender, key of C major. London: Schott & Co., c1918. S.&Co. 3472b.

VI, 48-50: 1-4, 21-32
Song for low voice with piano.
r: c^1 - f^2

Note: Except for the key, the music of RB582 is the same as RB583. A second copyright (c1918) is given for RB582.

RB583.   +—————. A Woman's Last Word, key of E-flat major. London: Schott & Co., c1916. S.&Co. 3472a. E411

VI, 48-50: 1-4, 21-32
Song for high voice with piano.
r: eb^1 - ab^2

Note: Except for the key and a second copyright given for RB582, the music of RB583 is the same as RB582.

RB584.   +Maclean, Alick. Hold Me with a Charm, key of F major. London: Boosey & Co, c1910. (H. 6673). E412

VI, 49-50: 21-40
Song for [medium] voice with piano.
r: b - f^2 t: c^1 - c^2

RB585.   +Raphael, Juliet. A Woman's Last Word, key of E major, [no. 6]. From Madrigal and Minstrelsy by Juliet Raphael. New York: Albert & Charles Boni, Thomas Seltzer c1927. No pl. no. E413

VI, 48-50: 1-40
Recitation for reader with keyboard.

Note: RB585 is bound in Madrigal and Minstrelsy.

RB586.   +Raymond, Ralph. A Last Word, key of E-flat major, no. 1. From Two Lyrics by Ralph Raymond. London: Lublin & Co., c1906. L.&Co. 33. E414

VI, 48-50: 1-4, 21-24, 37-40
Song for [medium high] voice with piano.
r: c^1 - eb^2 t: eb^1 - c^2

Note: RB586 is bound in Two Lyrics.

RB587.   —————. A Last Word, key of E-flat major, no. 1 [only]. London: Lublin & Co., Ltd., 1908. L. & Co. Ltd. 33.

VI, 48-50: 1-4, 21-24, 37-40
Song for [medium high] voice with piano.
r: c^1 - eb^2 t: eb^1 - c^2

RB588.   +Rogers, Clara Kathleen. A Woman's Last Word, key of A minor, no. 3. From Browning Songs, Second Series, op. 32. Edition Schmidt, no. 24b. Boston: Arthur P. Schmidt, c1900. A.P.S. 5037c. E415

VI, 48-50: 1-40
Song for [high] voice with keyboard.
r: c^1 - a^2 t: f^1 - f^2

Note: RB588 is bound in Browning Songs, Second Series.

RB589.   +Woolley, C. A Woman's Last Word, key of B minor. London: Novello and Company Limited, C. Woolley c1933. Pl. no. 15980. E416

VI, 48-50: 1-40
Song for [medium] voice with keyboard.
r: b - f#^{2} t: d^1 - d^2

WOMEN AND ROSES

RB590.   Lidgey, C. A. Women and Roses, key of D major, op. 5. 2nd edition. London: Pitt & Hatzfeld Ltd.; Boston: H. B. Stevens Coy., c1891. P. & H. 478.

VI, 180-182: 1-48
Choral setting for mixed chorus (soprano, alto, tenor, bass)
with orchestra. Piano-vocal score [only]. No parts.

THE WORST OF IT

RB591.   +Reinagle, Caroline. Would It Were I Had Been False, Not
You! key of A minor. Photostat copy, London: Addison &
Lucas, n.d. (A&L. 6121). E418

VII, 78: 1-6; 83-84: 85-90, 97-114
Song for [high] voice with piano.
r: d^1 - f^2 t: g^1 - d^2

Note: The ABL received RB591 Nov. 1, 1940. Broughton,
Bibliography gives 1864 as the date of publication.

RB592.   +Somervell, Arthur. The Worst of It, key of G-flat major, no. 5.
From the song cycle, A Broken Arc. London: Boosey & Co.,
c1923. H. 10770. E419

VII, 78-79: 1-6, 25-28; 84: 109-114
Song for [medium high] voice with piano.
r: bb - eb^2 t: db^1 - db^2

Note: RB592 is bound in A Broken Arc.

III

Musical Settings Related to Elizabeth Barrett Browning

Key to Abbreviations

ABL   Armstrong Browning Library

EBB   Elizabeth Barrett Browning

n.d.   no date

op.   opus

pl. no.   plate number

r   range

RB   Robert Browning

t   tessitura, i.e., the general compass of a song or where most of the notes lie

unacc.   unaccompanied

For the complete description and explanation of this chapter, read pages 1-4 of Chapter I.

AVENGE THE GOOD SHIP MAINE. *See* RB7.1

CASA GUIDI WINDOWS

EBB1.   Freer, Eleanor Everest. I Heard Last Night a Little Child Go Singing, key of G major. From the opera, The Brownings Go to Italy, (or) (A Love Story), op. 43. Libretto by G. A. Hawkins-Ambler. Chicago: The Music Library of Chicago, c1936. Pl. no. 38977.

     III, 237: 1-13
     Song for mezzo soprano with keyboard.
     r: c^1 - f^2 (optional g^2)

     Note: EBB1 is bound in The Brownings Go to Italy (piano-vocal score).

CATARINA TO CAMOENS;

Dying in His Absence abroad, and Referring to the Poem in Which He Recorded the Sweetness of Her Eyes

EBB2.   Philp, Elizabeth. Sweetest Eyes, key of D major. London: R. Mills & Sons, n.d. No pl. no.

III, 171-172: 1-32
Song for [medium] voice with piano.
r: d^1 - f^2 t: d^1 - d^2

CHANGE UPON CHANGE

EBB3.   Gabriel, Virginia. Change upon Change, key of F major, [no. 2]. From Hanover Square, a Magazine of New Copyright Music, edited by Lindsay Sloper, I, 2. London: Ashdown & Parry, 1867. No pl. no.

III, 145-146: 1-22
Song for [high] voice with piano.
r: c^1 - g^2 t: f^1 - f^2

Note: EBB3 is bound in Hanover Square.

A CHILD ASLEEP

EBB4.   Elgar, Edward. A Child Asleep, key of E-flat major. London: Novello & Co., Ltd., c1910. Pl. no. 13165.

II, 150-153: 1, 19-30, 49-54, 67-72
Song for [medium high] voice with keyboard.
r: d^1 - eb^2 t: f^1 - c^2

A CHILD'S GRAVE AT FLORENCE

EBB5.   Pascal, Florian. White Lilies, key of F major, no. 5. From Eight Songs (5th set) by Florian Pascal. London: Joseph Williams, Limited, c1905. J. W. 14240.

III, 166-167: 45-48, 57-60, 53-56
Song for [high] voice with piano.
r: c^1 - f^2 t: f^1 - e^2

Note: EBB5 is bound in Eight Songs (5th set).

A CHILD'S THOUGHT OF GOD

EBB6.   Treharne, Bryceson. A Child's Thought on God, key of G major, no. 1. From Five Songs by Bryceson Treharne. New York: G. Schirmer, c1918. Pl. no. 27994.

III, 102-103: 1-16
Song for high or medium voice with piano.
r: $c\#^1$ - $g\#^2$

COMFORT

EBB7. Broun, Harry. Comfort, key of A minor. Manuscript, no place: no publisher, n.d. No pl. no.

II, 270: 1-5
Hymn for soprano, alto, tenor, bass (unacc.).

EBB8. Coleridge-Taylor, S[amuel]. Comfort, key of F major, no. 4. From The Soul's Expression (Four Sonnets), op. 42. London: Novello & Co., Ltd., c1900. Pl. no. 11085.

II, 270: 1-14
Song for contralto with keyboard.
r: c^1 - e^2

Note: EBB8 is bound in The Soul's Expression.

EBB9. Ford, D. Rhys. Speak Low to Me, My Savior, key of C major. Xerox copy, Warren, Ohio: Melrose Music Co., c1937. No pl. no.

II, 270: 1-14, 1
Part-song for mixed chorus (soprano, alto, tenor, bass) with organ.

A DENIAL

EBB10. Lewando, Ralph. A Denial, key of F minor. Original manuscript, no place: no publisher, Sept. 9, 1932. No pl. no.

III, 179: 1-8
Song for [high] voice with keyboard.
r: db^1 - ab^2 t: f^1 - eb^2

Note: EBB10 is a gift of the composer.

A DRAMA OF EXILE

EBB11. Wiant, W[illiam] R. Exile. No place: no publisher, William R. Wiant c1957. No pl. no.

I, 1-92
Cantata for soloists, mixed chorus (soprano, alto, tenor, bass) and piano.

Characters

Lucifer [bass-baritone]	Bird Spirit (mezzo soprano)
Gabriel [mezzo soprano or tenor]	The Sylvan Spirit (soprano)
	Morning Star (lyric soprano)
Adam (tenor)	Earth Spirit (soprano)
Eve (soprano)	Earth Spirit (mezzo soprano)
God [bass]	Earth Spirit (alto)

Note: On the inside of the front cover is written "To Mrs. Armstrong and the Armstrong-Browning Library in gratitude for placing this work among compositions of [musicians far] more skilled than I. W. R. Wiant March 29, 1957."

EBB11.1.　————————. Prelude to Exile, key of C major. Photocopy, manuscript, no place: no publisher, W. R. Wiant c1957. No pl. no.

I, 1-92
Ballet-prelude [for orchestra]. Piano-conductor's score [only].

piccolo	bassoon	violins I and II
flute	trumpet I and II	viola
oboe	trombone	cello
English horn	horns I-IV	double bass
clarinet		timpani

Note: EBB11.1 is the gift of the composer.

EBB12.　Wood, Charles. Eden Spirits. London: H. F. W. Deane & Sons The Year Book Press Ltd., c1915. No pl. no.

I, 12-18: 227-242, 247-284, 296, 301-322, 327-348, 353-383, 388, 389
Cantata for women's chorus (soprano I and II, alto I and II) with piano.

EBB13.　Worth, John W. Three Songs. 1. Infant Voices, key of G major. 2. Song of the Morning Star to Lucifer, key of F major. 3. Bird Spirit, key of A-flat major. Manuscript, no place: no publisher, n.d. No pl. no.

Songs for medium voice with keyboard.
1.　I, 16-17: 329-354
　　r: d^1 - g^2
2.　I, 34-35: 810-824
　　r: d^1 - g^2
3.　I, 64-65: 1580-1594
　　r: d^1 - gb^2

FALSE STEP

EBB14.　Löhr, Hermann. Sweet, Thou Hast Trod on a Heart! key of F major. London: Chappell & Co, Ltd, c1912. Pl. no. 25298.

Last Poems, 5-6: 1-24
Song for [medium] voice with piano.
r: d^1 - f^2　　t: f^1 - c^2

GRIEF

EBB15.　Coleridge-Taylor, S[amuel]. Grief, key of F major, no. 3. From The Soul's Expression (Four Sonnets), op. 42. London: Novello & Co., Ltd., c1900. Pl. no. 11085.

II, 268: 1-14
Song for contralto with keyboard.
r: (optional g#) $c\#^1$ - e^2

Note: EBB15 is bound in The Soul's Expression.

THE HOUSE OF CLOUDS

EBB16. Pascal, Florian. The House of Clouds, key of D-flat major, no. 1. From Eight Songs (5th set) by Florian Pascal. London: Joseph Williams Limited, c1905. J.W. 14240.

III, 69-73: 1-8, 81-84, 101-104
Song for [high] voice with piano.
r: db^1 - f^2 (optional ab^2)   t: eb^1 - eb^2

Note: EBB16 is bound in Eight Songs (5th set).

INCLUSIONS

EBB17. Beach, Mrs. H[enry] H[arris] A[ubrey]. When Soul Is Joined to Soul, key of G-flat major, op. 62. Boston: The Arthur P. Schmidt Co., c1905. A.P.S. 6952.

III, 186: 1-9
Song for [high] voice with keyboard.
r: db^1 - bb^2 t: bb^1 - gb^2

EBB18. Gabriel, Virginia. O Wilt Thou Have My Hand, Dear (Inclusions), key of D-flat major. London: Duff & Stewart, n.d. (D & S.2874.)

III, 186: 1-9
Song for [high] voice with piano.
r: db^1 - gb^2 t: db^1 - db^2

EBB19. Miller, Karl. Inclusions, key of E-flat major. London: Augener & Co, c1903. Pl. no. 12418.

III, 186: 1-9
Song for [medium] voice with piano.
r: a - eb^2 t: c^1 - c^2

EBB20. Pascal, Florian. Inclusions, key of F major, no. 3. From Eight Songs (5th set) by Florian Pascal. London: Joseph Williams, Limited, c1905. H. W. 14240.

III, 186: 1-9
Song for [medium high] voice with piano.
r: c^1 - f^2 t: db^1 - d^2

Note: EBB20 is bound in Eight Songs (5th set).

EBB21. Philp, Elizabeth. "Inclusion," key of A-flat major. London: Hutchings & Romer, n.d. (H&R.2975).

III, 186: 1-9
Song for [high] voice with keyboard.
r: eb^1 - eb^2 t: ab^1 - db^2

EBB22.   Stothart, Herbert. "Wilt Thou Have My Hand," key of B-flat
major. Prod.749. 1058-Rev. 4-26-34. Photostat copy, manuscript, New York: Metro-Goldwyn-Mayer Corp., c1934. No
pl. no.

III, 186: 1-3
Song for [medium] voice with keyboard, specifically "on a
spinet."
r: bb - d²   t: c¹ - d²

Note: The music is the gift of the composer.

EBB23.   Treharne, Bryceson. Renunciation, key of A-flat major. From
Songs by Bryceson Treharne. Boston: The Boston Music Co.,
c1917. B.M.Co. 5555.

III, 186: 1-9
Song for high or medium voice with piano.
r: e¹ - f#²   t: ab¹ - eb²

EBB24.   Vannah, Kate. Questionings, key of F major. Boston: Oliver
Ditson Company, c1894. Pl. no. 81-57664.

III, 186: 1-9
Song for soprano with keyboard.
r: b - a²

INSUFFICIENCY

EBB25.   Cowen, Frederic H[ymen]. Insufficiency (Leaving Yet Lov-
ing) (Unzulänglichkeit), key of C minor, [no. 7]. [From
Album no. 50.] London: Joseph Williams, n.d. N.8162(7).
III, 187: 1-10
Song for [medium high] voice with piano.
r: d¹ - g²   t: eb¹ - e²

EBB26.   Hawley, Charles B[each]. I Only Can Love Thee, key of C
major. From Songs by Charles B. Hawley. Cincinnati: The
John Church Company, c1898. Pl. no. 12784.
III, 187: 1-10
Song for low voice with keyboard.
r: c¹ - f²

EBB27.   Marzials, Theo:[dor]. Leaving Yet Loving, key of E-flat major.
London: Boosey & Co, n.d. No pl. no.
III, 187: 1-10
Song for [medium high] voice with piano.
r: cb¹ - eb²   t: g¹ - eb²

Note: On the front cover is written "Florence Derby October
7th, 1884 Julia Ayrton."

EBB28. Marzials, Théo[dor]. Leaving Yet Loving, key of E-flat major, [no. 3]. From The World's Best Music, Famous Songs, vol. 6, edited by Victor Herbert, Henry H. Huss, Reginald De Koven, Fanny Morris Smith, Gerrit Smith, Louis R. Dressler, Joseph M. Priaulx, Louis C. Elson, Helen Kendrick Johnson, and others. Philharmonic edition, revised and enlarged. New York: The University Society, Inc., c1908. No pl. no.

III, 187: 1-10
Song for [medium high] voice with keyboard.
r: $cb^1 - eb^2$ t: $g^1 - eb^2$

Note: EBB28 is bound in The World's Best Music.

EBB29. Pascal, Florian. There Is No One Beside Thee, key of A major, no. 7. From Eight Songs (5th set) by Florian Pascal. London: Joseph Williams, Limited, c1905. J. W. 14240.

III, 187: 1-10
Song for [medium high] voice with piano.
r: $c\#^1 - f\#^2$ t: $f\#^1 - d\#^2$

Note: EBB29 is bound in Eight Songs (5th set).

EBB30. Patterson, Janie Alexander. "There Is No One Beside Thee," key of E-flat major. Xerox copy, manuscript, no place: no publisher, Janie Alexander Patterson c1935. No pl. no.

III, 187: 1-3, 1-5, 6-10
Song for [medium] voice with keyboard.
r: $db^1 - gb^2$ t: $g^1 - eb^2$

EBB31. Patton, Arthur. Insufficiency, key of G major. Dublin: Pohlmann & Son, n.d. No pl. no.

III, 187: 1-10
Song for [medium high] voice with piano.
r: $d^1 - g^2$ t: $g^1 - e^2$

Note: EBB31 is dedicated to R. Whately Ellis. On the front cover is written "from R. Whately Ellis." There is also an illegible name.

EBB32. Philp, Elizabeth. "Insufficiency," key of A-flat major. London: R. Mills, n.d. No pl. no.

III, 187: 1-10
Song for [medium] voice with keyboard.
r: $c^1 - eb^2$ t: $eb^1 - eb^2$

Note: On the front cover is written "Miss Clara Lacy With The Compo[. . .]."

THE LAST TRANSLATION. *See* PARAPHRASES ON HEINE

THE LAY OF THE BROWN ROSARY

EBB33.   Boyce, Ethel M[ary]. The Lay of the Brown Rosary. Novello's Original Octavo Edition. London: Novello, Ewer and Co., n.d. Pl. no. 8096.

II, 17-38: 1-10, 20-23, 36-40, 46-50, 61-65, 71-75, 86-90, 94-99, 101-105, 110-115, 130-134, 137-139, 152-156, 160, 161, 168, 169, 192-196, 200, 207, 212-222, 225, 230, 223, 229, 231, 232, 266-270, 293-295, 321, 322, 326-329, 333-337, 340, 348-355, 399, 400
Cantata for soloists (soprano, contralto), mixed chorus (soprano, alto, tenor, bass), and orchestra. Piano-vocal score [only]. No parts.

EBB34.   Carse, A[dam] von Ahn. The Lay of the Brown Rosary. Novello's Original Octavo Edition. London: Novello and Company, Limited, c1902. Pl. no. 11371.

II, 17-38
Dramatic cantata for soloists (soprano, mezzo soprano, tenor, baritone), mixed chorus (soprano, alto, tenor, bass), reader, and orchestra. Piano-vocal score [only]. No parts.

A LAY OF THE EARLY ROSE

EBB35.   Hammer, Marie von (Marie Sears). A Rose Once Grew, key of D-flat major. From Seven Songs by Marie von Hammer (Marie Sears). Boston: Oliver Ditson Company, c1900. Pl. no. 4-57-62321.

III, 40: 1-3, 9-12; 44: 105-108
Song for high voice with piano.
r: c^1 - gb^2

LET DOWN THE BARS, O DEATH[1]

EBB36.   Hall, William D. Let Down the Bars, O Death, key of C major, [no. 2]. Words by Emily Dickinson. From Reflectivity (Three Short Part-Songs). William Hall Choral Series. Glen Rock, N. J.: J. Fischer & Bro., c1967. J.F.&B.9732-3.

Part-song for mixed chorus (soprano, alto, tenor, bass), unacc.

Note: EBB36 is bound in Reflectivity. It was the gift of Belwin-Mills Publ. Corp. Jan. 26, 1972.

---

[1]This is not the title of an EBB poem; it is herein listed because the words are incorrectly attributed to her on the music; actually the words are by Emily Dickinson (poem 1,065).

LOVED ONCE

EBB37. Kellie, Lawrence. Say Never Ye Loved Once, key of D major. London: Metzler & Co., n.d. M. 7372.

III, 68: 49-55, 58-64
Song for [medium] voice with piano.
r: d^1 - e^2 t: f^1 - d^2

Note: The ABL received EBB37 Oct. 16, 1941.

A MAN'S REQUIREMENTS

EBB38. Clarke, Robert Coningsby. Love Me, key of G major. London: Cary & Co, c1911. Pl. no. 1643.

III, 140-141: 1-8, 29-32, 21-24
Song for [high] voice with piano.
r: d^1 - g^2 t: d^1 - e^2

EBB39. Giorza, Paolo. Love Me, key of D major. New York: G. Schirmer, c1889. Pl. no. 7337.

III, 141: 21-32
Song for mezzo soprano or baritone with piano.
r: a - d^2

EBB40. ————. Love Me, key of F major. New-York: G. Schirmer, c1889. Pl. no. 7338.

III, 141: 21-32
Song for soprano or tenor with piano.
r: c^1 - f^2

EBB41. Ormsby, George F. Love Me Sweet, key of G major. Photostat copy, Boston: Louis H. Ross & Co., c1897. Pl. no. 309.
III, 140-141: 1-8, 25-28, 21-24
Song for [medium high] voice with piano.
r: $c\#^1$ - g^2 t: d^1 - e^2

EBB42. Pascal, Florian. Love Me, Sweet, key of D-flat major, no. 4. From Eight Songs (5th set) by Florian Pascal. London: Joseph Williams, Limited, c1905. J. W. 14240.

III, 140-141: 1-4, 9-12, 25-28
Song for [high] voice with piano.
r: db^1 - gb^2 t: f^1 - eb^2

Note: EBB42 is bound in Eight Songs (5th set).

EBB43. White, Maude Valérie. Love Me, Sweet, with All Thou Art, key of D major. London: Boosey & Co., n.d. (H. 381).

III, 140-142: 1-12, 21-24, 29-32, 37-40
Song for [low] voice with piano.
r: $c\#^1$ - d^2 t: d^1 - b^1

Note: The ABL has 3 copies; on the front cover of copy 1 is written "Bradley."

THE MASK

EBB44.   Beta. "The Mask," key of D-flat major. London: Metzler & Co., n.d. M. 3549.

III, 84-86: 1-15, 36-40
Song for low voice with piano.
r: bb - db^2 t: db^1 - db^2

Note: On the front cover is written "Miss W. [V]al[p]y from [C]ast."

MAY'S LOVE

EBB45.   Stanford, C[harles] Villiers. May's Love, key of F major. London: Augener & Co., n.d. Pl. no. 9579.

Last Poems, 33: 1-15
Song for [high] voice with keyboard.
r: eb^1 - gb^2 t: g^1 - f^2

A MUSICAL INSTRUMENT

EBB46.   Ashford, Emma L. Pan Among the Reeds, key of F major. Xerox copy, New York: The Lorenz Publishing Company, c1908. No pl. no.

Last Poems, 55-56: 1-42
(Short) cantata for soloist (baritone or contralto), mixed chorus (soprano I and II, alto I and II, tenor I and II, bass I and II), and piano.

EBB47.   Busch, Carl. Pan's Flute. Boston: Oliver Ditson Company, c1920. Pl. no. 73802.

Last Poems, 55-56: 1-42
Cantata for women's chorus (soprano I and II, alto I and II), soloists (baritone voice, flute) and piano. Piano-vocal score. No parts.

EBB48.   Downing, Lulu Jones. A Musical Instrument, key of D-flat major. Manuscript, [New York: Bryant Music Co.], Lulu Jones Downing, n.d. No pl. no.

Last Poems, 55-56: 1-42
Recitation for reader with keyboard.

Note: On the front cover is written " 'A Musical Instrument' —Elizabeth Barrett Browning Description Music—Lulu Jones Downing. This manuscript written off for the Baylor University Browning Collection. Dr. A. J. Armstrong—in charge of this Collection. Lulu Jones Downing—1935."

EBB49. Godard, Benjamin. Pan Pastorale, key of G major, op. 50, no. 2 [only]. Revised by Wm. Scharfenberg. From Compositions for Pianoforte by Benjamin Godard. New York: G. Schirmer, Inc., c1894. Pl. no. 11423.

Last Poems, 55-56
Solo for piano.

EBB50. Perrin, H[arry] C[rane]. Pan's Pipes, key of C major. London: Breitkopf & Härtel, c1907. Pl. no. 25641.

Last Poems, 55-56: 1-42
Ballad for mixed chorus (soprano, alto, tenor, bass) and orchestra. Piano-vocal score. No parts.

EBB51. Sabin, Wallace A[rthur]. Pan, key of A major. From Two Songs by Wallace A. Sabin. New York: G. Schirmer, Inc., c1925. Pl. no. 32454.

Last Poems, 55-56: 1-12, 25-36
Song for high or medium voice with piano.
r: (optional c#^{1}) e^1 - f#^{2} (optional a^2)

EBB52. Smith, David Stanley. Pan, key of B-flat major, op. 32. G. Schirmer's Secular Choruses, no. 5631. New York: G. Schirmer, c1911. Pl. no. 23034.

Last Poems, 55-56: 1-42
Chorus for women's chorus (soprano I and II, alto), soprano soloist, oboe (or flute) obbligato, and piano. Piano-vocal score. No parts.

OUT IN THE FIELDS[2]

EBB53. Bond, Carrie Jacobs. Out in the Fields, key of F major. Words mistakenly attributed to EBB; actually the lyricist is unknown. Chicago: Carrie Jacobs-Bond & Son, Incorporated, c1919. No pl. no.

Song for [medium high] voice with keyboard.
r: c^1 - f^2 t: f^1 - d^2

EBB54. Dawson, William L. Out in the Fields, key of A major. Words mistakenly attributed to EBB; actually the lyricist is unknown. Chicago: Gamble Hinged Music Co., c1929. Pl. no. 876.

Song for low voice with keyboard.
r: a - d^2

---

[2]This is not the title of an EBB poem; it is herein listed because the words are incorrectly attributed to her on the music; according to *Granger's Index to Poetry,* ed. by William F. Bernhardt (5th ed., rev. and enl.; Morningside Heights, New York: Columbia University Press, 1962), p. 1006, *Out in the Fields with God* is of unknown authorship, but is attributed to Louis Imogen Guiney, *see A Song from "Sylvan,"* from *The Best Loved Poems of the American People,* selected by Hazel Felleman (Garden City: Garden City Publishing Co., 1936), p. 121, and to EBB, *see Cares,* from *A Book of Living Poems,* comp. and ed. by William R. Bowlin (Chicago: Albert Whitman & Company, 1934), p. 19.

EBB55.   French, Emma Weller. Out in the Fields, key of D-flat major.
         Words mistakenly attributed to EBB; actually the lyricist is
         unknown. Boston: C. W. Thompson & Co., c1913. T.&Co.
         269.

         Song for soprano or tenor with piano and violin (obbligato).
         With violin part.
         r: f^1 - ab^2

EBB56.   Metcalf, John W. The Cares of Yesterday, key of B-flat major.
         Words mistakenly attributed to EBB; actually the lyricist is
         unknown. Boston: The Arthur P. Schmidt Co., c1908. A.P.S.
         7898.

         Song for soprano or tenor with piano.
         r: f^1 - f^2

EBB57.   —————. The Cares of Yesterday, key of B-flat major.
         Words mistakenly attributed to EBB; actually the lyricist is
         unknown. London: Collard Moutrie; Boston: The Arthur
         P. Schmidt Co., c1908. C.M. 466.

         Song for [high] voice with keyboard.
         r: f^1 - f^2 t: g^1 - eb^2

EBB58.   Protheroe, Daniel. Out in the Fields, key of A-flat major. Words
         mistakenly attributed to EBB; actually the lyricist is unknown.
         From the Aeolian Series of Choral Music, no. 4013. Chicago:
         H. T. FitzSimons Company, Publishers of Music, c1926. Pl.
         no. 4013.

         Part-song for male chorus (tenor I and II, bass I and II) with
         piano (for rehearsal only).

EBB59.   —————. Out in the Fields, key of F major. Words mis-
         takenly attributed to EBB; actually the lyricist is unknown.
         From the Aeolian Series of Choral Music, no. 1010. Chicago:
         H. T. FitzSimons Company, Publishers of Music, c1927. Pl.
         no. 1010.

         Part-song for mixed chorus (soprano, alto, tenor, bass) with
         piano.

EBB60.   Warner, H. Waldo. The Cares of Yesterday, key of D major.
         Words mistakenly attributed to EBB; actually the lyricist is
         unknown. From Arthur P. Schmidt's Octavo Edition, Wom-
         ens Voices, Three and Four-Part Songs, [no.] 514. Boston:
         Arthur P. Schmidt, c1912. A.P.S. 9303-3.

         Trio for women's chorus (soprano I and II, alto) with key-
         board.

PARAPHRASES ON HEINE

[The Last Translation]

EBB61.   Carter, Ernest. "Thou Lov'st Me Not," key of D major. New York: G. Schirmer, c1901. Pl. no. 16240.

Last Poems, 140: 49-56
Song for [medium] voice with piano.
r: (optional a) c^1 - d^2 (optional $f\#^2$)

EBB62.   Rogers, Clara Kathleen. Out of My Own Great Woe, key of A-flat major, no. 1. From Browning Songs, First Series, op. 27. Edition Schmidt, no. 24a. Boston: Arthur P. Schmidt, c1893. A.P.S. 2910a.

Last Poems, 137: 1-8
Song for [medium] voice with piano.
r: c^1 - f^2 t: f^1 - db^2

Note: EBB62 is bound in Browning Songs, First Series.

PROOF AND DISPROOF

EBB63.   Cowen, Frederic H. Dost Thou Love Me (Bist du mein?), key of E-flat major, [no. 1]. [From Album no. 50.] London: Joseph Williams, Limited, n.d. N. 8162(1).

III, 85: 1-5; 184: 36-40, 46-50
Song for [high] voice with piano.
r: db^1 - f^2 t: f^1 - eb^2

EBB64.   Pascal, Florian. Proof and Disproof, key of A major, no. 6. From Eight Songs (5th set) by Florian Pascal. London: Joseph Williams, Limited, c1905. J. W. 14240.

III, 182: 1-5; 184: 36-40
Song for [medium] voice with piano.
r: c^1 - e^2 t: e^1 - e^2

Note: EBB64 is bound in Eight Songs (5th set).

EBB65.   Stisted, Maria E. H. Dost Thou Love Me, My Beloved? key of E-flat major. London: Metzler & Co., n.d. No pl. no.

III, 182: 1-5; 184: 41-50
Song for [medium] voice with piano.
r: c^1 - f^2 t: eb^1 - eb^2

QUESTION AND ANSWER

EBB66.   Ponssen, Mary Eleanor. Question and Answer, key of B-flat major. London: H. Davison, n.d. No pl. no.

III, 185: 1-14
Song for [high] voice with keyboard.
r: d^1 - g^2 t: gb^1 - eb^2

Note: On the front cover is written "Madame Ponssen of Medina Road Seven Sisters Road [J]insbury Park. [N.]"

RHYME OF THE DUCHESS MAY

EBB67.　Howe, Julia Ward. Oh, the Little Birds Sang East, key of G major, no. 10. From Songs by Julia Ward Howe. Edition De Luxe. Boston: The Boston Music Company, G. Schirmer, c1908. B.M.Co. 1852.

II, 78-79: 37-44
Song for [low] voice with piano.
r: b - b^1　　t: d^1 - b^1

Note: EBB67 is bound in Songs.

THE ROMAUNT OF MARGRET

EBB68.　Rogers, Clara Kathleen. I Have a More Than Friend, key of A major, no. 5. From Browning Songs, First Series, op. 27. Edition Schmidt, no. 24a. Boston: Arthur P. Schmidt, c1893. A.P.S. 2910e.

I, 286-287: 186-189, 195-198
Song for [medium] voice with piano.
r: c#^{1} - e^2　　t: e^1 - e^2

Note: EBB68 is bound in Browning Songs, First Series. On the music the lyricist is given as Elizabeth D. [sic] Browning.

A SABBATH MORNING AT SEA

EBB69.　Elgar, Edward. Sabbath Morning at Sea, key of C major, no. 3 [only]. From the song cycle, "Sea-Pictures," op. 37. London: Boosey & Co, c1899. H. 2670.

III, 74: 1-6, 13-18; 76-77: 61-78
Song for contralto with piano.
r: b - f^2 (optional g^2)

Note: The ABL has 2 copies. On the front cover of copy 2 is written "Sung before the N. Y. Browning Sociey [sic]—by Miss Veronica Govess. Dec. 1909. Florence Wier Gibson." EBB69 is the gift of Miss Gibson.

EBB70.　——————. Sabbath Morning at Sea, key of C major, op. 37, no. 3. From Songs in English, Nineteen Contemporary Settings by American and English Composers, edited by Bernard Taylor. New York: Carl Fischer, Inc., c1970. N 5203.

III, 74: 1-6, 13-18; 76-77: 61-78
Song for low voice with piano.
r: b - f^2 (optional g^2)

Note: EBB70 is bound in Songs in English.

EBB71. ———————. Sabbath Morning at Sea, key of E-flat major, op. 37, no. 3. From Songs in English, Nineteen Contemporary Settings by American and English Composers, edited by Bernard Taylor. New York: Carl Fischer, Inc., c1970. N5272.

III, 74: 1-6, 13-18; 76-77: 61-78
Song for high voice with piano.
r: d^1 - ab^2 (optional bb^2)

Note: EBB71 is bound in Songs in English.

THE SLEEP

EBB72. Austin, Torrington. Sleep Soft, Beloved, key of G major. London: Novello and Company, Limited, n.d. Pl. no. 12802.

III, 112: 19-24
Song for [high] voice with keyboard.
r: e^1 - g^2 t: g^1 - g^2

EBB73. Blumenthal, Jacques. Sleep (He Giveth His Beloved Sleep), key of E-flat major. London: Boosey & Co, n.d. H. 2211.

III, 111-113: 1-6, 13-18, 49-54
Song for [medium] voice with piano.
r: bb - eb^2 t: eb^1 - eb^2

EBB74. ———————. Sleep (He Giveth His Beloved Sleep), key of F major. London: Boosey & Co, n.d. H. 2212.

III, 111-113: 1-6, 13-18, 49-54
Song for [high] voice with piano.
r: c^1 - f^2 t: f^1 - f^2

EBB75. Bridge, J[ohn] Frederick. He Giveth His Beloved Sleep,[3] key of A-flat major. London: Novello and Company, Limited, n.d. No pl. no.

III, 111-112: 7-12, 25-36
Meditation for soprano soloist, mixed chorus (soprano, alto, tenor, bass), and organ (or unacc.).

EBB76. Cowen, Frederic H. He Giveth His Beloved Sleep, key of E-flat major. Novello's Original Octavo Edition. London: Novello & Co., Ltd., c1907. Pl. no. 12513.

III, 111-113: 1-54
Setting for contralto soloist, mixed chorus (soprano, alto, tenor, bass), and orchestra. Piano-vocal score. No parts.

---

[3]*He Giveth His Beloved Sleep* by Bridge was composed for and performed at the funeral of RB in Westminster Abbey, Dec. 31, 1889.

SLEEPING AND WATCHING

EBB77.   Gracey, W[illia]m Adolphe. Sleep on, Baby, on the Floor, key of C major. From Part-Songs for Mixed Voices, New Series, no. 2, series no. 9708. Oliver Ditson Company's Octavo Edition. Boston: Oliver Ditson Company, c1897. Pl. no. 4-111-60046.

II, 250: 1-16
Part-song for vocal quartet (soprano, alto, tenor, bass) with keyboard (for rehearsal only).

SONNETS FROM THE PORTUGUESE
I.

EBB78.   Branscombe, Gena. "I Thought Once How Theocritus Had Sung," key of C major, no. 1. From the song cycle, Love in a Life. New York: G. Schirmer, c1907. Pl. no. 19523.

III, 188: 1-14
Song for medium voice with piano.
r: c^1 - e^2

Note: EBB78 is bound in Love in a Life.

EBB79.   Castelnuovo-Tedesco, Mario. The Sweet Sad Years, key of F major, no. 1. From Three Sonnets from the Portuguese by Mario Castelnuovo-Tedesco. Edition Chester, no. 173. London: J. & W. Chester, Ltd., c1928. J. W. C. 3970.

III, 188: 1-14
Song for [medium] voice with piano.
r: $c\#^1$ - $f\#^2$ t: d^1 - d^2

Note: EBB79 is bound in Three Sonnets from the Portuguese.

EBB80.   Freer, Eleanor Everest. I Once Thought How Theocritus Had Sung, key of B-flat major, no. 1. From the song cycle, Sonnets from the Portuguese, op. 22, Book I. Milwaukee: Wm. A. Kaun, c1907. No pl. no.

III, 188: 1-14
Song for mezzo soprano with keyboard.
r: c^1 - eb^2 (optional g^2)

Note: EBB80 is bound in Sonnets from the Portuguese, Book I.

EBB81.   ————. I Thought Once How Theocritus Had Sung, key of B-flat major. From the opera, The Brownings Go to Italy, (or) (A Love Story), op. 43. Libretto by G. A. Hawkins-Ambler. Chicago: The Music Library of Chicago, c1936. Pl. no. 38977.

III, 188: 1-14
Song for mezzo soprano with keyboard.
r: c^1 - eb^2 (optional g^2)

Note: EBB81 is bound in The Brownings Go to Italy (piano-vocal score).

EBB82. ————————. I Thought Once How Theocritus Had Sung, key of B-flat major, no. 1. From the song cycle, Sonnets from the Portuguese, op. 22. French translation by Eleanor Everest Freer. Chicago: Music Library of Chicago, Eleanor Everest Freer c1939. No pl. no.

III, 188: 1-14
Song for medium voice with keyboard.
r: c^1 - eb^2 (optional g^2)

Note: EBB82 is bound in Sonnets from the Portuguese.

EBB83. ————————. I Thought Once How Theocritus Had Sung, key of B-flat major, no. 1. From the song cycle, Sonnets from the Portuguese, op. 22. Milwaukee: Wm. A. Kaun Music Co., c1910. No pl. no.

III, 188: 1-14
Song for medium voice with keyboard.
r: c^1 - eb^2 (optional g^2)

Note: EBB83 is bound in Sonnets from the Portuguese.

EBB84. Kaiser, Charles A. Not Death, but Love, key of D-flat major, no. 1. From the song cycle, Seven Sonnets from the Portuguese, op. 8. New York: Brietkopf & Härtel, Chas. A. Kaiser c1912. NY. 390.

III, 188: 1-14
Duet for soprano and tenor with keyboard.

Note: EBB84 is bound in Seven Sonnets from the Portuguese.

EBB85. Wellesz, Egon. Und es geschah mir einst, an Theokrit zu denken [I Thought Once How Theocritus], key of C major, no. 1. From Sonette der Elisabeth Barret-Browning, op. 52. Uebertragen von Rainer Maria Rilke. Photocopy, Vienna: Universal-Edition A. G., c1935. U.E. 10.281.

III, 188: 1-14
Song for soprano and string quartet. With parts.
r: bb - bb^2

Note: EBB85 is bound in Sonette.

II.

EBB86. Branscombe, Gena. "But Only Three in All God's Universe," key of E-flat major, op. 2. From the song cycle, Love in a Life. New York: G. Schirmer, c1907. Pl. no. 19523.

III, 189: 1-3, 9-14
Song for medium voice with piano.
r: $c\#^1$ - g^2 (optional eb^2)

Note: EBB86 is bound in Love in a Life.

EBB87.   Freer, Eleanor Everest. But Only Three in All God's Universe,
          key of E-flat major, no. 2. From the song cycle, Sonnets from
          the Portuguese, op. 22, Book I. Milwaukee: Wm. A. Kaun,
          c1907. No pl. no.

          III, 189: 1-14
          Song for mezzo soprano with keyboard.
          r: b - eb^2

          Note: EBB87 is bound in Sonnets from the Portuguese,
          Book I.

EBB88.   —————. But Only Three in All God's Universe, key of
          E-flat major, no. 2. From the song cycle, Sonnets from the
          Portuguese, op. 22. French translation by Eleanor Everest
          Freer. Chicago: Music Library of Chicago, Eleanor Everest
          Freer c1939. No pl. no.

          III, 189: 1-14
          Song for medium voice with keyboard.
          r: b - eb^2

          Note: EBB88 is bound in Sonnets from the Portuguese.

EBB89.   —————. But Only Three in All God's Universe, key of
          E-flat major, no. 2. From the song cycle, Sonnets from the
          Portuguese, op. 22. Milwaukee: Wm. A. Kaun Music Co.,
          c1910. No pl. no.

          III, 189: 1-14
          Song for medium voice with keyboard.
          r: b - eb^2

          Note: EBB89 is bound in Sonnets from the Portuguese.

EBB90.   Wellesz, Egon. Nur drei jedoch in Gottes ganzem All
          vernahmen es [But Only Three in All God's Universe], key
          of C major, no. 2. From Sonette der Elisabeth Barret-Brown-
          ing, op. 52. Uebertragen von Rainer Maria Rilke. Photocopy,
          Vienna: Universal-Edition A. G., c1935. U.E. 10.281.

          III, 189: 1-14
          Song for soprano and string quartet. With parts.
          r: bb - g^2

          Note: EBB90 is bound in Sonette.

III.

EBB91.   Freer, Eleanor Everest. Unlike Are We, Unlike, O Princely
          Heart! key of C major, no. 3. From the song cycle, Sonnets
          from the Portuguese, op. 22, Book I. Milwaukee: Wm. A.
          Kaun, c1907. No pl. no.

          III, 190: 1-14
          Song for mezzo soprano with keyboard.
          r: d^1 - e^2

          Note: EBB91 is bound in Sonnets from the Portuguese,
          Book I.

EBB92.   ————————. Unlike Are We, Unlike, O Princely Heart! key of
C major, no. 3. From the song cycle, Sonnets from the Portuguese, op. 22. French translation by Eleanor Everest Freer.
Chicago: Music Library of Chicago, Eleanor Everest Freer
c1939. No pl. no.

III, 190: 1-14
Song for medium voice with keyboard.
r: d^1 - e^2

Note: EBB92 is bound in Sonnets from the Portuguese.

EBB93.   ————————. Unlike Are We, Unlike, O Princely Heart! key of
C major, no. 3. From the song cycle, Sonnets from the Portu-
guese, op. 22. Milwaukee: Wm. A. Kaun Music Co., c1910.
No pl. no.

III, 190: 1-14
Song for medium voice with keyboard.
r: d^1 - e^2

Note: EBB93 is bound in Sonnets from the Portuguese.

IV.

EBB94.   Freer, Eleanor Everest. Thou Hast Thy Calling to Some
Palace-Floor, key of B major. From the opera, The Brownings
Go to Italy, (or) (A Love Story), op. 43. Libretto by G. A.
Hawkins-Ambler. Chicago: The Music Library of Chicago,
c1936. Pl. no. 38977.

III, 191: 1-14
Song for baritone with keyboard.
r: $d\#^1$ - e^2

Note: EBB94 is bound in The Brownings Go to Italy (piano-
vocal score).

EBB95.   ————————. Thou Hast Thy Calling to Some Palace-Floor, key
of B major, no. 4. From the song cycle, Sonnets from the Portuguese, op. 22, Book I. Milwaukee: Wm. A. Kaun, c1907.
No pl. no.

III, 191: 1-14
Song for mezzo soprano with keyboard.
r: $d\#^1$ - e^2

Note: EBB95 is bound in Sonnets from the Portuguese,
Book I.

EBB96.   ————————. Thou Hast Thy Calling to Some Palace-Floor, key
of B major, no. 4. From the song cycle, Sonnets from the
Portuguese, op. 22. French translation by Eleanor Everest
Freer. Chicago: Music Library of Chicago, Eleanor Everest
Freer c1939. No pl. no.

III, 191: 1-14
Song for medium voice with keyboard.
r: $d\#^1$ - e^2

Note: EBB96 is bound in Sonnets from the Portuguese.

EBB97. ———————. Thou Hast Thy Calling to Some Palace-Floor, key
of B major, no. 4. From the song cycle, Sonnets from the
Portuguese, op. 22. Milwaukee: Wm. A. Kaun Music Co.,
c1910. No pl. no.

III, 191: 1-14
Song for medium voice with keyboard.
r: d#^{1} - e^2

Note: EBB97 is bound in Sonnets from the Portuguese.

EBB98. Wellesz, Egon. Du bist da draben im Palast begehrt [Thou
Hast Thy Calling to Some Palace-Floor], key of C major, no.
3. From Sonnette der Elisabeth Barret-Browning, op. 52.
Uebertragen von Rainer Maria Rilke. Photocopy, Vienna:
Universal-Edition A. G., c1935. U.E. 10.281.

III, 191: 1-14
Song for soprano and string quartet. With parts.
r: c^1 - g#^{2}

Note: EBB98 is bound in Sonette.

V.

EBB99. Freer, Eleanor Everest. I Lift My Heavy Heart Up Solemnly,
key of A-flat major, no. 5. From the song cycle, Sonnets from
the Portuguese, op. 22, Book I. Milwaukee: Wm. A. Kaun,
c1907. No pl. no.

III, 192: 1-14
Song for mezzo soprano with keyboard.
r: eb^1 - f^2

Note: EBB99 is bound in Sonnets from the Portuguese,
Book I.

EBB100. ———————. I Lift My Heavy Heart Up Solemnly, key of
A-flat major, no. 5. From the song cycle, Sonnets from the
Portuguese, op. 22. French translation by Eleanor Everest
Freer. Chicago: Music Library of Chicago, Eleanor Everest
Freer c1939. No pl. no.

III, 192: 1-14
Song for medium voice with keyboard.
r: eb^1 - f^2

Note: EBB100 is bound in Sonnets from the Portuguese.

EBB101. ———————. I Lift My Heavy Heart Up Solemnly, key of
A-flat major, no. 5. From the song cycle, Sonnets from the
Portuguese, op. 22. Milwaukee: Wm. A. Kaun Music Co.,
c1910. No pl. no.

III, 192: 1-14
Song for medium voice with keyboard.
r: eb^1 - f^2

Note: EBB101 is bound in Sonnets from the Portuguese.

EBB102. Kaiser, Charles A. Ashes, key of F major, no. 2. From the
song cycle, Seven Sonnets from the Portuguese, op. 8. New
York: Breitkopf & Härtel, Chas. A. Kaiser c1912. NY. 391.

III, 192: 1-14
Song for soprano with keyboard.
r: c^1 - g^2

Note: EBB102 is bound in Seven Sonnets from the Portuguese.

VI.

EBB103. Branscombe, Gena. "The Widest Land," key of C major, no.
4. From the song cycle, Love in a Life. New York: G.
Schirmer, c1907. Pl. no. 19523.

III, 193: 8-14
Song for medium voice with piano.
r: c^1 - f^2

Note: EBB103 is bound in Love in a Life.

EBB104. Freer, Eleanor Everest. Go from Me. Yet I Feel That I Shall
Stand, key of C major, no. 6. From the song cycle, Sonnets
from the Portuguese, op. 22, Book I. Milwaukee: Wm. A.
Kaun, c1907. No pl. no.

III, 193: 1-14
Song for mezzo soprano with keyboard.
r: c^1 - $f\#^2$

Note: EBB104 is bound in Sonnets from the Portuguese,
Book I.

EBB105. —————. Go from Me. Yet I Feel That I Shall Stand,
key of C major, no. 6. From the song cycle, Sonnets from the
Portuguese, op. 22. French translation by Eleanor Everest
Freer. Chicago: Music Library of Chicago, Eleanor Everest
Freer c1939. No pl. no.

III, 193: 1-14
Song for medium voice with keyboard.
r: c^1 - $f\#^2$

Note: EBB105 is bound in Sonnets from the Portuguese.

EBB106. —————. Go from Me. Yet I Feel That I Shall Stand,
key of C major, no. 6. From the song cycle, Sonnets from the
Portuguese, op. 22. Milwaukee: Wm. A. Kaun Music Co.,
c1910. No pl. no.

III, 193: 1-14
Song for medium voice with keyboard.
r: c^1 - $f\#^2$

Note: EBB106 is bound in Sonnets from the Portuguese.

EBB107. Hadley, Henry K[imball]. Nevermore Alone, key of A minor, no. 2 [only]. From Five Songs, op. 20. Boston: Oliver Ditson Company, c1900. Pl. no. 4-54-62237.

III, 193: 1-14
Song for high voice with keyboard.
r: d#^{1} - a^2

EBB108. ————. Nevermore Alone, key of F minor, no. 2 [only]. From Five Songs, op. 20. Boston: Oliver Ditson Company, c1900. Pl. no. 4-54-62194.

III, 193: 1-14
Song for [medium] voice with keyboard.
r: b - f^2 t: db^1 - db^2

EBB109. White, Maude Valérie. What I Do, and What I Dream, key of G major. London: Chappell & Co., n.d. Pl. no. 17837.

III, 193: 10-14
Song for [medium] voice with piano.
r: b - e^2 t: e^1 - d^2

VII.

EBB110. Booth, Guy. Sonnet (Seven) from the Portuguese, key of C major. From Gamble's Collection of Secular Part Songs, no. 1464. Chicago: Gamble Hinged Music Co., c1939. Pl. no. 1464.

III, 194: 1-14
Part-song for mixed chorus (soprano, alto, tenor, bass) with keyboard (for rehearsal only).

EBB111. Branscombe, Gena. "The Face of All the World Is Changed," key of F major, no. 5. From the song cycle, Love in a Life. New York: G. Schirmer, c1907. Pl. no. 19523.

III, 194: 1-7, 10-14
Song for medium voice with piano.
r: c^1 - e^2

Note: EBB111 is bound in Love in a Life.

EBB112. Freer, Eleanor Everest. The Face of All the World Is Changed, I Think, key of C major, no. 7. From the song cycle, Sonnets from the Portuguese, op. 22, Book I. Milwaukee: Wm. A. Kaun, c1907. No pl. no.

III, 194: 1-14
Song for mezzo soprano with keyboard.
r: c^1 - f^2

Note: EBB112 is bound in Sonnets from the Portuguese, Book I.

EBB113. ——————. The Face of All the World Is Changed, I Think, key of C major, no. 7. From the song cycle, Sonnets from the Portuguese, op. 22. French translation by Eleanor Everest Freer. Chicago: Music Library of Chicago, Eleanor Everest Freer c1939. No pl. no.

III, 194: 1-14
Song for medium voice with keyboard.
r: $c^1 - f^2$

Note: EBB113 is bound in Sonnets from the Portugese.

EBB114. ——————. The Face of All the World Is Changed, I Think, key of C major, no. 7. From the song cycle, Sonnets from the Portuguese, op. 22. Milwaukee: Wm. A. Kaun Music Co., c1910. No pl. no.

III, 194: 1-14
Song for medium voice with keyboard.
r: $c^1 - f^2$

Note: EBB114 is bound in Sonnets from the Portuguese.

EBB115. Hadley, Henry. The Face of All the World Has Changed, key of D-flat major, no. 1 [only]. From Five Songs, op. 44. Cincinnati: The John Church Company, c1909. Pl. no. 16077.

III, 194: 1-14
Song for [high] voice with keyboard.
r: $eb^1 - ab^2$ t: $f^1 - gb^2$

EBB116. Kaiser, Charles A. A New Rhythm, key of G-flat major, no. 4. From the song cycle, Seven Sonnets from the Portuguese, op. 8. New York: Breitkopf & Härtel, Chas. A. Kaiser c1912. NY. 393.

III, 194: 1-14
Song for tenor with keyboard.
r: $db^1 - bb^2$

Note: EBB116 is bound in Seven Sonnets from the Portuguese.

EBB117. Surinach, Carlos. With Thee Anear, key of C major, no. 4 [only]. From Flamenco Meditations by Carlos Surinach. New York: Associated Music Publishers, Inc., c1966. AMP-96534.

III, 194: 1-14
Song for [high] voice with piano.
r: $e^1 - a^2$ t: $a^1 - gb^2$

EBB118. Wellesz, Egon. Mir scheint, das Angesicht der Welt verging—
in einem andern [The Face of All the World Is Changed, I
Think], key of C major, no. 5. From Sonette der Elisabeth
Barret-Browning, op. 52. Uebertragen von Ranier Maria Rilke.
Photocopy, Vienna: Universal-Edition A. G., c1935. U.E.
10.281.

III, 194: 1-14
Song for soprano and string quartet. With parts.
r: db^1 - bb^2

Note: EBB118 is bound in Sonette.

VIII.

EBB119. Freer, Eleanor Everest. What Can I Give Thee Back, O
Liberal, key of A-flat major, no. 8. From the song cycle,
Sonnets from the Portuguese, op. 22, Book I. Milwaukee:
Wm. A. Kaun, c1907. No pl. no.

III, 195: 1-14
Song for mezzo soprano with keyboard.
r: b - db^2

Note: EBB119 is bound in Sonnets from the Portuguese,
Book I.

EBB120. —————. What Can I Give Thee Back, O Liberal, key of
A-flat major, no. 8. From the song cycle, Sonnets from the
Portuguese, op. 22. French translation by Eleanor Everest
Freer. Chicago: Music Library of Chicago, Eleanor Everest
Freer c1939. No pl. no.

III, 195: 1-14
Song for medium voice with keyboard.
r: b - db^2

Note: EBB120 is bound in Sonnets from the Portuguese.

EBB121. —————. What Can I Give Thee Back, O Liberal, key of
A-flat major, no. 8. From the song cycle, Sonnets from the
Portuguese, op. 22. Milwaukee: Wm. A. Kaun Music Co.,
c1910. No pl. no.

III, 195: 1-14
Song for medium voice with keyboard.
r: b - db^2

Note: EBB121 is bound in Sonnets from the Portuguese.

IX.

EBB122.   Freer, Eleanor Everest. Can It Be Right to Give What I Can Give? key of B-flat major, no. 9. From the song cycle, Sonnets from the Portuguese, op. 22, Book I. Milwaukee: Wm. A. Kaun, c1907. No pl. no.

III, 196: 1-14
Song for mezzo soprano with keyboard.
r: c^1 - $f\#^2$

Note: EBB122 is bound in Sonnets from the Portuguese, Book I.

EBB123.   —————. Can It Be Right to Give What I Can Give? key of B-flat major, no. 9. From the song cycle, Sonnets from the Portuguese, op. 22. French translation by Eleanor Everest Freer. Chicago: Music Library of Chicago, Eleanor Everest Freer c1939. No pl. no.

III, 196: 1-14
Song for medium voice with keyboard.
r: c^1 - $f\#^2$

Note: EBB123 is bound in Sonnets from the Portuguese.

EBB124.   —————. Can It Be Right to Give What I Can Give? key of B-flat major, no. 9. From the song cycle, Sonnets from the Portuguese, op. 22. Milwaukee: Wm. A. Kaun Music Co., c1910. No pl. no.

III, 196: 1-14
Song for medium voice with keyboard.
r: c^1 - $f\#^2$

Note: EBB124 is bound in Sonnets from the Portuguese.

X.

EBB125.   Freer, Eleanor Everest. Yet, Love, Mere Love, Is Beautiful Indeed, key of C major. From the opera, The Brownings Go to Italy, (or) (A Love Story), op. 43. Libretto by G. A. Hawkins-Ambler. Chicago: The Music Library of Chicago, c1936. Pl. no. 38977.

III, 197: 1-14
Song for mezzo soprano with keyboard.
r: c^1 - e^2

Note: EBB125 is bound in The Brownings Go to Italy (piano-vocal score).

EBB126.   ————————. Yet, Love, Mere Love, Is Beautiful Indeed, key
of C major, no. 10. From the song cycle, Sonnets from the
Portuguese, op. 22, Book I. Milwaukee: Wm. A. Kaun, c1907.
No pl. no.

III, 197: 1-14
Song for mezzo soprano with keyboard.
r: c^1 - e^2

Note: EBB126 is bound in Sonnets from the Portuguese,
Book I.

EBB127.   ————————. Yet, Love, Mere Love, Is Beautiful Indeed, key
of C major, no. 10. From the song cycle, Sonnets from the
Portuguese, op. 22. French translation by Eleanor Everest
Freer. Chicago: Music Library of Chicago, Eleanor Everest
Freer c1939. No pl. no.

III, 197: 1-14
Song for medium voice with keyboard.
r: c^1 - e^2

Note: EBB127 is bound in Sonnets from the Portuguese.

EBB128.   ————————. Yet, Love, Mere Love, Is Beautiful Indeed, key
of C major, no. 10. From the song cycle, Sonnets from the
Portuguese, op. 22. Milwaukee: Wm. A. Kaun Music Co.,
c1910. No pl. no.

III, 197: 1-14
Song for medium voice with keyboard.
r: c^1 - e^2

Note: EBB128 is bound in Sonnets from the Portuguese.

EBB129.   Kaiser, Charles A. A Paean of Love, key of B major, no. 3.
From the song cycle, Seven Sonnets from the Portuguese, op.
8. New York: Breitkopf & Härtel, Chas. A. Kaiser c1912.
NY. 392.

III, 197: 1-14
Duet for soprano and tenor with keyboard.

Note: EBB129 is bound in Seven Sonnets from the Portuguese.

EBB130.   Surinach, Carlos. Yet, Love Is Beautiful Indeed, key of C
major, no. 2 [only]. From Flamenco Meditations. New York:
Associated Music Publisher, Inc., c1966. AMP-96532.

III, 194: 1-14
Song for [high] voice with piano.
r: $f\#^1$ - a^2 t: a^1 - f^2

XI.

EBB131. Freer, Eleanor Everest. And Therefore If to Love Can Be
Desert, key of F-sharp minor, no. 11. From the song cycle,
Sonnets from the Portuguese, op. 22, Book I. Milwaukee:
Wm. A. Kaun, c1907. No pl. no.

III, 198: 1-14
Song for mezzo soprano with keyboard.
r: $c\#^1$ - e^2

Note: EBB131 is bound in Sonnets from the Portuguese,
Book I.

EBB132. ————. And Therefore If to Love Can Be Desert, key of
F-sharp minor, no. 11. From the song cycle, Sonnets from the
Portuguese, op. 22. French translation by Eleanor Everest
Freer. Chicago: Music Library of Chicago, Eleanor Everest
Freer c1939. No pl. no.

III, 198: 1-14
Song for medium voice with keyboard.
r: $c\#^1$ - e^2

Note: EBB132 is bound in Sonnets from the Portuguese.

EBB133. ————. And Therefore If to Love Can Be Desert, key of
F-sharp minor, no. 11. From the song cycle, Sonnets from the
Portuguese, op. 22. Milwaukee: Wm. A. Kaun Music Co.,
c1910. No pl. no.

III, 198: 1-14
Song for medium voice with keyboard.
r: $c\#^1$ - e^2

Note: EBB133 is bound in Sonnets from the Portuguese.

XII.

EBB134. Freer, Eleanor Everest. Indeed This Very Love Which Is
My Boast, key of A minor, no. 12. From the song cycle,
Sonnets from the Portuguese, op. 22. French translation by
Eleanor Everest Freer. Chicago: Eleanor Everest Freer c1939.
No pl. no.

III, 199: 1-14
Song for medium voice with keyboard.
r: c^1 - e^2

Note: EBB134 is bound in Sonnets from the Portuguese.

EBB135.   ————————. Indeed This Very Love Which Is My Boast, key of A minor, no. 12. From the song cycle, Sonnets from the Portuguese, op. 22. Milwaukee: Wm. A. Kaun Music Co., c1910. No pl. no.

III, 199: 1-14
Song for medium voice with keyboard.
r: c^1 - e^2

Note: EBB135 is bound in Sonnets from the Portuguese.

XIII.

EBB136.   Freer, Eleanor Everest. And Wilt Thou Have Me Fashion into Speech, key of E major, no. 13. From the song cycle, Sonnets from the Portuguese, op. 22. French translation by Eleanor Everest Freer. Chicago: Music Library of Chicago, c1939. No pl. no.

III, 200: 1-14
Song for medium voice with keyboard.
r: b - d^2

Note: EBB136 is bound in Sonnets from the Portuguese.

EBB137.   ————————. And Wilt Thou Have Me Fashion into Speech, key of E major, no. 13. From the song cycle, Sonnets from the Portuguese, op. 22. Milwaukee: Wm. A. Kaun Music Co., c1910. No pl. no.

III, 200: 1-14
Song for medium voice with keyboard.
r: b - d^2

Note: EBB137 is bound in Sonnets from the Portuguese.

XIV.

EBB138.   Fisher, William Arms. For Love's Sake Only, key of C major, no. 4 [only]. From Five Songs, op. 9. Boston: Oliver Ditson Company, c1897. Pl. no. 4-19-60442.

III, 201: 1-4, 9-14
Song for high voice with piano.
r: g^1 - g^2

EBB139.   Freer, Eleanor Everest. If Thou Must Love Me, key of F major, no. 14. From the song cycle, Sonnets from the Portuguese, op. 22. French translation by Eleanor Everest Freer. Chicago: Music Library of Chicago, Eleanor Everest Freer c1939. No pl. no.

III, 201: 1-14
Song for medium voice with keyboard.
r: c^1 - f^2

Note: EBB139 is bound in Sonnets from the Portuguese.

EBB140.   —————. If Thou Must Love Me, key of F major, no. 14. From the song cycle, Sonnets from the Portuguese, op. 22. Milwaukee: Wm. A. Kaun Music Co., c1910. No pl. no.

III, 201: 1-14
Song for medium voice with keyboard.
r: c^1 - f^2

Note: EBB140 is bound in Sonnets from the Portuguese.

EBB141.   Goodeve, Mrs. Arthur. If Thou Must Love Me, key of C major. London: Robert Cocks & Co., n.d. Pl. no. 18,542.

III, 201: 1-14
Song for [low] voice with piano.
r: a - c^2 t: c^1 - c^2

EBB142.   MacMillan, Ernest. Sonnet, key of C major. London: The Frederick Harris Co., c1929. F.H.1916.

III, 201: 1-14
Song for [medium] voice with keyboard.
r: c^1 - f^2 t: e^1 - e^2

EBB143.   Surinach, Carlos. If Thou Must Love Me, key of C major, no. 5 [only]. From Flamenco Meditations by Carlos Surinach. New York: Associated Music Publishers, Inc., c1966. AMP-96535.

III, 201: 1-14
Song for [high] voice with piano.
r: f^1 - ab^2 (optional bb^2)   t: g^1 - g^2

XV.

EBB144.   Freer, Eleanor Everest. Accuse Me Not, Beseech Thee, key of C major, no. 15. From the song cycle, Sonnets from the Portuguese, op. 22. French translation by Eleanor Everest Freer. Chicago: Music Library of Chicago, Eleanor Everest Freer c1939. No pl. no.

III, 202: 1-14
Song for medium voice with keyboard.
r: c^1 - e^2

Note: EBB144 is bound in Sonnets from the Portuguese.

EBB145.   —————. Accuse Me Not, Beseech Thee, key of C major, no. 15. From the song cycle, Sonnets from the Portuguese, op. 22. Milwaukee: Wm. A. Kaun Music Co., c1910. No pl. no.

III, 202: 1-14
Song for medium voice with keyboard.
r: c^1 - e^2

Note: EBB145 is bound in Sonnets from the Portuguese.

XVI.

EBB146. Freer, Eleanor Everest. And Yet, Because Thou Overcomest So, key of C major, no. 16. From the song cycle, Sonnets from the Portuguese, op. 22. French translation by Eleanor Everest Freer. Chicago: Music Library of Chicago, Eleanor Everest Freer c1939. No pl. no.

III, 203: 1-14
Song for medium voice with keyboard.
r: d^1 - f^2

Note: EBB146 is bound in Sonnets from the Portuguese.

EBB147. —————. And Yet, Because Thou Overcomest So, key of C major, no. 16. From the song cycle, Sonnets from the Portuguese, op. 22. Milwaukee: Wm. A. Kaun Music Co., c1912. No pl. no.

III, 203: 1-14
Song for medium voice with keyboard.
r: d^1 - f^2

Note: EBB147 is bound in Sonnets from the Portuguese.

XVII.

EBB148. Freer, Eleanor Everest. My Poet, Thou Canst Touch on All the Notes, key of C major, no. 17. From the song cycle, Sonnets from the Portuguese, op. 22. French translation by Eleanor Everest Freer. Chicago: Music Library of Chicago, Eleanor Everest Freer c1939. No pl. no.

III, 204: 1-14
Song for medium voice with keyboard.
r: c^1 - e^2

Note: EBB148 is bound in Sonnets from the Portuguese.

EBB149. —————. My Poet, Thou Canst Touch on All the Notes, key of C major, no. 17. From the song cycle, Sonnets from the Portuguese, op. 22. Milwaukee: Wm. A. Kaun Music Co., c1910. No pl. no.

III, 204: 1-14
Song for medium voice with keyboard.
r: c^1 - e^2

Note: EBB149 is bound in Sonnets from the Portuguese.

XVIII.

EBB150. Freer, Eleanor Everest. I Never Gave a Lock of Hair Away, key of A major, no. 18. From the song cycle, Sonnets from the Portuguese, op. 22. French translation by Eleanor Everest Freer. Chicago: Music Library of Chicago, Eleanor Everest Freer c1939. No pl. no.

III, 205: 1-14
Song for medium voice with keyboard.
r: c^1 - f^2

Note: EBB150 is bound in Sonnets from the Portuguese.

EBB151. ——————. I Never Gave a Lock of Hair Away, key of A major, no. 18. From the song cycle, Sonnets from the Portuguese, op. 22. Milwaukee: Wm. A. Kaun Music Co., c1910. No pl. no.

III, 205: 1-14
Song for medium voice with keyboard.
r: c^1 - f^2

Note: EBB151 is bound in Sonnets from the Portuguese.

XIX.

EBB152. Freer, Eleanor Everest. The Soul's Rialto Hath Its Merchandise, key of C major, no. 19. From the song cycle, Sonnets from the Portuguese, op. 22. French translation by Eleanor Everest Freer. Chicago: Music Library of Chicago, Eleanor Everest Freer c1939. No pl. no.

III, 206: 1-14
Song for medium voice with keyboard.
r: b^b - e^{b2}

Note: EBB152 is bound in Sonnets from the Portuguese.

EBB153. ——————. The Soul's Rialto Hath Its Merchandise, key of C major, no. 19. From the song cycle, Sonnets from the Portuguese, op. 22. Milwaukee: Wm. A. Kaun Music Co., c1910. No pl. no.

III, 206: 1-14
Song for medium voice with keyboard.
r: b^b - e^{b2}

Note: EBB153 is bound in Sonnets from the Portuguese.

XX.

EBB154. Freer, Eleanor Everest. Beloved, My Beloved, When I Think, key of A-flat major, no. 20. From the song cycle, Sonnets from the Portuguese, op. 22. French translation by Eleanor Everest Freer. Chicago: Music Library of Chicago, Eleanor Everest Freer c1939. No pl. no.

III, 207: 1-14
Song for medium voice with keyboard.
r: bb - f^2

Note: EBB154 is bound in Sonnets from the Portuguese.

EBB155. ————. Beloved, My Beloved, When I Think, key of A-flat major, no. 20. From the song cycle, Sonnets from the Portuguese, op. 22. Milwaukee: Wm. A. Kaun Music Co., c1910. No pl. no.

III, 207: 1-14
Song for medium voice with keyboard.
r: bb - f^2

Note: EBB155 is bound in Sonnets from the Portuguese.

XXI.

EBB156. Bliss, James A. Sonnet Twenty-One, key of C major, op. 8, no. 1 [only]. From Songs and Ballads by American Composers. New York: G. Schirmer, c1919. Pl. no. 28981.

III, 208: 1-2, 7-14
Song for high voice with piano.
r: d^1 - a^2

EBB157. Cain, Noble. Say Thou Lovest Me! key of D major. From G. Schirmer's Secular Choruses, no. 7875. New York: G. Schirmer, Inc., c1935. Pl. no. 36681.

III, 208: 1-14
Chorus for mixed choir (soprano I and II, alto I and II, tenor I and II, bass I and II) with piano (for rehearsal only).

EBB158. Freer, Eleanor Everest. Say over Again, key of D-flat major. From the opera, The Brownings Go to Italy, (or) (A Love Story), op. 43. Libretto by G. A. Hawkins-Ambler. Chicago: The Music Library of Chicago, c1936. Pl. no. 38977.

III, 188: 1-14
Song for mezzo soprano with keyboard.
r: d^1 - d#^{2}

Note: EBB158 is bound in The Brownings Go to Italy (piano-vocal score).

EBB159. —————. Say over Again, key of D-flat major, no. 21. From the song cycle, Sonnets from the Portuguese, op. 22. French translation by Eleanor Everest Freer. Chicago: Music Library of Chicago, Eleanor Everest Freer c1939. No pl. no.

III, 208: 1-14
Song for medium voice with keyboard.
r: d^1 - $d\#^2$

Note: EBB159 is bound in Sonnets from the Portuguese.

EBB160. —————. Say over Again, key of D-flat major, no. 21. From the song cycle, Sonnets from the Portuguese, op. 22. Milwaukee: Wm. A. Kaun Music Co., c1910. No pl. no.

III, 188: 1-14
Song for medium voice with keyboard.
r: d^1 - $d\#^2$

Note: EBB160 is bound in Sonnets from the Portuguese.

EBB161. Kaiser, Charles A. A Cuckoo Song, key of E-flat major, no. 5. From the song cycle, Seven Sonnets from the Portuguese, op. 8. New York: Breitkopf & Härtel, Chas. A. Kaiser c1912. NY. 395.

III, 208: 1-14
Duet for soprano and tenor with keyboard.

Note: EBB161 is bound in Seven Sonnets from the Portuguese.

XXII.

EBB162. Freer, Eleanor Everest. When Our Two Souls Stand Up Erect and Strong, key of A major, no. 22. From the song cycle, Sonnets from the Portuguese, op. 22. French translation by Eleanor Everest Freer. Chicago: Music Library of Chicago, Eleanor Everest Freer c1939. No pl. no.

III, 209: 1-14
Song for medium voice with keyboard.
r: $c\#^1$ - e^2

Note: EBB162 is bound in Sonnets from the Portuguese.

EBB163. —————. When Our Two Souls Stand Up Erect and Strong, key of A major, no. 22. From the song cycle, Sonnets from the Portuguese, op. 22. Milwaukee: Wm. A. Kaun Music Co., c1910. No pl. no.

III, 209: 1-14
Song for medium voice with keyboard.
r: $c\#^1$ - e^2

Note: EBB163 is bound in Sonnets from the Portuguese.

EBB164. Kaiser, Charles A. United, key of G major, no. 7. From the song cycle, Seven Sonnets from the Portuguese, op. 8. New York: Breitkopf & Härtel, Chas. A. Kaiser c1912. NY. 396.

III, 209: 1-14
Duet for soprano and tenor with keyboard.

Note: EBB164 is bound in Seven Sonnets from the Portuguese.

EBB164.1. Robbins, Reginald C. Sonnet from the Portuguese, key of F major. Xerox copy, Paris: Editions Maurice Senart, c1923. E.M.S.6149.

III, 209: 1-14
Song for [medium low] voice with keyboard.
r: A - f^1 t: c - d^1

EBB165. Surinach, Carlos. Our Two Souls, key of C major, no. 3 [only]. From Flamenco Meditations by Carlos Surinach. New York: Associated Music Publishers, Inc., c1966. AMP-96533.

III, 209: 1-14
Song for [high] voice with piano.
r: eb^1 - ab^2 t: g^1 - g^2

EBB166. Willan, Healey. Sonnet, "When Our Two Souls Stand Up Erect and Strong," key of A-flat major, no. 3. From [the] Healey Willan Song Albums, no. 1. London: The Frederick Harris Co, c1925. F. H. 1505.

III, 209: 1-14
Song for [high] voice with piano.
r: c^1 - f#^{2} t: f^1 - eb^2

Note: EBB166 is bound in the Healey Willan Song Albums, no. 1.

XXIII.

EBB167. Freer, Eleanor Everest. Is It Indeed So? key of A major, no. 23. From the song cycle, Sonnets from the Portuguese, op. 22. French translation by Eleanor Everest Freer. Chicago: Music Library of Chicago, Eleanor Everest Freer c1939. No pl. no.

III, 210: 1-14
Song for medium voice with keyboard.
r: c^1 - d#^{2}

Note: EBB167 is bound in Sonnets from the Portuguese.

EBB168. ——————. Is It Indeed So? key of A major, no. 23. From the song cycle, Sonnets from the Portuguese, op. 22. Milwaukee: Wm. A. Kaun Music Co., c1910. No pl. no.

III, 210: 1-14
Song for medium voice with keyboard.
r: c^1 - d#^{2}

Note: EBB168 is bound in Sonnets from the Portuguese.

EBB169. Schaefer, [Harold Herman] Hal. "I Yield the Grave for Thy Sake," key of E-flat major. Xerox copy, manuscript, New York: no publisher, Miriam Music Corp. c1966. No pl. no.

III, 210: 1-14
Song for [medium high] voice with keyboard.
r: bb - f^2 t: eb^1 - c^2

Note: EBB169 was a gift of the composer Feb. 7, 1972.

XXIV.

EBB170. Freer, Eleanor Everest. Let the World's Sharpness, Like a Clasping Knife, key of A major, no. 24. From the song cycle, Sonnets from the Portuguese, op. 22. French translation by Eleanor Everest Freer. Chicago: Music Library of Chicago, Eleanor Everest Freer c1939. No pl. no.

III, 211: 1-14
Song for medium voice with keyboard.
r: $c^{\#1}$ - f^2

Note: EBB170 is bound in Sonnets from the Portuguese.

EBB171. —————. Let the World's Sharpness, Like a Clasping Knife, key of A major, no. 24. From the song cycle, Sonnets from the Portuguese, op. 22. Milwaukee: Wm. A. Kaun Music Co., c1910. No pl. no.

III, 211: 1-14
Song for medium voice with keyboard.
r: $c^{\#1}$ - f^2

Note: EBB171 is bound in Sonnets from the Portuguese.

XXV.

EBB172. Freer, Eleanor Everest. A Heavy Heart, Beloved, Have I Borne, key of C major, no. 25. From the song cycle, Sonnets from the Portuguese, op. 22. French translation by Eleanor Everest Freer. Chicago: Music Library of Chicago, Eleanor Everest Freer c1939. No pl. no.

III, 212: 1-14
Song for medium voice with keyboard.
r: b - eb^2

Note: EBB172 is bound in Sonnets from the Portuguese.

EBB173. —————. A Heavy Heart, Beloved, Have I Borne, key of C major, no. 25. From the song cycle, Sonnets from the Portuguese, op. 22. Milwaukee: Wm. A. Kaun Music Co., c1910. No pl. no.

III, 212: 1-14
Song for medium voice with keyboard.
r: b - eb^2

Note: EBB173 is bound in Sonnets from the Portuguese.

XXVI.

EBB174.   Freer, Eleanor Everest. I Lived with Visions for My Company, key of D-flat major, no. 26. From the song cycle, Sonnets from the Portuguese, op. 22. French translation by Eleanor Everest Freer. Chicago: Music Library of Chicago, Eleanor Everest Freer c1939. No pl. no.

III, 213: 1-14
Song for medium voice with keyboard.
r: b# - eb²

Note: EBB174 is bound in Sonnets from the Portuguese.

EBB175.   ——————. I Lived with Visions for My Company, key of D-flat major, no. 26. From the song cycle, Sonnets from the Portuguese, op. 22. Milwaukee: Wm. A. Kaun Music Co., c1910. No pl. no.

III, 213: 1-14
Song for medium voice with keyboard.
r: b# - eb²

Note: EBB175 is bound in Sonnets from the Portuguese.

XXVII.

EBB176.   Branscombe, Gena. "My Own Beloved," key of C major, no. 6. From the song cycle, Love in a Life. New York: G. Schirmer, c1907. Pl. no. 19523.

III, 214: 1-14
Song for medium voice with piano.
r: c¹ - f²

Note: EBB176 is bound in Love in a Life.

EBB177.   Freer, Eleanor Everest. My Own Beloved, Who Hast Lifted Me, key of E-flat major, no. 27. From the song cycle, Sonnets from the Portuguese, op. 22. French translation by Eleanor Everest Freer. Chicago: Music Library of Chicago, Eleanor Everest Freer c1939. No pl. no.

III, 214: 1-14
Song for medium voice with keyboard.
r: bb - f²

Note: EBB177 is bound in Sonnets from the Portuguese.

EBB178.   ——————. My Own Beloved, Who Hast Lifted Me, key of E-flat major, no. 27. From the song cycle, Sonnets from the Portuguese, op. 22. Milwaukee: Wm. A. Kaun Music Co., c1910. No pl. no.

III, 214: 1-14
Song for medium voice with keyboard.
r: bb - f²

Note: EBB178 is bound in Sonnets from the Portuguese.

XXVIII.

EBB179. Castelnuovo-Tedesco, Mario. Letters, key of G minor, no. 2. From Three Sonnets from the Portuguese by Mario Castelnuovo-Tedesco. Edition Chester, no. 173. London: J. & W. Chester, Ltd., c1928. J. W. C. 3970.

III, 215: 1-14
Song for [high] voice with piano.
r: c#^{1} - ab^2 t: g^1 - g^2

Note: EBB179 is bound in Three Sonnets from the Portuguese.

EBB180. Freer, Eleanor Everest. My Letters! All Dead Paper, Mute and White! key of C major, no. 28. From the song cycle, Sonnets from the Portuguese, op. 22. French translation by Eleanor Everest Freer. Chicago: Music Library of Chicago, Eleanor Everest Freer c1939. No pl. no.

III, 215: 1-14
Song for [high] voice with piano.
r: b - e^2

Note: EBB180 is bound in Sonnets from the Portuguese.

EBB181. —————. My Letters! All Dead Paper, Mute and White! key of C major, no. 28. From the song cycle, Sonnets from the Portuguese, op. 22. Milwaukee: Wm. A. Kaun Music Co., c1910. No pl. no.

III, 215: 1-14
Song for medium voice with keyboard.
r: b - e^2

Note: EBB181 is bound in Sonnets from the Portuguese.

XXIX.

EBB182. Freer, Eleanor Everest. I Think of Thee! My Thoughts Do Twine and Bud, key of A major, no. 29. From the song cycle, Sonnets from the Portuguese, op. 22. French translation by Eleanor Everest Freer. Chicago: Music Library of Chicago, Eleanor Everest Freer c1939. No pl. no.

III, 216: 1-14
Song for medium voice with keyboard.
r: c#^{1} - f^2

Note: EBB182 is bound in Sonnets from the Portuguese.

EBB183. —————. I Think of Thee! My Thoughts Do Twine and Bud, key of A major, no. 29. From the song cycle, Sonnets from the Portuguese, op. 22. Milwaukee: Wm. A. Kaun Music Co., c1910. No pl. no.

III, 216: 1-14
Song for medium voice with keyboard.
r: c#^{1} - f^2

Note: EBB183 is bound in Sonnets from the Portuguese.

EBB184.   Wellesz, Egon. Ich denk an dich, wie wilder Wein den Baum
spriessend umringt [I Think of Thee!—My Thoughts Do
Twine and Bud], key of C major, no. 4. From Sonette der
Elisabeth Barret-Browning, op. 52. Uebertragen von Rainer
Maria Rilke. Photocopy, Vienna: Universal-Edition, A. G.,
c1935. U.E. 10.281.

III, 216: 1-14
Song for soprano and string quartet. With parts.
r: c^1 - a^2

Note: EBB184 is bound in Sonette.

XXX.

EBB185.   Freer, Eleanor Everest. I See Thine Image thro' My Tears
Tonight, key of C major, no. 30. From the song cycle, Sonnets
from the Portuguese, op. 22. French translation by Eleanor
Everest Freer. Chicago: Music Library of Chicago, Eleanor
Everest Freer c1939. No pl. no.

III, 217: 1-14
Song for medium voice with keyboard.
r: b - f^2

Note: EBB185 is bound in Sonnets from the Portuguese.

EBB186.   —————. I See Thine Image thro' My Tears Tonight, key
of C major, no. 30. From the song cycle, Sonnets from the
Portuguese, op. 22. Milwaukee: Wm. A. Kaun Music Co.,
c1910. No pl. no.

III, 217: 1-14
Song for medium voice with keyboard.
r: b - f^2

Note: EBB186 is bound in Sonnets from the Portuguese.

XXXI.

EBB187.   Freer, Eleanor Everest. Thou Comest! All Is Said without a
Word, key of A major, no. 31. From the song cycle, Sonnets
from the Portuguese, op. 22. French translation by Eleanor
Everest Freer. Chicago: Music Library of Chicago, Eleanor
Everest Freer c1939. No pl. no.

III, 218: 1-14
Song for medium voice with keyboard.
r: $c\#^1$ - e^2 (optional $g\#^2$)

Note: EBB187 is bound in Sonnets from the Portuguese.

EBB188. ——————. Thou Comest! All Is Said without a Word, key of A major, no. 31. From the song cycle, Sonnets from the Portuguese, op. 22. Milwaukee: Wm. A. Kaun Music Co., c1910. No pl. no.

III, 218: 1-14
Song for medium voice with keyboard.
r: $c\#^1 - e^2$ (optional $g\#^2$)

Note: EBB188 is bound in Sonnets from the Portuguese.

XXXII.

EBB189. Freer, Eleanor Everest. The First Time That the Sun Rose on Thine Oath, key of C major, no. 32. From the song cycle, Sonnets from the Portuguese, op. 22. French translation by Eleanor Everest Freer. Chicago: Music Library of Chicago, Eleanor Everest Freer c1939. No pl. no.

III, 219: 1-14
Song for medium voice with keyboard.
r: $c^1 - f^2$

Note: EBB189 is bound in Sonnets from the Portuguese.

EBB190. ——————. The First Time That the Sun Rose on Thine Oath, key of C major, no. 32. From the song cycle, Sonnets from the Portuguese, op. 22. Milwaukee: Wm. A. Kaun Music Co., c1910. No pl. no.

III, 219: 1-14
Song for medium voice with keyboard.
r: $c^1 - f^2$

Note: EBB190 is bound in Sonnets from the Portuguese.

XXXIII.

EBB191. Freer, Eleanor Everest. Yes, Call Me by My Pet Name! key of C minor, no. 33. From the song cycle, Sonnets from the Portuguese, op. 22. French translation by Eleanor Everest Freer. Chicago: Music Library of Chicago, Eleanor Everest Freer c1939. No pl. no.

III, 220: 1-14
Song for medium voice with keyboard.
r: $b - eb^2$

Note: EBB191 is bound in Sonnets from the Portuguese.

EBB192. ——————. Yes, Call Me by My Pet Name! key of C minor, no. 33. From the song cycle, Sonnets from the Portuguese, op. 22. Milwaukee: Wm. A. Kaun Music Co., c1910. No pl. no.

III, 220: 1-14
Song for medium voice with keyboard.
r: $b - eb^2$

Note: EBB192 is bound in Sonnets from the Portuguese.

XXXIV.

EBB193. Freer, Eleanor Everest. With the Same Heart, I Said, I'll Answer Thee, key of D-flat major, no. 24. From the song cycle, Sonnets from the Portuguese, no. 22. French translation by Eleanor Everest Freer. Chicago: Music Library of Chicago, Eleanor Everest Freer c1939. No pl. no.

III, 221: 1-14
Song for medium voice with keyboard.
r: c^1 - f^2

Note: EBB193 is bound in Sonnets from the Portuguese.

EBB194. —————. With the Same Heart, I Said, I'll Answer Thee, key of D-flat major, no. 24. From the song cycle, Sonnets from the Portuguese, op. 22. Milwaukee: Wm. A. Kaun Music Co., c1910. No pl. no.

III, 221: 1-14
Song for medium voice with keyboard.
r: c^1 - f^2

Note: EBB194 is bound in Sonnets from the Portuguese.

XXXV.

EBB195. Freer, Eleanor Everest. If I Leave All for Thee, Wilt Thou Exchange, key of D major, no. 35. From the song cycle, Sonnets from the Portuguese, op. 22. French translation by Eleanor Everest Freer. Chicago: Music Library of Chicago, Eleanor Everest Freer c1939. No pl. no.

III, 222: 1-14
Song for medium voice with keyboard.
r: b - f^2

Note: EBB195 is bound in Sonnets from the Portuguese.

EBB196. —————. If I Leave All for Thee, Wilt Thou Exchange, key of D major, no. 35. From the song cycle, Sonnets from the Portuguese, op. 22. Milwaukee: Wm. A. Kaun Music Co., c1910. No pl. no.

III, 222: 1-14
Song for medium voice with keyboard.
r: b - f^2

Note: EBB196 is bound in Sonnets from the Portuguese.

EBB197. Klein, Bruno Oscar. If I Leave All for Thee (Lass' Alles ich für dich), no. 9 [only]. From Ten Songs (Zehn Lieder), op. 59. German words by Helen D. Tretbar. New-York: Edward Schuberth & Co., Charles F. Tretbar c1898. C.F.T. 189.

III, 222: 1-14
Song for [high] voice with piano.
r: c^1 - a^2 t: g^1 - g^2

XXXVI.

EBB198. Freer, Eleanor Everest. When We First Met and Loved, I Did Not Build, key of C major, no. 36. From the song cycle, Sonnets from the Portuguese, op. 22. French translation by Eleanor Everest Freer. Chicago: Music Library of Chicago, Eleanor Everest Freer c1939. No pl. no.

III, 223: 1-14
Song for medium voice with keyboard.
r: b - f#^{2}

Note: EBB198 is bound in Sonnets from the Portuguese.

EBB199. —————. When We First Met and Loved, I Did Not Build, key of C major, no. 36. From the song cycle, Sonnets from the Portuguese, op. 22. Milwaukee: Wm. A. Kaun Music Co., c1910. No pl. no.

III, 223: 1-14
Song for medium voice with keyboard.
r: b - f#^{2}

Note: EBB199 is bound in Sonnets from the Portuguese.

XXXVII.

EBB200. Freer, Eleanor Everest. Pardon, oh, Pardon, That My Soul Should Make, key of C major, no. 37. From the song cycle, Sonnets from the Portuguese, op. 22. French translation by Eleanor Everest Freer. Chicago: Music Library of Chicago, Eleanor Everest Freer c1939. No pl. no.

III, 224: 1-14
Song for medium voice with keyboard.
r: a - f^2

Note: EBB200 is bound in Sonnets from the Portuguese.

EBB201. —————. Pardon, oh, Pardon, That My Soul Should Make, key of C major, no. 37. From the song cycle, Sonnets from the Portuguese, op. 22. Milwaukee: Wm. A. Kaun Music Co., c1910. No pl. no.

III, 224: 1-14
Song for medium voice with keyboard.
r: a - f^2

Note: EBB201 is bound in Sonnets from the Portuguese.

XXXVIII.

EBB202. Barbour, Florence Newell. Love's Ecstasy, key of E-flat major. From Songs by Florence Newell Barbour. Boston: The Arthur P. Schmidt Co., c1922. A.P.S. 12434.

III, 225: 1-14
Song for mezzo soprano or baritone with keyboard.
r: c^1 - eb^2

EBB203.	————————. Love's Ecstasy, key of G major. From Songs by Florence Newell Barbour. Boston: The Arthur P. Schmidt Co., c1922. A.P.S. 12433.

III, 225: 1-14
Song for soprano or tenor with keyboard.
r: e^1 - g^2

EBB204.	Freer, Eleanor Everest. First Time He Kissed Me, He but Only Kissed, key of D-flat major, no. 38. From the song cycle, Sonnets from the Portuguese, op. 22. French translation by Eleanor Everest Freer. Chicago: Music Library of Chicago, Eleanor Everest Freer c1939. No pl. no.

III, 225: 1-14
Song for medium voice with keyboard.
r: c^1 - eb^2

Note: EBB204 is bound in Sonnets from the Portuguese.

EBB205.	————————. First Time He Kissed Me, He but Only Kissed, key of D-flat major, no. 38. From the song cycle, Sonnets from the Portuguese, op. 22. Milwaukee: Wm. A. Kaun Music Co., c1910. No pl. no.

III, 225: 1-14
Song for medium voice with keyboard.
r: c^1 - eb^2

EBB206.	Kaiser, Charles A. Three Kisses, key of B-flat major, no. 6. From the song cycle, Seven Sonnets from the Portuguese, op. 8. New York: Breitkopf & Härtel, Chas. A. Kaiser c1912. NY. 395.

III, 225: 1-14
Song for soprano with keyboard.
r: eb^1 - a^2 (optional c^3)

Note: EBB206 is bound in Seven Sonnets from the Portuguese.

XXXIX.

EBB207.	Freer, Eleanor Everest. Because Thou Hast the Pow'r and Own'st the Grace, key of G major, no. 39. From the song cycle, Sonnets from the Portuguese, op. 22. French translation by Eleanor Everest Freer. Chicago: Music Library of Chicago, Eleanor Everest Freer c1939. No pl. no.

III, 226: 1-14
Song for medium voice with keyboard.
r: b - f^2

Note: EBB207 is bound in Sonnets from the Portuguese.

EBB208.　————. Because Thou Hast the Pow'r and Own'st the Grace, key of G major, no. 39. From the song cycle, Sonnets from the Portuguese, op. 22. Milwaukee: Wm. A. Kaun Music Co., c1910. No pl. no.

III, 226: 1-14
Song for medium voice with keyboard.
r: b - f²

Note: EBB208 is bound in Sonnets from the Portuguese.

XL.

EBB209.　Freer, Eleanor Everest. Oh, Yes! They Love through All This World of Ours! key of E minor, no. 40. From the song cycle, Sonnets from the Portuguese, op. 22. French translation by Eleanor Everest Freer. Chicago: Music Library of Chicago, Eleanor Everest Freer c1939. No pl. no.

III, 227: 1-14
Song for medium voice with keyboard.
r: b - f²

Note: EBB209 is bound in Sonnets from the Portuguese.

EBB210.　————. Oh, Yes! They Love through All This World of Ours! key of E minor, no. 40. From the song cycle, Sonnets from the Portuguese, op. 22. Milwaukee: Wm. A. Kaun Music Co., c1910. No pl. no.

III, 227: 1-14
Song for medium voice with keyboard.
r: b - f²

Note: EBB210 is bound in Sonnets from the Portuguese.

XLI.

EBB211.　Freer, Eleanor Everest. I Thank All Who Have Loved Me in Their Hearts, key of E-flat major, no. 41. From the song cycle, Sonnets from the Portuguese, op. 22. French translation by Eleanor Everest Freer. Chicago: Music Library of Chicago, Eleanor Everest Freer c1939. No pl. no.

III, 228: 1-14
Song for medium voice with keyboard.
r: c¹ - eb²

Note: EBB211 is bound in Sonnets from the Portuguese.

EBB212.　————. I Thank All Who Have Loved Me in Their Hearts, key of E-flat major, no. 41. From the song cycle, Sonnets from the Portuguese, op. 22. Milwaukee: Wm. A. Kaun Music Co., c1910. No pl. no.

III, 228: 1-14
Song for medium voice with keyboard.
r: c¹ - eb²

Note: EBB212 is bound in Sonnets from the Portuguese.

XLII.

EBB213. Freer, Eleanor Everest. "My Future Will Not Copy Fair My Past," key of A major, no. 42. From the song cycle, Sonnets from the Portuguese, op. 22. French translation by Eleanor Everest Freer. Chicago: Music Library of Chicago, Eleanor Everest Freer c1939. No pl. no.

III, 229: 1-14
Song for medium voice with keyboard.
r: b - e^2

Note: EBB213 is bound in Sonnets from the Portuguese.

EBB214. —————. "My Future Will Not Copy Fair My Past," key of A major, no. 42. From the song cycle, Sonnets from the Portuguese, op. 22. Milwaukee: Wm. A. Kaun Music Co., c1910. No pl. no.

III, 229: 1-14
Song for medium voice with keyboard.
r: b - e^2

Note: EBB214 is bound in Sonnets from the Portuguese.

XLIII.

EBB215. Barnett, Alice. Sonnet, key of G major. From Three Songs by Alice Barnett. Songs and Ballads by American Composers. New York: G. Schirmer, c1918. Pl. no. 28551.

III, 230: 1-14
Song for high voice with piano.
r: d^1 - ab^2

EBB216. Beecher, Carl. How Do I Love Thee? key of F major. From Songs by Carl Beecher. 2 Sheet Music Edition, V. 537. New York: Carl Fischer, c1921. Pl. no. 22040.

III, 230: 1-14
Song for medium voice with piano.
r: c^1 - g^2

EBB217. Branscombe, Gena. "How Do I Love Thee," key of F major, no. 3. From the song cycle, Love in a Life. New York: G. Schirmer, c1907. Pl. no. 19523.

III, 230: 1-14
Song for medium voice with piano.
r: c^1 - f^2

Note: EBB217 is bound in Love in a Life.

EBB218. Cain, Noble. How Do I Love Thee, key of A major. From G. Schirmer, Octavo No. 7910. Xerox copy, [New York]: G. Schirmer, Inc., c1936. Pl. no. 36796.

III, 230: 1-4, 1, 5-10, 1, 11-14, 1
Part-song for mixed chorus (soprano I and II, alto I and II, tenor I and II, bass I and II) with piano (for rehearsal only).

Note: EBB218 is the gift of the Library of Congress.

EBB219. Colvin, Herbert. How Do I Love Thee, key of C major. Manuscript, no place: no publisher, 1952. No pl. no.

III, 230: 1-14
Song for [high] voice with keyboard.
r: $c^1 - bb^2$ t: $f^1 - e^2$

EBB220. ————————. How Do I Love Thee, key of C major. Manuscript, no place: no publisher, 1970. No pl. no.

III, 230: 1-14
Song for [high] voice with keyboard.
r: $eb^1 - bb^2$ t: $ab^1 - g^2$

EBB221. Davis, Blevins. "How Do I Love Thee," key of D-flat major. Xerox copy, New York City: Handy Brothers Music Co., Inc., c1936. No pl. no.

III, 230: 1-14
Song for [medium] voice with keyboard.
r: $db^1 - gb^2$ t: $f^1 - eb^2$

EBB222. Dello Joio, Norman. How Do I Love Thee? key of C major. From Songs in English, Nineteen Contemporary Settings by American and English Composers, edited by Bernard Taylor. New York: Carl Fischer, Inc., c1954. N5203.

III, 230: 1-14
Song for low voice with piano.
r: $b - e^2$

Note: EBB222 is bound in Songs in English.

EBB223. ————————. How Do I Love Thee? key of C major. From Songs in English, Nineteen Contemporary Settings by American and English Composers, edited by Bernard Taylor. New York: Carl Fischer, Inc., c1954. N5272.

III, 230: 1-14
Song for high voice with keyboard.
r: $d^1 - g^2$

Note: EBB223 is bound in Songs in English.

EBB224.   ——————. How Do I Love Thee? key of C major. V 2230.
New York: Carl Fischer, Inc., c1954. Pl. no. 31066.

III, 230: 1-14
Song for high voice with keyboard.
r: d^1 - g^2

EBB225.   Freer, Eleanor Everest. How Do I Love Thee, key of C major.
From the opera, The Brownings Go to Italy, (or) (A Love
Story), op. 43. Libretto by G. A. Hawkins-Ambler. Chicago:
The Music Library of Chicago, c1936. Pl. no. 38977.

III, 230: 1-14
Duet for mezzo soprano and baritone with keyboard.

Note: EBB225 is bound in The Brownings Go to Italy (piano-
vocal score).

EBB226.   ——————. How Do I Love Thee? key of C major, no. 43.
From the song cycle, Sonnets from the Portuguese, op. 22.
French translation by Eleanor Everest Freer. Chicago: Music
Library of Chicago, Eleanor Everest Freer c1939. No pl. no.

III, 230: 1-14
Song for medium voice with keyboard.
r: b^b - f^2

Note: EBB226 is bound in Sonnets from the Portuguese.

EBB227.   ——————. How Do I Love Thee? key of C major, no. 43.
From the song cycle, Sonnets from the Portuguese, op. 22.
Milwaukee: Wm. A. Kaun Music Co., c1910. No pl. no.

III, 230: 1-14
Song for medium voice with keyboard.
r: b^b - f^2

Note: EBB227 is bound in Sonnets from the Portuguese.

EBB228.   Gabert, Abel. How Do I Love Thee, key of G major. Edition
no. 2. Photostat copy, New York: J. Fischer & Bro., Abel
Gabert c1908. No pl. no.

III, 230: 1-14
Song for medium voice with keyboard.
r: d^1 - g^2

EBB229.   Gaul, Harvey B[artlett]. A Sonnet from the Portuguese, key
of D major. From G. Schirmer's Secular Choruses, no. 7162.
New York: G. Schirmer, Inc., c1926. Pl. no. 32670.

III, 230: 1-14
Chorus for men's choir (tenor I and II, bass I and II) with
piano.

EBB230.   Glarum, L. Stanley. How Do I Love Thee, key of C major. From Choral Compositions, no. SG51. New York: Bourne Co., c1964. Pl. no. 3094.

III, 230: 1-14, 1
Part-song for mixed chorus (soprano, alto, tenor, bass) with piano (for rehearsal only).

EBB231.   Goldsworthy, W. A. How Do I Love Thee, key of G minor. Xerox copy, no place: G. Ricordi & Co., Inc., c1932. N.Y.886.

III, 208: 1-14; 209: 1-9; 230: 1-3, 5-14
Setting for women's chorus and alto soloist with piano:

> Part-song for women's chorus (soprano I and II, alto) with piano.
>
> Song for alto with piano.
> r: b♭ - f
>
> Part-song for women's chorus (soprano I and II, alto) with piano.

Note: Although the music is written to be performed successively, the three sections can be performed separately.

EBB232.   Hadley, Henry K[imball]. How Do I Love Thee? key of B-flat major, no. 3 [only]. From Five Songs, op. 20. Boston: Oliver Ditson Company, c1900. ML-696.

III, 230: 1-14
Song for high voice with piano.
r: c^1 - g^2 (optional a^2 and bb^2)

EBB233.   Hopkins, Franklin. How Do I Love Thee, key of A-flat major. Photostat copy, no place: [Cecil Mackie, Inc.], c1913. No pl. no.

III, 230: 1-14
Song for [high] voice with keyboard.
r: b - ab^2 t: g^1 - g^2

EBB234.   Hopkins, Joseph M. How Do I Love Thee? key of D major. No. 131-41004. Bryn Mawr: Oliver Ditson Company, c1949. Pl. no. 78913.

III, 230: 1-14
Song for high voice with piano.
r: $c\#^1$ - $f\#^2$

Note: Above the first line of music is written "Dear Mr. Lewando. Thank you for the nice write-up on my anthem. Hope you will like this new song as well. Joseph M. Hopkins." EBB234 is a gift from Ralph Lewando.

EBB235.   Lippé, Edouard. How Do I Love Thee, key of D-flat major. Boston: Boston Music Company, c1941. B.M.Co.9880.

III, 230: 1-14
Song for low or medium voice with piano.
r: db^1 - e^2 (optional gb^2)

EBB236.   ————. How Do I Love Thee, key of E-flat major. Boston: Boston Music Company, c1941. B.M.Co.9881.

III, 230: 1-14
Song for high voice with piano.
r: eb^1 - gb^2 (optional ab^2)

EBB237.   McDaniel, William J. How Do I Love Thee, key of C major. Manuscript, no place: no publisher, Wm. J. McDaniel c1961-1969. No pl. no.

III, 230: 1-14
Song for [high] voice with keyboard.
r: c^1 - a^2 (optional bb^2)   t: g^1 - g^2

Note: EBB237 was a gift from the composer March 15, 1972. The letter of presentation from the composer says that the song is published by Composers' Autograph Publication in Shaker Heights, Ohio.

EBB238.   Madsen, Mrs. J. Chester. Sonnet, key of G-flat major. Manuscript, no place: no publisher, n.d. No pl. no.

III, 230: 1-14
Song for [high] voice with keyboard.
r: $c\#^1$ - a^2 t: f^1 - $f\#^2$

Note: The ABL received EBB238 Aug. 4, 1943.

EBB239.   Markham, Robert Alexander. How Do I Love Thee, key of B-flat major. Manuscript, no place: no publisher, n.d. No pl. no.

III, 230: 1-14
Song for soprano with piano.
r: c^1 - f^2

Note: EBB239 is the gift of the composer.

EBB240.   Passailaigue, Mary [Flournoy]. How Do I Love Thee, key of A-flat major. Arranged by Elizabeth Jenkins. No place: no publisher, Mary Passailaigue c1965. No pl. no.

III, 230: 1-3, 5-14
Song for [medium] voice with keyboard.
r: f - bb^2 t: c^1 - db^2

Note: EBB240 was the gift of the composer June 21, 1972.

EBB241. Pierce, Allie Coleman. How Do I Love Thee, key of G major. Manuscript, no place: no publisher, n.d. No pl. no.

III, 230: 1-3, 5, 6, 11, 12, 9, 10, 11-14
Song for [high] voice with keyboard.
r: d^1 - g^2 t: e^1 - e^2

Note: EBB241 is a gift of the composer.

EBB242. Protheroe, Daniel. How Do I Love Thee, key of D major. From Songs by Daniel Protheroe. Chicago: The Gamble Hinged Music Company, c1913. G.H.M.Co. 271.

III, 230: 1-14
Song for medium voice with keyboard.
r: d^1 - e^2

EBB243. Rhodes, Harold. A Woman's Love, key of C major, op. 6, no. 2 [only]. London: Novello & Co., Ltd., c1919. Pl. no. 14616.

III, 230: 1-14
Song for [high] voice with keyboard.
r: eb^1 - g^2 t: f^1 - f^2

EBB245. Roy, William. How Do I Love Thee, key of C major. New York: G. Schirmer, Inc., c1948. Pl. no. 41697.

III, 230: 1-14
Song for medium voice with piano.
r: c^1 - g^2

EBB246. —————————. How Do I Love Thee, key of E-flat major. New York: G. Schirmer, Inc., c1948. Pl. no. 41696.

III, 230: 1-14
Song for high voice with piano.
r: eb^1 - bb^2

Note: On the front cover is written "To the Browning Library Cordially Gladys Swarthout   February 9th, 1948   1st radio performance."

EBB247. Surinach, Carlos. How Do I Love Thee? key of C major, no. 1 [only]. From Flamenco Meditations by Carlos Surinach. New York: Associated Music Publishers, Inc., c1966. AMP-9653.

III, 230: 1-14
Song for [high] voice with piano.
r: f^1 - ab^2 t: f^1 - f^2

EBB248. Threlkeld, Beulah. How Do I Love Thee, key of B-flat major. Xerox copy, manuscript, no place: no publisher, Beulah Threlkeld cSept. 5, 1935. No pl. no.

III, 230: 1-14
Song for [medium high] voice with keyboard.
r: d^1 - a^2 t: f^1 - f^2

EBB249. Ware, Harriet. How Do I Love Thee, key of B-flat major.
Philadelphia: Theodore Presser Co. The John Church Division, c1930. Pl. no. 30128.

III, 230: 1-3, 5, 6, 11, 12, 7-10, 12-14
Song for high voice with keyboard.
r: c^1 - e^2

EBB250. Ware, Harriett [*sic*]. How Do I Love Thee, key of B-flat
major. Cincinnati: The John Church Company, c1912. Pl. no.
16600.

III, 230: 1-3, 5, 6, 11, 12, 7-10, 12-14
Song for high voice with piano.
r: c^1 - e^2

Note: The ABL has 3 copies. On the front cover of copy 3
is written "presented to Baylor University by Harriet Ware
At the request of Mrs. F. W. Vaughan of San Francisco."

EBB251. Weems, Mrs. J. Eddie. How Do I Love Thee, key of D major.
From the song cycle, The Browning Cycle of Love Lyrics.
Manuscript, no place: no publisher, n.d. No pl. no.

III, 230: 1-14
Song for [low] voice with keyboard.
r: a - d^2 t: d^1 - b^1

EBB252. White, Maude Valérie. How Do I Love Thee, key of D-flat
major. From Selected English Songs and Ballads. New York:
G. Schirmer, c1899. Pl. no. 15238.

III, 230: 1-3, 8, 5, 6, 12-14
Song for mezzo soprano or baritone with piano.
r: db^1 - db^2

EBB253. ——————. How Do I Love Thee, key of D-flat major. From
The World's Best Music, Famous Songs, Vol. 6, edited by
Victor Herbert, Henry H. Huss, Reginald De Koven, Fanny
Morris Smith, Gerrit Smith, Louis R. Dressler, Joseph M.
Priaulx, Louis C. Elson, Helen Kendrick Johnson, and others.
Philharmonic Edition, revised and enlarged. New York: The
University Society, Inc., c1908. No pl. no.

III, 230: 1-3, 8, 5, 6, 12-14
Song for [medium] voice with keyboard.
r: db^1 - db^2 t: db^1 - db^2

Note: EBB253 is bound in The World's Best Music, Vol. 6.

EBB254. ——————. How Do I Love Thee, key of D-flat major. Milan:
Tito di Gio. Ricordi, n.d. d 49677 d.

III, 230: 1-3, 8, 5, 6, 12-14
Song for [medium] voice with keyboard.
r: db^1 - db^2 t: db^1 - db^2

EBB255.   ————————. How Do I Love Thee, key of F major. Milan: G. Ricordi & C., n.d. d 49676 d.

III, 230: 1-3, 8, 5, 6, 12-14
Song for [high] voice with keyboard.
r: f^1 - f^2 t: f^1 - f^2

XLIV.

EBB256.   Castelnuovo-Tedesco, Mario. Poems and Flowers, key of G major, no. 3. From Three Sonnets from the Portuguese by Mario Castelnuovo-Tedesco. Edition Chester, no. 173. London: J. & W. Chester, Ltd., c1928. J. W. C. 3970.

III, 231: 1-14
Song for [medium] voice with piano.
r: $c\#^1$ - g^2 t: d^1 - e^2

Note: EBB256 is bound in Three Sonnets from the Portuguese.

EBB257.   Freer, Eleanor Everest. Beloved, Thou Hast Brought Me Many Flowers, key of G major, no. 44. From the song cycle, Sonnets from the Portuguese, op. 22. French translation by Eleanor Everest Freer. Chicago: Music Library of Chicago, Eleanor Everest Freer c1939. No pl. no.

III, 231: 1-14
Song for medium voice with keyboard.
r: c^1 - e^2 (optional $g\#^2$)

Note: EBB257 is bound in Sonnets from the Portuguese.

EBB258.   ————————. Beloved, Thou Hast Brought Me Many Flowers, key of G major, no. 44. From the song cycle, Sonnets from the Portuguese, op. 22. Milwaukee: Wm. A. Kaun Music Co., c1910. No pl. no.

III, 231: 1-14
Song for medium voice with keyboard.
r: c^1 - e^2 (optional $g\#^2$)

Note: EBB258 is bound in Sonnets from the Portuguese.

THE SOUL'S EXPRESSION

EBB259.   Coleridge-Taylor, S[amuel]. The Soul's Expression, key of G major, no. 1. From The Soul's Expression (Four Sonnets), op. 42. London: Novello & Co., Ltd., c1900. Pl. no. 11085.

II, 259: 1-14
Song for contralto with keyboard.
r: $a\#$ - e^2

Note: EBB259 is bound in The Soul's Expression (Four Sonnets).

SUBSTITUTION

EBB260. Coleridge-Taylor, S[amuel]. "Substitution," key of B major, no. 2. From In Memoriam, Three Rhapsodies, op. 24. Augener's Edition, no. 8868. London: Augener Limited, n.d. Pl. no. 11278.

II, 269: 1-14
Song for low voice with piano.
r: b - e^2

Note: EBB260 is bound in In Memoriam.

EBB261. —————. Substitution, key of B major, no. 2 [only]. From In Memoriam, Three Rhapsodies, op. 24. London: Augener Ltd., n.d. Pl. no. 11278b.

II, 269: 1-14
Song for low voice with piano.
r: b - e^2

TEARS

EBB262. Coleridge-Taylor, S[amuel]. Tears, key of A major, no. 2. From The Soul's Expression (Four Sonnets), op. 42. London: Novello & Co., Ltd., c1900. Pl. no. 11085.

II, 267: 1-14
Song for contralto with keyboard.
r: c#^{1} - d#^{2}

Note: EBB262 is bound in The Soul's Expression.

EBB263. Harris, Russell G. "Tears," key of C major. Photostat copy, manuscript, New York: Independent Music Publishers, n.d. No pl. no.

II, 267: 1-14
Setting for [high] voice with violin I and II, flute, oboe, clarinet, bassoon, cymbal, and piano. Conductor's score. No parts.
r: d^1 - bb^2 t: f^1 - a^2

Note: Inside the front cover is written *To Dr. & Mrs. A. J. Armstrong. In whom the Spirit of the Brownings finds its true reincarnation. Russell G. Harris 2/23/45.* Below the last line of the music is the date (12/44).

THAT DAY

EBB264. Nicholson, Alfred. That Day, key of D minor. London: Addison & Hollier, n.d. Pl. no. 2883.

III, 147: 1-15
Song for [medium] voice with keyboard.
r: d^1 - d^2 t: e^1 - c^2

THE VIRGIN MARY TO THE CHILD JESUS

EBB265. Damrosch, Walter. The Virgin Mary to the Child Jesus, op. 4, no. 1, key of B-flat major and op. 4, no. 2, key of F major. No. 2011. Cincinnati: The John Church Company, c1899. Pl. nos. 12939 and 12940.

II, 174-175: 1-20
(2) motets for mixed chorus (soprano I and II, alto I and II, tenor I and II, bass I and II), unacc. (To be performed successively, although can be performed separately.)

A VISION OF POETS

EBB266. Pascal, Florian. No Little Flower, key of D major, no. 8. From Eight Songs (5th set) by Florian Pascal. London: Joseph Williams, Limited, c1905. J. W. 14240.

I, 223: 457-465
Song for [medium] voice with piano.
r: $c\#^1 - d^2$ t: $d^1 - d^2$

Note: EBB266 is bound in Eight Songs (5th set).

THE WISDOM OF FOLLY[4]

EBB267. Warburg, Frederic S. Silver Linings, key of E-flat major, no. 2. Words by Ellen Thorneycroft Fowler. From Eight Songs by Frederic S. Warburg. Vol. I, op. 16. London: Weekes & Co., n.d. W. 5340.

Song for [medium] voice with piano.
r: $b^b - g^2$ t: $e^{b1} - d^2$

Note: EBB267 is bound in Eight Songs. On the front cover is written "With the Composer's compliments. Nov 1907."

WISDOM UNAPPLIED

EBB268. Hammer, Marie von. If I Were Thou, key of A-flat major. From Five Songs by Marie von Hammer. Boston: Oliver Ditson Company, c1900. Pl. no. 4-57-62322.

III, 92-93: 1-12, 25, 26, 28, 29
Song for high voice with piano.
r: $d^{b1} - g^2$

---

[4]This is not the title of an EBB poem; it is herein listed because the words are incorrectly attributed to her on the music; according to *Granger's Index to Poetry* (5th ed., rev. and enl.), p. 1565, the words on which Warburg's *Silver Linings* is based are from *The Wisdom of Folly* by Ellen Thorneycroft Fowler, *see A Book of Living Poems,* p. 87.

EBB269.   Pascal, Florian. Wisdom Unapplied, key of A-flat major, no. 2.
           From Eight Songs (5th set) by Florian Pascal. London:
           Joseph Williams, Limited, c1905. J. W. 14240.

           III, 92: 1-6, 25-30
           Song for [high] voice with piano.
           r: eb^1 - f#^{2} t: f^1 - e^2

           Note: EBB269 is bound in Eight Songs (5th set).

A WOMAN'S SHORTCOMINGS

EBB270.   Beningfield, Ethel. Unless, key of G major. London: Chap-
           pell & Co., Ltd., c1897. Pl. no. 20396.

           III, 139: 25-40
           Song for [low] voice with piano.
           r: b - e^2 t: d^1 - d^2

EBB271.   Bennett, Howard. "Unless," key of E major. From Two
           Songs by Howard Bennett. New York: G. Schirmer, c1908.
           Pl. no. 20235.

           III, 139: 25-40
           Song for low voice with piano.
           r: b - e^2

EBB272.   ————. "Unless," key of G major. From Two Songs by
           Howard Bennett. New York: G. Schirmer, c1908. Pl. no.
           20234.

           III, 139: 25-40
           Song for high voice with piano.
           r: d^1 - g^2

EBB273.   Brooke, Carol Kelley. True Love, key of G major. Chicago:
           F E. Hathaway Music Publisher, c1911. No pl. no.

           III, 139: 25-40
           Song for [medium] voice with keyboard.
           r: bb - db^2 t: d^1 - b^1

EBB274.   Caldicott, Alfred J. Unless, key of B-flat major. London:
           Metzler & Co., Ltd., n.d. M.6012.

           III, 139: 25-40
           Song for [low] voice with violin or cello obbligato and piano.
           With parts.
           r: bb - f^2 t: bb - bb^1

EBB275.   ————. Unless, key of D major. London: Metzler &
           Co., Ltd., n.d. M.5914.

           III, 139: 25-40
           Song for [medium] voice with violin or cello obbligato and
           piano. With parts.
           r: d^1 - a^2 t: d^1 - d^2

EBB276. Caracciolo, Luigi. Unless, key of B-flat major. Milan: Tito di Gio. Ricordi, n.d. r 49438 r.

III, 139: 25-40
Song for [medium high] voice with keyboard.
r: b^b - g^2 t: f^1 - f^2

EBB277. ——————. Unless, key of C major. Milan: Tito di Gio. Ricordi, n.d. n 51197 n.

III, 139: 25-40
Song for [high] voice with keyboard.
r: c^1 - a^2 t: g^1 - g^2

EBB278. ——————. Unless, key of G major, [no. 6]. From The World's Best Music, Famous Songs, Vol. 6, edited by Victor Herbert, Henry H. Huss, Reginald De Koven, Fanny Morris Smith, Gerrit Smith, Louis R. Dressler, Joseph M. Priaulx, Louis C. Elson, Helen Kendrick Johnson and others. Philharmonic Edition, revised and enlarged. New York: The University Society, Inc., c1908. No pl. no.

III, 139: 25-40
Song for [low] voice with keyboard.
r: g - e^2 t: d^1 - d^2

Note: EBB278 is bound in The World's Best Music, Vol. 6.

EBB279. Hervey, Augusta E. Unless, key of C major. London: C. Lonsdale, Musical Circulating Library, n.d. Pl. no. 3730.

III, 139: 25-40
Song for [medium] voice with piano.
r: c^1 - e^2 t: c^1 - c^2

EBB280. Mills, Edward. Never Call It Loving, key of G major. London: Webster & Waddington, Ltd., n.d. No pl. no.

III, 139: 25-40
Song for [medium] voice with piano.
r: b - e^2 t: d^1 - d^2

EBB281. Needham, Alicia Adélaïda. Unless, key of A-flat major, no. 3. From Twelve Lyrics for Lovers by Alicia Adélaïda Needham. London: Boosey & Co., c1902. H.3395.

III, 139: 25-40
Song for [high] voice with piano.
r: eb^1 - f^2 t: eb^1 - eb^2

Note: EBB281 is bound in Twelve Lyrics for Lovers.

EBB282. Parker, Phyllis Norman. Unless, key of B-flat major. London: Keith, Prowse & Co. Ltd., c1917. (K.P&Co.2183).

III, 139: 25-40
Song for [medium] voice with piano.
r: c^1 - eb^2 t: d^1 - bb^1

EBB283. —————. Unless, key of D-flat major. London: Keith, Prowse & Co. Ltd., c1917. (K.P&Co.2184).

III, 139: 25-40
Song for [high] voice with piano.
r: eb^1 - g^2 t: f^1 - db^2

EBB284. Schlesinger, Sebastian B. Unless, key of C major. London: Novello, Ewer & Co., c1893. Pl. no. 96232.

III, 139: 25-40
Song for [medium] voice with keyboard.
r: (optional a) b - f^2 (optional g^2)   t: d^1 - d^2

EBB285. Spencer, Fanny M. Unless, key of D major. Cleveland: J. H. Rogers, c1893. J.H. 215 R.

III, 139: 25-40
Song for mezzo soprano or baritone with keyboard.
r: c#^{1} - e^2 (optional a^2)

EBB286. —————. Unless, key of F major. Cleveland: J. H. Rogers, c1893. J.H. 214 R.

III, 139: 25-40
Song for tenor or soprano with keyboard.
r: e^1 - g^2 (optional c^3)

EBB287. Troup, Emily Josephine. Unless, key of A major. New Edition. London: Stanley Lucas, Weber & Co., n.d. S. L. W. 2833.

III, 139: 25-40
Song for [medium high] voice with piano.
r: c^1 - g^2 t: e^1 - e^2

Note: The ABL received EBB287 Jan. 20, 1941.

A YEAR'S SPINNING

EBB288. Metcalfe, W. A Year's Spinning (Die Spinnerin), key of G minor, no. 4. German words by Willy Kastner. From Six Songs by W. Metcalfe. London: Joseph Williams, c1899. N.12790.

III, 143-144: 1-10, 26-35
Song for [medium] voice with piano.
r: d^1 - e^2 t: d^1 - d^2

Note: EBB288 is bound in Six Songs.

EBB289. Pease, Alfred H. A Year's Spinning, key of C-sharp minor. New York: G. Schirmer, 1865. Pl. no. 437.

III, 143-144: 1-15, 26-35
Song for [high] voice with keyboard.
r: (optional c#^{1}) e^1 - g^2 t: g#^{1} - f#^{2}

IV

Composer, Arranger, and Editor Entry

Key to Abbreviations

acc.	accompanied
SA	soprano, alto
SAB	soprano, alto, bass
SATB	soprano, alto, tenor, bass
SATBB	soprano, alto, tenor, bass I, bass II
SS	soprano I, soprano II
SSA	soprano I, soprano II, alto
SSAA	soprano I, soprano II, alto I, alto II
SS-AA	soprano, soprano-alto, alto
SSAATTBB	soprano I, soprano II, alto I, alto II, tenor I, tenor II, bass I, bass II
TTBB	tenor I, tenor II, bass I, bass II
TTBBBB	tenor I, tenor II, baritone I, baritone II, bass I, bass II
unacc.	unaccompanied

For the complete description and explanation of this chapter, read page 5 of Chapter I.

Ackert, Bernard G. Rabbi Ben Ezra. Song for [medium] voice with keyboard. RB469

Aiken, Walter H. The Pied Piper of Hamelin. Operetta. Piano-vocal score. RB306

Akerman, Martin, editor. RB48

Aldrich, Leslie. Paean, "One Who Never Turn'd His Back." Song for [medium] voice with keyboard. RB72

Alsop, Marion. The Year's at the Spring. Song for soprano with piano. RB340

Andrews, Jessie, lyricist. RB219

Anglia. *See* Galsworthy, Ada

[Armes, Nancy.] Meeting at Night. Song for [medium] voice with keyboard. RB234

Arnott, A. Davidson. Give a Rouse. Song for baritone or bass with keyboard. RB32

Ashford, Emma L. Pan Among the Reeds. Cantata with piano. EBB46

Atkins, Evelyn Harper. My Star. Song for [high] voice with violin. RB250

Atkins, Ivor. The Year's at the Spring. Song for [high] voice with keyboard. RB341

Austin, Frederic. Home-Thoughts from Abroad. Song for [high] voice with keyboard. RB113

Austin, Torrington. Sleep Soft, Beloved. Song for [high] voice with keyboard. EBB72

Avison, Charles. "Grand March." Solo for unspecified keyboard (?) instrument. RB294

—————. [March]. Solo for unspecified keyboard (?) instrument. RB295

Aylwin, Josephine Crew. The Pied Piper of Hamelin. Cantata with piano. RB307

Ayres, Harold. I Loved You. Song for [medium] voice with keyboard. RB82

—————. I Send My Heart. Song for [high] voice with keyboard. RB132

Bantock, Granville. Amphibian. Piano solo. RB106

—————. As I Ride ("Through the Metidja to Abd-el-Kadr"). Song for [medium] voice with piano. RB527

—————. Ballade (Childe Roland to the Dark Tower Came.) Piano solo. RB61

—————. A Bean-Stripe: Also, Apple Eating. Song for [high] voice with piano. RB101

—————. Boot and Saddle. Part-song for male chorus (TTBB), unacc. RB43

—————. By the Fireside. Song for high voice with piano. RB17

————————. By the Fireside. Song for low voice with piano. RB18

————————. Caliban upon Setebos. Piano solo. RB19

————————. A Camel-Driver. Song for [medium] voice with piano. RB94

————————. Cherries. Song for [high] voice with piano. RB96

————————. The Eagle. Song for [high] voice with piano. RB85

————————. Epilogue. Song for [high] voice with piano. RB102

————————. The Family. Song for [high] voice with piano. RB91

————————. Fifine at the Fair. Orchestral drama with a prologue. Miniature score. RB105

————————. Give a Rouse. Part-song for male chorus (TTBB), unacc. RB33

————————. Gold Hair. Piano solo. RB109

————————. The Guardian Angel. Song for high voice with piano. RB111

————————. The Guardian Angel. Song for low voice with piano. RB110

————————. Home Thoughts. Song for high voice with piano. RB114

————————. Home Thoughts. Song for low voice with piano. RB115

————————. I Go to Prove My Soul. Song for [high] voice with piano. RB282

————————. I Go to Prove My Soul. Song for [high] voice with piano. RB281

————————. In a Gondola. Piano solo. RB133

————————. In a Year. Song for high voice with piano. RB169

————————. In a Year. Song for low voice with piano. RB170

————————. Life in a Love. Song for high voice with piano. RB220

————————. Life in a Love. Song for low voice with piano. RB221

————————. The Lost Leader. Part-song for male chorus (TTBB), unacc. RB224

————————. Marching Along. Part-song for male chorus (TTBB), unacc. RB20

————————. Master Hughes of Saxe-Gotha. Piano solo. RB232

————————. The Melon-Seller. Song for [high] voice with piano. RB89

————————. Midnight. Part-song for male chorus (TTBBBB), unacc. RB73

————————. Mihrab Shah. Song for [high] voice with piano. RB93

—————. My Star. Song for high voice with piano. RB252

—————. My Star. Song for low voice with piano. RB251

—————. Never the Time and the Place. Song for high voice with piano. RB272

—————. Never the Time and the Place. Song for low voice with piano. RB271

—————. Now. Song for high voice with piano. RB274

—————. Now. Song for low voice with piano. RB273

—————. O Zeus the King. Part-song for male chorus (TTBB), with short score for keyboard. RB5

—————. Pan and Luna. Piano solo. RB280

—————. Paracelsus. Part-song for male chorus (TTBBBB), unacc. RB283

—————. A Pearl, a Girl. Song for high voice with piano. RB305

—————. A Pearl, a Girl. Song for low voice with piano. RB304

—————. A Pillar at Sebzevah. Song for [high] voice with piano. RB98

—————. Pippa Passes. Song for high voice with piano. RB343

—————. Pippa Passes. Song for medium voice with piano. RB342

—————. Plot-Culture. Song for [high] voice with piano. RB97

—————. Red Cotton Night-Cap Country. Piano solo. RB482

—————. A Serenade at the Villa. Piano solo. RB492

—————. Shah Abbas. Song for [high] voice with piano. RB90

—————. Soliloquy of the Spanish Cloister. Piano solo. RB496

—————. Song of the Galleys from "Paracelsus." Part-song for male chorus (TTBB), unacc. RB284

—————. Summum Bonum. Song for high voice with piano. RB515

—————. Summum Bonum. Song for low voice with piano. RB516

—————. The Sun. Song for [high] voice with piano. RB92

—————. A Toccata of Galuppi's. Piano solo. RB528

—————. Two Camels. Song for [high] voice with piano. RB95

—————. Wanting Is—What? Song for high voice with piano. RB208

—————. Wanting Is—What? Song for low voice with piano. RB207

——————. A Woman's Last Word. Song for high voice with piano. RB566

——————. A Woman's Last Word. Song for low voice with piano. RB565

Barbour, Florence Newell. Love's Ecstasy. Song for mezzo soprano or baritone with keyboard. EBB202

——————. Love's Ecstasy. Song for soprano or tenor with keyboard. EBB203

Barlow, Emily. Entreaty. Song for [medium] voice with piano. RB567

Barnett, Alice. Boat-Song. Song for high voice with piano. RB134

——————. Dip Your Arm o'er the Boatside. Song for high voice with piano. RB135

——————. He Muses—Drifting. Song for high voice with piano. RB136

——————. In a Gondola. Song cycle for high voice with piano. RB134-RB141

——————. It Was Ordained to Be So, Sweet. Song for high voice with piano. RB137

——————. The Moth's Kiss. Song for high voice with piano. RB138

——————. Serenade. Song for high voice with piano. RB139

——————. Sonnet. Song for high voice with piano. EBB215

——————. To-morrow, If a Harp-string, Say. Song for high voice with piano. RB140

——————. What Are We Two. Song for high voice with piano. RB141

Bartholeyns, A. O'D., librettist. RB317

Bateman, Alice. In My Sleep, "Last Night I Saw You in My Sleep." Song for [low] voice with keyboard. RB8

Bates, Anna Craig. Apparitions. Song for [high] voice with keyboard. RB538

Beach, Mrs. H. H. A. Ah, Love, but a Day. Duet for soprano and tenor with keyboard. RB175

——————. Ah, Love, but a Day. Edited and arranged by William Creston. Part-song for women's chorus (SSA) with piano. RB178

——————. Ah, Love, but a Day. Song for mezzo soprano or baritone with piano. RB176 and RB177

——————. Ah, Love, but a Day! Song for soprano or tenor with keyboard. RB174

—————. I Send My Heart Up to Thee! Song for low voice with keyboard. RB142

—————. I Send My Heart Up to Thee! Song for soprano or tenor with keyboard. RB143

—————. When Soul Is Joined to Soul. Song for [high] voice with keyboard. EBB17

—————. The Year's at the Spring. Arranged by Francis Moore. Part-song for male chorus (TTBB) with piano. RB348

—————. The Year's at the Spring. Part-song for mixed chorus (SATB) with keyboard. RB349

—————. The Year's at the Spring. Part-song for women's chorus (SSAA) with keyboard. RB346

—————. The Year's at the Spring. Song for low voice with keyboard. RB345

—————. The Year's at the Spring. Song for [medium] voice with piano. RB344

—————. The Year's at the Spring. Song for soprano or tenor with piano. RB347

Beach, John. In a Gondola. Dramatic monologue for baritone with keyboard. RB144

—————. Is She Not Pure Gold. Song for [medium] voice with piano. RB497

—————. New Year's Hymn. Song for [medium] voice with keyboard. RB350

—————. A Woman's Last Word. Song for [medium high] voice with piano. RB568

Beckett, Bessie D. Submission. Song for [medium] voice with piano. RB569

Beecher, Carl. How Do I Love Thee? Song for medium voice with piano. EBB216

Behrend, A. H. All's Right, "The Year's at the Spring." Song for soprano with keyboard. RB351

Beiswenger, Anna J., librettist. RB313

Bending, Edwin. In a Gondola. Duet for soprano and tenor with cello or violin obbligato and piano. RB145

Beningfield, Ethel. Unless. Song for [low] voice with piano. EBB270

Bennett, Howard. "Unless." Song for high voice with piano. EBB272

—————. "Unless." Song for low voice with piano. EBB271

Berdahl, Arthur C. Epithalamium. Song for [high] voice with keyboard. RB539

Bergh, Arthur. The Pied Piper of Hamelin. Recitation for reader with piano. RB308

Beringer, Marjorie. The Boy and the Angel. Chant for [unison] voice[s] with unspecified keyboard [?] instrument. RB16

St. Bernard of Clairvaux. *See* Harwood, Basil

Bernhoff-Leipzig, Joh., translator. RB85, RB89-RB98, RB101, and RB102

Beta. "The Mask." Song for low voice with piano. EBB44

Bickford, Zahr Myron. I Find Earth Not Gray but Rosy. Song for soprano or tenor with keyboard. RB7

Birge, Edward Bailey, [compiler]. RB395

Black, Kate Gilmore. Pippa's Song. Song for high voice with piano. RB352

——————. The Year's at the Spring. Song for [high] voice, unacc. RB353

Blair, William. The Year's at the Spring. Song for [medium] voice with piano. RB354

Bliss, James A. Sonnet Twenty-One. Song for high voice with piano. EBB156

Bliss, Paul. Thy Face. Song for [medium low] voice with keyboard. RB540

Bloem, Walter, librettist. RB322

Blumenthal, Jacques. Sleep (He Giveth His Beloved Sleep). Song for [high] voice with piano. EBB74

——————. Sleep (He Giveth His Beloved Sleep). Song for [medium] voice with piano. EBB73

Bode, Alice M. The Year's at the Spring. Song for [high] voice with piano. RB355

Bollinger, Sam'l. Pompilia e Caponsacchi. Overture for orchestra. Conductor's score. RB483

——————. Pompilia e Caponsacchi. Overture for orchestra. Conductor's score with parts. RB484

Bond, Carrie Jacobs. Out in the Fields. Song for [medium high] voice with keyboard. EBB53

Booth, Guy. Sonnet (Seven) from the Portuguese. Part-song for mixed chorus (SATB), unacc. EBB110

Borton, Alice. Ah, Love, but a Day. Song for high voice with keyboard. RB179

Boughton, Rutland. Prospice. Part-song for male chorus (TTBB), unacc. RB456

Boyce, Ethel M. The Lay of the Brown Rosary. Cantata. Piano-vocal score. EBB33

Boyle, George F. Marching Along. Song for bass with piano. RB21

——————. The Pied Piper of Hamelin. Cantata. Piano-vocal score. RB309

Boys, Reginald S. Devotion. Song for [medium] voice with keyboard. RB570

Brahe, May H. Oh, to Be in England! Song for medium voice with piano. RB116

——————. The Year's at the Spring. Song for [high] voice with piano. RB358

——————. The Year's at the Spring. Song for medium voice with piano. RB356 and RB357

Brahms, Johannes. There's Heaven Above, and Night by Night. Hymn for SATB, unacc. RB213

Branscombe, Gena. The Best Is Yet to Be. Song for soprano or tenor with keyboard. RB470

——————. Boot and Saddle. Song for medium voice with piano. RB44

——————. "But Only Three in All God's Universe." Song for medium voice with piano. EBB86

——————. "The Face of All the World Is Changed." Song for medium voice with piano. EBB111

——————. "How Do I Love Thee." Song for medium voice with piano. EBB217

——————. I Send My Heart Up to Thee (Serenade). Song for soprano or tenor with keyboard. RB146

——————. "I Thought Once How Theocritus Had Sung." Song for medium voice with piano. EBB78

——————. Love in a Life. Song cycle for medium voice with piano. EBB78, EBB86, EBB103, EBB111, EBB176, and EBB217

——————. Marching Along! Song for medium voice with piano. RB22

——————. "My Own Beloved." Song for medium voice with piano. EBB176

————————. Serenade (I Send My Heart Up to Thee). Song for mezzo soprano or baritone with keyboard. RB148

————————. Serenade (I Send My Heart Up to Thee). Song for soprano or tenor with keyboard. RB147

————————. There's a Woman Like a Dew-drop. Song for high voice with piano. RB9

————————. What Are We Two? Song for [medium] voice with keyboard. RB149

————————. "The Widest Land." Song for medium voice with piano. EBB103

Bridge, J. Frederick. He Giveth His Beloved Sleep. Meditation for solo soprano, mixed chorus (SATB) and organ (or unacc.). EBB75

Brooke, Carol Kelley. True Love. Song for [medium] voice with keyboard. EBB273

Brooks, C. J., librettist. RB306

Broun, Harry. Comfort. Hymn for SATB, unacc. EBB7

Browne, Marmaduke E., librettist. RB318

Browning, Robert. O Bell' Andare. Two-part chorus for children's voices [SA], unacc. RB510, RB511, and RB512

Browning, [Robert and Elizabeth Barrett]. Avenge the Good Ship Maine. Arranged by R. M. Stults. Song for [medium high] voice with keyboard. RB7.1

Bruguiere, E. A. Life in a Love. Song for [medium] voice with piano. RB222

Brumleu, Ernest. The Pied Piper. Musical play with keyboard. RB310

Brydson, John C. The Bells of Hamelin. Piano solo. RB311

————————. The Children. Piano solo. RB311

————————. The Mayor and Corporation. Piano solo. RB311

————————. The Pied Piper. Piano solo. RB311

————————. The Pied Piper of Hamelin. Suite for piano. RB311

————————. The Rats. Piano solo. RB311

————————. The River Weser. Piano solo. RB311

Bryson, Ernest. So, the Year's Done With! Song for high voice with piano. RB64

————————. So, the Year's Done With! Song for medium voice with piano. RB65

Bullard, Frederic Field. There's a Woman Like a Dewdrop. Song for high voice, violin, and piano. RB10

Burnside, R. H., lyricist. RB325

Busch, Carl. Pan's Flute. Cantata with flute and piano. EBB47

Butt, Frances Mary, lyricist. RB394

Cain, Noble. Ah, Love, but a Day. Part-song for women's chorus (SSA) with piano. RB180

——————. How Do I Love Thee. Part-song for mixed chorus (SS AATTBB), unacc. EBB218

——————. Say Thou Lovest Me! Chorus for mixed choir (SSAA TTBB), unacc. EBB157

——————. The Year's at the Spring. Chorus for women's voices (SS-AA) with piano. RB359

Caldicott, Alfred J. Unless. Song for [low] voice with violin or cello obbligato and piano. EBB274

——————. Unless. Song for [medium] voice with violin or cello obbligato and piano. EBB275

Caldwell, Mary E. Year's at the Spring. Part-song for mixed chorus (SAB) with keyboard. RB361

——————. Year's at the Spring. Song for unison chorus with organ or piano. RB360

Cantor, Otto. Lov'd by Thee. Song for alto or baritone with piano. RB571

——————. Loved by Thee. Song for soprano or tenor or high voice with piano. RB572, RB573, and RB574

Caracciolo, Luigi. Unless. Song for [high] voice with keyboard. EBB277

——————. Unless. Song for [low] voice with keyboard. EBB278

——————. Unless. Song for [medium high] voice with keyboard. EBB276

Carse, A. von Ahn. The Lay of the Brown Rosary. Cantata. Piano-vocal score. EBB34

Carter, Ernest. "Thou Lov'st Me Not." Song for [medium] voice with piano. EBB61

Carter, Esther May. The Year's at the Spring. Song for [medium] voice with piano. RB362

Caruana, Iris, transcriber. RB530

Caruthers, Julia Lois. Pippa's Spring Song. Song for [high] voice with keyboard. RB363

Castelnuovo-Tedesco, Mario. Letters. Song for [high] voice with piano. EBB179

————. Poems and Flowers. Song for [medium] voice with piano. EBB256

————. The Sweet Sad Years. Song for [medium] voice with piano. EBB79

Chanter, Arthur. There's a Woman Like a Dewdrop. Song for bass or contralto with piano. RB11

Chao, T. C., translator and editor. RB480 and RB481

Christopher, Carol. The Magic Piper. Operetta. Piano-vocal score. RB312

Church, Frank M. A Passacaglia. Solo for unspecified keyboard (?) instrument. RB300

Clark, Ruth Kinney. The Year's at the Spring. Song for [medium high] voice with keyboard. RB364

Clarke, Helen A. Apparitions. Song for [medium high] voice with keyboard. RB541

————. My Star. Song for [high] voice with piano. RB253 and RB254

————. One Way of Love. Song for high voice, cello obbligato, and keyboard. RB276

————. Round Us the Wild Creatures. Song for [high] voice with keyboard. RB86

————. Song: Ask Not One Least Word of Praise. Song for [medium] voice with piano. RB99

————. You'll Love Me Yet. Song for [high] voice, cello, and piano. RB365

Clarke, Henry Leland. The Year's at the Spring. Song for [medium] voice with keyboard. RB366

Clarke, Hugh A. Give Her but a Least Excuse. Song for [high] voice with keyboard. RB367

————. Overhead the Treetops Meet. Song for [high] voice with keyboard. RB368

Clarke, Reginald. Home Thoughts from Abroad. Song for [high] voice with piano. RB117

Clarke, Robert Coningsby. Love Me. Song for [high] voice with piano. EBB38

Clokey, Joseph W. The Pied Piper of Hamelin. Opera. Piano-vocal score. RB313

Coleridge-Taylor, S. Comfort. Song for contralto with keyboard. EBB8

——————. Earth Fades! Heaven Breaks on Me. Song for low voice with piano. RB513 and RB514

——————. Grief. Song for contralto with keyboard. EBB15

——————. The Soul's Expression. Song for contralto with keyboard. EBB259

——————. "Substitution." Song for low voice with piano. EBB260 and EBB261

——————. Tears. Song for contralto with keyboard. EBB262

——————. You'll Love Me Yet. Song for contralto or baritone with keyboard. RB369

Colvin, Herbert. How Do I Love Thee. Song for [high] voice with keyboard. EBB219 and EBB220

Cooke, Greville. Oh, to Be in England. Part-song for mixed chorus (SSAATTBB), unacc. RB118

Cooley, Carlton. "Caponsacchi." Epic poem for orchestra. Conductor's score. RB485

Coombs, C. Whitney. Thy Face. Song for medium voice with piano. RB542

Cowen, Frederic H. Dost Thou Love Me. Song for [high] voice with piano. EBB63

——————. He Giveth His Beloved Sleep. Setting for contralto solo, mixed chorus (SATB), orchestra. Piano-vocal score. EBB76

——————. Insufficiency, (Leaving Yet Loving). Song for [medium high] voice with piano. EBB25

Cowley, Elsie M. But Love. Song for [low] voice with piano. RB131

Craddock, Reginald W. Apparitions. Song for medium voice with piano. RB543

Creston, William, editor and arranger. Ah, Love, but a Day. Mrs. H. H. A. Beach. Part-song for women's chorus (SSA) with piano. RB178

Cripps, A. Redgrave. The Year's at the Spring. Song for [medium] voice with keyboard. RB370

Croft, William. O God, Our Help. Hymn for SATB, unacc. RB275

Crumpler, Mary Frances. You'll Love Me Yet! Song for [medium high] voice with piano. RB371

Curtis, Natalie. Song from Pippa Passes. Song for [medium] voice with piano. RB372

Damrosch, Walter. The Virgin Mary to the Child Jesus. Two motets for mixed chorus (SSAATTBB), unacc. EBB265

Dansie, Redgewell. Boot and Saddle. Song for [medium high] voice with piano. RB45

————. Give a Rouse. Song for [medium high] voice with piano. RB34

————. Marching Along. Song for [medium] voice with piano. RB23

David, Elizabeth Harbison. Pippa's Song. Song for [medium high] voice with flute, violin and keyboard. RB373

Davidson, Frank. Summum Bonum. Song for tenor with piano. RB517

Davies, H. Walford. Hervé Riel. Choral setting for baritone solo, mixed chorus (SSAATTBB), and orchestra. Piano-vocal score. RB112

————. The Pied Piper. Chamber cantata. Piano-vocal score. RB314

————. Prospice. Song for baritone and string quartet. RB457

Davis, Blevins. "How Do I Love Thee." Song for [medium] voice with keyboard. EBB221

Davis, Carlyle. Heart's-Ease. Piano solo. RB374

————. The King's Dancer. Piano solo. RB374

————. Morning at Asolo. Piano solo. RB374

————. Ottima's Regret. Piano solo. RB374

————. Pippa Passes, Four Moods from Browning. Suite for piano. RB374

Dawson, William L. Out in the Fields. Song for low voice with keyboard. EBB54

Dearmer, Percy, editor. RB213, RB444, and RB479

De Francesco, Louis E. Ah, Love but a Day. Ballad for high voice with keyboard. RB181

————. Ah, Love but a Day. Ballad for medium voice with keyboard. RB182

————. Ah, Love but a Day. Song for [medium] voice with keyboard. RB183

De Koven, Reginald. There's a Woman Like a Dewdrop. Song for soprano or tenor with piano. RB12

————, editor. The World's Best Music. EBB28, EBB253, and EBB278

de Lacey, Robert. I Stoop into a Dark Tremendous Sea of Cloud. Anthem for bass and alto soloists, mixed chorus (SATB), and organ. RB285

Dello Joio, Norman. How Do I Love Thee? Song for high voice with keyboard. EBB223 and EBB224

——————. How Do I Love Thee? Song for low voice with piano. EBB222

——————. Meeting at Night. Song for high voice with keyboard. RB235

del Riego, Teresa. All's Right with the World. Song for [medium] voice with piano. RB375

——————. June, and My Lady. Song for [high] voice with piano. RB108

——————. June, and My Lady. Song for [medium] voice with piano. RB107

Demuth, Norman. Boot and Saddle. Song for unison chorus with piano. RB46

de Sousa, Leon. Give a Rouse! Song for [medium] voice with piano. RB35

DeVane, William Clyde, editor. RB533

Dichmont, William. Be a God and Hold Me. Song for high voice with piano. RB575

——————. Let's Contend No More. Song for high voice with piano. RB575

——————. What So Wild. Song for high voice with piano. RB575

——————. A Woman's Last Word. Songs for high voice with piano. RB575

Dickinson, Bertha Lovewell, [librettist]. RB491

Dickinson, Clarence. Summum Bonum. Duet for [medium] voices with keyboard. RB518

Dillon, Fannie Charles. Porphyria. Song for [high] voice with keyboard. RB455

——————. Saul. Recitation for reader with keyboard. RB488

Dittenhaver, Sarah Louise. Pied Piper's Tune. Piano solo. RB315

Dougherty, Celius. Portrait. Song for medium voice with piano. RB544

Downing, Lulu Jones. Apparitions. Song for medium voice with keyboard. RB545

——————. A Musical Instrument. Recitation for reader with keyboard. EBB48

Drakeford, Louis. Boot and Saddle. Song for [medium high] voice with piano. RB47

——————. Give a Rouse. Song for [medium high] voice with piano. RB36

——————. Marching Along. Song for [medium] voice with piano. RB24

Dressler, Louis R., editor. EBB28, EBB53, and EBB278

Duncan, Edmondstoune. Good News to Aix. Song for [high] voice with piano. RB128

——————. Prospice. Song for [low] voice with keyboard. RB458

——————. The Year's at the Spring. Song for [medium high] voice with piano. RB376

Dunhill, Thomas F. The Children Follow. Piano solo. RB316

——————. Hamelin Town's in Brunswick. Piano solo. RB316

——————. Into the Street. Piano solo. RB316

——————. The Mayor Expostulates. Piano solo. RB316

——————. The Pied Piper. Piano [suite]. RB316

——————. Rats! Piano solo. RB316

——————. Ringing the Bells. Piano solo. RB316

Dyson, George. Boot, Saddle, to Horse, and Away! Song for unison chorus with piano. RB48

Easson, James. Boot, Saddle, to Horse and Away. Song for unison chorus with piano. RB49

——————. God's in His Heaven. Two-part round, unacc. RB377 and RB378

Ehrmann, Mary B. Pippa's Song. Chorus for unison children's voices with keyboard. RB379

Elgar, Edward. A Child Asleep. Song for [medium high] voice with keyboard. EBB4

——————. Sabbath Morning at Sea. Song for contralto or low voice with piano. EBB69 and EBB70

——————. Sabbath Morning at Sea. Song for high voice with piano. EBB71

Ellingham, Harry. Evelyn. Song for [medium high] voice with keyboard. RB83

——————. Her Tresses. Song for [medium] voice with keyboard. RB498

Elman, Mischa. In a Gondola. Impromptu for violin and piano. RB150

Elson, Louis C., editor. EBB28, EBB253, and EBB278

Emerson, [Ralph Waldo], lyricist. RB393 and RB394

England, Nick. The All-Loving. Song for baritone, reader, and piano. RB80

Farley, Roland. God's Own Smile. Song for high voice with piano. RB546

Farmer, John. Epilogue, "At the Midnight in the Silence of the Sleep-time." Song for unison chorus with piano. RB74

——————. Epilogue [from *Asolando*]. Song for unison chorus with piano. RB75

——————. Heroes. Song for unison male chorus with piano. RB103 and RB104

——————. The Pied Piper; or The Rat-Catcher of Hamelin. Opera. Piano-vocal score. RB317

Farrington, Frederick W. The Piper of Hamelin. Cantata with flageolet or flute, piano, and harmonium. Piano-vocal score. RB318

Fergus, Phyllis. Thoughts. Recitation for reader with violin and piano. RB151

Fisher, Charles R. Meeting at Night. Song for [medium high] voice with piano. RB236

Fisher, William Arms. For Love's Sake Only. Song for high voice with piano. EBB138

Floyd, A. E. The Year's at the Spring. Part-song for women's chorus (SSA), unacc. RB380

Foote, David. A Woman's Last Word. Song for [medium high] voice with keyboard. RB576

Forbes, J. Winchell. Toccata. Solo for unspecified keyboard instrument. RB529

Ford, D. Rhys. Speak Low to Me, My Savior. Part-song for mixed chorus (SATB) with organ. EBB9

Forrester, J. Cliffe. Devotion. Song for [high] voice with piano. RB499

Forster, Beatrice. Wanting Is—What? Song for [high] voice with piano. RB209

Fowler, Ellen Thorneycroft, lyricist. EBB267

Freer, Eleanor Everest. Accuse Me Not, Beseech Thee. Song for medium voice with keyboard. EBB144 and EBB145

——————. All That I Know of a Certain Star. Song for baritone with keyboard. RB255

—————. And Therefore If to Love Can Be Desert. Song for mezzo soprano or medium voice with keyboard. EBB131, EBB132, and EBB133

—————. And Wilt Thou Have Me Fashion into Speech. Song for medium voice with keyboard. EBB136 and EBB137

—————. And Yet, Because Thou Overcomest So. Song for medium voice with keyboard. EBB146 and EBB147

—————. Apparitions. Song for [high] voice or tenor with keyboard. RB547 and RB548

—————. Because Thou Hast the Pow'r and Own'st the Grace. Song for medium voice with keyboard. EBB207 and EBB208

—————. Beloved, My Beloved, When I Think. Song for medium voice with keyboard. EBB154 and EBB155

—————. Beloved, Thou Hast Brought Me Many Flowers. Song for medium voice with keyboard. EBB257 and EBB258

—————. But Only Three in All God's Universe. Song for medium voice or mezzo soprano with keyboard. EBB87, EBB88, and EBB89

—————. Can It Be Right to Give What I Can Give? Song for mezzo soprano or medium voice with keyboard. EBB122, EBB123, and EBB124

—————. The Face of All the World Is Changed, I Think. Song for mezzo soprano or medium voice with keyboard. EBB112, EBB113, and EBB114

—————. First Time He Kissed Me, He but Only Kissed. Song for medium voice with keyboard. EBB204 and EBB205

—————. The First Time That the Sun Rose on Thine Oath. Song for medium voice with keyboard. EBB189 and EBB190

—————. Go from Me. Yet I Feel That I Shall Stand. Song for mezzo soprano or medium voice with keyboard. EBB104, EBB105, and EBB106

—————. A Heavy Heart, Beloved, Have I Borne. Song for medium voice with keyboard. EBB172 and EBB173

—————. How Do I Love Thee. Duet for mezzo soprano and baritone with keyboard. EBB225

—————. How Do I Love Thee. Song for medium voice with keyboard. EBB226 and EBB227

—————. I Heard Last Night a Little Child Go Singing. Song for mezzo soprano with keyboard. EBB1

—————. I Lift My Heavy Heart Up Solemnly. Song for medium voice or mezzo soprano with keyboard. EBB99, EBB100 and EBB101

—————. I Lived with Visions for My Company. Song for medium voice with keyboard. EBB174 and EBB175

—————. I Never Gave a Lock of Hair Away. Song for medium voice with keyboard. EBB150 and EBB151

—————. I Once Thought How Theocritus Had Sung. Song for mezzo soprano with keyboard. EBB80

—————. I See Thine Image thro' My Tears Tonight. Song for medium voice with keyboard. EBB185 and EBB186

—————. I Thank All Who Have Loved Me in Their Hearts. Song for medium voice with keyboard. EBB211 and EBB212

—————. I Think of Thee! My Thoughts Do Twine and Bud. Song for medium voice with keyboard. EBB182 and EBB183

—————. I Thought Once How Theocritus Had Sung. Song for medium voice or mezzo soprano with keyboard. EBB81, EBB82, and EBB83

—————. If I Leave All for Thee, Wilt Thou Exchange. Song for medium voice with keyboard. EBB195 and EBB196

—————. If Thou Must Love Me. Song for medium voice with keyboard. EBB139 and EBB140

—————. Indeed This Very Love Which Is My Boast. Song for medium voice with keyboard. EBB134 and EBB135

—————. Is It Indeed So? Song for medium voice with keyboard. EBB167 and EBB168

—————. The Legend of the Piper. [Opera.] Piano-vocal score. RB319

—————. Let the World's Sharpness Like a Clasping Knife. Song for medium voice with keyboard. EBB170 and EBB171

—————. "My Future Will Not Copy Fair My Past." Song for medium voice with keyboard. EBB213 and EBB214

—————. My Letters! All Dead Paper, Mute and White! Song for medium voice with keyboard. EBB180 and EBB181

—————. My Own Beloved, Who Hast Lifted Me. Song for medium voice with keyboard. EBB177 and EBB178

—————. My Poet, Thou Canst Touch on All the Notes. Song for medium voice with keyboard. EBB148 and EBB149

——————. My Star. Song for baritone or [medium] voice with key-board. RB256 and RB257

——————. Nay! But You Do Not Love Her. Song for low voice with piano. RB500

——————. Nay, but You, Who Do Not Love Her. Song for baritone with keyboard. RB501

——————. Oh, Yes! They Love through All This World of Ours! Song for medium voice with keyboard. EBB209 and EBB210

——————. Pardon, oh, Pardon, That My Soul Should Make. Song for medium voice with keyboard. EBB200 and EBB201

——————. Say over Again. Song for mezzo soprano or medium voice with keyboard. EBB158-EBB160

——————. Sonnets from the Portuguese, op. 22. Book I. Song cycle for mezzo soprano with keyboard. EBB80, EBB87, EBB91, EBB95, EBB99, EBB104, EBB112, EBB119, EBB122, EBB126, and EBB131.

——————. Sonnets from the Portuguese, op. 22. French translation by Eleanor Everest Freer. Song cycle for medium voice with keyboard. EBB82, EBB88, EBB92, EBB96, EBB100, EBB105, EBB113, EBB120, EBB123, EBB127, EBB132, EBB134, EBB136, EBB139, EBB144, EBB146, EBB148, EBB150, EBB152, EBB154, EBB159, EBB162, EBB167, EBB170, EBB172, EBB174, EBB177, EBB180, EBB182, EBB185, EBB187, EBB189, EBB191, EBB193, EBB195, EBB198, EBB200, EBB204, EBB207, EBB209, EBB211, EBB213, EBB226, and EBB257

——————. Sonnets from the Portuguese, op. 22. Song cycle for medium voice with keyboard. EBB83. EBB89, EBB93, EBB97, EBB101, EBB106, EBB114, EBB121, EBB124, EBB128, EBB133, EBB135, EBB137, EBB140, EBB145, EBB147, EBB149, EBB151, EBB153, EBB155, EBB160, EBB163, EBB168, EBB171, EBB173, EBB175, EBB178, EBB181, EBB183, EBB186, EBB188, EBB190, EBB192, EBB194, EBB196, EBB199, EBB201, EBB205, EBB208, EBB210, EBB212, EBB214, EBB227, and EBB258

——————. The Soul's Rialto Hath Its Merchandise. Song for medium voice with keyboard. EBB152 and EBB153

——————. Such a Starved Bank of Moss. Song for baritone with key-board. RB549

——————. Thou Comest! All Is Said without a Word. Song for medium voice with keyboard. EBB187 and EBB188

——————. Thou Hast Thy Calling to Some Palace-Floor. Song for medium voice, baritone, or mezzo soprano with keyboard. EBB94, EBB95, EBB96, and EBB97

—————. Unlike Are We, Unlike, O Princely Heart! Song for medium voice or mezzo soprano with keyboard. EBB91, EBB92, and EBB93

—————. What Can I Give Thee Back, O Liberal. Song for mezzo soprano or medium voice with keyboard. EBB119, EBB120, and EBB121

—————. When Our Two Souls Stand Up Erect and Strong. Song for medium voice with keyboard. EBB162 and EBB163

—————. When We First Met and Loved, I Did Not Build. Song for medium voice with keyboard. EBB198 and EBB199

—————. With the Same Heart, I Said, I'll Answer Thee. Song for medium voice with keyboard. EBB193 and EBB194

—————. The Year's at the Spring. Song for baritone with keyboard. RB382

—————. The Year's at the Spring. Song for low voice with keyboard. RB381

—————. The Year's at the Spring. Song for medium voice with keyboard. RB383

—————. Yes, Call Me by My Pet Name! Song for medium voice with keyboard. EBB191 and EBB192

—————. Yet, Love, Mere Love, Is Beautiful Indeed. Song for mezzo soprano or medium voice with keyboard. EBB125, EBB126, EBB127, and EBB128

French, Emma Weller. Out in the Fields. Song for soprano or tenor with piano and violin (obbligato). EBB55

Frey, Adolf. Apparitions. Song for [high] voice with keyboard. RB550

Fuller, Caroline M. The Changing Year. Song for contralto or bass with keyboard. RB184

—————. Over-head the Tree-tops Meet. Song for mezzo soprano with keyboard. RB384

—————. The Year's at the Spring. Song for soprano with keyboard. RB384

Gabert, Abel. How Do I Love Thee. Song for mezzo soprano or baritone with piano. EBB228

Gabriel, Virginia. At the Window. Song for [high] voice with piano. RB185

—————. At the Window. Song for [medium low] voice with piano. RB186

————————. Change upon Change. Song for [high] voice with piano. EBB3

————————. O Wilt Thou Have My Hand, Dear, (Inclusions). Song for [high] voice with piano. EBB18

Galsworthy, Ada. In the Doorway. Song for [medium] voice with piano. RB202

————————. Pippa's Song. Song for [high] voice with keyboard. RB385 and RB386

Galuppi, Baldassare. Sei Sonate. Four sonatas and two toccatas for harpsichord. RB530

————————. Sonata in A major. Edited and revised by Joseph Henius. Piano sonata. RB531

————————. Sonata in B-flat major. Sonata for harpsichord. RB530

————————. Sonata in C major. Sonata for harpsichord. RB530

————————. Sonata in D major. Edited and revised by Joseph Henius. Piano sonata. RB532

————————. Sonata in G major. Sonata for harpsichord. RB530

————————. Toccata in D minor. Toccata for harpsichord. RB530

————————. Toccata in F major. Toccata for harpsichord. RB530

[————————. Toccata] in G major. [Toccata for clavichord.] RB533

Ganz, Rudolf. A Woman's Last Word. Song for [high] voice with piano. RB578

————————. A Woman's Last Word. Song for [medium] voice with piano. RB577

Gaul, Harvey B. A Sonnet from the Portuguese. Chorus for male choir (TTBB) with piano. EBB229

Geisler, Paul. Der Rattenfänger von Hameln. Piano solo for four hands. RB320

Gelrud, Paul. Love. Song for [medium] voice, unacc. RB66

Gilberté, Hallett. Ah! Love but a Day. Song for high voice with piano. RB188

————————. Ah! Love but a Day. Song for low voice with piano. RB187

Gilchrist, W. W. All Service Ranks the Same with God. Song for [medium] voice with keyboard. RB387

————————. Pippa's Song. Chorus for unison voices with piano. RB388

Giorza, Paolo. Love Me. Song for mezzo soprano or baritone with piano. EBB39

—————. Love Me. Song for soprano or tenor with piano. EBB40

Glarum, L. Stanley. How Do I Love Thee. Part-song for mixed chorus (SATB), unacc. EBB230

Goatley, Alma. Now That April's There. Song for soprano or tenor with piano. RB119

Godard, Benjamin. Pan Pastorale. Piano solo. EBB49

Goldsworthy, W. A. How Do I Love Thee. Setting for women's chorus (SSA) and alto soloist with piano. Two part-songs and one song. EBB231

Goodeve, Mrs. Arthur. If Thou Must Love Me. Song for [low] voice with piano. EBB141

Goodrich, Arthur, librettist. RB486

Gow, George Coleman. "Colombe." Piano solo. RB62

—————. "Colombe's Birthday," Intermezzo Music. RB62, RB245, and RB389

—————. "Give Her but a Least Excuse to Love Me." Part-song for women's voices (SSAA), unacc. RB389

—————. Intermezzo Music to "Colombe's Birthday." Piano solo. RB62

—————. Misconceptions. Part-song for women's voices (SSAA), unacc. RB245

—————. "Valence." Piano solo. RB62

—————. Wedding March. Piano solo. RB62

—————. "The Year's at the Spring." Song for [medium high] voice with piano. RB389

—————. "You'll Love Me Yet." Part-song for women's voices (SSAA) with piano. RB389

Grace, Harvey. The Year's at the Spring. Song for mezzo soprano with piano. RB390

Gracey, Wm. Adolphe. Sleep on, Baby, on the Floor. Part-song for vocal quartet (SATB), unacc. EBB77

Graham, A. Cyril. Love Has Come. Song for [high] voice with keyboard. RB228

—————. The Piper of Hamelin. Cantata. Piano-vocal score. RB321

Gregory, E. C. Apparitions. Song for [medium] voice with keyboard. RB551

—————. James Lee's Wife. Song for [high] voice with keyboard. RB189

————————. A Lover's Quarrel. Song for [medium high] voice with keyboard. RB229

————————. Misconceptions. Song for [medium] voice with keyboard. RB246

————————. One Way of Loving. Song for [medium] voice with keyboard. RB277

————————. Song. Song for [medium high] voice with keyboard. RB502

Hadley, Henry. The Face of All the World Has Changed. Song for [high] voice with keyboard. EBB115

————————. How Do I Love Thee? Song for high voice with piano. EBB232

————————. Nevermore Alone. Song for high voice with keyboard. EBB107

————————. Nevermore Alone. Song for [medium] voice with keyboard. EBB108

————————. Prospice. Song for medium voice with piano. RB459

————————. Rabbi Ben Ezra. Part-song for mixed chorus (SATB), unacc. RB471

————————. There's a Woman Like a Dew-drop. Song for [medium] voice with keyboard. RB13

————————. The Year's at the Spring. Song for [medium] voice with keyboard. RB391

————————. You'll Love Me Yet. Song for high voice with keyboard. RB392

Hageman, Richard. Tragödie in Arezzo (Caponsacchi). Opera. Piano-vocal score. RB486

Hall, William D. Let Down the Bars, O Death. Part-song for mixed chorus (SATB), unacc. EBB36

Halley, Margaret A. "As Flowers in Rain." RB393 and RB394

————————. To Perfect the Summer. Song for [high] voice with piano. RB211

————————. To Perfect the Summer. Song for [medium] voice with keyboard. RB210

————————. The Year's at the Spring. Song for [high] voice with piano. RB394

————————. The Year's at the Spring. Song for [medium] voice with piano. RB393

Hawley, Charles B. I Only Can Love Thee. Song for low voice with keyboard. EBB26

Henius, Joseph, editor. Sonata in A major. Baldassare Galuppi. Piano sonata. RB531

——————. Sonata in D major. Baldassare Galuppi. Piano sonata. RB532

Herbert, Victor, editor. EBB28, EBB253, and EBB278

Hervey, Augusta E. Unless. Song for [medium] voice with piano. EBB279

Herz, Maria. Pippa Passes (Pippa's Lied). Song for [medium] voice with piano. RB399

Hill, Mildred J. My Star. Song for [medium] voice with piano. RB258

Hinkle, Daisy. Home Thoughts from Abroad. Song for mezzo soprano with piano. RB120 and RB121

Hirsch, Carl. Der Rattenfänger von Hameln. [Cantata] with piano and organ. RB322

Hoberg, Margaret. Such a Starved Bank of Moss (Apparitions). Song for soprano or tenor with keyboard. RB552

Hoffman, Rud. RB338

Hollander, Benoit. Summum Bonum. Song for [medium] voice with piano. RB519

Hollins, Dorothea. Boot and Saddle. Song for [medium] voice with keyboard. RB52

——————. The Year's at the Spring. Song for mezzo soprano with keyboard. RB400

Homer, Sidney. My Star. Song for high voice with piano. RB259

——————. My Star. Song for low voice with piano. RB260

——————. Prospice. Song for high voice with piano. RB460

——————. Prospice. Song for low voice with piano. RB461

——————. There's Heaven Above. Song for high voice with piano. RB214

——————. A Woman's Last Word. Song for high voice with piano. RB579

Hopkins, Franklin. How Do I Love Thee. Song for [high] voice with keyboard. EBB233

——————. The Isle Enchantress. Song for [high] voice with piano. RB173

Hopkins, Joseph M. How Do I Love Thee? Song for high voice with piano. EBB234

Howe, Julia Ward. Oh, the Little Birds Sang East. Song for [low] voice with piano. EBB67

Howorth, Wayne, arranger. Ah, Love, but a Day. Daniel Protheroe. Part-song for male chorus (TTBB) with piano. RB195

Hubrich, N. Mitchell, librettist. RB312

Hudson, Henry. The Pied Piper of Hamelin. Cantata. Piano-vocal score. RB323

Hughes, Rupert. A Gondolier's Song. Song for [high] voice with piano. RB153

Huhn, Bruno. Faith. Song for [high] voice with keyboard. RB289

——————. A Meditation. Part-song for male chorus (TTBB) with organ or piano. RB215

Hullah, John. The Lost Leader. Song for [medium low] voice with piano. RB226

——————. The Lost Leader, "Just for a Handful of Silver He Left Us." Song for [medium low] voice with piano. RB225

Hurless, Don. The Pied Piper of Hamelin. Cantata. Piano-vocal score. RB324

Huss, Henry H., editor. EBB28, EBB253, and EBB278

Iles, Edward. Nay but Do You Not Love Her. Song for [medium] voice with piano. RB503

Inches, Charles. Summum Bonum. Song for [medium] voice with piano. RB520

Italiener, H., librettist. RB331

Ives, Charles. From "Paracelsus." Song for [medium] voice with keyboard. RB290

——————. Robert Browning Overture. Overture for orchestra. Study score. RB487

Jenkins, Elizabeth, arranger. How Do I Love Thee. Mary Passailaigue. Song for [medium] voice with keyboard. EBB240

Jervis-Read, H. V. My Mistress. Song for [medium] voice with piano. RB504

Johnson, F. Arthur. Song from Pippa Passes. Song for [high] voice with piano. RB401-RB403

Johnson, Helen Kendrick, editor. EBB28, EBB253, and EBB278

Johnson, Leslie. "Only Sleep," a Slumber Song. Song for [medium high] voice with keyboard. RB580

——————. A Woman's Last Word. Song for [medium low] voice with piano. RB581

Johnson, Noel. All the Bloom of the Year (Summum Bonum). Song for [high] voice with piano. RB521

Johnstone, Harry. Pippa's Song. Song for [medium high] voice with keyboard. RB404

Jordan, Jules. Love's Confidence. Song for soprano or tenor with piano. RB405

Jowett, Albert. Love's Surrender. Song for low voice with piano. RB582

——————. A Woman's Last Word. Song for high voice with piano. RB583

Kaiser, Charles A. Ashes. Song for soprano with keyboard. EBB102

——————. A Cuckoo Song. Duet for soprano and tenor with keyboard. EBB161

——————. A New Rhythm. Song for tenor with keyboard. EBB116

——————. Not Death, but Love. Duet for soprano and tenor with keyboard. EBB84

——————. A Paean of Love. Duet for soprano and tenor with keyboard. EBB129

——————. Seven Sonnets from the Portuguese. Song cycle for soprano and tenor with keyboard. EBB84, EBB102, EBB116, EBB129, EBB161, EBB164, and EBB206

——————. Three Kisses. Song for soprano with keyboard. EBB206

——————. United. Duet for soprano and tenor with keyboard. EBB164

Kastner, Willy, translator. EBB288

Kellie, Lawrence. Say Never Ye Loved Once. Song for [medium] voice with piano. EBB37

Kernochan, Marshall Rogers. Ah, Love, but a Day. Revised edition. Song for medium voice with keyboard. RB191

——————. At the Window. Song for medium voice with piano. RB192

——————. Give a Rouse! Song for medium voice with piano. RB38

——————. King Charles. Part-song for male chorus (TTBB) with piano. RB39

——————. Round Us the Wild Creatures. Song for medium voice with piano. RB87

——————. A Serenade at the Villa. Song for medium voice with piano. RB493

——————. Wanting Is—What? Song for [high] voice with piano. RB212

——————. You'll Love Me Yet. Song for [medium high] voice with piano. RB406 and RB407

Klein, Bruno Oscar. If I Leave All for Thee. Song for [high] voice with piano. EBB197

Klein, Manuel. The Pied Piper. Operatic fantasy. Piano-vocal score. RB325

Knickerbocker, Kenneth Leslie, editor. RB533

Kobbé, Gustav. To Horse! Song for [medium] voice with keyboard. RB53

Komter, Jan Maarten. In a Gondola. Song for [medium] voice with guitar. RB154

Kramer, A. Walter. At Evening. Prelude for piano. RB227

——————. The Patriot. Song for high voice with piano. RB302

——————. The Patriot. Song for low voice with piano. RB301

Krug, Arnold. The Pied Piper of Hamelin Pipes and Disappears with the Children in the Mountain. Piano solo. RB326

Krull, Fritz. Epilogue. Song for [medium high] voice with keyboard. RB76 and RB77

——————. I Go to Prove My Soul. Song for [high] voice with keyboard. RB291

——————. Round Us the Wild Creatures. Song for [high] voice with keyboard. RB88

——————. Such a Starved Bank of Moss. Song for [high] voice with keyboard. RB553

Lee, E. Markham. The Year's at the Spring. Part-song for women's chorus (SA) with piano. RB408

Lehmann, Liza. Incident of the French Camp. Song for [low] voice with piano. RB172

——————. Love, If You Knew the Light. Song for low voice with piano. RB230

——————. Prospice. Song for low voice with piano. RB462

Lewando, Ralph. A Denial. Song for [high] voice with keyboard. EBB10

Lewis, Ella V. The Year's at the Spring. Song for [medium] voice with piano. RB409

Lewis, Leo Rich. A King Lived Long Ago. Song for medium voice with piano. RB410

————. Symphonic Prelude to Robert Browning's Tragedy, a Blot in the 'Scutcheon. Symphonic prelude for orchestra. Full score. RB14

Liddle, Samuel. King Charles. Song for [high] voice with piano. RB40

Lidgey, C. A. Women and Roses. Choral setting for mixed chorus (SATB) and orchestra. Piano-vocal score. RB590

Lippé, Edouard. How Do I Love Thee. Song for high voice with piano. EBB236

————. How Do I Love Thee. Song for low or medium voice with piano. EBB235

Löhr, Harvey. Summum Bonum. Song for [high] voice with piano. RB522

Löhr, Hermann. Sweet, Thou Hast Trod on a Heart! Song for [medium] voice with piano. EBB14

Loomis, Harvey Worthington. Morning Song. Song for [high] voice with keyboard. RB411

Loughridge, Jean M. Pippa's Song. Song for unison children's chorus with piano. RB412 and RB413

Lynes, Frank. Apparitions. Song for high voice with keyboard. RB554

Mc Conathy, Osbourne, [compiler]. RB395

McDaniel, William J. How Do I Love Thee. Song for [high] voice with keyboard. EBB237

Mc. Hardy, James M. P. Life in a Love. Song for [high] voice with piano. RB223

McLeod, Robert. March Them Along. Song for unison boys chorus with piano. RB26

Mackenzie, Alexander C. "One Who Never Turned His Back." Song for [medium] voice with piano. RB78 and RB79

————. There's a Woman Like a Dew-drop. Song for [high] voice with harp or piano. RB15

Maclean, Alick. Hold Me with a Charm. Song for [medium] voice with piano. RB584

MacMillan, Ernest. Sonnet. Song for [medium] voice with keyboard. EBB142

Macmillen, Francis. The Year's at the Spring. Song for high voice with piano. RB414

Madsen, Dora L. Rabbi Ben Ezra. [Song for medium voice] with keyboard. RB472

——————————. Sonnet. Song for [high] voice with keyboard. EBB238

Mallinson, Albert. All the Breath and the Bloom of the Year. Song for [high] voice with piano. RB523

Mana-Zucca. A Query. Song for high voice with piano. RB100

——————————. That Was I. Song for high voice with piano. RB494

Manney, Charles Fonteyn. Transformations ("Such a Starved Bank of Moss"). Song for mezzo soprano or baritone with keyboard. RB555

Markham, Robert Alexander. How Do I Love Thee. Song for soprano with piano. EBB239

Martin, Margaret R. The Children's Skipping Dance. Dance for children, flute, and keyboard. RB327

——————————. The Dance of the Rats. Dance for children with flute or piccolo and keyboard. RB328

——————————. The Pied Piper of Hamelin. [Musical play] with flute or piccolo and keyboard. RB327-RB329

——————————. The Story. Recitation for reader, children, and keyboard. RB329

Marzials, Théo. Leaving Yet Loving. Song for [medium high] voice with keyboard. EBB27 and EBB28

Mason, Mrs. Alexander O. The Year's at the Spring (Song from Pippa Passes). Song for soprano with keyboard. RB415

Mayer, Max. Pippa's Song. Song for [medium] voice with piano. RB416

Metcalf, C. S. Ah Love, but a Day. Song for [medium] voice with piano. RB193

Metcalf, John W. The Cares of Yesterday. Song for soprano or tenor with piano. EBB56 and EBB57

Metcalfe, W. A Year's Spinning. Song for [medium] voice with piano. EBB288

Miessner, W. Otto, [compiler]. RB395

Millar, A. F. My Star. Song for [low] voice with piano. RB261

Miller, Anne Stratton. Parting at Morning. Song for [medium] voice with piano. RB296

Miller, Karl. Inclusions. Song for [medium] voice with piano. EBB19

Miller, Lewis. Suite for Pied Piper. Trio for flute, double bass, and piano. Piano-conductor's score. RB330

Mills, Edward. Never Call It Loving. Song for [medium] voice with piano. EBB280

Mokrejs, John. You'll Love Me Yet (Song from Pippa Passes). Song for [medium] voice with keyboard. RB417

Molineux, Maria Ada. In the Campagna. Arranged by Harry Lawson Harts. Song for [medium] voice with keyboard. RB534 and RB535

—————. In the Campagna. Song for [medium] voice, unacc. RB536

—————. Thy Face. Arranged by Harry Lawson Harts. Song for [high] voice with keyboard. RB556 and RB558

—————. Thy Face. Song for [high] voice with keyboard. RB557

Moore, Francis, arranger. The Year's at the Spring. Mrs. H. H. A. Beach. Part-song for male chorus (TTBB) with piano. RB348

Moore, Mary Carr. Saul. Setting for reader, violin, cello, and piano. RB489

—————. Suite for Strings and Piano. Suite for string quartet and piano. RB490

Morgan, W. A., compiler. RB404

Mozart, W. A. You'll Love Me Yet. Song for [medium] voice, unacc. RB418

Mueller, Carl F. Grow Old Along with Me. Part-song for mixed chorus [SATBB], unacc. RB473

Neale, (Rev.) J. M., translator. RB81

Needham, Alicia Adélaïda. Unless. Song for [high] voice with piano. EBB281

Neidlinger, W. H. My Star: "All That I Know of a Certain Star." Song for soprano or tenor with piano. RB262

—————. Thy Face. Song for baritone or mezzo soprano with piano. RB559

—————. The Year's at the Spring. Song for soprano or tenor with piano. RB419

Neuendorff, Adolf. The Rat-Charmer of Hamelin. Comic opera. Piano-vocal score. RB331

Nevin, Ethelbert. The Lark Is on the Wing. Piano solo. RB420

—————. The Wedding Morn. Song for high voice with piano. RB421

Nichols, Robert, lyricist. RB422

Nicholson, Alfred. That Day. Song for [medium] voice with keyboard. RB264

Nicholson, Mary E. That May Morn. Song for [medium] voice with piano. RB560

Nisbet, Ola Jones, adaptor. All Service Ranks the Same with God. Mary E. Watson. Song for [medium] voice, unacc. RB447

——————, editor. *Browning's Pippa Passes.* RB353, RB418, RB446-RB449

Nisbet, Ola Jones; and Watson, Mary E. A King Lived Long Ago. Song for [high] voice, unacc. RB448 and RB449

Norén, Helmer. "Alone." RB422

——————. The Year's at the Spring. Song for [high] voice with piano. RB422

Oldroyd, George. Tresses. Song for [high] voice with piano. RB505

Olds, W. B. A King Lived Long Ago. Song for medium voice with keyboard. RB423

——————. The Page's Song. Song for [medium] voice with keyboard. RB424

Ormerod, H. J. How They Brought the Good News from Ghent to Aix. Song for baritone with piano. RB130

Ormsby, George F. Love Me Sweet. Song for [medium high] voice with piano. EBB41

Parker, Horatio, [compiler]. RB395

Parker, Phyllis Norman. Unless. Song for [high] voice with piano. EBB283

——————. Unless. Song for [medium] voice with piano. EBB282

Parker, Willetta. Pippa's Song. Song for [medium] voice with piano. RB425

Parry, C. Hubert H. The Pied Piper of Hamelin. [Cantata.] Piano-vocal score. RB332

Pascal, Florian. The House of Clouds. Song for [high] voice with piano. EBB16

——————. Inclusions. Song for [medium high] voice with piano. EBB20

——————. Love Me, Sweet. Song for [high] voice with piano. EBB42

——————. No Little Flower. Song for [medium] voice with piano. EBB266

——————. Proof and Disproof. Song for [medium] voice with piano. EBB64

——————. There Is No One Beside Thee. Song for [medium high] voice with piano. EBB29

——————. White Lilies. Song for [high] voice with piano. EBB5

——————. Wisdom Unapplied. Song for [high] voice with piano. EBB269

Pascal, Julian. Ah, Love, but a Day. Song for medium voice with piano. RB194

Passailaigue, Mary. How Do I Love Thee. Song for [medium] voice with keyboard. Arranged by Elizabeth Jenkins. EBB240

Patterson, Janie Alexander. "There Is No One Beside Thee." Song for [medium] voice with keyboard. EBB30

Patton, Arthur. Insufficiency. Song for [medium high] voice with piano. EBB31

Paulsen, P. Marinus. The Tale of the Pied Piper. Operetta-pageant with keyboard. RB333

Peabody, Josephine Preston, librettist. RB319

Pease, Alfred H. A Year's Spinning. Song for [high] voice with keyboard. EBB289

Peel, Graham. Boot, Saddle, to Horse. Song for [high] voice with piano. RB54

Perrin, H. C. Pan's Pipes. Ballad for mixed chorus (SATB) and orchestra. Piano-vocal score. EBB50

Philp, Elizabeth. "Inclusions." Song for [high] voice with keyboard. EBB21

——————. "Insufficiency." Song for [medium] voice with keyboard. EBB32

——————. Sweetest Eyes. Song for [medium] voice with piano. EBB2

Pickard-Cambridge, W. A. Nay, but You Who Do Not Love Her. Song for low or middle voice with keyboard. RB506

Pierce, Allie Coleman. How Do I Love Thee. Song for [high] voice with keyboard. EBB241

Ponssen, Mary Eleanor. Question and Answer. Song for [high] voice with keyboard. EBB66

Porter, Charlotte, editor. RB99, RB253, and RB511

Priaulx, Joseph M., editor. EBB28, EBB253, and EBB278

Protheroe, Daniel. Ah, Love, but a Day. Arranged by Wayne Howorth. Part-song for male chorus (TTBB) with piano. RB195

—————————. Ah, Love, but a Day. Song for high voice with keyboard. RB196

—————————. How Do I Love Thee. Song for medium voice with keyboard. EBB242

—————————. I Send My Heart Up to Thee. Song for high voice with keyboard. RB155

—————————. Out in the Fields. Part-song for male chorus (TTBB), unacc. EBB58

—————————. Out in the Fields. Part-song for mixed chorus (SATB) with piano. EBB59

—————————. The Year's at the Spring. Song for high voice with keyboard. RB426

Raif, Oscar, [transcriber]. RB336

Ralston, Frances Marion. Ay! Note That Potter's Wheel. Piano solo with choral monotone accompaniment (SSAA) and soprano soloist. RB475

—————————. But I Need Now As Then. Song for alto with piano. RB475

—————————. For Note When Evening Shuts. Part-song for women's chorus (SSAA) with piano. RB475

—————————. For Pleasant Is This Flesh. Song for soprano with piano. RB475

—————————. Grow Old Along with Me. Part-song for women's chorus (SSAA) with piano. RB475

—————————. Not That, Amassing Flowers. Part-song for women's chorus (SSAA) with piano. RB475

—————————. Now Who Shall Arbitrate. Song for [medium high] voice with keyboard. RB474

—————————. Now Who Shall Arbitrate. Song for soprano with piano. RB475

—————————. Rabbi Ben Ezra. [Cantata] with piano. RB475. *See also* RB474

—————————. Saul. Oratorio with pipe organ or piano. RB491

—————————. So Still within This Life. Vocal quartet for two treble voices and two bass voices, unacc. RB475

—————————. So Take and Use Thy Work. Part-song for two women's choruses (SSAA) (SSAA) with piano. RB475

—————————. Then Welcome Each Rebuff. Song for alto with piano. RB475

————————. Yet Gifts Should Prove Their Use. Part-song for women's chorus (SSAA) with piano. RB475

————————. Youth Ended. Song for mezzo soprano with piano. RB475

Raphael, Juliet. A Woman's Last Word. Recitation for reader with keyboard. RB585

Rathbone, George. The Pied Piper of Hamelin. Cantata. Piano-vocal score. RB334

Raymond, Ralph. A Last Word. Song for [medium high] voice with piano. RB586 and RB587

Reed, C. H. Cavalier Song. Song for [high] voice with piano. RB55

————————. Meeting at Night. Song for [high] voice with piano. RB237

————————. Parting at Morning. Song for [high] voice with piano. RB297

Reinagle, Caroline. I Would That You Were All to Me. Song for [medium] voice with piano. RB537

————————. In a Year. Song for [medium] voice with piano. RB171

————————. This Is a Spray the Bird Clung To. Song for [medium] voice with piano. RB247

————————. Would It Were I Had Been False, Not You! Song for [high] voice with piano. RB591

Renaud, Emiliano. All's Right with the World. Song for [high] voice with piano. RB427

————————. Love Me Forever. Song for [high] voice with piano. RB67

————————. My Star. Song for [high] voice with piano. RB263

————————. You'll Love Me Yet. Song for [high] voice with piano. RB428

Rhodes, Harold. A Woman's Love. Song for [high] voice with keyboard. EBB243

Rilke, Rainer Maria, translator. EBB85, EBB90, EBB98, EBB118, and EBB184

Robbins, Reginald C. Sonnet from the Portuguese. Song for [medium low] voice with keyboard. EBB164.1

————————. The Wanderers. Song for [medium low] voice with keyboard. RB291.1

Robyn, Alfred G. "Good to Forgive." Song for mezzo soprano or baritone with piano. RB216

Rogers, Clara Kathleen. Ah, Love, but a Day. Song for [medium] voice with piano. RB197

—————————. Apparitions. Song for [medium] voice with piano. RB561

—————————. Appearances. Song for [high] voice with keyboard. RB6

—————————. Good to Forgive. Song for [high] voice with keyboard. RB217

—————————. I Have a More Than Friend. Song for [medium] voice with piano. EBB68

—————————. Love. Song for [high] voice with piano. RB68

—————————. My Star. Song for [high] voice with keyboard. RB264

—————————. One Way of Love. Song for [high] voice with keyboard. RB278

—————————. Out of My Own Great Woe. Song for [medium] voice with piano. EBB62

—————————. "Overhead the Tree-tops Meet." Song for [medium] voice with keyboard. RB429

—————————. Summum Bonum. Song for [medium] voice with piano. RB524

—————————. A Woman's Last Word. Song for [high] voice with keyboard. RB588

—————————. The Year's at the Spring. Song for [medium high] voice with piano. RB430

Rogers, James H. Boot and Saddle—Cavalier Song. Song for high voice with piano. RB57

—————————. Boot and Saddle—Cavalier Song by Robert Browning. Song for tenor with piano. RB56

—————————. I Go to Prove My Soul. Song for [medium high] voice with keyboard. RB293

—————————. I Go to Prove My Soul. Song for medium voice with piano. RB292

Rohrer, Mildred. Pippa Passes. Song for [low] voice with keyboard. RB431

Roper, E. Stanley, editor. RB63

Rorem, Ned. In a Gondola. Song for high voice with piano. RB156

—————————. Pippa's Song. Song for high voice with piano. RB432

Rossman, Floy Adele. The Year's at the Spring. Part-song for women's chorus (SSAA) with piano. RB433

Rowley, Alec. Oh to Be in England. Duet for [high] voice and [medium low] voice with keyboard. RB122

Roy, William. How Do I Love Thee. Song for high voice with piano. EBB246

——————. How Do I Love Thee. Song for medium voice with piano. EBB245

Royle, Popplewell. Summum Bonum. Song for [high] voice with piano. RB525

Ryan, Margaret. Meeting at Night. Song for high voice with piano. RB238

Saar, Louis Victor. Browning Song Cycle from Letters of R. B. to E. B. B. Song cycle for high voice with piano. RB219

——————. The Rose Tree. Song for high voice with piano. RB219

——————. Some Happy Day. Song for high voice with piano. RB219

——————. This Little Flower. Song for high voice with piano. RB219

——————. Thou Shalt Know Me. Song for high voice with piano. RB219

——————. Thou Wilt Know. Song for high voice with piano. RB219

Sabin, Wallace A. Pan. Song for high or medium voice with piano. EBB51

Saminsky, Lazare. Venezia. [Symphonic poem] for orchestra. Conductor's score. RB157

Sarson, H. M. The Year's at the Spring. Part-song for children's chorus (SS), unacc. RB434

Sarson, May. Cavalier Song. Song for unison voices with keyboard. RB57.1

Schaefer, Hal. "I Yield the Grave for Thy Sake." Song for [medium high] voice with keyboard. EBB169

Scharfenberg, Wm., revisor. EBB49

Scheu-Riesz, Helene, lyricist. RB338

Schlesinger, Sebastian B. Unless. Song for [medium] voice with keyboard. EBB284

Schmidt, Louis. All's Right with the World. Song for [medium] voice with piano. RB435

Schneider, F. H., translator. RB222

Schuyler, Georgina. Grow Old Along with Me. Song for mezzo soprano or contralto with piano. RB476 and RB477

——————. In a Gondola. Song for mezzo soprano or contralto with piano. RB158

————————. In a Gondola. Song for mezzo soprano with piano. RB159

————————. The Page Sings to the Queen. Song for mezzo soprano or contralto with piano. RB436

————————. This Is a Spray the Bird Clung To. Song for mezzo soprano or contralto with piano. RB248

————————. Venetian Serenade. Song for contralto or baritone with piano. RB160

Sears, Marie. *See* Hammer, Marie von

Shapleigh, Bertram. O to Be in England. Song for contralto with piano. RB123

Sharpe, Cedric. The Year's at the Spring. Song for [medium high] voice with piano. RB437

Shaw, Martin, editor. RB213, RB444, and RB479

Shillington, Mary. Apparitions. Song for [medium] voice with piano. RB562

Simon, E., transcriber. RB338

Slater, Gordon. For Life, with All It Yields. Short anthem for mixed chorus (SATB) with organ. RB63

Sloper, Lindsay, editor. EBB3

Smith, David Stanley. Pan. Chorus for women's choir (SSA), soprano solo, oboe (or flute) obbligato with piano. EBB52

Smith, Fannie Morris, editor. EBB28, EBB253, and EBB278

Smith, Gerrit, editor. EBB28, EBB253, and EBB278

Smith, Leo. My Star. Song for [high] voice with piano. RB265

Smith, Lewis Worthington. In a Gondola. Duet for tenor and alto with keyboard. RB161

Somervell, Arthur. After. Song for [medium] voice with piano. RB4

————————. Among the Rocks. Song for contralto solo with orchestra. Piano-vocal score. RB205

————————. A Broken Arc. Song cycle for [medium] voice or [medium high] voice with piano. RB4, RB70, RB239, RB266, RB438, RB507, RB563, and RB592

————————. By the Fireside. Song for contralto solo with orchestra. Piano-vocal score. RB201

————————. From "Easter Day." Song for [medium] voice with piano. RB70

—————. In the Doorway. Song for contralto solo with orchestra. Piano-vocal score. RB203

—————. James Lee's Wife. Song cycle for contralto solo with orchestra. Piano-vocal score. RB198, RB201, and RB203-RB205

—————. James Lee's Wife Speaks at the Window. Song for contralto solo with orchestra. Piano-vocal score. RB198

—————. Meeting at Night. Song for [medium high] voice with piano. RB239

—————. My Star. Song for [medium high] voice with piano. RB266

—————. Nay, but You, Who Do Not Love Her. Song for [medium high] voice with piano. RB507

—————. On the Cliff. Song for contralto solo with orchestra. Piano-vocal score. RB204

—————. Such a Starved Bank of Moss. Song for [medium high] voice with piano. RB563

—————. The Worst of It. Song for [medium high] voice with piano. RB592

—————. The Year's at the Spring. Song for [medium high] voice with piano. RB438

Spencer, Fanny M. Unless. Song for mezzo soprano or baritone with keyboard. EBB285

—————. Unless. Song for tenor or soprano with keyboard. EBB286

Spencer-Welch, Sylvia, translator. RB338

Spier, La Salle. And You Are Ever by Me. Song for [medium high] voice with string quartet and piano. RB439

—————. But Winter Hastens at Summer's End. Song for [medium high] voice with string quartet and piano. RB439

—————. A Cycle of Six Songs from Pippa Passes. Song cycle for [medium high] voice with string quartet and piano. RB439

—————. Day! Song for [medium high] voice with string quartet and piano. RB439

—————. New-Year's Hymn. Song for [medium high] voice with string quartet and piano. RB439

—————. Oh, What a Drear, Dark Close to My Poor Day! Song for [medium high] voice with string quartet and piano. RB439

—————. Overhead the Treetops Meet. Song for [medium high] voice with string quartet and piano. RB439

Stanford, Charles Villiers. Boot, Saddle, to Horse and Away. Song for baritone solo, male chorus (TTBB), with piano. RB58

—————. King Charles. Song for baritone solo, male chorus (TTBB) with piano. RB41

—————. Marching Along. Song for baritone solo, male chorus (TTBB) with piano. RB28

—————. May's Love. Song for [high] voice with keyboard. EBB45

—————. Prospice. Song for [medium high] voice with piano. RB463 and RB464

Stebbins, G. Waring. Meeting. Song for high voice with piano. RB240

Stephens, Ward. You'll Love Me Yet. Song for [high] voice with piano. RB440

Sternberg, Daniel Arie. Pippa's Song. Song for high voice with keyboard. RB441

Stewart, Humphrey J. Best of All. Song for [high] voice with piano. RB526

Stisted, Maria E. H. Dost Thou Love Me, My Beloved? Song for [medium] voice with piano. EBB65

Stock, E. Elliot, librettist. RB310

Stoker, Richard. Here's the Spring Back. Part-song for women's chorus (SSA), unacc. RB231

Stothart, Herbert. "Wilt Thou Have My Hand." Song for medium voice with keyboard, specifically "on a spinet." EBB22

Stratton, G. R. Boot, Saddle, to Horse, and Away. Song for [high] voice with piano. RB59

—————. Boot, Saddle, to Horse, and Away. Song for [medium high] voice with piano. RB60

Stults, R. M., arranger. Avenge the Good Ship Maine. [Robert and Elizabeth Barrett] Browning. Song for [medium high] voice with keyboard. RB7.1

Surinach, Carlos. How Do I Love Thee? Song for [high] voice with piano. EBB247

—————. If Thou Must Love Me. Song for [high] voice with piano. EBB143

—————. Our Two Souls. Song for [high] voice with piano. EBB165

—————. With Thee Anear. Song for [high] voice with piano. EBB117

——————. I Send My Heart Up to Thee. Song for [high] voice with keyboard. RB163

——————. The Moth's Kiss and the Bee's Kiss. Song for [high] voice with keyboard. RB164

——————. My Star. Song for [medium] voice with keyboard. RB267

——————. Overhead the Treetops Meet. Song for [medium] voice with keyboard. RB443.

——————. Prospice. Song for [high] voice with keyboard. RB468

——————. Prospice. Song for [medium] voice with keyboard. RB467

Truman, Ernest. The Pied Piper. Cantata Grotesque. Piano-vocal score. RB335

Turner, Nancy Byrd, lyricist. RB71

Urban, Heinrich. Der Rattenfänger von Hameln. Fantasy for piano. RB336

Vaille, Clara Hinman. Death Is a Door. Song for [high] voice with keyboard. RB71

Vannah, Kate. Questionings. Song for soprano with keyboard. EBB24

Vaughan Williams, Ralph, editor. Songs of Praise. RB213, RB444, and RB479

——————. Spring. Hymn for SATB, unacc. RB444

——————. Then Welcome Each Rebuff. Hymn for SATB, unacc. RB479

Versel, Louis. Since We Parted. Song for high voice with piano. RB495

Vogler, [Georg Joseph]. The Request. Song for [high] voice with keyboard. RB2 and RB3

Walthew, Richard H. The Pied Piper of Hamelin. [Cantata.] Piano-vocal score. RB337

Warburg, Frederic S. Silver Linings. Song for [medium] voice with piano. EBB267

Ware, Harriet. How Do I Love Thee. Song for high voice with piano. EBB249 and EBB250

Warner, H. Waldo. The Cares of Yesterday. Trio for women's chorus (SSA) with keyboard. EBB60

Warren, Jeanne. Pippa's Holiday (Danse Grotesque). Piano solo. RB445

Watson, Mary E. All Service Ranks the Same with God. Adapted by Ola Jones Nisbet. Song for [medium] voice, unacc. RB447

__________. All Service Ranks the Same with God. Hymn for [medium] voice, unacc. RB447

__________. And More of It. Recitation for speaker, violin, and harp. RB447

__________. Day. Recitation for speaker, violin, and harp. RB447

__________. Give Her but a Least Excuse to Love Me. Song for [high] voice, unacc. RB446 and RB447

__________. I Am Queen of Thee, Floweret! Song for [high] voice, unacc. RB447

__________. Incidental Music to *Pippa's Soliloquy*. Incidental music for speaker, [high] voice, [medium] voice, violin, and harp. RB447

__________. Let the Watching Lids Wink. Song for [medium] voice, unacc. RB447

__________. Overhead the Tree Tops Meet. Song for [high] voice, unacc. RB447

__________. Worship Whom Else? Recitation for speaker, violin, and harp. RB447

Watson, Mary E.; and Nisbet, Ola Jones. A King Lived Long Ago. Song for [high] voice, unacc. RB448 and RB449

Watts, Isaac, lyricist. RB275

Weems, Mrs. J. Eddie. The Browning Cycle of Love Lyrics. Song cycle for [low] voice, [medium] voice, or [medium high] voice with keyboard. EBB251, RB69, and RB268

__________. How Do I Love Thee. Song for [low] voice with keyboard. EBB251

__________. Love. Song for [medium high] voice with keyboard. RB69

__________. My Star. Song for [medium] voice with keyboard. RB268

Weigl, Karl. Der Rattenfänger von Hameln. Operetta. Piano-vocal score. RB338

Welch, Jay. All Service Ranks the Same with God. Song for soprano, oboe, harp, and clarinet. RB450

__________. [Give Her the Least Excuse to Love Me.] Clarinet solo with oboe and harp. RB450

__________. Give Her the Least Excuse to Love Me. Song for soprano, oboe, clarinet, and harp. RB450

__________. A King Lived Long Ago. Song for soprano with oboe and harp. RB450

—————. Music for Robert Browning's Pippa Passes. Incidental music for oboe, clarinet, harp, soprano, [medium] voice, and [low] voice. RB450

—————. Night Wind. Prelude for harp. RB450

—————. Overhead the Treetops Meet. Song for soprano with harp. RB450

—————. Prelude. Prelude for oboe, clarinet, and harp. RB450

—————. The Year's at the Spring. Song for soprano with harp. RB450

—————. You'll Love Me Yet. Song for [medium] voice, unacc. RB450

Wellesz, Egon. Du bist da draben im Palast begehrt. Song for soprano and string quartet. EBB98

—————. Ich denk an dich, wie wilder Wein den Baum spriessend umringt. Song for soprano and string quartet. EBB184

—————. Mir scheint, das Angesicht der Welt verging—in einem andern. Song for soprano and string quartet. EBB118

—————. Nur drei jedoch in Gottes ganzem All vernahmen es. Song for soprano and string quartet. EBB90

—————. Sonette der Elisabeth Barret-Browning. Songs for soprano and string quartet. EBB85, EBB90, EBB98, EBB118, and EBB184

—————. Und es geschah mir einst, an Theokrit zu denken. Song for soprano and string quartet. EBB85

White, Grace. Three Descriptions from Browning, no. 1. Solo for violin with piano. RB241

—————. Three Descriptions from Browning, no. 2. Solo for violin with piano. RB124

—————. Three Descriptions from Browning, no. 3. Solo for violin with piano. RB298

White, Maude Valérie. Home Thoughts from Abroad. Song for [medium high] voice with piano. RB125

—————. How Do I Love Thee. Song for [high] voice with keyboard. EBB255

—————. How Do I Love Thee. Song for mezzo soprano, baritone, or [medium] voice with keyboard. EBB252, EBB253, and EBB254

—————. King Charles, Cavalier Song. Song for [medium] voice with piano. RB42

—————. Love Me, Sweet, with All Thou Art. Song for [low] voice with piano. EBB43

__________. Marching Along. Song for [high] voice with piano. RB31

__________. Marching Along. Song for [medium] voice with piano. RB30

__________. What I Do, and What I Dream. Song for [medium] voice with piano. EBB109

Whitmer, T. Carl. "Ah! Love, but a Day." Song for mezzo soprano with piano. RB199

__________. "My Star." Song for mezzo soprano with piano. RB269

__________. Song from Pippa Passes. Song for mezzo soprano with piano. RB451

Whitney, Maurice C. Meeting at Night. Part-song for mixed chorus (SATB) with piano. RB242

__________. Meeting at Night. Part-song for women's chorus (SSA) with piano. RB243

Wiant, Bliss, editor. Then Welcome Each Rebuff. Hymn for SATB, unacc. RB480 and RB481

Wiant, W. R. Exile. Cantata with piano. EBB11

__________. Prelude to Exile. Ballet-prelude. Piano-conductor's score. EBB11.1

Wickins, Florence. Oh, to Be in England! Duet for mezzo soprano and baritone with piano. RB126

Willan, Healey. Sonnet, "When Our Two Souls Stand Up Erect and Strong." Song for [high] voice with piano. EBB166

Williams, Fred, librettist. RB331

Wilson, Alec. Oh! To Be in England. Song for [high] voice with piano. RB127

Wilson, Harry Robert. All's Right with the World. Part-song for mixed chorus (SATB) with piano. RB452

Wodell, Frederick W. A Venetian Night. Cantata with piano. RB165

Wood, Charles. Eden Spirits. Cantata with piano. EBB12

Woolley, C. A Woman's Last Word. Song for [medium] voice with keyboard. RB589

Worth, John W. Ah Love, but a Day. Song for [medium] voice with keyboard. RB200

__________. Barcarola. Piano solo. RB166

__________. Bird Spirit. Song for medium voice with keyboard. EBB13

—————————. Dip Your Arm o'er the Boatside. Song for soprano with piano. RB166

—————————. Evelyn Hope. Song for [high] voice with keyboard. RB84

—————————. Four Songs from Pippa Passes. Songs for [high] voice with keyboard. RB453

—————————. Give Her but a Least Excuse to Love Me. Song for [high] voice with keyboard. RB453

—————————. Gondoliera in Lontanza. Piano solo. RB166

—————————. Good to Forgive. Song for [high] voice with keyboard. RB218

—————————. I Send My Heart Up to Thee. Song for tenor with piano. RB166

—————————. In a Gondola. [Song cycle] for soprano, tenor, reader, and piano. RB166

—————————. Infant Voices. Song for medium voice with keyboard. EBB13

—————————. It Was Ordained to Be So. Song for tenor with piano. RB166

—————————. A King Lived Long Ago. Song for [high] voice with keyboard. RB453

—————————. Meeting at Night. Song for [medium] voice with keyboard. RB244

—————————. Misconceptions. Song for [high] voice with keyboard. RB249

—————————. The Moth's Kiss, First. Song for soprano with piano. RB166

—————————. My Star. Song for [high] voice with keyboard. RB270

—————————. Oh, Which Were Best to Roam or Rest. Recitation for reader with piano. RB166

—————————. Overhead the Tree-tops Meet. Song for [high] voice with keyboard. RB453

—————————. Parting at Morning. Song for [high] voice with keyboard. RB299

—————————. Past We Glide. Song for tenor with piano. RB166

—————————. The Patriot. Song for [high] voice with keyboard. RB303

—————————. Prelude. Piano solo. RB166

—————————. Row Home? Must We Row Home. Recitation for reader with piano. RB166

————————. Say after Me, and Try to Say My Very Words. Recitation for reader with piano. RB166

————————. Song of the Morning Star to Lucifer. Song for medium voice with keyboard. EBB13

————————. Three Songs. Songs for medium voice with keyboard. EBB13

————————. To-morrow, If a Harp-String, Say. Song for soprano with piano. RB166

————————. What Are We Two. Song for tenor with piano. RB166

————————. What If the Three. Recitation for reader with piano. RB166

————————. The Year's at the Spring. Song for [high] voice with keyboard. RB453

Woyrsch, Felix von. Erinnerung. Song for medium voice with piano. RB339

————————. Nach Hameln! Song for medium voice with piano. RB339

————————. Die Nächste. Song for medium voice with piano. RB339

————————. Nun stellt euch auf, ihr Kinderlein. Song for medium voice with piano. RB339

————————. Rattenfänger Lieder. Songs for medium voice with piano. RB339

————————. Eine Rose gepflückt! Song for medium voice with piano. RB339

————————. Röslein, wann blühst du auf? Song for medium voice with piano. RB339

————————. Stelldichein. Song for medium voice with piano. RB339

————————. Waldesruh. Song for medium voice with piano. RB339

————————. Wenn du kein Spielmann wärst! Song for medium voice with piano. RB339

————————. Wo ich mich zeige. Song for medium voice with piano. RB339

Young, Dal. Dip Your Arm o'er the Boatside. Song for soprano with piano. RB167

————————. I Send My Heart Up to Thee. Song for tenor with piano. RB167

————————. In a Gondola. Song cycle for tenor and soprano with piano. RB167

————————. In a Gondola. Song for soprano with piano. RB168

——————. The Moth's Kiss. Song for soprano with piano. RB167 and RB168

——————. Past We Glide. Song for tenor with piano. RB167

——————. Pippa's Song ("The Year's at the Spring"). Song for [high] voice with piano. RB454

——————. Say after Me. Duet for soprano and tenor with piano. RB167

——————. There's Zanse's Vigilant Taper. Duet for soprano and tenor with piano. RB167

——————. What Are We Two? Song for tenor with piano. RB167

——————. What If the Three. Song for tenor with piano. RB167

Zuckerman, Augusta. *See* Mana-Zucca

V

Title Entry

Key to Abbreviations

acc.	accompanied
SA	soprano, alto
SAB	soprano, alto, bass
SATB	soprano, alto, tenor, bass
SATBB	soprano, alto, tenor, bass I, bass II
SS	soprano I, soprano II
SSA	soprano I, soprano II, alto
SSAA	soprano I, soprano II, alto I, alto II
SS-AA	soprano, soprano-alto, alto
SSAATTBB	soprano I, soprano II, alto I, alto II, tenor I, tenor II, bass I, bass II
TTBB	tenor I, tenor II, bass I, bass II
TTBBBB	tenor I, tenor II, baritone I, baritone II, bass I, bass II
unacc.	unaccompanied

For the complete description and explanation of this chapter, read page 5 of Chapter I.

Abt Vogler. True, Latham. Recitation for reader with piano. RB1

Accompanied Readings. RB1

Accuse Me Not, Beseech Thee. Freer, Eleanor Everest. Song for medium voice with keyboard. EBB144 and EBB145

Der Adler. *See* The Eagle

Advanced Piano Compositions for Small Hands. RB315

Aeolian Series of Choral Music. EBB58 and EBB59

After. Somervell, Arthur. Song for [medium] voice with piano. RB4

Ah, Love, but a Day. Beach, Mrs. H. H. A. Duet for soprano and tenor with keyboard. RB175

——————. Beach, Mrs. H. H. A. Edited and arranged by William Creston. Part-song for women's chorus (SSA) with piano. RB178

——————. Beach, Mrs. H. H. A. Song for mezzo soprano or baritone with piano. RB176 and RB177

——————. Beach, Mrs. H. H. A. Song for soprano or tenor with keyboard. RB174

——————. Borton, Alice. Song for high voice with keyboard. RB179

——————. Cain, Noble. Part-song for women's chorus (SSA) with piano. RB180

——————. De Francesco, Louis E. Ballad for high voice with keyboard. RB181

——————. De Francesco, Louis E. Ballad for medium voice with keyboard. RB182

——————. De Francesco, Louis E. Song for [medium] voice with keyboard. RB183

——————. Gilberté, Hallett. Song for high voice with piano. RB188

——————. Gilberté, Hallett. Song for low voice with piano. RB187

——————. Kernochan, Marshall Rogers. Revised edition. Song for medium voice with keyboard. RB191

——————. Metcalf, C. S. Song for [medium] voice with piano. RB193

——————. Pascal, Julian. Song for medium voice with piano. RB194

——————. Protheroe, Daniel. Arranged by Wayne Howorth. Part-song for male chorus (TTBB) with piano. RB195

——————. Protheroe, Daniel. Song for high voice with keyboard. RB196

——————. Rogers, Clara Kathleen. Song for [medium] voice with piano. RB197

——————. Whitmer, T. Carl. Song for mezzo soprano with piano. RB199

——————. Worth, John W. Song for [medium] voice with keyboard. RB200

Album No. Fifty. EBB25 and EBB63

Album of Songs. RB158, RB248, RB436, and RB476

Album of Ten Songs. RB522

The All-Loving. England, Nick. Song for baritone, reader, and piano. RB80

All Service Ranks the Same with God. Gilchrist, W. W. Song for [medium] voice with keyboard. RB387

——————. Watson, Mary E. Adapted by Ola Jones Nisbet. Song for [medium] voice, unacc. RB447

——————. Watson, Mary E. Hymn for [medium] voice, unacc. RB447

——————. Welch, Jay. Song for soprano, oboe, harp, and clarinet. RB450

All That I Know of a Certain Star. *See also* My Star

All That I Know of a Certain Star. Freer, Eleanor Everest. Song for baritone with keyboard. RB255

All the Bloom of the Year (Summum Bonum). Johnson, Noel. Song for [high] voice with piano. RB521

All the Breath and the Bloom of the Year. Mallinson, Albert. Song for [high] voice with piano. RB523

All's Right, "The Year's at the Spring." Behrend, A. H. Song for soprano with keyboard. RB351

All's Right with the World. del Riego, Teresa. Song for [meduim] voice with piano. RB375

——————. Renaud, Emiliano. Song for [high] voice with piano. RB427

——————. Schmidt, Louis. Song for [medium] voice with piano. RB435

——————. Wilson, Harry Robert. Part-song for mixed chorus (SATB) with piano. RB452

"Alone." RB422

Among the Rocks. Somervell, Arthur. Song for contralto solo with orchestra. Piano-vocal score. RB205

——————. True, Latham. Song for [medium] voice with keyboard. RB206

Amphibian. Bantock, Granville. Piano solo. RB106

And More of It. Watson, Mary E. Recitation for speaker, violin, and harp. RB447

And Therefore If to Love Can Be Desert. Freer, Eleanor Everest. Song for mezzo soprano or medium voice with keyboard. EBB131, EBB132, and EBB133

And Wilt Thou Have Me Fashion into Speech. Freer, Eleanor Everest. Song for medium voice with keyboard. EBB136 and EBB137

And Yet, Because Thou Overcomest So. Freer, Eleanor Everest. Song for medium voice with keyboard. EBB146 and EBB147

And You Are Ever by Me. Spier, La Salle. Song for [medium high] voice with string quartet and piano. RB439

The Anglo French Unison and Part Songs. RB408

Apparitions. *See also* Such a Starved Bank of Moss

Apparitions. Bates, Anna Craig. Song for [high] voice with keyboard. RB538

——————. Clarke, Helen A. Song for [medium high] voice with keyboard. RB541

——————. Craddock, Reginald W. Song for medium voice with piano. RB543

——————. Downing, Lulu Jones. Song for medium voice with keyboard. RB545

——————. Freer, Eleanor Everest. Song for [high] voice or tenor with keyboard. RB547 and RB548

——————. Frey, Adolf. Song for [high] voice with keyboard. RB550

——————. Gregory, E. C. Song for [medium] voice with keyboard. RB551

——————. Lynes, Frank. Song for high voice with keyboard. RB554

——————. Rogers, Clara Kathleen. Song for [medium] voice with piano. RB561

——————. Shillington, Mary. Song for [medium] voice with piano. RB562

——————. Tedaldi, F. Song for [medium] voice with keyboard. RB564

Appearances. Rogers, Clara Kathleen. Song for [high] voice with keyboard. RB6

Arthur P. Schmidt's Octavo Edition. EBB60

"As Flowers in Rain." RB394

As I Ride ("Through the Metidja to Abd-el-Kadr"). Bantock, Granville. Song for [medium] voice with piano. RB527

Ashes. Kaiser, Charles A. Song for soprano with keyboard. EBB102

At Evening. Kramer, A. Walter. Prelude for piano. RB227

At the Midnight in the Silence of the Sleep-time. *See* Epilogue, "At the Midnight in the Silence of the Sleep-time"

At the Window. Gabriel, Virginia. Song for [high] voice with piano. RB185

—————. Gabriel, Virginia. Song for [medium low] voice with piano. RB186

—————. Kernochan, Marshall. Song for medium voice with piano. RB192

Ausonia (Italian Pages). RB157

Avenge the Good Ship Maine. Browning, [Robert and Elizabeth Barrett]. Arranged by R. M. Stults. Song for [medium high] voice with keyboard. RB7.1

Ay! Note That Potter's Wheel. Ralston, Frances Marion. Piano solo with choral monotone accompaniment (SSAA) and soprano soloist. RB475

Ballade (Childe Roland to the Dark Tower Came). Bantock, Granville. Piano solo. RB61

Balliol College Song Book. RB74

The Balliol Song Book. RB103

Barcarola. Worth, John W. Piano solo. RB166

Be a God and Hold Me. Dichmont, William. Song for high voice with piano. RB575

A Bean-Stripe: Also, Apple Eating. Bantock, Granville. Song for [high] voice with piano. RB101

Because Thou Hast the Pow'r and Own'st the Grace. Freer, Eleanor Everest. Song for medium voice with keyboard. EBB207 and EBB208

The Bells of Hamelin. Brydson, John C. Piano solo. RB311

Beloved, My Beloved, When I Think. Freer, Eleanor Everest. Song for medium voice with keyboard. EBB154 and EBB155

Beloved, Thou Hast Brought Me Many Flowers. Freer, Eleanor Everest. Song for medium voice with keyboard. EBB257 and EBB258

Belwin Choral Series. RB178

The Best Is Yet to Be. Branscombe, Gena. Song for soprano or tenor with keyboard. RB470

Best of All. Stewart, Humphrey J. Song for [high] voice with piano. RB526

Bird Spirit. Worth, John W. Song for medium voice with keyboard. EBB13

Bist du mein? *See* Dost Thou Love Me

Boat-Song. Barnett, Alice. Song for high voice with piano. RB134

Ein Bohnenstreifen. *See* A Bean-Stripe: Also, Apple Eating

Boot and Saddle. Bantock, Granville. Part-song for male chorus (TTBB), unacc. RB43

—————————. Branscombe, Gena. Song for medium voice with piano. RB44

—————————. Dansie, Redgewell. Song for [medium high] voice with piano. RB45

—————————. Demuth, Norman. Boot and Saddle. Song for unison chorus with piano. RB46

—————————. Drakeford, Louis. Song for [medium high] voice with piano. RB47

—————————. Hollins, Dorothea. Song for [medium] voice with keyboard. RB52

Boot and Saddle—Cavalier Song. Rogers, James H. Song for high voice with piano. RB57

Boot and Saddle—Cavalier Song by Robert Browning. Rogers, James H. Song for tenor with piano. RB56

Boot, Saddle, to Horse. Peel, Graham. Song for [high] voice with piano. RB54

Boot, Saddle, to Horse, and Away! Dyson, George. Song for unison chorus with piano. RB48

—————————. Easson, James. Song for unison chorus with piano. RB49

—————————. Harrison, Julius. Song for baritone with piano. RB51

—————————. Harrison, Julius. Song for tenor or baritone with piano. RB50

—————————. Stanford, Charles Villiers. Song for baritone solo, male chorus (TTBB), and piano. RB58

—————————. Stratton, G. R. Song for [high] voice with piano. RB59

—————————. Stratton, G. R. Song for [medium high] voice with piano. RB60

The Boy and the Angel. Beringer, Marjorie. Chant for [unison] voice[s] with unspecified keyboard [?] instrument. RB16

Breitkopf and Härtel's Choruses for Mens Voices. RB224

A Broken Arc. Somervell, Arthur. Song cycle for [medium] voice or [medium high] voice with piano. RB4, RB70, RB239, RB266, RB438, RB507, RB563, and RB592

The Browning Cycle of Love Lyrics. Weems, Mrs. J. Eddie. Song cycle for [low] voice, [medium] voice, or [medium high] voice with keyboard. EBB251, RB69, and RB268

Browning Song Cycle from Letters of R. B. to E. B. B. Saar, Louis Victor. Song cycle for high voice with piano. RB219

Browning Songs. RB163, RB164, RB206, RB267, RB442, RB443, RB467, and RB468

Browning Songs, First Series. EBB62, EBB68, RB197, RB430, RB524, and RB561

Browning Songs, Second Series. RB6, RB68, RB217, RB264, RB278, and RB588

The Brownings Go to Italy. EBB1, EBB81, EBB94, EBB125, EBB158, EBB225, RB255, RB382, RB501, and RB549

Browning's Pippa Passes. RB353, RB418, and RB446-RB449

But I Need Now As Then. Ralston, Frances Marion. Song for alto with piano. RB475

But Love. Cowley, Elsie M. Song for [low] voice with piano. RB131

"But Only Three in All God's Universe." Branscombe, Gena. Song for medium voice with piano. EBB86

————. Freer, Eleanor Everest. Song for mezzo soprano or medium voice with keyboard. EBB87, EBB88, and EBB89

[But Only Three in All God's Universe.] Nur drei jedoch in Gottes ganzem All vernahmen es. Wellesz, Egon. Song for soprano and string quartet. EBB90

But Winter Hastens at Summer's End. Spier, La Salle. Song for [medium high] voice with string quartet and piano. RB439

By the Fireside. Bantock, Granville. Song for high voice with piano. RB17

————. Bantock, Granville. Song for low voice with piano. RB18

————. Somervell, Arthur. Solo for contralto with orchestra. Piano-vocal score. RB201

Caliban upon Setebos. Bantock, Granville. Piano solo. RB19

A Camel-Driver. Bantock, Granville. Song for [medium] voice with piano. RB94

Can It Be Right to Give What I Can Give? Freer, Eleanor Everest. Song for mezzo soprano or medium voice with keyboard. EBB122, EBB123, and EBB124

Caponsacchi. *See also* Tragödie in Arezzo (Caponsacchi)

"Caponsacchi." Cooley, Carlton. Epic poem for orchestra. Conductor's score. RB485

The Cares of Yesterday. Metcalf, John W. Song for soprano or tenor with piano. EBB56 and EBB57

——————. Warner, H. Waldo. Trio for women's chorus (SSA) with keyboard. EBB60

Cavalier Song. Reed, C. H. Song for [high] voice with piano. RB55

——————. Sarson, May. Song for unison voices with keyboard. RB57.1

Cavalier Tunes by Robert Browning. RB23, RB34, and RB45

Change upon Change. Gabriel, Virginia. Song for [high] voice with piano. EBB3

The Changing Year. Fuller, Caroline M. Song for contralto or bass with keyboard. RB184

Cherries. Bantock, Granville. Song for [high] voice with piano. RB96

A Child Asleep. Elgar, Edward. Song for [medium high] voice with keyboard. EBB4

Childe Roland to the Dark Tower Came. *See* Ballade (Childe Roland to the Dark Tower Came)

The Children. Brydson, John C. Piano solo. RB311

The Children Follow. Dunhill, Thomas F. Piano solo. RB316

The Children's Skipping Dance. Martin, Margaret R. Dance for children, flute, and keyboard. RB327

A Child's Thought on God. Treharne, Bryceson. Song for high or medium voice with piano. EBB6

Choral Compositions. EBB230

Christian Fellowship Hymns. RB480 and RB481

A Collection of Glees and Part-Songs for Male Voices. *See* The Orpheus

"Colombe." Gow, George Coleman. Piano solo. RB62

"Colombe's Birthday," Intermezzo Music. RB62, RB245, and RB389

Comfort. Broun, Harry. Hymn for SATB, unacc. EBB7

——————. Coleridge-Taylor, S. Song for contralto with keyboard. EBB8

Compositions. RB417

Compositions for Pianoforte. EBB49

A Cuckoo Song. Kaiser, Charles A. Duet for soprano and tenor with keyboard. EBB161

A Cycle of Six Songs from Pippa Passes. Spier, La Salle. Song cycle for [medium high] voice with string quartet and piano. RB439

The Dance of the Rats. Martin, Margaret R. Dance for children with flute or piccolo and keyboard. RB328

Day! Spier, La Salle. Song for [medium high] voice with string quartet and piano. RB439

——————. Watson, Mary E. Recitation for speaker, violin, and harp. RB447

Death Is a Door. Vaille, Clara Hinman. Song for [high] voice with keyboard. RB71

A Denial. Lewando, Ralph. Song for [high] voice with keyboard. EBB10

Devotion. Boys, Reginald S. Song for [medium] voice with keyboard. RB570

——————. Forrester, J. Cliffe. Song for [high] voice with piano. RB499

Dip Your Arm o'er the Boatside. Barnett, Alice. Song for high voice with piano. RB135

——————. Worth, John W. Song for soprano with piano. RB166

——————. Young, Dal. Song for soprano with piano. RB167

Dost Thou Love Me. Cowen, Frederic H. Song for [high] voice with piano. EBB63

Dost Thou Love Me, My Beloved? Stisted, Maria E. H. Song for [medium] voice with piano. EBB65

Dramatic Lyrics by Robert Browning. RB110, RB111, RB114, RB115, RB169, RB170, RB251, RB252, RB273, and RB274

Du bist da draben im Palast begehrt. Wellesz, Egon. Song for soprano and string quartet. EBB98

Duets. RB518

The Eagle. Bantock, Granville. Song for [high] voice with piano. RB85

The Early Sonata Forms . . . of the Seventeenth and Eighteenth Centuries. RB531 and RB532

Earth Fades! Heaven Breaks on Me. Coleridge-Taylor, S. Song for low voice with piano. RB513 and RB514

Easter Day. *See* From "Easter Day"

Eden Spirits. Wood, Charles. Cantata with piano. EBB12

Eight Songs. Mayer, Max. RB416

————————. Pascal, Florian. EBB5, EBB16, EBB20, EBB29, EBB42, EBB64, EBB266, and EBB269

————————. Warburg, Frederic S. EBB267

English Songs, Book II. RB376

English Songs, Book III. RB128

English Songs, Second Series. RB397

Entreaty. Barlow, Emily. Song for [medium] voice with piano. RB567

Epilog. *See* Epilogue [from Ferishtah's Fancies]

Epilogue, "At the Midnight in the Silence of the Sleep-time." Farmer, John. Song for unison chorus with piano. RB74

Epilogue [from *Asolando*]. Farmer, John. Song for unison chorus with piano. RB75

————————. Krull, F. Song for [medium high] voice with keyboard. RB76 and RB77

Epilogue [from Ferishtah's Fancies]. Song for [high] voice with piano. RB102

Epithalamium. Berdahl, Arthur C. Song for [high] voice with keyboard. RB539

Erinnerung. Woyrsch, Felix von. Song for medium voice with piano. RB339

Evelyn. Ellingham, Harry. Song for [medium high] voice with keyboard. RB83

Evelyn Hope. Worth, John W. Song for [high] voice with keyboard. RB84

Exile. Wiant, W. R. Cantata with piano. EBB11

The Face of All the World Has Changed. Hadley, Henry. Song for [high] voice with keyboard. EBB115

"The Face of All the World Is Changed." Branscombe, Gena. Song for medium voice with piano. EBB111

The Face of All the World Is Changed, I Think. Freer, Eleanor Everest. Song for mezzo soprano or medium voice with keyboard. EBB112, EBB113, and EBB114

[The Face of All the World Is Changed, I Think.] Mir scheint, das Angesicht, der Welt verging—in einem andern. Wellesz, Egon. Song for soprano and string quartet. EBB118

Faith. Huhn, Bruno. Song for [high] voice with keyboard. RB289

Die Familie. *See* The Family

The Family. Bantock, Granville. Song for [high] voice with piano. RB91

Festival Music. RB73

Fifine at the Fair. Bantock, Granville. Orchestral drama with a prologue. Miniature score. RB105

Fifty Rote-Songs for Little Singers. RB412 and RB413

Fifty Unaccompanied Love Songs for Solo Voice. *See* Two Leaves of Green

First Time He Kissed Me, He but Only Kissed. Freer, Eleanor Everest. Song for medium voice with keyboard. EBB204 and EBB205

The First Time That the Sun Rose on Thine Oath. Freer, Eleanor Everest. Song for medium voice with keyboard. EBB189 and EBB190

Five Songs. Fisher, William Arms. EBB138

————————. Hadley, Henry K., op. 20. EBB107, EBB108, EBB232, and RB392

————————. Hadley, Henry [K.], op. 44. EBB115 and RB391

————————. Hammer, Marie von. EBB268

————————. Smith, Leo. RB265

————————. Treharne, Bryceson. EBB6

Flamenco Meditations. EBB117, EBB130, EBB143, EBB165, and EBB247

For Life, with All It Yields. Slater, Gordon. Short anthem for mixed chorus (SATB) with organ. RB63

For Love's Sake Only. Fisher, William Arms. Song for high voice with piano. EBB138

For Note When Evening Shuts. Ralston, Frances Marion. Part-song for women's chorus (SSAA) with piano. RB475

For Pleasant Is This Flesh. Ralston, Frances Marion. Song for soprano with piano. RB475

Four Cavalier Tunes. RB25, RB37, RB50, and RB51

Four Moods from Browning. *See* Pippa Passes, Four Moods from Browning

Four Songs. Freer, Eleanor Everest. RB547

————————. Frey, Adolf. RB550

————————. Manney, Charles Fonteyn. RB553

Four Songs by Robert Browning. RB67, RB263, RB427, and RB428

Four Songs from Pippa Passes. Worth, John W. Songs for [high] voice with keyboard. RB453

Four Sonnets. *See* The Soul's Expression (Four Sonnets)

From "Easter Day." Somervell, Arthur. Song for [medium] voice with piano. RB70

From "Paracelsus." Ives, Charles. Song for [medium] voice with keyboard. RB290

G. S. Octavo Choruses. RB473

G. Schirmer's Secular Choruses. EBB52, EBB157, and EBB229

Gamble's Collection of Secular Part Songs. EBB110

Gaudeamus: Songs for Colleges and Schools. RB75 and RB104

Give a Rouse. Arnott, A. Davidson. Song for baritone or bass with keyboard. RB32

——————. Bantock, Granville. Part-song for male chorus (TTBB), unacc. RB33

——————. Dansie, Redgewell. Song for [medium high] voice with piano. RB34

——————. de Sousa, Leon. Song for [medium] voice with piano. RB35

——————. Drakeford, Louis. Song for [medium high] voice with piano. RB36

——————. Kernochan, Marshall. Song for medium voice with piano. RB38

Give Her but a Least Excuse. Clarke, H[ugh] A. Song for [high] voice with keyboard. RB367

"Give Her but a Least Excuse to Love Me." Gow, George Coleman. Part-song for women's voices (SSAA), unacc. RB389

——————. Watson, Mary E. Song for [high] voice, unacc. RB446 and RB447

——————. Worth, John W. Song for [high] voice with keyboard. RB453

Give Her but the Least Excuse to Love Me. True, Latham. Song for [medium] voice with keyboard. RB442

[Give Her the Least Excuse to Love Me.] Welch, Jay. Clarinet solo with oboe and harp. RB450

——————. Welch, Jay. Song for soprano, oboe, clarinet, and harp. RB450

Go from Me. Yet I Feel That I Shall Stand. Freer, Eleanor Everest. Song for mezzo soprano or medium voice with keyboard. EBB104, EBB105, and EBB106

God's in His Heaven. Easson, James. Two-part round, unacc. RB377 and RB378

God's Own Smile. Farley, Roland. Song for high voice with piano. RB546

Gold Hair. Bantock, Granville. Piano solo. RB109

Gondoliera in Lontanza. Worth, John W. Piano solo. RB166

A Gondolier's Song. Hughes, Rupert. Song for [high] voice with piano. RB153

Good News from Ghent. Hattersley, F. Kilvington. Ballad for mixed chorus (SATB) with keyboard. RB129

Good News to Aix. Duncan, Edmondstoune. Song for [high] voice with piano. RB128

"Good to Forgive." Robyn, Alfred G. Song for mezzo soprano or baritone with piano. RB216

——————. Rogers, Clara Kathleen. Song for [high] voice with keyboard. RB217

——————. Worth, John W. Song for [high] voice with keyboard. RB218

"Grand March." Avison, Charles. Solo for unspecified keyboard [?] instrument. RB294

Grief. Coleridge-Taylor, S. Song for contralto with keyboard. EBB15

Grow Old Along with Me. Mueller, Carl F. Part-song for mixed chorus [SATBB], unacc. RB473

——————. Ralston, Frances Marion. Part-song for women's chorus (SSAA) with piano. RB475

——————. Schuyler, Georgina. Song for mezzo soprano or contralto with piano. RB476 and RB477

——————. True, Latham. Song for [medium] voice with keyboard. RB478

The Guardian Angel. Bantock, Granville. Song for high voice with piano. RB111

——————. Bantock, Granville. Song for low voice with piano. RB110

Hamelin Town's in Brunswick. Dunhill, Thomas F. Piano solo. RB316

Hanover Square, a Magazine of New Copyright Music. EBB3

Harold Flammer Choral Series, Secular Three-Part Choruses for Women's Voices. RB180 and RB359

————————. Cain, Noble. Part-song for mixed chorus (SSAATTBB), unacc. EBB218

————————. Colvin, Herbert. Song for [high] voice with keyboard. EBB219 and EBB220

————————. Davis, Blevins. Song for [medium] voice with keyboard. EBB221

————————. Dello Joio, Norman. Song for high voice with keyboard. EBB223 and EBB224

————————. Dello Joio, Norman. Song for low voice with piano. EBB222

————————. Freer, Eleanor Everest. Duet for mezzo soprano and baritone with keyboard. EBB225

————————. Freer, Eleanor Everest. Song for medium voice with keyboard. EBB226 and EBB227

————————. Gabert, Abel. Song for mezzo soprano or baritone with piano. EBB228

————————. Glarum, L. Stanley. Part-song for mixed chorus (SATB), unacc. EBB230

————————. Goldsworthy, W. A. Setting for women's chorus (SSA), alto solo, and piano. Two-part songs and one song. EBB231

————————. Hadley, Henry K. Song for high voice with piano. EBB232

————————. Hopkins, Franklin. Song for [high] voice with keyboard. EBB233

————————. Hopkins, Joseph M. Song for high voice with piano. EBB234

————————. Lippé, Edouard. Song for high voice with piano. EBB236

————————. Lippé, Edouard. Song for low or medium voice with piano. EBB235

————————. McDaniel, William J. Song for [high] voice with keyboard. EBB237

————————. Markham, Robert Alexander. How Do I Love Thee. Song for soprano with piano. EBB239

————————. Passailaigue, Mary. Arranged by Elizabeth Jenkins. Song for [medium] voice with keyboard. EBB240

————————. Pierce, Allie Coleman. Song for [high] voice with keyboard. EBB241

————————. Protheroe, Daniel. Song for medium voice with keyboard. EBB242

————————. Roy, William. Song for high voice with piano. EBB246

I Lift My Heavy Heart Up Solemnly. Freer, Eleanor Everest. Song for mezzo soprano or medium voice with keyboard. EBB99, EBB100, and EBB101

I Lived with Visions for My Company. Freer, Eleanor Everest. Song for medium voice with keyboard. EBB174 and EBB175

I Loved You. Ayres, Harold. Song for [medium] voice with keyboard. RB82

I Never Gave a Lock of Hair Away. Freer, Eleanor Everest. Song for medium voice with keyboard. EBB150 and EBB151

I Once Thought How Theocritus Had Sung. Freer, Eleanor Everest. Song for mezzo soprano with keyboard. EBB80

I Only Can Love Thee. Hawley, Charles B. Song for low voice with keyboard. EBB26

I See Thine Image thro' My Tears Tonight. Freer, Eleanor Everest. Song for medium voice with keyboard. EBB185 and EBB186

I Send My Heart. Ayres, Harold. Song for [high] voice with keyboard. RB132

I Send My Heart Up to Thee! Beach, Mrs. H. H. A. Song for low voice with keyboard. RB142

—————————. Beach, Mrs. H. H. A. Song for soprano or tenor with keyboard. RB143

—————————. Protheroe, Daniel. Song for high voice with keyboard. RB155

—————————. True, Latham. Song for [high] voice with keyboard. RB163

—————————. Worth, John W. Song for tenor with piano. RB166

—————————. Young, Dal. Song for tenor with piano. RB167

I Send My Heart Up to Thee (Serenade). Branscombe, Gena. Song for soprano or tenor with keyboard. RB146

I Stoop into a Dark Tremendous Sea of Cloud. De Lacey, Robert. Anthem for bass and alto soloists, mixed chorus (SATB), and organ. RB285

I Thank All Who Have Loved Me in Their Hearts. Freer, Eleanor Everest. Song for medium voice with keyboard. EBB211 and EBB212

I Think of Thee! My Thoughts Do Twine and Bud. Freer, Eleanor Everest. Song for medium voice with keyboard. EBB182 and EBB183

[I Think of Thee!—My Thoughts Do Twine and Bud.] Ich denk an dich, wie wilder Wein den Baum spriessend umringt. Wellesz, Egon. Song for soprano and string quartet. EBB184

[I Thought Once How Theocritus.] Und es geschah mir einst, an Theokrit zu denken. Wellesz, Egon. Song for soprano and string quartet. EBB85

"I Thought Once How Theocritus Had Sung." Branscombe, Gena. Song for medium voice with piano. EBB78

—————. Freer, Eleanor Everest. Song for medium voice or mezzo soprano with keyboard. EBB81, EBB82, and EBB83

I Would That You Were All to Me. Reinagle, Caroline. Song for [medium] voice with piano. RB537

"I Yield the Grave for Thy Sake." Schaefer, Hal. Song for [medium high] voice with keyboard. EBB169

Ich denk an dich, wie wilder Wein den Baum spriessend umringt. Wellesz, Egon. Song for soprano and string quartet. EBB184

If I Leave All for Thee. Klein, Bruno Oscar. Song for [high] voice with piano. EBB197

If I Leave All for Thee, Wilt Thou Exchange. Freer, Eleanor Everest. Song for medium voice with keyboard. EBB195 and EBB196

If I Were Thou. Hammer, Marie von. Song for high voice with piano. EBB268

If Thou Must Love Me. Freer, Eleanor Everest. Song for medium voice with keyboard. EBB139 and EBB140

—————. Goodeve, Mrs. Arthur. Song for [low] voice with piano. EBB141

—————. Surinach, Carlos. Song for [high] voice with piano. EBB143

In a Gondola. Bantock, Granville. Piano solo. RB133

—————. Barnett, Alice. Song cycle for high voice with piano. RB134-RB141

—————. Beach, John. Dramatic monologue for baritone with keyboard. RB144

—————. Bending, Edwin. Duet for soprano and tenor with cello or violin obbligato and piano. RB145

—————. Elman, Mischa. Impromptu for violin with piano. RB150

—————. Hartmann, Arthur. Song for [medium low] voice with keyboard. RB152

—————. Komter, Jan Maarten. Song for [medium] voice with guitar. RB154

—————. Rorem, Ned. Song for high voice with piano. RB156

————————. Schuyler, Georgina. Song for mezzo soprano or contralto with piano. RB158

————————. Schuyler, Georgina. Song for mezzo soprano with piano. RB159

————————. Smith, Lewis Worthington. Duet for tenor and alto with keyboard. RB161

————————. Treharne, Bryceson. Song for [high] voice with piano. RB162

————————. Worth, John W. [Song cycle] for soprano, tenor, reader, and piano. RB166

————————. Young, Dal. Song cycle for tenor, soprano, and piano. RB167

————————. Young, Dal. Song for soprano with piano. RB168

In a Year. Bantock, Granville. Song for high voice with piano. RB169

————————. Bantock, Granville. Song for low voice with piano. RB170

————————. Reinagle, Caroline. Song for [medium] voice with piano. RB171

In Memoriam, Three Rhapsodies. EBB260, EBB261, RB513, and RB514

In My Sleep, "Last Night I Saw You in My Sleep." Bateman, Alice. Song for [low] voice with keyboard. RB8

In the Campagna. Molineux, Marie Ada. Arranged by Harry Lawson Harts. Song for [medium] voice with keyboard. RB534 and RB535

————————. Molineux, Marie Ada. Song for [medium] voice, unacc. RB536

In the Doorway. Galsworthy, Ada. Song for [medium] voice with piano. RB202

————————. Somervell, Arthur. Contralto solo with orchestra. Piano-vocal score. RB203

Incident of the French Camp. Lehmann, Liza. Song for [low] voice with piano. RB172

Incidental Music to *Pippa's Soliloquy.* Watson, Mary E. Incidental music for speaker, [high] voice, [medium] voice, violin, and harp. RB447

Inclusions. *See also* O Wilt Thou Have My Hand, Dear

Inclusions. Pascal, Florian. Song for [medium high] voice with piano. EBB20

————————. Philp, Elizabeth. Song for [high] voice with keyboard. EBB21

————————. Miller, Karl. Song for [medium] voice with piano. EBB19

Indeed This Very Love Which Is My Boast. Freer, Eleanor Everest. Song for medium voice with keyboard. EBB134 and EBB135

Infant Voices. Worth, John W. Song for medium voice with keyboard. EBB13

Insufficiency. Patton, Arthur. Song for [medium high] voice with piano. EBB31

——————. Philp, Elizabeth. Song for [medium] voice with keyboard. EBB32

Insufficiency, (Leaving Yet Loving). Cowen, Frederic H. Song for [medium high] voice with piano. EBB25

Intermezzo Music to "Colombe's Birthday." Gow, George Coleman. Piano solo. RB62

Into the Street. Dunhill, Thomas F. Piano solo. RB316

Is It Indeed So? Freer, Eleanor Everest. Song for medium voice with keyboard. EBB167 and EBB168

Is She Not Pure Gold. Beach, John. Song for [medium] voice with piano. RB497

The Isle Enchantress. Hopkins, Franklin. Song for [high] voice with piano. RB173

It Was Ordained to Be So. Worth, John W. Song for tenor with piano. RB166

It Was Ordained to Be So, Sweet. Barnett, Alice. Song for high voice with piano. RB137

Italian Pages. *See* Ausonia (Italian Pages)

James Lee's Wife. Gregory, E. C. Song for [high] voice with keyboard. RB189

——————. Somervell, Arthur. Song cycle for contralto solo and orchestra. Piano-vocal score. RB198, RB201, and RB203-RB205

James Lee's Wife Speaks at the Window. Somervell, Arthur. Contralto solo with orchestra. Piano-vocal score. RB198

"Jesu, Dulcis Memoria." *See* Love Incarnate

June, and My Lady. del Riego, Teresa. Song for [high] voice with piano. RB108

——————. del Riego, Teresa. Song for [medium] voice with piano. RB107

Just for a Handful of Silver He Left Us. *See* The Lost Leader

Ein Kameltreiber. *See* A Camel-Driver

Kent County Song Book. RB434

King Albert's Book. RB78 and RB79

King Charles. Harrison, Julius. Song for baritone with piano. RB37

——————. Kernochan, Marshall. Part-song for male chorus (TTBB) with piano. RB39

——————. Liddle, Samuel. Song for [high] voice with piano. RB40

——————. Stanford, C. Villiers. Song for baritone solo, male voices (TTBB) with piano. RB41

King Charles, Cavalier Song. White, Maude Valérie. Song for [medium] voice with piano. RB42

A King Lived Long Ago. Lewis, Leo Rich. Song for medium voice with piano. RB410

——————. Olds, W. B. Song for medium voice with keyboard. RB423

——————. Watson, Mary E.; and Nisbet, Ola Jones. Song for [high] voice, unacc. RB448 and RB449

——————. Welch, Jay. Song for soprano with oboe and harp. RB450

——————. Worth, John W. Song for [high] voice with keyboard. RB453

The King's Dancer. Davis, Carlyle. Piano solo. RB374

Kirschen. *See* Cherries

Landbau. *See* Plot-Culture

The Lark Is on the Wing. Nevin, Ethelbert. Piano solo. RB420

Lass Alles ich für dich. *See* If I Leave All for Thee

A Last Word. Raymond, Ralph. Song for [medium high] voice with piano. RB586 and RB587

The Laurel Music-Reader. RB388

The Laurel Song Book. RB471

The Lay of the Brown Rosary. Boyce, Ethel M. Cantata. Piano-vocal score. EBB33

——————. Carse, A. von Ahn. Cantata. Piano-vocal score. EBB34

Leaving Yet Loving. Marzials, Théo. Song for [medium high] voice with keyboard. EBB27 and EBB28

The Legend of the Piper. Freer, Eleanor Everest. Opera. Piano-vocal score. RB319

Let Down the Bars, O Death. Hall, William D. Part-song for mixed chorus (SATB), unacc. EBB36

Let the Watching Lids Wink. Watson, Mary E. Song for [medium] voice, unacc. RB447

Let the World's Sharpness, Like a Clasping Knife. Freer, Eleanor Everest. Song for medium voice with keyboard. EBB170 and EBB171

Let's Contend No More. Dichmont, William. Song for high voice with piano. RB575

Letters. Castelnuovo-Tedesco, Mario. Song for [high] voice with piano. EBB179

Liebesringen. *See* Life in a Love. Bruguiere, E. A.

Life in a Love. Bantock, Granville. Song for high voice with piano. RB220

——————. Bantock, Granville. Song for low voice with piano. RB221

——————. Bruguiere, E. A. Song for [medium] voice with piano. RB222

——————. Mc. Hardy, James M. P. Song for [high] voice with piano. RB223

Little Songs for Little Folks. RB379

The Lost Leader. Bantock, Granville. Part-song for male chorus (TTBB), unacc. RB224

——————. Hullah, John. Song for [medium low] voice with piano. RB226

The Lost Leader, "Just for a Handful of Silver He Left Us." Hullah, John. Song for [medium low] voice with piano. RB225

Lov'd by Thee. Cantor, Otto. Song for alto or baritone with piano. RB571

Love. Gelrud, Paul. Song for [medium] voice, unacc. RB66

——————. Rogers, Clara Kathleen. Song for [high] voice with piano. RB68

——————. Weems, Mrs. J. Eddie. Song for [medium high] voice with keyboard. RB69

Love Has Come. Graham, A. Cyril. Song for [high] voice with keyboard. RB228

Love, If You Knew the Light. Lehmann, Liza. Song for low voice with piano. RB230

Love in a Life. Branscombe, Gena. Song cycle for medium voice with piano. EBB78, EBB86, EBB103, EBB111, EBB176, and EBB217

Love Incarnate. Harwood, Basil. Choral setting for mixed chorus (SSAATTBB), boy sopranos, and organ. RB81

Love Me. Clarke, Robert Coningsby. Song for [high] voice with piano. EBB38

——————. Giorza, Paolo. Song for mezzo soprano or baritone with piano. EBB39

——————. Giorza, Paolo. Song for soprano or tenor with piano. EBB40

Love Me Forever. Renaud, Emiliano. Song for [high] voice with piano. RB67

Love Me Sweet. Ormsby, George F. Song for [medium high] voice with piano. EBB41

——————. Pascal, Florian. Song for [high] voice with piano. EBB42

Love Me, Sweet, with All Thou Art. White, Maude Valérie. Song for [low] voice with piano. EBB43

A Love Story. *See* The Brownings Go to Italy

Loved by Thee. Cantor, Otto. Song for soprano or tenor or high voice with piano. RB572-RB574

A Lover's Quarrel. Gregory, E. C. Song for [medium high] voice with keyboard. RB229

Love's Confidence. Jordan, Jules. Song for soprano or tenor with piano. RB405

Love's Ecstasy. Barbour, Florence Newell. Song for mezzo soprano or baritone with keyboard. EBB202

——————. Barbour, Florence Newell. Song for soprano or tenor with keyboard. EBB203

Love's Surrender. Jowett, Albert. Song for low voice with piano. RB582

Lyrical Songs. RB162

Lyrics from Ferishtah's Fancies. RB85, RB89-RB98, RB101, and RB102

Lyrische Gedichte aus Ferishtah's Fantasien. *See* Lyrics from Ferishtah's Fancies

Madrigal and Minstrelsy. RB585

A Magazine of New Copyright Music. *See* Hanover Square

The Magic Piper. Christopher, Carol. Operetta. Piano-vocal score. RB312

[March.] Avison, Charles. Solo for unspecified keyboard [?] instrument. RB295

March Them Along. McLeod, Robert. Song for unison boys chorus with piano. RB26

Marching Along. Bantock, Granville. Part-song for male chorus (TTBB), unacc. RB20

—————. Boyle, George F. Song for bass with piano. RB21

—————. Branscombe, Gena. Song for medium voice with piano. RB22

—————. Dansie, Redgewell. Song for [medium] voice with piano. RB23

—————. Drakeford, Louis. Song for [medium] voice with piano. RB24

—————. Harrison, Julius. Song for tenor or baritone with piano. RB25

—————. Stanford, C. Villiers. Song for baritone solo, male voices (TTBB) with piano. RB28

—————. Sykes, Harold H. Song for unison chorus (with optional descant) with keyboard. RB29

—————. White, Maude Valèrie. Song for [high] voice with piano. RB31

—————. White, Maude Valèrie. Song for [medium] voice with piano. RB30

"The Mask." Beta. Song for low voice with piano. EBB44

Master Hughes of Saxe-Gotha. Bantock, Granville. Piano solo. RB232

—————. Hathaway, Joseph W. G. Choral rhapsody for mixed chorus (SSAATTBB) with piano. RB233

The Mayor and Corporation. Brydson, John C. Piano solo. RB311

The Mayor Expostulates. Dunhill, Thomas F. Piano solo. RB316

May's Love. Stanford, C. Villiers. Song for [high] voice with keyboard. EBB45

Mazurka. RB528

A Meditation. Huhn, Bruno. Part-song for male chorus (TTBB) with organ or piano. RB215

Meeting. Stebbins, G. Waring. Song for high voice with piano. RB240

Meeting at Night. [Armes, Nancy.] Song for [medium] voice with keyboard. RB234

—————. Dello Joio, Norman. Song for high voice with keyboard. RB235

—————. Fisher, Charles R. Song for [medium high] voice with piano. RB236

—————. Reed, C. H. Song for [high] voice with piano. RB237

—————. Ryan, Margaret. Song for high voice with piano. RB238

————————. Somervell, Arthur. Song for [medium high] voice with piano. RB239

————————. Whitney, Maurice C. Part-song for mixed chorus (SATB) with piano. RB242

————————. Whitney, Maurice C. Part-song for women's chorus (SSA) with piano. RB243

————————. Worth, John W. Song for [medium] voice with keyboard. RB244

The Melon-Seller. Bantock, Granville. Song for [high] voice with piano. RB89

Der Melonenhändler. *See* The Melon-Seller

Midnight. Bantock, Granville. Part-song for male chorus (TTBBBB), unacc. RB73

Mihrab Schach. *See* Mihrab Shah

Mihrab Shah. Bantock, Granville. Song for [high] voice with piano. RB93

Mir scheint, das Angesicht der Welt verging—in einem andern. Wellesz, Egon. Song for soprano and string quartet. EBB118

Misconceptions. Gow, George Coleman. Part-song for women's voices (SSAA), unacc. RB245

————————. Gregory, E. C. Song for [medium] voice with keyboard. RB246

————————. Worth, John W. Song for [high] voice with keyboard. RB249

Modern Piano Solos. RB445

A Monthly Magazine. *See* Music, a Monthly Magazine

Morning at Asolo. Davis, Carlyle. Piano solo. RB374

Morning Song. Loomis, Harvey Worthington. Song for [high] voice with keyboard. RB411

The Moth's Kiss. Barnett, Alice. Song for high voice with piano. RB138

————————. Young, Dal. Song for soprano with piano. RB167 and RB168

The Moth's Kiss and the Bee's Kiss. True, Latham. Song for [high] voice with keyboard. RB164

The Moth's Kiss, First. Worth, John W. Song for soprano with piano. RB166

Music, a Monthly Magazine. RB363

Music for Robert Browning's Pippa Passes. Welch, Jay. Incidental music for oboe, clarinet, harp, soprano, [medium] voice, and [low] voice. RB450

Music for the Examinations of Trinity College of Music, London. RB528

The Music of Tufts College. RB14 and RB410

A Musical Instrument. Downing, Lulu Jones. Recitation for reader with keyboard. EBB48

"My Future Will Not Copy Fair My Past." Freer, Eleanor Everest. Song for medium voice with keyboard. EBB213 and EBB214

My Letters! All Dead Paper, Mute and White! Freer, Eleanor Everest. Song for medium voice with keyboard. EBB180 and EBB181

My Mistress. Jervis-Read, H. V. Song for [medium] voice with piano. RB504

"My Own Beloved." Branscombe, Gena. Song for [medium] voice with piano. EBB176

My Own Beloved, Who Hast Lifted Me. Freer, Eleanor Everest. Song for medium voice with keyboard. EBB177 and EBB178

My Poet, Thou Canst Touch on All the Notes. Freer, Eleanor Everest. Song for medium voice with keyboard. EBB148 and EBB149

My Star. Atkins, Evelyn Harper. Song for [high] voice with violin. RB250

—————. Bantock, Granville. Song for high voice with piano. RB252

—————. Bantock, Granville. Song for low voice with piano. RB251

—————. Clarke, Helen A. Song for [high] voice with piano. RB253 and RB254

—————. Freer, Eleanor Everest. Song for baritone or [medium] voice with keyboard. RB256 and RB257

—————. Hill, Mildred J. Song for [medium] voice with piano. RB258

—————. Homer, Sidney. Song for high voice with piano. RB259

—————. Homer, Sidney. Song for low voice with piano. RB260

—————. Millar, A. F. Song for [low] voice with piano. RB261

—————. Renaud, Emiliano. Song for [high] voice with piano. RB263

—————. Rogers, Clara Kathleen. Song for [high] voice with keyboard. RB264

—————. Smith, Leo. Song for [high] voice with piano. RB265

—————. Somervell, Arthur. Song for [medium high] voice with piano. RB266

—————. True, Latham. Song for [medium] voice with keyboard. RB267

—————. Weems, Mrs. J. Eddie. Song for [medium] voice with keyboard. RB268

—————. Whitmer, T. Carl. Song for mezzo soprano with piano. RB269

—————. Worth, John W. Song for [high] voice with keyboard. RB270

My Star: "All That I Know of a Certain Star." Neidlinger, W. H. Song for soprano or tenor with piano. RB262

Nach Hameln! Woyrsch, Felix von. Song for medium voice with piano. RB339

Die Nächste. Woyrsch, Felix von. Song for medium voice with piano. RB339

Nay but Do You Not Love Her. Iles, Edward. Song for [medium] voice with piano. RB503

Nay but You. Thayer, Arthur W. Song for high voice with piano. RB508

Nay! But You Do Not Love Her. Freer, Eleanor Everest. Song for low voice with piano. RB500

Nay, but You, Who Do Not Love Her. Freer, Eleanor Everest. Song for baritone with keyboard. RB501

—————. Pickard-Cambridge, W. A. Song for low or middle voice with keyboard. RB506

—————. Somervell, Arthur. Song for [medium high] voice with piano. RB507

—————. Toye, Francis. Song for [medium] voice with piano. RB509

Never Call It Loving. Mills, Edward. Song for [medium] voice with piano. EBB280

Never the Time and the Place. Bantock, Granville. Song for high voice with piano. RB272

—————. Bantock, Granville. Song for low voice with piano. RB271

Nevermore Alone. Hadley, Henry K. Song for high voice with keyboard. EBB107

—————. Hadley, Henry K. Song for [medium] voice with keyboard. EBB108

New Letters of Robert Browning. RB533

A New Rhythm. Kaiser, Charles A. Song for tenor with keyboard. EBB116

New Year's Hymn. Beach, John. Song for [medium] voice with keyboard. RB350

————————. Spier, La Salle. Song for [medium high] voice with string quartet and piano. RB439

Night Wind. Welch, Jay. Prelude for harp. RB450

Nine Compositions. RB403

Nine Songs. RB40

Nineteen Songs. RB290

No Little Flower. Pascal, Florian. Song for [medium] voice with piano. EBB266

Not Death, but Love. Kaiser, Charles A. Duet for soprano and tenor with keyboard. EBB84

Not That, Amassing Flowers. Ralston, Frances Marion. Part-song for women's chorus (SSAA) with piano. RB475

Novello's School Songs. RB57.1

Now. Bantock, Granville. Song for high voice with piano. RB274

————————. Bantock, Granville. Song for low voice with piano. RB273

Now That April's There. Goatley, Alma. Song for soprano or tenor with piano. RB119

Now Who Shall Arbitrate. Ralston, Frances Marion. Song for [medium high] voice with keyboard. RB474

————————. Ralston, Frances Marion. Song for soprano with piano. RB475

Nun stellt euch auf, ihr Kinderlein. Woyrsch, Felix von. Song for medium voice with piano. RB339

Nur drei jedoch in Gottes ganzem All vernahmen es. Wellesz, Egon. Song for soprano and string quartet. EBB90

O Bell' Andare. Browning, Robert. Two-part chorus for children's voices [SA], unacc. RB510, RB511, and RB512

O God, Our Help. Croft, William. Hymn for SATB, unacc. RB275

O Wilt Thou Have My Hand, Dear, (Inclusions). Gabriel, Virginia. Song for [high] voice with piano. EBB18

O Zeus the King. Bantock, Granville. Part-song for male chorus (TTBB), with short score for keyboard. RB5

Octavo Series. RB346, RB348, and RB349

"O'er Hill and Dale." RB420

Oh, the Little Birds Sang East. Howe, Julia Ward. Song for [low] voice with piano. EBB67

Oh, to Be in England! Brahe, May H. Song for medium voice with piano. RB116

————. Cooke, Greville. Part-song for mixed chorus (SSAATTBB), unacc. RB118

————. Rowley, Alec. Duet for [high] voice and [medium low] voice with keyboard. RB122

————. Shapleigh, Bertram. Song for contralto with piano. RB123

————. Wickins, Florence. Duet for mezzo soprano and baritone with piano. RB126

————. Wilson, Alec. Song for [high] voice with piano. RB127

Oh, What a Drear, Dark Close to My Poor Day! Spier, La Salle. Song for [medium high] voice with string quartet and piano. RB439

Oh, Which Were Best to Roam or Rest. Worth, John W. Recitation for reader with piano. RB166

Oh, Yes! They Love through All This World of Ours! Freer, Eleanor Everest. Song for medium voice with keyboard. EBB209 and EBB210

On the Cliff. Somervell, Arthur. Contralto solo with orchestra. Piano-vocal score. RB204

One Way of Love. Clarke, Helen A. Song for high voice, cello obbligato, and keyboard. RB276

————. Rogers, Clara Kathleen. Song for [high] voice with keyboard. RB278

————. Thayer, Arthur W. Song for high voice with piano. RB279

One Way of Loving. Gregory, E. C. Song for [medium] voice with keyboard. RB277

"One Who Never Turned His Back." *See also* Paean "One Who Never Turn'd His Back"

"One Who Never Turned His Back." Mackenzie, Alexander C. Song for [medium] voice with piano. RB78 and RB79

"Only Sleep," a Slumber Song. Johnson, Leslie. Song for [medium high] voice with keyboard. RB580

The Orpheus, a Collection of Glees and Part-Songs for Male Voices. RB20, RB33, and RB43

Ottima's Regret. Davis, Carlyle. Piano solo. RB374

Our Two Souls. Surinach, Carlos. Song for [high] voice with piano. EBB165

Out in the Fields. Bond, Carrie Jacobs. Song for [medium high] voice with keyboard. EBB53

————————. Dawson, William L. Song for low voice with keyboard. EBB54

————————. French, Emma Weller. Song for soprano or tenor with piano and violin (obbligato). EBB55

————————. Protheroe, Daniel. Part-song for male chorus (TTBB), unacc. EBB58

————————. Protheroe, Daniel. Part-song for mixed chorus (SATB) with piano. EBB59

Out of My Own Great Woe. Rogers, Clara Kathleen. Song for [medium] voice with piano. EBB62

"Over the Sea Our Galleys Went," (Paracelsus). Harraden, Ethel. Part-song for male chorus (TTBB) with piano. RB288

Overhead the Treetops Meet. Clarke, Hugh A. Song for [high] voice with keyboard. RB368

————————. Fuller, Caroline M. Song for mezzo soprano with keyboard. RB384

————————. Rogers, Clara Kathleen. Song for [medium] voice with keyboard. RB429

————————. Spier, La Salle. Song for [medium high] voice with string quartet and piano. RB439

————————. True, Latham. Song for [medium] voice with keyboard. RB443

————————. Watson, Mary E. Song for [high] voice, unacc. RB447

————————. Welch, Jay. Song for soprano with harp. RB450

————————. Worth, John W. Song for [high] voice with keyboard. RB453

The Oxford Choral Songs. RB5, RB46, and RB283

The Oxford Series of Modern Anthems. RB63

A Paean of Love. Kaiser, Charles A. Duet for soprano and tenor with keyboard. EBB129

Paean, "One Who Never Turn'd His Back." Aldrich, Leslie. Song for [medium] voice with keyboard. RB72

The Page Sings to the Queen. Schuyler, Georgina. Song for mezzo soprano or contralto with piano. RB436

The Page's Song. Olds, W. B. Song for [medium] voice with keyboard. RB424

Pan. Sabin, Wallace A. Song for high or medium voice with piano. EBB51

——————. Smith, David Stanley. Chorus for women's choir (SSA), soprano solo, oboe (or flute obbligato), and piano. EBB52

Pan among the Reeds. Ashford, Emma L. Cantata with piano. EBB46

Pan and Luna. Bantock, Granville. Piano solo. RB280

Pan Pastorale. Godard, Benjamin. Piano solo. EBB49

Pan's Flute. Busch, Carl. Cantata with flute and piano. EBB47

Pan's Pipes. Perrin, H. Ballad for chorus (SATB) and orchestra. Piano-vocal score. EBB50

Paracelsus. Bantock, Granville. Part-song for male chorus (TTBBBB), unacc. RB283

Pardon, oh, Pardon, That My Soul Should Make. Freer, Eleanor Everest. Song for medium voice with keyboard. EBB200 and EBB201

Part-Songs for Mens Voices. RB215

Part-Songs for Mixed Voices. EBB77

Parting at Morning. Miller, Anne Stratton. Song for [medium] voice with piano. RB296

——————. Reed, C. H. Song for [high] voice with piano. RB297

——————. Worth, John W. Song for [high] voice with keyboard. RB299

A Passacaglia. Church, Frank M. Solo for unspecified keyboard (?) instrument. RB300

Past We Glide. Worth, John W. Song for tenor with piano. RB166

——————. Young, Dal. Song for tenor with piano. RB167

The Patriot. Kramer, A. Walter. Song for high voice with piano. RB302

——————. Kramer, A. Walter. Song for low voice with piano. RB301

——————. Worth, John W. Song for [high] voice with keyboard. RB303

A Pearl, a Girl. Bantock, Granville. Song for high voice with piano. RB305

——————. Bantock, Granville. Song for low voice with piano. RB304

The Pied Piper. Brumleu, Ernest. Musical play with keyboard. RB310

——————. Brydson, John C. Piano solo. RB311

——————. Davies, Walford. Chamber cantata. Piano-vocal score. RB314

——————. Dunhill, Thomas F. Piano [suite]. RB316

——————. Klein, Manuel. Operatic fantasy. Piano-vocal score. RB325

——————. Truman, Ernest. Cantata Grotesque. Piano-vocal score. RB335

The Pied Piper of Hamelin. Aiken, Walter H. Operetta. Piano-vocal score. RB306

——————. Aylwin, Josephine Crew. Cantata with piano. RB307

——————. Bergh, Arthur. Recitation for reader with piano. RB308

——————. Boyle, George F. Cantata. Piano-vocal score. RB309

——————. Brydson, John C. Suite for piano. RB311

——————. Clokey, Joseph W. Opera. Piano-vocal score. RB313

——————. Hudson, Henry. Cantata. Piano-vocal score. RB323

——————. Hurless, Don. Cantata. Piano-vocal score. RB324

——————. Martin, Margaret R. [Musical play] with flute or piccolo and keyboard. RB327-RB329

——————. Parry, C. Hubert H. [Cantata.] Piano-vocal score. RB332

——————. Rathbone, George. Cantata. Piano-vocal score. RB334

——————. Walthew, Richard. [Cantata.] Piano-vocal score. RB337

The Pied Piper of Hamelin Pipes and Disappears with the Children in the Mountain. Krug, Arnold. Piano solo. RB326

The Pied Piper; or The Rat-Catcher of Hamelin. Farmer, John. Opera. Piano-vocal score. RB317

Pied Piper's Tune. Dittenhaver, Sarah Louise. Piano solo. RB315

A Pillar at Sebzevah. Bantock, Granville. Song for [high] voice with piano. RB98

The Piper of Hamelin. Farrington, Frederick W. Cantata with flageolet or flute, piano, and harmonium. Piano-vocal score. RB318

——————. Graham, A. Cyril. Cantata. Piano-vocal score. RB321

Pippa Passes. Bantock, Granville. Song for high voice with piano. RB343

——————. Bantock, Granville. Song for medium voice with piano. RB342

——————. Rohrer, Mildred. Song for [low] voice with keyboard. RB431

Pippa Passes, Four Moods from Browning. Davis, Carlyle. Suite for piano. RB374

Pippa Passes (Pippa's Lied). Herz, Maria. Song for [medium] voice with piano. RB399

Pippa's Holiday. RB350

Pippa's Holiday (Danse Grotesque). Warren, Jeanne. Piano solo. RB445

(Pippa's Lied). *See* Pippa Passes (Pippa's Lied)

Pippa's Song. Black, Kate Gilmore. Song for high voice with piano. RB352

——————. David, Elizabeth Harbison. Song for [medium high] voice with flute, violin and keyboard. RB373

——————. Ehrmann, Mary. Chorus for unison children's voices with keyboard. RB379

——————. Galsworthy, Ada. Song for [high] voice with keyboard. RB385 and RB386

——————. Gilchrist, W. W. Chorus for unison voices with piano. RB388

——————. Hammond, William G. Two-part song for children's chorus, unacc. RB395

——————. Johnstone, Harry. Song for [medium high] voice with keyboard. RB404

——————. Loughridge, Jean M. Song for unison children's chorus with piano. RB412 and RB413

——————. Mayer, Max. Song for [medium] voice with piano. RB416

——————. Parker, Willetta. Song for [medium] voice with piano. RB425

——————. Rorem, Ned. Song for high voice with piano. RB432

——————. Sternberg, Daniel Arie. Song for high voice with keyboard. RB441

Pippa's Song ("The Year's at the Spring"). Young, Dalhousie. Song for [high] voice with piano. RB454

Pippa's Spring Song. Caruthers, Julia Lois. Song for [high] voice with keyboard. RB363

Plot-Culture. Bantock, Granville. Song for [high] voice with piano. RB97

Poems and Flowers. Castelnuovo-Tedesco, Mario. Song for [medium] voice with piano. EBB256

Poet-Lore. RB99, RB253, and RB511

The Poetical Works of Robert Browning. RB295

Pompilia e Caponsacchi. Bollinger, Sam'l. Overture for orchestra. Conductor's score. RB483

——————. Bollinger, Sam'l. Overture for orchestra. Conductor's score with parts. RB484

Porphyria. Dillon, Fannie Charles. Song for [high] voice with keyboard. RB455

Portrait. Dougherty, Celius. Song for medium voice with piano. RB544

Prelude. Welch, Jay. Prelude for oboe, clarinet, and harp. RB450

——————. Worth, John W. Piano solo. RB166

Prelude to Exile. Wiant, W. R. Ballet-prelude. Piano-conductor's score. EBB11.1

The Progressive Music Series. RB395

Proof and Disproof. Pascal, Florian. Song for [medium] voice with piano. EBB64

Prospice. Boughton, Rutland. Part-song for male chorus (TTBB), unacc. RB456

——————. Davies, H. Walford. Song for baritone and string quartet. RB457

——————. Duncan, Edmondstoune. Song for [low] voice with keyboard. RB458

——————. Hadley, Henry. Song for medium voice with piano. RB459

——————. Homer, Sidney. Song for high voice with piano. RB460

——————. Homer, Sidney. Song for low voice with piano. RB461

——————. Lehmann, Liza. Song for low voice with piano. RB462

——————. Stanford, C. Villiers. Song for [medium high] voice with piano. RB463 and RB464

——————. Thomas, Adelaida. Song for [medium] voice with piano. RB465

——————. Thomas, D. Vaughan. Part-song for male chorus (TTBB), unacc. RB466

——————. True, Latham. Song for [high] voice with keyboard. RB468

——————. True, Latham. Song for [medium] voice with keyboard. RB467

A Query. Mana-Zucca. Song for high voice with piano. RB100

Question and Answer. Ponssen, Mary Eleanor. Song for [high] voice with keyboard. EBB66

Questionings. Vannah, Kate. Song for soprano with keyboard. EBB24

Rabbi Ben Ezra. Ackert, Bernard G. Song for [medium] voice with keyboard. RB469

——————. Hadley, Henry K. Part-song for mixed chorus (SATB), unacc. RB471

——————. Madsen, Dora L. [Song for medium voice] with keyboard. RB472

——————. Ralston, Frances Marion. [Cantata] with piano. RB475. *See also* RB474

Radio Choral Series. RB195

The Rat-Charmer of Hamelin. Neuendorff, Adolf. Comic opera. Piano-vocal score. RB331

The Rats. Brydson, John C. Piano solo. RB311

——————. Dunhill, Thomas F. Piano solo. RB316

Rattenfänger Lieder. Woyrsch, Felix von. Songs for medium voice with piano. RB339

Der Rattenfänger von Hameln. *See also* The Rat-Charmer of Hamelin

Der Rattenfänger von Hameln. Geisler, Paul. Piano solo for four hands. RB320

Der Rattenfänger von Hameln. Hirsch, Carl. [Cantata] with piano and organ. RB322

——————. Urban, Heinrich. Fantasy for piano. RB336

——————. Weigl, Karl. Operetta. Piano-vocal score. RB338

Readings with Musical Settings. RB151

Red Cotton Night-Cap Country. Bantock, Granville. Piano solo. RB482

Reflectivity (Three Short Part-Songs). EBB36

Renunciation. Treharne, Bryceson. Song for high voice or medium voice with piano. EBB23

The Request. Vogler, [Georg Joseph]. Song for [high] voice with keyboard. RB2 and RB3

Ringing the Bells. Dunhill, Thomas F. Piano solo. RB316

The River Weser. Brydson, John C. Piano solo. RB311

Robert Browning Overture. Ives, Charles E. Overture for orchestra. Study score. RB487

Eine Rose gepflückt! Woyrsch, Felix von. Song for medium voice with piano. RB339

A Rose Once Grew. Hammer, Marie von. Song for high voice with piano. EBB35

The Rose Tree. Saar, Louis Victor. Song for high voice with piano. RB219

Röslein, wann blühst du auf? Woyrsch, Felix von. Song for medium voice with piano. RB339

Round Us the Wild Creatures. Clarke, Helen A. Song for [high] voice with keyboard. RB86

—————————. Kernochan, Marshall. Song for medium voice with piano. RB87

—————————. Krull, Fritz. Song for [high] voice with keyboard. RB88

Row Home? Must We Row Home. Worth, John W. Recitation for reader with piano. RB166

Sabbath Morning at Sea. Elgar, Edward. Song for contralto or low voice with piano. EBB69 and EBB70

—————————. Elgar, Edward. Song for high voice with piano. EBB71

Saul. Dillon, Fannie Charles. Recitation for reader with keyboard. RB488

—————————. Moore, Mary Carr. Setting for reader, violin, cello, and piano. RB489

—————————. Ralston, Frances Marion. Oratorio with pipe organ or piano. RB491

Eine Säule in Sebzevar. *See* A Pillar at Sebzevah

Say after Me. Young, Dal. Duet for soprano and tenor with piano. RB167

Say after Me, and Try to Say My Very Words. Worth, John W. Recitation for reader with piano. RB166

Say Never Ye Loved Once. Kellie, Lawrence. Song for [medium] voice with piano. EBB37

Say over Again. Freer, Eleanor Everest. Song for mezzo soprano or medium voice with keyboard. EBB158-EBB160

Say Thou Lovest Me! Cain, Noble. Chorus for mixed choir (SSAA TTBB), unacc. EBB157

Scenes from Fairy-Land. RB326

Schach Abbas. *See* Shah Abbas

The School Music Review. RB351

"Sea-Pictures." EBB69

Sleep Soft, Beloved. Austin, Torrington. Song for [high] voice with keyboard. EBB72

A Slumber Song. *See* "Only Sleep," a Slumber Song

So Still within This Life. Ralston, Frances Marion. Vocal quartet for two treble voices and two bass voices, unacc. RB475

So Take and Use Thy Work. Ralston, Frances Marion. Part-song for two women's choruses (SSAA) (SSAA) with piano. RB475

So, the Year's Done With! Bryson, Ernest. Song for high voice with piano. RB64

——————. Bryson, Ernest. Song for medium voice with piano. RB65

Soliloquy of the Spanish Cloister. Bantock, Granville. Piano solo. RB496

Some Happy Day. Saar, Louis Victor. Song for high voice with piano. RB219

Sonata in A major. Galuppi, Baldassare. Edited and revised by Joseph Henius. Piano sonata. RB531

Sonata in B-flat major. Galuppi, Baldassare. Sonata for harpsichord. RB530

Sonata in C major. Galuppi, Baldassare. Sonata for harpsichord. RB530

Sonata in D major. Galuppi, Baldassare. Edited and revised by Joseph Henius. Piano sonata. RB532

Sonata in G major. Galuppi, Baldassare. Sonata for harpsichord. RB530

Sonette der Elisabeth Barret-Browning. Wellesz, Egon. Songs for soprano and string quartet. EBB85, EBB90, EBB98, EBB118, and EBB184

Song. Gregory, E. C. Song for [medium high] voice with keyboard. RB502

Song: Ask Not One Least Word of Praise. Clarke, Helen Archibald. Song for [medium] voice with piano. RB99

A Song-Book for Adolescent Boys. *See* A Heritage of Song

Song from Pippa Passes. Curtis, Natalie. Song for [medium] voice with piano. RB372

——————. Johnson, F. Arthur. Song for [high] voice with piano. RB401-RB403

——————. Whitmer, T. Carl. Song for mezzo soprano with piano. RB451

Song of the Galleys from "Paracelsus." Bantock, Granville. Part-song for male chorus (TTBB), unacc. RB284

Song of the Morning Star to Lucifer. Worth, John W. Song for medium voice with keyboard. EBB13

Songs in English, Nineteen Contemporary Settings by American and English Composers. EBB70, EBB71, EBB222, and EBB223

Songs of Praise. RB213, RB444, and RB479

Songs of Spring. RB231

Die Sonne. *See* The Sun

Sonnet. Barnett, Alice. Song for high voice with piano. EBB215

———————. MacMillan, Ernest. Song for [medium] voice with keyboard. EBB142

———————. Madsen, Dora L. Song for [high] voice with keyboard. EBB238

A Sonnet from the Portuguese. Gaul, Harvey. Chorus for male choir (TTBB) with piano. EBB229

———————. Robbins, Reginald C. Song for [medium low] voice with keyboard. RB164.1

Sonnet (Seven) from the Portuguese. Booth, Guy. Part-song for mixed chorus (SATB), unacc. EBB110

Sonnet Twenty-One. Bliss, James A. Song for high voice with piano. EBB156

Sonnet, "When Our Two Souls Stand Up Erect and Strong." Willan, Healey. Song for [high] voice with piano. EBB166

Sonnets from the Portuguese, op. 22. Book I. Freer, Eleanor Everest. Song cycle for mezzo soprano with keyboard. EBB80, EBB87, EBB91, EBB95, EBB99, EBB104, EBB112, EBB119, EBB122, EBB126, and EBB131

Sonnets from the Portuguese, op. 22. Freer, Eleanor Everest. French translation by Eleanor Everest Freer. Song cycle for medium voice with keyboard. EBB82, EBB88, EBB92, EBB96, EBB100, EBB105, EBB113, EBB120, EBB123, EBB127, EBB132, EBB134, EBB136, EBB139, EBB144, EBB146, EBB148, EBB150, EBB152, EBB154, EBB159, EBB162, EBB167, EBB170, EBB172, EBB174, EBB177, EBB180, EBB182, EBB185, EBB187, EBB189, EBB191, EBB193, EBB195, EBB198, EBB200, EBB204, EBB207, EBB209, EBB211, EBB213, EBB226, and EBB257

———————. Freer, Eleanor Everest. Song cycle for medium voice with keyboard. EBB83, EBB89, EBB93, EBB97, EBB101, EBB106, EBB114, EBB121, EBB124, EBB128, EBB133, EBB135, EBB137, EBB140, EBB145, EBB147, EBB149, EBB151, EBB153, EBB155, EBB160, EBB163, EBB168, EBB171, EBB173, EBB175, EBB178, EBB181, EBB183, EBB186, EBB188, EBB190, EBB192, EBB194, EBB196, EBB199, EBB201, EBB205, EBB208, EBB210, EBB212, EBB214, EBB227, and EBB258

The Soul's Expression. Coleridge-Taylor, S. Song for contralto with keyboard. EBB259

The Soul's Expression (Four Sonnets). EBB8, EBB15, EBB259, and EBB262

The Soul's Rialto Hath Its Merchandise. Freer, Eleanor Everest. Song for medium voice with keyboard. EBB152 and EBB153

Speak Low to Me, My Savior. Ford, D. Rhys. Part-song for mixed chorus (SATB) with organ. EBB9

Spring. Vaughan Williams, Ralph. Hymn for SATB, unacc. RB444

Stelldichein. Woyrsch, Felix von. Song for medium voice with piano. RB339

The Stock Exchange Christmas Annual. RB404

The Story. Martin, Margaret R. Recitation for reader, children, and keyboard. RB329

Submission. Beckett, Bessie D. Song for [medium] voice with piano. RB569

"Substitution." Coleridge-Taylor, S. Song for low voice with piano. EBB260 and EBB261

Such a Starved Bank of Moss. *See also* Transformations ("Such a Starved Bank of Moss")

Such a Starved Bank of Moss. Freer, Eleanor Everest. Song for baritone with keyboard. RB549

——————. Krull, Fritz. Song for [high] voice with keyboard. RB553

——————. Somervell, Arthur. Song for [medium high] voice with piano. RB563

Such a Starved Bank of Moss (Apparitions). Hoberg, Margaret. Song for soprano or tenor with keyboard. RB552

Suite for Pied Piper. Miller, Lewis. Trio for flute, piano, and double bass. Piano-conductor's score. RB330

Suite for Strings and Piano. Moore, Mary Carr. Suite for string quartet and piano. RB490

Summum Bonum. Bantock, Granville. Song for high voice with piano. RB515

——————. Bantock, Granville. Song for low voice with piano. RB516

——————. Davidson, Frank. Song for tenor with piano. RB517

——————. Dickinson, Clarence. Duet for [medium] voices with keyboard. RB518

—————. Hollander, Benoit. Song for [medium] voice with piano. RB519

—————. Inches, Charles. Song for [medium] voice with piano. RB520

—————. Löhr, Harvey. Song for [high] voice with piano. RB522

—————. Rogers, Clara Kathleen. Song for [medium] voice with piano. RB524

—————. Royle, Popplewell. Song for [high] voice with piano. RB525

The Sun. Bantock, Granville. Song for [high] voice with piano. RB92

The Sweet Sad Years. Castelnuovo-Tedesco, Mario. Song for [medium] voice with piano. EBB79

Sweet, Thou Hast Trod on a Heart! Löhr, Hermann. Song for [medium] voice with piano. EBB14

Sweetest Eyes. Philp, Elizabeth. Song for [medium] voice with piano. EBB2

Symphonic Prelude to Robert Browning's Tragedy, a Blot in the 'Scutcheon. Lewis, Leo Rich. Symphonic prelude for orchestra. Full score. RB14

The Tale of the Pied Piper. Paulsen, P. Marinus. Operetta-pageant with keyboard. RB333

Tears. Coleridge-Taylor, S. Song for contralto with keyboard. EBB262

—————. Harris, Russell G. Setting for [high] voice with violin I, violin II, flute, oboe, clarinet, bassoon, cymbal, and piano. EBB263

Ten Songs. EBB197

Teresa del Riego Album. RB375

That May. Nicholson, Alfred. Song for [medium] voice with keyboard. EBB264

That May Morn. Nicholson, Mary E. Song for [medium] voice with piano. RB560

That Was I. Mana-Zucca. Song for high voice with piano. RB494

Then Welcome Each Rebuff. Ralston, Frances Marion. Song for alto with piano. RB475

—————. Vaughan Williams, Ralph. Hymn for SATB, unacc. RB479

—————. Wiant, Bliss, editor. Hymn for SATB, unacc. RB480 and RB481

There Is No One Beside Thee. Pascal, Florian. Song for [medium high] voice with piano. EBB29

——————. Patterson, Janie Alexander. Song for [medium] voice with keyboard. EBB30

There's a Woman Like a Dew-drop. Branscombe, Gena. Song for high voice with piano. RB9

——————. Bullard, Frederic Field. Song for high voice, violin, and piano. RB10

——————. Chanter, Arthur. Song for bass or contralto with piano. RB11

——————. De Koven, Reginald. Song for soprano or tenor with piano. RB12

——————. Hadley, Henry K. Song for [medium] voice with keyboard. RB13

——————. Mackenzie, A. C. Song for [high] voice with harp or piano. RB15

There's Heaven Above. Homer, Sidney. Song for high voice with piano. RB214

There's Heaven Above, and Night by Night. Brahms, Johannes. Hymn for SATB, unacc. RB213

There's Zanse's Vigilant Taper. Young, Dal. Duet for soprano and tenor with piano. RB167

This Is a Spray the Bird Clung To. Reinagle, Caroline. Song for [medium] voice with piano. RB247

——————. Schuyler, Georgina. Song for mezzo soprano or contralto with piano. RB248

This Little Flower. Saar, Louis Victor. Song for high voice with piano. RB219

Thou Comest! All Is Said without a Word. Freer, Eleanor Everest. Song for medium voice with keyboard. EBB187 and EBB188

Thou Hast Thy Calling to Some Palace-Floor. Freer, Eleanor Everest. Song for medium voice, baritone, or mezzo soprano with keyboard. EBB94, EBB95, EBB96, and EBB97

[Thou Hast Thy Calling to Some Palace-Floor]. Du bist da draben im Palast begehrt. Wellesz, Egon. Song for soprano and string quartet. EBB98

"Thou Lov'st Me Not." Carter, Ernest. Song for [medium] voice with piano. EBB61

Thou Shalt Know Me. Saar, Louis Victor. Song for high voice with piano. RB219

Thou Wilt Know. Saar, Louis Victor. Song for high voice with piano. RB219

Thoughts. Fergus, Phyllis. Recitation for reader with violin and piano. RB151

Three Browning Songs. RB142, RB143, RB174, RB176, RB345, and RB347

Three Cavalier Songs. RB28, RB41, and RB58

Three Cavalier Tunes by Robert Browning. RB24, RB36, and RB47

Three Choruses for Male Voices. *See* The Oxford Choral Songs, Three Choruses for Male Voices

Three Descriptions from Browning. White, Grace. Violin solos with piano. RB124, RB241, and RB298

Three Descriptions from Browning, no. 1. White, Grace. Violin solo with piano. RB241

Three Descriptions from Browning, no. 2. White, Grace. Violin solo with piano. RB124

Three Descriptions from Browning, no. 3. White, Grace. Violin solo with piano. RB298

Three English Songs. RB123

Three Kisses. Kaiser, Charles A. Song for soprano with keyboard. EBB206

Three Lyrics by Robert Browning. RB155, RB196, and RB426

Three Preludes. RB227

Three Rhapsodies. *See* In Memoriam (Three Rhapsodies)

Three Short Part-Songs. *See* Reflectivity (Three Short Part-Songs)

Three Songs. Barnett, Alice. EBB215

——————. Craddock, Reginald. RB543

——————. Homer, Sidney. RB259, RB260, RB460, RB461, and RB579

——————. Iles, Edward. RB503

——————. Krull, Fritz. RB88, RB291, and RB553

——————. Lehmann, Liza. RB230 and RB462

——————. Lewis, Leo Rich. RB410

——————. Parker, Willetta. RB425

——————. Reinagle, Caroline. RB171, RB247, and RB537

——————. Thayer, Arthur W. RB279 and RB508

——————. Whitmer, T. Carl. RB199 and RB451

——————. Worth, John W. Songs for medium voice with keyboard. EBB13

Three Songs from Robert Browning. RB184 and RB384

Three Songs with Piano Accompaniment. RB352

Three Sonnets from the Portuguese. EBB79, EBB179, and EBB256

Thy Face. Bliss, Paul. Song for [medium low] voice with keyboard. RB540

——————. Coombs, C. Whitney. Song for medium voice with piano. RB542

——————. Molineux, Marie Ada. Arranged by Harry Lawson Harts. Song for [high] voice with keyboard. RB556 and RB558

——————. Molineux, Marie Ada. Song for [high] voice with keyboard. RB557

——————. Neidlinger, W. H. Song for baritone or mezzo soprano with piano. RB559

To Horse! Kobbé, Gustav. Song for [medium] voice with keyboard. RB53

To Perfect the Summer. Halley, Margaret A. Song for [high] voice with piano. RB211

——————. Halley, Margaret A. Song for [medium] voice with keyboard. RB210

Toccata. Forbes, J. Winchell. Solo for unspecified keyboard instrument. RB529

Toccata in D minor. Galuppi, Baldassare. Toccata for harpsichord. RB530

Toccata in F major. Galuppi, Baldassare. Toccata for harpsichord. RB530

[Toccata] in G major. [Galuppi, Baldassare]. [Toccata for clavichord]. RB533

A Toccata of Galuppi's. Bantock, Granville. Piano solo. RB528

To-morrow, If a Harp-String, Say. Barnett, Alice. Song for high voice with piano. RB140

——————. Worth, John W. Song for soprano with piano. RB166

Tragödie in Arezzo (Caponsacchi). Hageman, Richard. Opera. Piano-vocal score. RB486

Transformations ("Such a Starved Bank of Moss"). Manney, Charles Fonteyn. Song for mezzo soprano or baritone with keyboard. RB555

Tresses. Oldroyd, George. Song for [high] voice with piano. RB505

Troubadour Song Book. RB377 and RB378

True Love. Brooke, Carol Kelley. Song for [medium] voice with keyboard. EBB273

Twelve Lyrics for Lovers. EBB281

Twelve Songs. RB55, RB237, and RB297

Twelve Songs by Browning. RB84, RB200, RB218, RB244, RB249, RB270, RB299, RB303, and RB453

Two Camels. Bantock, Granville. Song for [high] voice with piano. RB95

Two Ecstasies. RB504

Two Leaves of Green—Fifty Unaccompanied Love Songs for Solo Voice. RB66

Two Lyrics. RB586

Two Poems by Robert Browning. Kernochan, Marshall. RB38 and RB192

——————. Mana-Zucca. RB100 and RB494

Two Short Songs. RB340

Two Songs. Bennett, Howard. EBB271 and EBB272

——————. Brahe, May H. RB116 and RB357

——————. Cantor, Otto. RB571 and RB572

——————. Galsworthy, Mrs. John. RB202 and RB386

——————. Goatley, Alma. RB119

——————. Herz, Maria. RB399

——————. Hollander, Benoit. RB519

——————. Inches, Charles. RB520

——————. Jordan, Jules. RB405

——————. Kernochan, Marshall. RB493

——————. Neidlinger, W. H. RB559

——————. Ryan, Margaret. RB238

——————. Sabin, Wallace A. EBB51

Two Songs with Piano Accompaniment. RB21

Und es geschah mir einst, an Theokrit zu denken. Wellesz, Egon. Song for soprano and string quartet. EBB85

United. Kaiser, Charles A. Duet for soprano and tenor with keyboard. EBB164

Unless. Beningfield, Ethel. Song for [low] voice with piano. EBB270

——————. Bennett, Howard. Song for high voice with piano. EBB272

—————. Bennett, Howard. Song for low voice with piano. EBB271

—————. Caldicott, Alfred J. Song for [low] voice with violin or cello obbligato and piano. EBB274

—————. Caldicott, Alfred J. Song for [medium] voice with violin or cello obbligato and piano. EBB275

—————. Caracciolo, Luigi. Song for [high] voice with keyboard. EBB277

—————. Caracciolo, Luigi. Song for [low] voice with keyboard. EBB278

—————. Caracciolo, Luigi. Song for [medium high] voice with keyboard. EBB276

—————. Hervey, Augusta E. Song for [medium] voice with piano. EBB279

—————. Needham, Alicia Adélaïda. Song for [high] voice with piano. EBB281

—————. Parker, Phyllis Norman. Song for [high] voice with piano. EBB283

—————. Parker, Phyllis Norman. Song for [medium] voice with piano. EBB282

—————. Schlesinger, Sebastian B. Song for [medium] voice with keyboard. EBB284

—————. Spencer, Fanny M. Song for mezzo soprano or baritone with keyboard. EBB285

—————. Spencer, Fanny M. Song for tenor or soprano with keyboard. EBB286

—————. Troup, Emily Josephine. Song for [medium high] voice with piano. EBB287

Unlike Are We, Unlike, O Princely Heart! Freer, Eleanor Everest. Song for mezzo soprano or medium voice with keyboard. EBB91-EBB93

Unzulänglichkeit. *See* Insufficiency (Leaving Yet Loving)

"Valence." Gow, George Coleman. Piano solo. RB62

A Venetian Night. Wodell, Frederick W. Cantata with piano. RB165

Venetian Serenade. Schuyler, Georgina. Song for contralto or baritone with piano. RB160

Venezia. Saminsky, Lazare. [Symphonic poem] for orchestra. Conductor's score. RB157

The Virgin Mary to the Child Jesus. Damrosch, Walter. Two motets for mixed chorus (SSAATTBB), unacc. EBB265

Vocal Duets. RB175

Waldesruh. Woyrsch, Felix von. Song for medium voice with piano. RB339

The Wanderers. Robbins, Reginald C. Song for [medium low] voice with keyboard. RB291.1

Wanting Is—What? Bantock, Granville. Song for high voice with piano. RB208

——————. Bantock, Granville. Song for low voice with piano. RB207

——————. Forster, Beatrice. Song for [high] voice with piano. RB209

——————. Kernochan, Marshall. Song for [high] voice with piano. RB212

Wa-Wan Series of American Compositions. RB144

Wedding March. Gow, George Coleman. Piano solo. RB62

The Wedding Morn. Nevin, Ethelbert. Song for high voice with piano. RB421

Wenn du kein Spielmann wärst! Woyrsch, Felix von. Song for medium voice with piano. RB339

What Are We Two. Barnett, Alice. Song for high voice with piano. RB141

——————. Branscombe, Gena. Song for [medium] voice with keyboard. RB149

——————. Worth, John W. Song for tenor with piano. RB166

——————. Young, Dal. Song for tenor with piano. RB167

What Can I Give Thee Back, O Liberal. Freer, Eleanor Everest. Song for mezzo soprano or medium voice with keyboard. EBB119, EBB120, and EBB121

What I Do, and What I Dream. White, Maude Valérie. Song for [medium] voice with piano. EBB109

What If the Three. Worth, John W. Recitation for reader with piano. RB166

——————. Young, Dal. Song for tenor with piano. RB167

What So Wild. Dichmont, William. Song for high voice with piano. RB575

When Our Two Souls Stand Up Erect and Strong. *See also* Sonnet, "When Our Two Souls Stand Up Erect and Strong"

When Our Two Souls Stand Up Erect and Strong. Freer, Eleanor Everest. Song for medium voice with keyboard. EBB162 and EBB163

When Soul Is Joined to Soul. Beach, Mrs. H. H. A. Song for [high] voice with keyboard. EBB17

When We First Met and Loved, I Did Not Build. Freer, Eleanor Everest. Song for medium voice with keyboard. EBB198 and EBB199

White Lilies. Pascal, Florian. Song for [high] voice with piano. EBB5

"The Widest Land." Branscombe, Gena. Song for medium voice with piano. EBB103

Wilt Thou Change Too? Harraden, Ethel. Song for [medium] voice with piano. RB190

"Wilt Thou Have My Hand." Stothart, Herbert. Song for medium voice with keyboard, specifically "on a spinet." EBB22

The Winthrop Rogers Edition of Choral Music for Festivals. RB118

Wisdom Unapplied. Pascal, Florian. Song for [high] voice with piano. EBB269

With the Same Heart, I Said, I'll Answer Thee. Freer, Eleanor Everest. Song for medium voice with keyboard. EBB193 and EBB194

With Thee Anear. Surinach, Carlos. Song for [high] voice with piano. EBB117

Wo ich mich zeige. Woyrsch, Felix von. Song for medium voice with piano. RB339

A Woman's Last Word. Bantock, Granville. Song for high voice with piano. RB566

——————. Bantock, Granville. Song for low voice with piano. RB565

——————. Beach, John Parsons. Song for [medium high] voice with piano. RB568

——————. Dichmont, William. Songs for high voice with piano. RB575

——————. Foote, David. Song for [medium high] voice with keyboard. RB576

——————. Ganz, Rudolf. Song for [high] voice with piano. RB578

——————. Ganz, Rudolf. Song for [medium] voice with piano. RB577

——————. Homer, Sidney. Song for high voice with piano. RB579

——————. Johnson, Leslie. Song for [medium low] voice with piano. RB581

——————. Jowett, Albert. Song for high voice with piano. RB583

——————. Raphael, Juliet. Recitation for reader with keyboard. RB585

——————. Rogers, Clara Kathleen. Song for [high] voice with keyboard. RB588

——————. Woolley, C. Song for [medium] voice with keyboard. RB589

A Woman's Love. Rhodes, Harold. Song for [high] voice with keyboard. EBB243

Women and Roses. Lidgey, C. A. Choral setting for mixed voices (SATB) and orchestra. Piano-vocal score. RB590

The World's Best Music. EBB28, EBB253, and EBB278

Worship Whom Else? Watson, Mary E. Recitation for speaker, violin, and harp. RB447

The Worst of It. Somervell, Arthur. Song for [medium high] voice with piano. RB592

Would It Were I Had Been False, Not You! Reinagle, Caroline. Song for [high] voice with piano. RB591

The Year Book Press Series of Unison and Part-Songs. RB48

The Year's at the Spring. *See also* All's Right *and* Pippa's Song

The Year's at the Spring. Alsop, Marion. Song for soprano with piano. RB340

——————. Atkins, Ivor. Song for [high] voice with keyboard. RB341

——————. Beach, Mrs. H. H. A. Arranged by Francis Moore. Part-song for male chorus (TTBB) with piano. RB348

——————. Beach, Mrs. H. H. A. Part-song for mixed chorus (SATB) with keyboard. RB349

——————. Beach, Mrs. H. H. A. Part-song for women's chorus (SSAA) with keyboard. RB346

——————. Beach, Mrs. H. H. A. Song for low voice with keyboard. RB345

——————. Beach, Mrs. H. H. A. Song for [medium] voice with piano. RB344

——————. Beach, Mrs. H. H. A. Song for soprano or tenor with piano. RB347

——————. Black, Kate Gilmore. Song for [high] voice, unacc. RB353

——————. Blair, William. Song for [medium] voice with piano. RB354

——————. Bode, Alice M. Song for [high] voice with piano. RB355

——————. Brahe, May H. Song for [high] voice with piano. RB358

——————. Brahe, May H. Song for medium voice with piano. RB356 and RB357

——————. Cain, Noble. Chorus for women's voices (SS-AA) with piano. RB359

————. Caldwell, Mary E. Part-song for mixed chorus (SAB) with keyboard. RB361

————. Caldwell, Mary E. Song for unison chorus with organ or piano. RB360

————. Carter, Esther May. Song for [medium] voice with piano. RB362

————. Clark, Ruth Kinney. Song for [medium high] voice with keyboard. RB364

————. Clarke, Henry Leland. Song for [medium] voice with keyboard. RB366

————. Cripps, A. Redgrave. Song for [medium] voice with keyboard. RB370

————. Duncan, Edmondstoune. Song for [medium high] voice with piano. RB376

————. Floyd, A. E. Part-song for women's chorus (SSA), unacc. RB380

————. Freer, Eleanor Everest. Song for baritone with keyboard. RB382

————. Freer, Eleanor Everest. Song for low voice with keyboard. RB381

————. Freer, Eleanor Everest. Song for medium voice with keyboard. RB383

————. Fuller, Caroline M. Song for soprano with keyboard. RB384

————. Gow, George Coleman. Song for [medium high] voice with piano. RB389

————. Grace, Harvey. Song for mezzo soprano with piano. RB390

————. Hadley, Henry. Song for [medium] voice with keyboard. RB391

————. Halley, Margaret A. Song for [high] voice with piano. RB394

————. Halley, Margaret A. Song for [medium] voice with piano. RB393

————. Hartog, Cécile S. Song for high voice with piano. RB396, RB397, and RB398

————. Hollins, Dorothea. Song for mezzo soprano with keyboard. RB400

————. Lee, E. Markham. Part-song for women's chorus (SA) with piano. RB408

—————————. Lewis, Ella V. Song for [medium] voice with piano. RB409

—————————. Macmillen, Francis. Song for high voice with piano. RB414

—————————. Neidlinger, W. H. Song for soprano or tenor with piano. RB419

—————————. Norén, Helmer. Song for [high] voice with piano. RB422

—————————. Protheroe, Daniel. Song for high voice with keyboard. RB426

—————————. Rogers, Clara Kathleen. Song for [medium high] voice with piano. RB430

—————————. Rossman, Floy Adele. Part-song for women's chorus (SS AA) with piano. RB433

—————————. Sarson, H. M. Part-song for children's chorus (SS), unacc. RB434

—————————. Sharpe, Cedric. Song for [medium high] voice with piano. RB437

—————————. Somervell, Arthur. Song for [medium high] voice with piano. RB438

—————————. Welch, Jay. Song for soprano with harp. RB450

—————————. Worth, John W. Song for [high] voice with keyboard. RB453

The Year's at the Spring (Song from Pippa Passes). Mason, Alexander O. Song for soprano with keyboard. RB415

The Year's Spinning. Metcalfe, W. Song for [medium] voice with piano. EBB288

—————————. Pease, Alfred H. Song for [high] voice with keyboard. EBB289

Yes, Call Me by My Pet Name! Freer, Eleanor Everest. Song for medium voice with keyboard. EBB191 and EBB192

Yet Gifts Should Prove Their Use. Ralston, Frances Marion. Part-song for women's chorus (SSAA) with piano. RB475

Yet, Love Is Beautiful Indeed. Surinach, Carlos. Song for [high] voice with piano. EBB130

Yet, Love, Mere Love, Is Beautiful Indeed. Freer, Eleanor Everest. Song for mezzo soprano or medium voice with keyboard. EBB125, EBB126, EBB127, and EBB128

You'll Love Me Yet. Clarke, Helen A. Song for [high] voice, cello, and piano. RB365

————————. Coleridge-Taylor, S. Song for contralto or baritone with keyboard. RB369

————————. Crumpler, Mary Frances. Song for [medium high] voice with piano. RB371

————————. Gow, George Coleman. Part-song for women's voices (SS AA) with piano. RB389

————————. Hadley, Henry K. Song for high voice with keyboard. RB392

————————. Kernochan, Marshall. Song for [medium high] voice with piano. RB406 and RB407

————————. Mozart, W. A. Song for [medium] voice, unacc. RB418

————————. Renaud, Emiliano. Song for [high] voice with piano. RB428

————————. Stephens, Ward. Song for [high] voice with piano. RB440

————————. Welch, Jay. Song for [medium] voice, unacc. RB450

You'll Love Me Yet (Song from Pippa Passes). Mokrejs, John. Song for [medium] voice with keyboard. RB417

Youth Ended. Ralston, Frances Marion. Song for mezzo soprano with piano. RB475

Zehn Lieder. *See* Ten Songs

Zwei Kamels. *See* Two Camels

VI

Performance Medium Entry

Key to Abbreviations

acc.	accompanied
SA	soprano, alto
SAB	soprano, alto, bass
SATB	soprano, alto, tenor, bass
SATBB	soprano, alto, tenor, bass I, bass II
SS	soprano I, soprano II
SSA	soprano I, soprano II, alto
SSAA	soprano I, soprano II, alto I, alto II
SS-AA	soprano, soprano-alto, alto
SSAATTBB	soprano I, soprano II, alto I, alto II, tenor I, tenor II, bass I, bass II
TTBB	tenor I, tenor II, bass I, bass II
TTBBBB	tenor I, tenor II, baritone I, baritone II, bass I, bass II
unacc.	unaccompanied

For the complete description and explanation of this chapter, read pages 5-7 of Chapter I.

Vocal Music: Solo High Voice

Alsop, Marion. The Year's at the Spring. Song for soprano with piano. RB340

Atkins, Evelyn Harper. My Star. Song for [high] voice with violin. RB250

Atkins, Ivor. The Year's at the Spring. Song for [high] voice with keyboard. RB341

Austin, Frederic. Home-Thoughts from Abroad. Song for [high] voice with keyboard. RB113

Austin, Torrington. Sleep Soft, Beloved. Song for [high] voice with
keyboard. EBB72

Ayres, Harold. I Send My Heart. Song for [high] voice with keyboard.
RB132

Bantock, Granville. A Bean-Stripe: Also, Apple Eating. Song for [high]
voice with piano. RB101

——————. By the Fireside. Song for high voice with piano. RB17

——————. Cherries. Song for [high] voice with piano. RB96

——————. The Eagle. Song for [high] voice with piano. RB85

——————. Epilogue. Song for [high] voice with piano. RB102

——————. The Family. Song for [high] voice with piano. RB91

——————. The Guardian Angel. Song for high voice with piano. RB111

——————. Home Thoughts. Song for high voice with piano. RB114

——————. I Go to Prove My Soul. Song for [high] voice with piano.
RB282

——————. In a Year. Song for high voice with piano. RB169

——————. Life in a Love. Song for high voice with piano. RB220

——————. The Melon-Seller. Song for [high] voice with piano. RB89

——————. Mihrab Shah. Song for [high] voice with piano. RB93

——————. My Star. Song for high voice with piano. RB252

——————. Never the Time and the Place. Song for high voice with
piano. RB272

——————. Now. Song for high voice with piano. RB274

——————. A Pearl, a Girl. Song for high voice with piano. RB305

——————. A Pillar at Sebzevah. Song for [high] voice with piano.
RB98

——————. Pippa Passes. Song for high voice with piano. RB343

——————. Plot-Culture. Song for [high] voice with piano. RB97

——————. Shah Abbas. Song for [high] voice with piano. RB90

——————. Summum Bonum. Song for high voice with piano. RB515

——————. The Sun. Song for [high] voice with piano. RB92

——————. Two Camels. Song for [high] voice with piano. RB95

——————. Wanting Is—What? Song for high voice with piano. RB208

——————. A Woman's Last Word. Song for high voice with piano. RB566

Barbour, Florence Newell. Love's Ecstasy. Song for soprano or tenor with keyboard. EBB203

Barnett, Alice. Boat-Song. Song for high voice with piano. RB134

——————. Dip Your Arm o'er the Boatside. Song for high voice with piano. RB135

——————. He Muses—Drifting. Song for high voice with piano. RB136

——————. In a Gondola. Song cycle for high voice with piano. RB134-RB141

——————. It Was Ordained to Be So, Sweet. Song for high voice with piano. RB137

——————. The Moth's Kiss, First. Song for high voice with piano. RB138

——————. Serenade. Song for high voice with piano. RB139

——————. Sonnet. Song for high voice with piano. EBB215

——————. To-morrow, If a Harp-String, Say. Song for high voice with piano. RB140

——————. What Are We Two. Song for high voice with piano. RB141

Bates, Anna Craig. Apparitions. Song for [high] voice with keyboard. RB538

Beach, Mrs. H. H. A. Ah, Love, but a Day! Song for soprano or tenor with keyboard. RB174

——————. I Send My Heart Up to Thee! Song for soprano or tenor with keyboard. RB143

——————. When Soul Is Joined to Soul. Song for [high] voice with keyboard. EBB17

——————. The Year's at the Spring. Song for soprano or tenor with piano. RB347

Behrend, A. H. All's Right, "The Year's at the Spring." Song for soprano with keyboard. RB351

Bennett, Howard. "Unless." Song for high voice with piano. EBB272

Berdahl, Arthur C. Epithalamium. Song for [high] voice with keyboard. RB539

Bickford, Zahr Myron. I Find Earth Not Gray but Rosy. Song for soprano or tenor with keyboard. RB7

Black, Kate Gilmore. Pippa's Song. Song for high voice with piano. RB352

——————. The Year's at the Spring. Song for [high] voice, unacc. RB353

Bliss, James A. Sonnet Twenty-One. Song for high voice with piano. EBB156

Blumenthal, Jacques. Sleep (He Giveth His Beloved Sleep). Song for [high] voice with piano. EBB74

Bode, Alice M. The Year's at the Spring. Song for [high] voice with piano. RB355

Borton, Alice. Ah, Love, but a Day. Song for high voice with keyboard. RB179

Brahe, May H. The Year's at the Spring. Song for [high] voice with piano. RB358

Branscombe, Gena. The Best Is Yet to Be. Song for soprano or tenor with keyboard. RB470

——————. I Send My Heart Up to Thee (Serenade). Song for soprano or tenor with keyboard. RB146

——————. Serenade (I Send My Heart Up to Thee). Song for soprano or tenor with keyboard. RB147

——————. There's a Woman Like a Dew-drop. Song for high voice with piano. RB9

Bridge, J. Frederick. He Giveth His Beloved Sleep. Meditation for soprano soloist, mixed chorus (SATB), and organ (or unacc.). EBB75

Bryson, Ernest. So, the Year's Done With! Song for high voice with piano. RB64

Bullard, Frederic Field. There's a Woman Like a Dewdrop. Song for high voice, violin, and piano. RB10

Cantor, Otto. Loved by Thee. Song for soprano or tenor or high voice with piano. RB572, RB573, and RB574

Caracciolo, Luigi. Unless. Song for [high] voice with keyboard. EBB277

Caruthers, Julia Lois. Pippa's Spring Song. Song for [high] voice with keyboard. RB363

Castelnuovo-Tedesco, Mario. Letters. Song for [high] voice with piano. EBB179

Clarke, Helen A. My Star. Song for [high] voice with piano. RB253 and RB254

——————. One Way of Love. Song for [high] voice with cello obbligato and keyboard. RB276

————————. Round Us the Wild Creatures. Song for [high] voice with keyboard. RB86

————————. You'll Love Me Yet. Song for [high] voice with cello and piano. RB365

Clarke, H[ugh] A. Give Her but a Least Excuse. Song for [high] voice with keyboard. RB367

————————. Overhead the Treetops Meet. Song for [high] voice with keyboard. RB368

Clarke, Reginald. Home Thoughts from Abroad. Song for [high] voice with piano. RB117

Clarke, Robert Coningsby. Love Me. Song for [high] voice with piano. EBB38

Colvin, Herbert. How Do I Love Thee. Song for [high] voice with keyboard. EBB219 and EBB220

Cowen, Frederic H. Dost Thou Love Me (Bist du Mein?). Song for [high] voice with piano. EBB63

Davidson, Frank. Summum Bonum. Song for tenor with piano. RB517

De Francesco, Louis E. Ah, Love but a Day. Ballad for high voice with keyboard. RB181

De Koven, Reginald. There's a Woman Like a Dewdrop. Song for soprano or tenor with piano. RB12

Dello Joio, Norman. How Do I Love Thee? Song for high voice with keyboard. EBB223 and EBB224

————————. Meeting at Night. Song for high voice with keyboard. RB235

del Riego, Teresa. June, and My Lady. Song for [high] voice with piano. RB108

Dichmont, William. Be a God and Hold Me. Song for high voice with piano. RB575

————————. Let's Contend No More. Song for high voice with piano. RB575

————————. What So Wild. Song for high voice with piano. RB575

————————. A Woman's Last Word. Songs for high voice with piano. RB575

Dillon, Fannie Charles. Porphyria. Song for [high] voice with keyboard. RB455

Duncan, Edmondstoune. Good News to Aix. Song for [high] voice with piano. RB128

Elgar, Edward. Sabbath Morning at Sea. Song for high voice with piano. EBB71

Farley, Roland. God's Own Smile. Song for high voice with piano. RB546

Fisher, William Arms. For Love's Sake Only. Song for high voice with piano. EBB138

Forrester, J. Cliffe. Devotion. Song for [high] voice with piano. RB499

Forster, Beatrice. Wanting Is—What? Song for [high] voice with piano. RB209

Freer, Eleanor Everest. Apparitions. Song for [high] voice or tenor with keyboard. RB547 and RB548

French, Emma Weller. Out in the Fields. Song for soprano or tenor with piano and violin obbligato. EBB55

Frey, Adolf. Apparitions. Song for [high] voice with keyboard. RB550

Fuller, Caroline M. The Year's at the Spring. Song for soprano with keyboard. RB384

Gabriel, Virginia. At the Window. Song for [high] voice with piano. RB185

—————. Change upon Change. Song for [high] voice with piano. EBB3

—————. O Wilt Thou Have My Hand, Dear (Inclusions). Song for [high] voice with piano. EBB18

Galsworthy, Ada. Pippa's Song. Song for [high] voice with keyboard. RB385 and RB386

Ganz, Rudolf. A Woman's Last Word. Song for [high] voice with piano. RB578

Gilberté, Hallett. Ah! Love but a Day. Song for high voice with piano. RB188

Giorza, Paolo. Love Me. Song for soprano or tenor with piano. EBB40

Goatley, Alma. Now That April's There. Song for soprano or tenor with piano. RB119

Graham, A. Cyril. Love Has Come. Song for [high] voice with keyboard. RB228

Gregory, E. C. James Lee's Wife. Song for [high] voice with keyboard. RB189

Hadley, Henry. The Face of All the World Has Changed. Song for [high] voice with keyboard. EBB115

—————. How Do I Love Thee? Song for high voice with piano. EBB232

————————. Nevermore Alone. Song for high voice with keyboard. EBB107

————————. You'll Love Me Yet. Song for high voice with keyboard. RB392

Halley, Margaret A. To Perfect the Summer. Song for [high] voice with piano. RB211

————————. The Year's at the Spring. Song for [high] voice with piano. RB394

Hammer, Marie von. If I Were Thou. Song for high voice with piano. EBB268

————————. A Rose Once Grew. Song for high voice with piano. EBB35

Harraden, Ethel. I Go to Prove My Soul. Edited by Emma L. Taussig. Song for soprano or tenor with keyboard. RB286

————————. I Go to Prove My Soul. Song for [high] voice with piano. RB287

Harris, Russell G. "Tears." Setting for [high] voice with violin I and II, flute, oboe, clarinet, bassoon, cymbal, and piano. EBB263

Harrison, Julius. Boot, Saddle, to Horse and Away. Song for tenor or baritone with piano. RB50

————————. Marching Along. Song for tenor or baritone with piano. RB25

Hartog, Cécile S. The Year's at the Spring. Song for high voice with piano. RB396, RB397, and RB398

Hoberg, Margaret. Such a Starved Bank of Moss (Apparitions). Song for soprano or tenor with keyboard. RB552

Homer, Sidney. My Star. Song for high voice with piano. RB259

————————. Prospice. Song for high voice with piano. RB460

————————. There's Heaven Above. Song for high voice with piano. RB214

————————. A Woman's Last Word. Song for high voice with piano. RB579

Hopkins, Franklin. How Do I Love Thee. Song for [high] voice with keyboard. EBB233

————————. The Isle Enchantress. Song for [high] voice with piano. RB173

Hopkins, Joseph M. How Do I Love Thee? Song for high voice with piano. EBB234

Hughes, Rupert. A Gondolier's Song. Song for [high] voice with keyboard. RB153

Huhn, Bruno. Faith. Song for [high] voice with keyboard. RB289

Johnson, F. Arthur. Song from Pippa Passes. Song for [high] voice with piano. RB401, RB402, and RB403

Johnson, Noel. All the Bloom of the Year (Summum Bonum). Song for [high] voice with piano. RB521

Jordan, Jules. Love's Confidence. Song for soprano or tenor with piano. RB405

Jowett, Albert. A Woman's Last Word. Song for high voice with piano. RB583

Kaiser, Charles A. Ashes. Song for soprano with keyboard. EBB102

——————. A New Rhythm. Song for tenor with keyboard. EBB116

——————. Seven Sonnets from the Portuguese. Song cycle for soprano and tenor with keyboard. EBB84, EBB102, EBB116, EBB129, EBB161, EBB164, and EBB206

——————. Three Kisses. Song for soprano with keyboard. EBB206

Kernochan, Marshall. Wanting Is—What? Song for [high] voice with piano. RB212

Klein, Bruno Oscar. If I Leave All for Thee. Song for [high] voice with piano. EBB197

Kramer, A. Walter. The Patriot. Song for high voice with piano. RB302

Krull, Fritz. I Go to Prove My Soul. Song for [high] voice with keyboard. RB291

——————. Round Us the Wild Creatures. Song for [high] voice with keyboard. RB88

——————. Such a Starved Bank of Moss. Song for [high] voice with keyboard. RB553

Lewando, Ralph. A Denial. Song for [high] voice with keyboard. EBB10

Liddle, Samuel. King Charles. Song for [high] voice with piano. RB40

Lippé, Edouard. How Do I Love Thee. Song for high voice with piano. EBB236

Löhr, Harvey. Summum Bonum. Song for [high] voice with piano. RB522

Loomis, Harvey Worthington. Morning Song. Song for [high] voice with keyboard. RB411

Lynes, Frank. Apparitions. Song for high voice with keyboard. RB554

McDaniel, William J. How Do I Love Thee. Song for [high] voice with keyboard. EBB237

Mc. Hardy, James M. P. Life in a Love. Song for [high] voice with piano. RB223

Mackenzie, A. C. There's a Woman Like a Dew-drop. Song for [high] voice with harp or piano. RB15

Macmillen, Francis. The Year's at the Spring. Song for high voice with piano. RB414

Madsen, Dora L. Sonnet. Song for [high] voice with keyboard. EBB238

Mallinson, Albert. All the Breath and the Bloom of the Year. Song for [high] voice with piano. RB523

Mana-Zucca. A Query. Song for high voice with piano. RB100

——————. That Was I. Song for high voice with piano. RB494

Markham, Robert Alexander. How Do I Love Thee. Song for soprano with piano. EBB239

Mason, Mrs. Alexander O. The Year's at the Spring (Song from Pippa Passes). Song for soprano with keyboard. RB415

Metcalf, John W. The Cares of Yesterday. Song for soprano or tenor with piano. EBB56 and EBB57

Molineux, Marie Ada. Thy Face. Arranged by Harry Lawson Harts. Song for [high] voice with keyboard. RB556 and RB558

——————. Thy Face. Song for [high] voice with keyboard. RB557

Needham, Alicia Adélaïda. Unless. Song for [high] voice with piano. EBB281

Neidlinger, W. H. My Star: "All That I Know of a Certain Star." Song for soprano or tenor with piano. RB262

——————. The Year's at the Spring. Song for soprano or tenor with piano. RB419

Nevin, Ethelbert. The Wedding Morning. Song for high voice with piano. RB421

Norén, Helmer. The Year's at the Spring. Song for [high] voice with piano. RB422

Oldroyd, George. Tresses. Song for [high] voice with piano. RB505

Parker, Phyllis Norman. Unless. Song for [high] voice with piano. EBB283

Pascal, Florian. The House of Clouds. Song for [high] voice with piano. EBB16

——————. Love Me, Sweet. Song for [high] voice with piano. EBB42

—————. White Lilies. Song for [high] voice with piano. EBB5

—————. Wisdom Unapplied. Song for [high] voice with piano. EBB269

Pease, Alfred H. A Year's Spinning. Song for [high] voice with keyboard. EBB289

Peel, Graham. Boot, Saddle, to Horse. Song for [high] voice with piano. RB54

Philp, Elizabeth. "Inclusion." Song for [high] voice with keyboard. EBB21

Pierce, Allie Coleman. How Do I Love Thee. Song for [high] voice with keyboard. EBB241

Ponssen, Mary Eleanor. Question and Answer. Song for [high] voice with keyboard. EBB66

Protheroe, Daniel. Ah, Love, but a Day. Song for high voice with keyboard. RB196

—————. I Send My Heart Up to Thee. Song for high voice with keyboard. RB155

—————. The Year's at the Spring. Song for high voice with keyboard. RB426

Ralston, Frances Marion. Ay! Note That Potter's Wheel. Piano solo with choral monotone accompaniment (SSAA) and soprano soloist. RB475

—————. For Pleasant Is This Flesh. Song for soprano with piano. RB475

—————. Now Who Shall Arbitrate. Song for soprano with piano. RB475

Reed, C. H. Cavalier Song. Song for [high] voice with piano. RB55

—————. Meeting at Night. Song for [high] voice with piano. RB237

—————. Parting at Morning. Song for [high] voice with piano. RB297

Reinagle, Caroline. Would It Were I Had Been False, Not You! Song for [high] voice with piano. RB591

Renaud, Emiliano. All's Right with the World. Song for [high] voice with piano. RB427

—————. Love Me Forever. Song for [high] voice with piano. RB67

—————. My Star. Song for [high] voice with piano. RB263

—————. You'll Love Me Yet. Song for [high] voice with piano. RB428

Rhodes, Harold. A Woman's Love. Song for [high] voice with keyboard. EBB243

Rogers, Clara Kathleen. Appearances. Song for [high] voice with keyboard. RB6

—————. Good to Forgive. Song for [high] voice with keyboard. RB217

—————. Love. Song for [high] voice with piano. RB68

—————. My Star. Song for [high] voice with keyboard. RB264

—————. One Way of Love. Song for [high] voice with keyboard. RB278

—————. A Woman's Last Word. Song for [high] voice with keyboard. RB588

Rogers, James H. Boot and Saddle—Cavalier Song. Song for high voice with piano. RB57

—————. Boot and Saddle—Cavalier Song by Robert Browning. Song for tenor with piano. RB56

Rorem, Ned. In a Gondola. Song for high voice with piano. RB156

—————. Pippa's Song. Song for high voice with piano. RB432

Roy, William. How Do I Love Thee. Song for high voice with piano. EBB246

Royle, Popplewell. Summum Bonum. Song for [high] voice with piano. RB525

Ryan, Margaret. Meeting at Night. Song for high voice with piano. RB238

Saar, Louis Victor. Browning Song Cycle from Letters of R. B. to E. B. B. Song cycle for high voice with piano. RB219

—————. The Rose Tree. Song for high voice with piano. RB219

—————. Some Happy Day. Song for high voice with piano. RB219

—————. This Little Flower. Song for high voice with piano. RB219

—————. Thou Shalt Know Me. Song for high voice with piano. RB219

—————. Thou Wilt Know. Song for high voice with piano. RB219

Sabin, Wallace A. Pan. Song for high or medium voice with piano. EBB51

Smith, David Stanley. Chorus for women's choir (SSA), soprano solo, oboe (or flute) obbligato, and piano. EBB52

Smith, Leo. My Star. Song for [high] voice with piano. RB265

Spencer, Fanny M. Unless. Song for tenor or soprano with keyboard. EBB286

Stanford, C. Villiers. May's Love. Song for [high] voice with keyboard. EBB45

Stebbins, G. Waring. Meeting. Song for high voice with piano. RB240

Stephens, Ward. You'll Love Me Yet. Song for [high] voice with piano. RB440

Sternberg, Daniel Arie. Pippa's Song. Song for high voice with keyboard. RB441

Stewart, Humphrey J. Best of All. Song for [high] voice with piano. RB526

Stratton, G. R. Boot, Saddle, to Horse, and Away. Song for [high] voice with piano. RB59

Surinach, Carlos. How Do I Love Thee? Song for [high] voice with piano. EBB247

——————. If Thou Must Love Me. Song for [high] voice with piano. EBB143

——————. Our Two Souls. Song for [high] voice with piano. EBB165

——————. With Thee Anear. Song for [high] voice with piano. EBB117

——————. Yet, Love Is Beautiful Indeed. Song for [high] voice with piano. EBB130

Taussig, Emma L., editor. I Go to Prove My Soul. Ethel Harraden. Song for soprano or tenor with keyboard. RB286

Thayer, Arthur W. Nay but You. Song for high voice with piano. RB508

——————. One Way of Love. Song for high voice with piano. RB279

Treharne, Bryceson. A Child's Thought on God. Song for high or medium voice with piano. EBB6

——————. In a Gondola. Song for [high] voice with piano. RB162

——————. Renunciation. Song for high or medium voice with piano. EBB23

True, Latham. I Send My Heart Up to Thee. Song for [high] voice with keyboard. RB163

——————. The Moth's Kiss and the Bee's Kiss. Song for [high] voice with keyboard. RB164

——————. Prospice. Song for [high] voice with keyboard. RB468

Vaille, Clara Hinman. Death Is a Door. Song for [high] voice with keyboard. RB71

Vannah, Kate. Questionings. Song for soprano with keyboard. EBB24

Versel, Louis. Since We Parted. Song for high voice with piano. RB495

Vogler, [Georg Joseph]. The Request. Song for [high] voice with keyboard. RB2 and RB3

Ware, Harriet. How Do I Love Thee. Song for high voice with piano. EBB249 and EBB250

Watson, Mary E. Give Her but a Least Excuse to Love Me. Song for [high] voice, unacc. RB446 and RB447

——————. I Am Queen of Thee, Floweret! Song for [high] voice, unacc. RB447

——————. Incidental Music to *Pippa's Soliloquy*. Incidental music for speaker, [high] voice, [medium] voice, violin, and harp. RB447

——————. Overhead the Tree Tops Meet. Song for [high] voice, unacc. RB447

Watson, Mary E.; and Nisbet, Ola Jones. A King Lived Long Ago. Song for [high] voice, unacc. RB448 and RB449

Welch, Jay. All Service Ranks the Same with God. Song for soprano, oboe, harp, and clarinet. RB450

——————. Give Her the Least Excuse to Love Me. Song for soprano, oboe, clarinet, and harp. RB450

——————. A King Lived Long Ago. Song for soprano with oboe and harp. RB450

——————. Music for Robert Browning's Pippa Passes. Incidental music for oboe, clarinet, harp, soprano, [medium] voice, and [low] voice. RB450

——————. Overhead the Treetops Meet. Song for soprano with harp. RB450

——————. The Year's at the Spring. Song for soprano with harp. RB450

Wellesz, Egon. Du bist da draben im Palast begehrt. Song for soprano and string quartet. EBB98

——————. Ich denk an dich, wie wilder Wein den Baum spriessend umringt. Song for soprano and string quartet. EBB184

——————. Mir scheint, das Angesicht der Welt verging—in einem andern. Song for soprano and string quartet. EBB118

——————. Nur drei jedoch in Gottes ganzem All vernahmen es. Song for soprano and string quartet. EBB90

——————. Sonette der Elisabeth Barret-Browning. Songs for soprano and string quartet. EBB85, EBB90, EBB98, EBB118, and EBB184

——————. Und es geschah mir einst, an Theokrit zu denken. Song for soprano and string quartet. EBB85

White, Maude Valérie. How Do I Love Thee. Song for [high] voice with keyboard. EBB255

——————. Marching Along. Song for [high] voice with piano. RB31

Willan, Healey. Sonnet, "When Our Two Souls Stand Up Erect and Strong." Song for [high] voice with piano. EBB166

Wilson, Alec. Oh! To Be in England. Song for [high] voice with piano. RB127

Worth, John W. Dip Your Arm o'er the Boatside. Song for soprano with piano. RB166

——————. Evelyn Hope. Song for [high] voice with keyboard. RB84

——————. Four Songs from Pippa Passes. Songs for high voice with keyboard. RB453

——————. Give Her but a Least Excuse to Love Me. Song for [high] voice with keyboard. RB453

——————. Good to Forgive. Song for [high] voice with keyboard. RB218

——————. I Send My Heart Up to Thee. Song for tenor with piano. RB166

——————. In a Gondola. [Song cycle] for soprano, tenor, reader, and piano. RB166

——————. It Was Ordained to Be So. Song for tenor with piano. RB166

——————. A King Lived Long Ago. Song for [high] voice with keyboard. RB453

——————. Misconceptions. Song for [high] voice with keyboard. RB249

——————. The Moth's Kiss, First. Song for soprano with piano. RB166

——————. My Star. Song for [high] voice with keyboard. RB270

——————. Overhead the Tree-tops Meet. Song for [high] voice with keyboard. RB453

——————. Parting at Morning. Song for [high] voice with keyboard. RB299

——————. Past We Glide. Song for tenor with piano. RB166

——————. The Patriot. Song for [high] voice with keyboard. RB303

——————. To-morrow, If a Harp-String, Say. Song for soprano with piano. RB166

————. What Are We Two. Song for tenor with piano. RB166

————. The Year's at the Spring. Song for [high] voice with keyboard. RB453

Young, Dal. Dip Your Arm o'er the Boatside. Song for soprano with piano. RB167

————. I Send My Heart Up to Thee. Song for tenor with piano. RB167

————. In a Gondola. Song cycle for tenor and soprano with piano. RB167

————. In a Gondola. Song for soprano with piano. RB168

————. The Moth's Kiss. Song for soprano with piano. RB167 and RB168

————. Past We Glide. Song for tenor with piano. RB167

————. Pippa's Song ("The Year's at the Spring"). Song for [high] voice with piano. RB454

————. What Are We Two? Song for tenor with piano. RB167

————. What If the Three. Song for tenor with piano. RB167

Vocal Music: Solo Medium High Voice

Beach, John Parsons. A Woman's Last Word. Song for [medium high] voice with piano. RB568

Bond, Carrie Jacobs. Out in the Fields. Song for [medium high] voice with keyboard. EBB53

Browning, [Robert and Elizabeth Barrett]. Avenge the Good Ship Maine. Arranged by R. M. Stults. Song for [medium high] voice with keyboard. RB7.1

Caracciolo, Luigi. Unless. Song for [medium high] voice with keyboard. EBB276

Clark, Ruth Kinney. The Year's at the Spring. Song for [medium high] voice with keyboard. RB364

Clarke, Helen A. Apparitions. Song for [medium high] voice with keyboard. RB541

Cowen, Frederic H. Insufficiency (Leaving Yet Loving). Song for [medium high] voice with piano. EBB25

Crumpler, Mary Frances. You'll Love Me Yet! Song for [medium high] voice with piano. RB371

Dansie, Redgewell. Boot and Saddle. Song for [medium high] voice with piano. RB45

————. Give a Rouse. Song for [medium high] voice with piano. RB34

David, Elizabeth Harbison. Pippa's Song. Song for [medium high] voice with flute, violin, and keyboard. RB373

Drakeford, Louis. Boot and Saddle. Song for [medium high] voice with piano. RB47

————. Give a Rouse. Song for [medium high] voice with piano. RB36

Duncan, Edmondstoune. The Year's at the Spring. Song for [medium high] voice with piano. RB376

Elgar, Edward. A Child Asleep. Song for [medium high] voice with keyboard. EBB4

Ellingham, Harry. Evelyn. Song for [medium high] voice with keyboard. RB83

Fisher, Charles R. Meeting at Night. Song for [medium high] voice with piano. RB236

Foote, David. A Woman's Last Word. Song for [medium high] voice with keyboard. RB576

Gow, George Coleman. The Year's at the Spring. Song for [medium high] voice with piano. RB389

Gregory, E. C. A Lover's Quarrel. Song for [medium high] voice with keyboard. RB229

————. Song. Song for [medium high] voice with keyboard. RB502

Harrison, Julius. Boot, Saddle, to Horse and Away. Song for tenor or baritone with piano. RB50

————. Marching Along. Song for tenor or baritone with piano. RB25

Johnson, Leslie. "Only Sleep," a Slumber Song. Song for [medium high] voice with keyboard. RB580

Johnstone, Harry. Pippa's Song. Song for [medium high] voice with keyboard. RB404

Kernochan, Marshall. You'll Love Me Yet. Song for [medium high] voice with piano. RB406 and RB407

Krull, F. Epilogue. Song for [medium high] voice with keyboard. RB76 and RB77

Marzials, Théo. Leaving Yet Loving. Song for [medium high] voice with keyboard. EBB27 and EBB28

Ormsby, George F. Love Me Sweet. Song for [medium high] voice with piano. EBB41

Pascal, Florian. Inclusions. Song for [medium high] voice with piano. EBB20

——————. There Is No One Beside Thee. Song for [medium high] voice with piano. EBB29

Patton, Arthur. Insufficiency. Song for [medium high] voice with piano. EBB31

Ralston, Frances Marion. Now Who Shall Arbitrate. Song for [medium high] voice with keyboard. RB474

Raymond, Ralph. A Last Word. Song for [medium high] voice with piano. RB586 and RB587

Rogers, Clara Kathleen. The Year's at the Spring. Song for [medium high] voice with piano. RB430

Rogers, James H. I Go to Prove My Soul. Song for [medium high] voice with keyboard. RB293

Sabin, Wallace A. Pan. Song for high or medium high voice with piano. EBB51

Schaefer, Hal. "I Yield the Grave for Thy Sake." Song for [medium high] voice with keyboard. EBB169

Sharpe, Cedric. The Year's at the Spring. Song for [medium high] voice with piano. RB437

Somervell, Arthur. A Broken Arc. Song cycle for [medium] voice or [medium high] voice with piano. RB4, RB70, RB239, RB266, RB438, RB507, RB563, and RB592

——————. Meeting at Night. Song for [medium high] voice with piano. RB239

——————. My Star. Song for [medium high] voice with piano. RB266

——————. Nay, but You, Who Do Not Love Her. Song for [medium high] voice with piano. RB507

——————. Such a Starved Bank of Moss. Song for [medium high] voice with piano. RB563

——————. The Worst of It. Song for [medium high] voice with piano. RB592

——————. The Year's at the Spring. Song for [medium high] voice with piano. RB438

Spier, La Salle. And You Are Ever by Me. Song for [medium high] voice with string quartet and piano. RB439

——————. But Winter Hastens at Summer's End. Song for [medium high] voice with string quartet and piano. RB439

—————. A Cycle of Six Songs from *Pippa Passes*. Song cycle for [medium high] voice with string quartet and piano. RB439

—————. Day! Song for [medium high] voice with string quartet and piano. RB439

—————. New-Year's Hymn. Song for [medium high] voice with string quartet and piano. RB439

—————. Oh, What a Drear, Dark Close to My Poor Day! Song for [medium high] voice with string quartet and piano. RB439

—————. Overhead the Tree-tops Meet. Song for [medium high] voice with string quartet and piano. RB439

Stanford, C. Villiers. Prospice. Song for [medium high] voice with piano. RB463 and RB464

Stratton, G. R. Boot, Saddle, to Horse, and Away. Song for [medium high] voice with piano. RB60

Threlkeld, Beulah. How Do I Love Thee. Song for [medium high] voice with keyboard. EBB248

Treharne, Bryceson. A Child's Thought on God. Song for high or medium voice with piano. EBB6

—————. Renunciation. Song for high or medium voice with piano. EBB23

Troup, Emily Josephine. Unless. Song for [medium high] voice with piano. EBB287

Weems, Mrs. J. Eddie. The Browning Cycle of Love Lyrics. Song cycle for [low] voice, [medium] voice, or [medium high] voice with keyboard. EBB251, RB69, and RB268

—————. Love. Song for [medium high] voice with keyboard. RB69

White, Maude Valérie. Home Thoughts from Abroad. Song for [medium high] voice with piano. RB125

Vocal Music: Solo Medium Voice

Ackert, Bernard G. Rabbi Ben Ezra. Song for [medium] voice with keyboard. RB469

Aldrich, Leslie. Paean, "One Who Never Turn'd His Back." Song for [medium] voice with keyboard. RB72

[Armes, Nancy.] Meeting at Night. Song for [medium] voice with keyboard. RB234

Arnott, A. Davidson. Give a Rouse. Song for baritone or bass with keyboard. RB32

Ayres, Harold. I Loved You. Song for [medium] voice with keyboard. RB82

Bantock, Granville. As I Ride ("Through the Metidja to Abd-el-Kadr"). Song for [medium] voice with piano. RB527

——————. A Camel-Driver. Song for [medium] voice with piano. RB94

——————. Pippa Passes. Song for medium voice with piano. RB342

Barbour, Florence Newell. Love's Ecstasy. Song for mezzo soprano or baritone with keyboard. EBB202

Barlow, Emily. Entreaty. Song for [medium] voice with piano. RB567

Beach, Mrs. H. H. A. Ah, Love, but a Day! Song for mezzo soprano or baritone with piano. RB176 and RB177

——————. The Year's at the Spring. Song for [medium] voice with piano. RB344

Beach, John. In a Gondola. Dramatic monologue for baritone with keyboard. RB144

——————. Is She Not Pure Gold. Song for [medium] voice with piano. RB497

——————. New Year's Hymn. Song for [medium] voice with keyboard. RB350

Beckett, Bessie D. Submission. Song for [medium] voice with piano. RB569

Beecher, Carl. How Do I Love Thee? Song for medium voice with piano. EBB216

Blair, William. The Year's at the Spring. Song for [medium] voice with piano. RB354

Blumenthal, Jacques. Sleep (He Giveth His Beloved Sleep). Song for [medium] voice with piano. EBB73

Boys, Reginald S. Devotion. Song for [medium] voice with keyboard. RB570

Brahe, May H. Oh, to Be in England! Song for medium voice with piano. RB116

——————. The Year's at the Spring. Song for medium voice with piano. RB356 and RB357

Branscombe, Gena. Boot and Saddle. Song for medium voice with piano. RB44

——————. "But Only Three in All God's Universe." Song for medium voice with piano. EBB86

——————. "The Face of All the World Is Changed." Song for medium voice with piano. EBB111

——————. "How Do I Love Thee." Song for medium voice with piano. EBB217

——————. "I Thought Once How Theocritus Had Sung." Song for medium voice with piano. EBB78

——————. Love in a Life. Song cycle for medium voice with piano. EBB78, EBB86, EBB103, EBB111, EBB176, and EBB217

——————. Marching Along! Song for medium voice with piano. RB22

——————. "My Own Beloved." Song for medium voice with piano. EBB176

——————. Serenade (I Send My Heart Up to Thee). Song for mezzo soprano or baritone with keyboard. RB148

——————. What Are We Two? Song for [medium] voice with keyboard. RB149

——————. "The Widest Land." Song for medium voice with piano. EBB103

Brooke, Carol Kelley. True Love. Song for [medium] voice with keyboard. EBB273

Bruguiere, E. A. Life in a Love. Song for [medium] voice with piano. RB222

Bryson, Ernest. So, the Year's Done With! Song for medium voice with piano. RB65

Caldicott, Alfred J. Unless. Song for [medium] voice with violin or cello obbligato and piano. EBB275

Cantor, Otto. Lov'd by Thee. Song for alto or baritone with piano. RB571

Carter, Ernest. "Thou Lov'st Me Not." Song for [medium] voice with piano. EBB61

Carter, Esther May. The Year's at the Spring. Song for [medium] voice with piano. RB362

Castelnuovo-Tedesco, Mario. Poems and Flowers. Song for [medium] voice with piano. EBB256

——————. The Sweet Sad Years. Song for [medium] voice with piano. EBB79

Clarke, Helen Archibald. Song: Ask Not One Least Word of Praise. Song for [medium] voice with piano. RB99

Clarke, Henry Leland. The Year's at the Spring. Song for [medium] voice with keyboard. RB366

Coleridge-Taylor, S. You'll Love Me Yet. Song for contralto or baritone with keyboard. RB369

Coombs, C. Whitney. Thy Face. Song for medium voice with piano. RB542

Craddock, Reginald W. Apparitions. Song for medium voice with piano. RB543

Cripps, A. Redgrave. The Year's at the Spring. Song for [medium] voice with keyboard. RB370

Curtis, Natalie. Song from Pippa Passes. Song for [medium] voice with piano. RB372

Dansie, Redgewell. Marching Along. Song for [medium] voice with piano. RB23

Davies, H. Walford. Hervé Riel. Choral setting for baritone solo, mixed chorus (SSAATTBB), and orchestra. Piano-vocal score. RB112

————. Prospice. Song for baritone with string quartet. RB457

Davis, Blevins. "How Do I Love Thee." Song for [medium] voice with keyboard. EBB221

De Francesco, Louis E. Ah, Love but a Day. Ballad for medium voice with keyboard. RB182 and RB183

del Riego, Teresa. All's Right with the World. Song for [medium] voice with piano. RB375

————. June, and My Lady. Song for [medium] voice with piano. RB107

de Sousa, Leon. Give a Rouse! Song for [medium] voice with piano. RB35

Dougherty, Celius. Portrait. Song for medium voice with piano. RB544

Downing, Lulu Jones. Apparitions. Song for medium voice with keyboard. RB545

Drakeford, Louis. Marching Along. Song for [medium] voice with piano. RB24

Ellingham, Harry. Her Tresses. Song for [medium] voice with keyboard. RB498

England, Nick. The All-Loving. Song for baritone, reader, and piano. RB80

Freer, Eleanor Everest. Accuse Me Not, Beseech Thee. Song for medium voice with keyboard. EBB144 and EBB145

————. All That I Know of a Certain Star. Song for baritone with keyboard. RB255

————. And Therefore If to Love Can Be Desert. Song for mezzo soprano or medium voice with keyboard. EBB131, EBB132, and EBB133

————. And Wilt Thou Have Me Fashion into Speech. Song for medium voice with keyboard. EBB136 and EBB137

————. And Yet, Because Thou Overcomest So. Song for medium voice with keyboard. EBB146 and EBB147

————————. Because Thou Hast the Pow'r and Own'st the Grace. Song for medium voice with keyboard. EBB207 and EBB208

————————. Beloved, My Beloved, When I Think. Song for medium voice with keyboard. EBB154 and EBB155

————————. Beloved, Thou Hast Brought Me Many Flowers. Song for medium voice with keyboard. EBB257 and EBB258

————————. But Only Three in All God's Universe. Song for medium voice or mezzo soprano with keyboard. EBB87, EBB88, and EBB89

————————. Can It Be Right to Give What I Can Give? Song for mezzo soprano or medium voice with keyboard. EBB122, EBB123, and EBB124

————————. The Face of All the World Is Changed, I Think. Song for mezzo soprano or medium voice with keyboard. EBB112, EBB113, and EBB114

————————. First Time He Kissed Me, He but Only Kissed. Song for medium voice with keyboard. EBB204 and EBB205

————————. The First Time That the Sun Rose on Thine Oath. Song for medium voice with keyboard. EBB189 and EBB190

————————. Go from Me. Yet I Feel That I Shall Stand. Song for mezzo soprano or medium voice with keyboard. EBB104, EBB105, and EBB106

————————. A Heavy Heart, Beloved, Have I Borne. Song for medium voice with keyboard. EBB172 and EBB173

————————. How Do I Love Thee? Song for medium voice with keyboard. EBB226 and EBB227

————————. I Heard Last Night a Little Child Go Singing. Song for mezzo soprano with keyboard. EBB1

————————. I Lift My Heavy Heart Up Solemnly. Song for medium voice or mezzo soprano with keyboard. EBB99, EBB100, and EBB101

————————. I Lived with Visions for My Company. Song for medium voice with keyboard. EBB174 and EBB175

————————. I Never Gave a Lock of Hair Away. Song for medium voice with keyboard. EBB150 and EBB151

————————. I Once Thought How Theocritus Had Sung. Song for mezzo soprano with keyboard. EBB80

————————. I See Thine Image thro' My Tears Tonight. Song for medium voice with keyboard. EBB185 and EBB186

————————. I Thank All Who Have Loved Me in Their Hearts. Song for medium voice with keyboard. EBB211 and EBB212

—————. I Think of Thee! My Thoughts Do Twine and Bud. Song for medium voice with keyboard. EBB182 and EBB183

—————. I Thought Once How Theocritus Had Sung. Song for medium voice or mezzo soprano with keyboard. EBB81, EBB82, and EBB83

—————. If I Leave All for Thee, Wilt Thou Exchange. Song for medium voice with keyboard. EBB195 and EBB196

—————. If Thou Must Love Me. Song for medium voice with keyboard. EBB139 and EBB140

—————. Indeed This Very Love Which Is My Boast. Song for medium voice with keyboard. EBB134 and EBB135

—————. Is It Indeed So? Song for medium voice with keyboard. EBB167 and EBB168

—————. Let the World's Sharpness, Like a Clasping Knife. Song for medium voice with keyboard. EBB170 and EBB171

—————. "My Future Will Not Copy Fair My Past." Song for medium voice with keyboard. EBB213 and EBB214

—————. My Letters! All Dead Paper, Mute and White! Song for medium voice with keyboard. EBB180 and EBB181

—————. My Own Beloved, Who Hast Lifted Me. Song for medium voice with keyboard. EBB177 and EBB178

—————. My Poet, Thou Canst Touch on All the Notes. Song for medium voice with keyboard. EBB148 and EBB149

—————. My Star. Song for baritone or [medium] voice with keyboard. RB256 and RB257

—————. Nay, but You, Who Do Not Love Her. Song for baritone with keyboard. RB501

—————. Oh, Yes! They Love through All This World of Ours! Song for medium voice with keyboard. EBB209 and EBB210

—————. Pardon, oh, Pardon, That My Soul Should Make. Song for medium voice with keyboard. EBB200 and EBB201

—————. Say over Again. Song for mezzo soprano or medium voice with keyboard. EBB158, EBB159, and EBB160

—————. Sonnets from the Portuguese, op. 22. Book I. Song cycle for mezzo soprano with keyboard. EBB80, EBB87, EBB91, EBB95, EBB99, EBB104, EBB112, EBB119, EBB122, EBB126, and EBB131

——————. Sonnets from the Portuguese, op. 22. French translation by Eleanor Everest Freer. Song cycle for medium voice with keyboard. EBB82, EBB88, EBB92, EBB96, EBB100, EBB105, EBB113, EBB120, EBB123, EBB127, EBB132, EBB134, EBB136, EBB139, EBB144, EBB146, EBB148, EBB150, EBB152, EBB154, EBB159, EBB162, EBB167, EBB170, EBB172, EBB174, EBB177, EBB180, EBB182, EBB185, EBB187, EBB189, EBB191, EBB193, EBB195, EBB198, EBB200, EBB204, EBB207, EBB209, EBB211, EBB213, EBB226, and EBB257

——————. Sonnets from the Portuguese, op. 22. Song cycle for medium voice with keyboard. EBB83, EBB89, EBB93, EBB97, EBB101, EBB106, EBB114, EBB121, EBB124, EBB128, EBB133, EBB135, EBB137, EBB140, EBB145, EBB147, EBB149, EBB151, EBB153, EBB155, EBB160, EBB163, EBB168, EBB171, EBB173, EBB175, EBB178, EBB181, EBB183, EBB186, EBB188, EBB190, EBB192, EBB194, EBB196, EBB199, EBB201, EBB205, EBB208, EBB210, EBB212, EBB214, EBB227, and EBB258

——————. The Soul's Rialto Hath Its Merchandise. Song for medium voice with keyboard. EBB152 and EBB153

——————. Such a Starved Bank of Moss. Song for baritone with keyboard. RB549

——————. Thou Comest! All Is Said without a Word. Song for medium voice with keyboard. EBB187 and EBB188

——————. Thou Hast Thy Calling to Some Palace-Floor. Song for medium voice, baritone, or mezzo soprano with keyboard. EBB94, EBB95, EBB96, and EBB97

——————. Unlike Are We, Unlike, O Princely Heart! Song for medium voice or mezzo soprano with keyboard. EBB91, EBB92, and EBB93

——————. What Can I Give Thee Back, O Liberal. Song for mezzo soprano or medium voice with keyboard. EBB119, EBB120, and EBB121

——————. When Our Two Souls Stand Up Erect and Strong. Song for medium voice with keyboard. EBB162 and EBB163

——————. When We First Met and Loved, I Did Not Build. Song for medium voice with keyboard. EBB198 and EBB199

——————. With the Same Heart, I Said, I'll Answer Thee. Song for medium voice with keyboard. EBB193 and EBB194

——————. The Year's at the Spring. Song for baritone or medium voice with keyboard. RB382 and RB383

——————. Yes, Call Me by My Pet Name! Song for medium voice with keyboard. EBB191 and EBB192

——————. Yet, Love, Mere Love, Is Beautiful Indeed. Song for mezzo soprano or medium voice with keyboard. EBB125, EBB126, EBB127, and EBB128

Fuller, Caroline M. Over-head the Tree-tops Meet. Song for mezzo soprano with keyboard. RB384

Gabert, Abel. How Do I Love Thee. Song for mezzo soprano or baritone with piano. EBB228

Galsworthy, Ada. In the Doorway. Song for [medium] voice with piano. RB202

Ganz, Rudolf. A Woman's Last Word. Song for [medium] voice with piano. RB577

Gelrud, Paul. Love. Song for [medium] voice, unacc. RB66

Gilchrist, W. W. All Service Ranks the Same with God. Song for [medium] voice with keyboard. RB387

Giorza, Paolo. Love Me. Song for mezzo soprano or baritone with piano. EBB39

Grace, Harvey. The Year's at the Spring. Song for mezzo soprano with piano. RB390

Gregory, E. C. Apparitions. Song for [medium] voice with keyboard. RB551

——————. Misconceptions. Song for [medium] voice with keyboard. RB246

——————. One Way of Loving. Song for [medium] voice with keyboard. RB277

Hadley, Henry K. Nevermore Alone. Song for [medium] voice with keyboard. EBB108

——————. Prospice. Song for medium voice with piano. RB459

——————. There's a Woman Like a Dew-drop. Song for [medium] voice with keyboard. RB13

——————. The Year's at the Spring. Song for [medium] voice with keyboard. RB391

Halley, M. A. To Perfect the Summer. Song for [medium] voice with keyboard. RB210

——————. The Year's at the Spring. Song for [medium] voice with piano. RB393

Harraden, Ethel. Wilt Thou Change Too? Song for [medium] voice with piano. RB190

Harrison, Julius. Boot, Saddle, to Horse and Away. Song for tenor or baritone with piano. RB50 and RB51

—————. King Charles. Song for baritone with piano. RB37

—————. Marching Along. Song for tenor or baritone with piano. RB25

Hervey, Augusta E. Unless. Song for [medium] voice with piano. EBB279

Herz, Maria. Pippa Passes (Pippa's Lied). Song for [medium] voice with piano. RB399

Hill, Mildred J. My Star. Song for [medium] voice with piano. RB258

Hinkle, Daisy. Home Thoughts from Abroad. Song for mezzo soprano with piano. RB120 and RB121

Hollander, Benoit. Summum Bonum. Song for [medium] voice with piano. RB519

Hollins, Dorothea. Boot and Saddle. Song for [medium] voice with keyboard. RB52

—————. The Year's at the Spring. Song for mezzo soprano with keyboard. RB400

Iles, Edward. Nay but Do You Not Love Her. Song for [medium] voice with piano. RB503

Inches, Charles. Summum Bonum. Song for [medium] voice with piano. RB520

Ives, Charles. From "Paracelsus." Song for [medium] voice with keyboard. RB290

Jenkins, Elizabeth, arranger. How Do I Love Thee. Mary Passailaigue. Song for [medium] voice with keyboard. EBB240

Jervis-Read, H. V. My Mistress. Song for [medium] voice with piano. RB504

Kellie, Lawrence. Say Never Ye Loved Once. Song for [medium] voice with piano. EBB37

Kernochan, Marshall Rogers. Ah, Love, but a Day. Revised edition. Song for medium voice with keyboard. RB191

—————. At the Window. Song for medium voice with piano. RB192

—————. Give a Rouse. Song for medium voice with piano. RB38

—————. Round Us the Wild Creatures. Song for medium voice with piano. RB87

—————. A Serenade at the Villa. Song for medium voice with piano. RB493

Kobbé, Gustav. To Horse! Song for [medium] voice with keyboard. RB53

Komter, Jan Maarten. In a Gondola. Song for [medium] voice with guitar. RB154

Lewis, Ella V. The Year's at the Spring. Song for [medium] voice with piano. RB409

Lewis, Leo Rich. A King Lived Long Ago. Song for medium voice with piano. RB410

Lippé, Edouard. How Do I Love Thee. Song for low or medium voice with piano. EBB235

Löhr, Hermann. Sweet, Thou Hast Trod on a Heart! Song for [medium] voice with piano. EBB14

Mackenzie, Alexander C. "One Who Never Turned His Back." Song for [medium] voice with piano. RB78 and RB79

Maclean, Alick. Hold Me with a Charm. Song for [medium] voice with piano. RB584

MacMillan, Ernest. Sonnet. Song for [medium] voice with keyboard. EBB142

Madsen, Dora L. Rabbi Ben Ezra. [Song for medium voice] with keyboard. RB472

Manney, Charles Fonteyn. Transformations ("Such a Starved Bank of Moss"). Song for mezzo soprano or baritone with keyboard. RB555

Mayer, Max. Pippa's Song. Song for [medium] voice with piano. RB416

Metcalf, C. S. Ah Love, but a Day. Song for [medium] voice with piano. RB193

Metcalfe, W. A Year's Spinning. Song for [medium] voice with piano. EBB288

Miller, Anne Stratton. Parting at Morning. Song for [medium] voice with piano. RB296

Miller, Karl. Inclusions. Song for [medium] voice with piano. EBB19

Mills, Edward. Never Call It Loving. Song for [medium] voice with piano. EBB280

Mokrejs, John. You'll Love Me Yet (Song from Pippa Passes). Song for [medium] voice with keyboard. RB417

Molineux, Marie Ada. In the Campagna. Arranged by Harry Lawson Harts. Song for [medium] voice with keyboard. RB534 and RB535

—————. In the Campagna. Song for [medium] voice, unacc. RB536

Mozart, W. A. You'll Love Me Yet. Song for [medium] voice, unacc. RB418

Neidlinger, W. H. Thy Face. Song for baritone or mezzo soprano with piano. RB559

Nicholson, Alfred. That Day. Song for [medium] voice with keyboard. EBB264

Nicholson, Mary E. That May Morn. Song for [medium] voice with piano. RB560

Olds, W. B. A King Lived Long Ago. Song for medium voice with keyboard. RB423

—————. The Page's Song. Song for [medium] voice with keyboard. RB424

Ormerod, H. J. How They Brought the Good News to Aix. Song for baritone with piano. RB130

Parker, Phyllis Norman. Unless. Song for [meduim] voice with piano. EBB282

Parker, Willetta. Pippa's Song. Song for [medium] voice with piano. RB425

Pascal, Florian. No Little Flower. Song for [medium] voice with piano. EBB266

—————. Proof and Disproof. Song for [medium] voice with piano. EBB64

Pascal, Julian. Ah, Love, but a Day. Song for medium voice with piano. RB194

Passailaigue, Mary. How Do I Love Thee. Arranged by Elizabeth Jenkins. Song for [medium] voice with keyboard. EBB240

Patterson, Janie Alexander. "There Is No One Beside Thee." Song for [medium] voice with keyboard. EBB30

Philp, Elizabeth. "Insufficiency." Song for [medium] voice with keyboard. EBB32

—————. Sweetest Eyes. Song for [medium] voice with piano. EBB2

Pickard-Cambridge, W. A. Nay, but You Who Do Not Love Her. Song for low or middle voice with keyboard. RB506

Protheroe, Daniel. How Do I Love Thee. Song for medium voice with keyboard. EBB242

Ralston, Frances Marion. Youth Ended. Song for mezzo soprano with piano. RB475

Reinagle, Caroline. I Would That You Were All to Me. Song for [medium] voice with piano. RB537

—————. In a Year. Song for [medium] voice with piano. RB171

—————. This Is a Spray the Bird Clung To. Song for [medium] voice with piano. RB247

Robyn, Alfred G. "Good to Forgive." Song for mezzo soprano or baritone with piano. RB216

Rogers, Clara Kathleen. Ah, Love, but a Day. Song for [medium] voice with piano. RB197

—————. Apparitions. Song for [medium] voice with piano. RB561

—————. I Have a More Than Friend. Song for [medium] voice with piano. EBB68

—————. Out of My Own Great Woe. Song for [medium] voice with piano. EBB62

—————. "Overhead the Tree-tops Meet." Song for [medium] voice with keyboard. RB429

—————. Summum Bonum. Song for [medium] voice with piano. RB524

Rogers, James H. I Go to Prove My Soul. Song for medium voice with piano. RB292

Roy, William. How Do I Love Thee. Song for medium voice with piano. EBB245

Sabin, Wallace A. Pan. Song for high or medium voice with piano. EBB51

Schlesinger, Sebastian B. Unless. Song for [medium] voice with keyboard. EBB284

Schmidt, Louis. All's Right with the World. Song for [medium] voice with piano. RB435

Schuyler, Georgina. Grow Old Along with Me. Song for mezzo soprano or contralto with piano. RB476 and RB477

—————. In a Gondola. Song for mezzo soprano or contralto with piano. RB158 and RB159

—————. The Page Sings to the Queen. Song for mezzo soprano or contralto with piano. RB436

—————. This Is a Spray the Bird Clung To. Song for mezzo soprano or contralto with piano. RB248

—————. Venetian Serenade. Song for contralto or baritone with piano. RB160

Shillington, Mary. Apparitions. Song for [medium] voice with piano. RB562

Somervell, Arthur. After. Song for [medium] voice with piano. RB4

——————. A Broken Arc. Song cycle for [medium] voice or [medium high] voice with piano. RB4, RB70, RB239, RB266, RB438, RB507, RB563, and RB592

——————. From "Easter Day." Song for [medium] voice with piano. RB70

Spencer, Fanny M. Unless. Song for mezzo soprano or baritone with keyboard. EBB285

Stanford, Charles Villiers. Boot, Saddle, to Horse and Away. Song for baritone solo, male chorus (TTBB) with piano. RB58

——————. King Charles. Song for baritone solo, male chorus (TTBB) with piano. RB41

——————. Marching Along. Song for baritone solo, male chorus (TTBB) with piano. RB28

Stisted, Maria E. H. Dost Thou Love Me, My Beloved? Song for [medium] voice with piano. EBB65

Stothart, Herbert. "Wilt Thou Have My Hand." Song for [medium] voice with keyboard, specifically "on a spinet." EBB22

Tedaldi, F. Apparitions. Song for [medium] voice with keyboard. RB564

Thomas, Adelaida. Prospice. Song for [medium] voice with piano. RB465

Toye, Francis. Nay but You Who Do Not Love Her. Song for [medium] voice with piano. RB509

Treharne, Bryceson. A Child's Thought on God. Song for high or medium voice with piano. EBB6

——————. Renunciation. Song for high or medium voice with piano. EBB23

True, Latham. Among the Rocks. Song for [medium] voice with keyboard. RB206

——————. Give Her but the Least Excuse to Love Me. Song for [medium] voice with keyboard. RB442

——————. Grow Old Along with Me. Song for [medium] voice with keyboard. RB478

——————. My Star. Song for [medium] voice with keyboard. RB267

——————. Overhead the Treetops Meet. Song for [medium] voice with keyboard. RB443

——————. Prospice. Song for [medium] voice with keyboard. RB467

Warburg, Frederic S. Silver Linings. Song for [medium] voice with piano. EBB267

Watson, Mary E. All Service Ranks the Same with God. Hymn for [medium] voice, unacc. RB447

—————. All Service Ranks the Same with God. Song for [medium] voice, unacc. RB447

—————. Incidental Music to *Pippa's Soliloquy*. Incidental music for speaker, [high] voice, [medium] voice, violin, and harp. RB447

—————. Let the Watching Lids Wink. Song for [medium] voice, unacc. RB447

Weems, Mrs. J. Eddie. The Browning Cycle of Love Lyrics. Song cycle for [low] voice, [medium] voice, or [medium high] voice with keyboard. EBB251, RB69, and RB268

—————. My Star. Song for [medium] voice with keyboard. RB268

Welch, Jay. Music for Robert Browning's Pippa Passes. Incidental music for oboe, clarinet, harp, soprano, [medium] voice, and [low] voice. RB450

—————. You'll Love Me Yet. Song for [medium] voice, unacc. RB450

White, Maude Valérie. How Do I Love Thee. Song for mezzo soprano, baritone, or [medium] voice with keyboard. EBB252, EBB253, and EBB254

—————. King Charles, Cavalier Song. Song for [medium] voice with piano. RB42

—————. Marching Along. Song for [medium] voice with piano. RB30

—————. What I Do, and What I Dream. Song for [medium] voice with piano. EBB109

Whitmer, T. Carl. "Ah! Love, but a Day." Song for mezzo soprano with piano. RB199

—————. "My Star." Song for mezzo soprano with piano. RB269

—————. Song from Pippa Passes. Song for mezzo soprano with piano. RB451

Woolley, C. A Woman's Last Word. Song for [medium] voice with keyboard. RB589

Worth, John W. Ah Love, but a Day. Song for [medium] voice with keyboard. RB200

—————. Bird Spirit. Song for medium voice with keyboard. EBB13

—————. Infant Voices. Song for medium voice with keyboard. EBB13

————. Meeting at Night. Song for [medium] voice with keyboard. RB244

————. Song of the Morning Star to Lucifer. Song for medium voice with keyboard. EBB13

————. Three Songs. Songs for medium voice with keyboard. EBB13

Woyrsch, Felix von. Erinnerung. Song for medium voice with piano. RB339

————. Nach Hameln! Song for medium voice with piano. RB339

————. Die Nächste. Song for medium voice with piano. RB339

————. Nun stellt euch auf, ihr Kinderlein. Song for medium voice with piano. RB339

————. Rattenfänger Lieder. Songs for medium voice with piano. RB339

————. Eine Rose gepflückt! Song for medium voice with piano. RB339

————. Röslein, wann blühst du auf? Song for medium voice with piano. RB339

————. Stelldichein. Song for medium voice with piano. RB339

————. Waldesruh. Song for medium voice with piano. RB339

————. Wenn du kein Spielmann wärst! Song for medium voice with piano. RB339

————. Wo ich mich zeige. Song for medium voice with piano. RB339

Vocal Music: Solo Medium Low Voice

Arnott, A. Davidson. Give a Rouse. Song for baritone or bass with keyboard. RB32

Bliss, Paul. Thy Face. Song for [medium low] voice with keyboard. RB540

Gabriel, Virginia. At the Window. Song for [medium low] voice with piano. RB186

Hartmann, Arthur. In a Gondola. Song for [medium low] voice with keyboard. RB152

Hullah, John. The Lost Leader. Song for [medium low] voice with piano. RB226

——————. The Lost Leader, "Just for a Handful of Silver He Left Us." Song for [medium low] voice with piano. RB225

Johnson, Leslie. A Woman's Last Word. Song for [medium low] voice with piano. RB581

Lippé, Edouard. How Do I Love Thee. Song for low or medium voice with piano. EBB235

Pickard-Cambridge, W. A. Nay, but You Who Do Not Love Her. Song for low or middle voice with keyboard. RB506

Robbins, Reginald C. Sonnet from the Portuguese. Song for [medium low] voice with keyboard. RB164.1

——————. The Wanderers. Song for [medium low] voice with keyboard. RB291.1

Schuyler, Georgina. Grow Old Along with Me. Song for mezzo soprano or contralto with piano. RB476 and RB477

——————. In a Gondola. Song for mezzo soprano or contralto with piano. RB158

——————. The Page Sings to the Queen. Song for mezzo soprano or contralto with piano. RB436

——————. This Is a Spray the Bird Clung To. Song for mezzo soprano or contralto with piano. RB248

——————. Venetian Serenade. Song for contralto or baritone with piano. RB160

Weems, Mrs. J. Eddie. The Browning Cycle of Love Lyrics. Song cycle for [low] voice, [medium] voice, or [medium high] voice with keyboard. EBB251, RB69, and RB268

Vocal Music: Solo Low Voice

Arnott, A. Davidson. Give a Rouse. Song for baritone or bass with keyboard. RB32

Bantock, Granville. By the Fireside. Song for low voice with piano. RB18

——————. The Guardian Angel. Song for low voice with piano. RB110

——————. Home Thoughts. Song for low voice with piano. RB115

——————. I Go to Prove My Soul. Song for [low] voice with piano. RB281

——————. In a Year. Song for low voice with piano. RB170

——————. Life in a Love. Song for low voice with piano. RB221

————————. My Star. Song for low voice with piano. RB251

————————. Never the Time and the Place. Song for low voice with piano. RB271

————————. Now. Song for low voice with piano. RB273

————————. A Pearl, a Girl. Song for low voice with piano. RB304

————————. Summum Bonum. Song for low voice with piano. RB516

————————. Wanting Is—What? Song for low voice with piano. RB207

————————. A Woman's Last Word. Song for low voice with piano. RB565

Bateman, Alice. In My Sleep, "Last Night I Saw You in My Sleep." Song for [low] voice with keyboard. RB8

Beach, Mrs. H. H. A. I Send My Heart Up to Thee! Song for low voice with keyboard. RB142

————————. The Year's at the Spring. Song for low voice with keyboard. RB345

Beningfield, Ethel. Unless. Song for [low] voice with piano. EBB270

Bennett, Howard. "Unless." Song for low voice with piano. EBB271

Beta. "The Mask." Song for low voice with piano. EBB44

Boyle, George F. Marching Along. Song for bass with piano. RB21

Caldicott, Alfred J. Unless. Song for [low] voice with violin or cello obbligato and piano. EBB274

Cantor, Otto. Lov'd by Thee. Song for alto or baritone with piano. RB571

Caracciolo, Luigi. Unless. Song for [low] voice with keyboard. EBB278

Chanter, Arthur. There's a Woman Like a Dewdrop. Song for bass or contralto with piano. RB11

Coleridge-Taylor, S. Comfort. Song for contralto with keyboard. EBB8

————————. Earth Fades! Heaven Breaks on Me. Song for low voice with piano. RB513 and RB514

————————. Grief. Song for contralto with keyboard. EBB15

————————. The Soul's Expression. Song for contralto with keyboard. EBB259

————————. "Substitution." Song for low voice with piano. EBB260 and EBB261

————————. Tears. Song for contralto with keyboard. EBB262

————————. You'll Love Me Yet. Song for contralto or baritone with keyboard. RB369

Cowen, Frederic H. He Giveth His Beloved Sleep. Setting for contralto soloist, mixed chorus (SATB) and orchestra. Piano-vocal score. EBB76

Cowley, Elsie M. But Love. Song for [low] voice with piano. RB131

Dawson, William L. Out in the Fields. Song for low voice with keyboard. EBB54

de Lacey, Robert. I Stoop into a Dark Tremendous Sea of Cloud. Anthem for bass and alto soloists, mixed chorus (SATB) and organ. RB285

Dello Joio, Norman. How Do I Love Thee? Song for low voice with piano. EBB222

Duncan, Edmondstoune. Prospice. Song for [low] voice with keyboard. RB458

Elgar, Edward. Sabbath Morning at Sea. Song for contralto or low voice with piano. EBB69 and EBB70

Freer, Eleanor Everest. Nay! But You Do Not Love Her. Song for low voice with piano. RB500

————————. The Year's at the Spring. Song for low voice with keyboard. RB381

Fuller, Caroline M. The Changing Year. Song for contralto or bass with keyboard. RB184

Gilberté, Hallett. Ah! Love but a Day. Song for low voice with piano. RB187

Goldsworthy, W. A. How Do I Love Thee. Setting for women's chorus (SSA) and alto soloist with piano. Two part-songs and one song. EBB231

Goodeve, Mrs. Arthur. If Thou Must Love Me. Song for [low] voice with piano. EBB141

Hawley, Charles B. I Only Can Love Thee. Song for low voice with keyboard. EBB26

Homer, Sidney. My Star. Song for low voice with piano. RB260

————————. Prospice. Song for low voice with piano. RB461

Howe, Julia Ward. Oh, the Little Birds Sang East. Song for [low] voice with piano. EBB67

Jowett, Albert. Love's Surrender. Song for low voice with piano. RB582

Kramer, A. Walter. The Patriot. Song for low voice with piano. RB301

Lehmann, Liza. Incident of the French Camp. Song for [low] voice with piano. RB172

————————. Love, If You Knew the Light. Song for low voice with piano. RB230

————————. Prospice. Song for low voice with piano. RB462

Lippé, Edouard. How Do I Love Thee. Song for low or medium voice with piano. EBB235

Millar, A. F. My Star. Song for [low] voice with piano. RB261

Pickard-Cambridge, W. A. Nay, but You Who Do Not Love Her. Song for low or middle voice with keyboard. RB506

Ralston, Frances Marion. But I Need Now As Then. Song for alto with piano. RB475

————————. Then Welcome Each Rebuff. Song for alto with piano. RB475

Rohrer, Mildred. Pippa Passes. Song for [low] voice with keyboard. RB431

Schuyler, Georgina. Grow Old Along with Me. Song for mezzo soprano or contralto with piano. RB476 and RB477

————————. In a Gondola. Song for mezzo soprano or contralto with piano. RB158

————————. The Page Sings to the Queen. Song for mezzo soprano or contralto with piano. RB436

————————. This Is a Spray the Bird Clung To. Song for mezzo soprano or contralto with piano. RB248

————————. Venetian Serenade. Song for contralto or baritone with piano. RB160

Shapleigh, Bertram. O to Be in England. Song for contralto with piano. RB123

Somervell, Arthur. Among the Rocks. Song for contralto with orchestra. Piano-vocal score. RB205

————————. By the Fireside. Song for contralto with orchestra. Piano-vocal score. RB201

————————. In the Doorway. Song for contralto with orchestra. Piano-vocal score. RB203

————————. James Lee's Wife. Song cycle for contralto solo and orchestra. Piano-vocal score. RB198, RB201, and RB203-RB205

————————. James Lee's Wife Speaks at the Window. Song for contralto with orchestra. Piano-vocal score. RB198

——————. On the Cliff. Song for contralto with orchestra. Piano-vocal score. RB204

Weems, Mrs. J. Eddie. The Browning Cycle of Love Lyrics. Song cycle for [low] voice, [medium] voice, or [medium high] voice with keyboard. EBB251, RB69, and RB268

——————. How Do I Love Thee. Song for [low] voice with keyboard. EBB251

Welch, Jay. Music for Robert Browning's Pippa Passes. Incidental music for oboe, clarinet, harp, soprano, [medium] voice, and [low] voice. RB450

White, Maude Valérie. Love Me, Sweet, with All Thou Art. Song for [low] voice with piano. EBB43

Vocal Music: Duets

Beach, Mrs. H. H. A. Ah, Love, but a Day. Duet for soprano and tenor with keyboard. RB175

Bending, Edwin. In a Gondola. Duet for soprano and tenor with cello or violin obbligato and piano. RB145

Dickinson, Clarence. Summum Bonum. Duet for [medium] voices with keyboard. RB518

Freer, Eleanor Everest. How Do I Love Thee. Duet for mezzo soprano and baritone with keyboard. EBB225

Kaiser, Charles A. A Cuckoo Song. Duet for soprano and tenor with keyboard. EBB161

——————. Not Death, but Love. Duet for soprano and tenor with keyboard. EBB84

——————. A Paean of Love. Duet for soprano and tenor with keyboard. EBB129

——————. United. Duet for soprano and tenor with keyboard. EBB164

Rowley, Alec. Oh to Be in England. Duet for [high] voice and [medium low] voice with keyboard. RB122

Smith, Lewis Worthington. In a Gondola. Duet for tenor and alto with keyboard. RB161

Wickins, Florence. Oh, to Be in England. Duet for mezzo soprano and baritone with piano. RB126

Young, Dal. Say after Me. Duet for soprano and tenor with piano. RB167

——————. There's Zanse's Vigilant Taper. Duet for soprano and tenor with piano. RB167

Vocal Music: Quartets

Gracey, Wm. Adolphe. Sleep on, Baby, on the Floor. Part-song for vocal
quartet (SATB), unacc. EBB77

Ralston, Frances Marion. So Still within This Life. Vocal quartet for
two treble voices and two bass voices, unacc. RB475

Vocal Music: Women's Chorus

Beach, Mrs. H. H. A. Ah, Love, but a Day. Edited and arranged by
William Creston. Part-song for women's chorus (SSA) with
piano. RB178

——————. The Year's at the Spring. Part-song for women's chorus
(SSAA) with keyboard. RB346

Cain, Noble. Ah, Love, but a Day. Part-song for women's chorus
(SSA) with piano. RB180

——————. The Year's at the Spring. Chorus for women's voices
(SS-AA) with piano. RB359

Floyd, A. E. The Year's at the Spring. Part-song for women's chorus
(SSA) with piano, unacc. RB380

Goldsworthy, W. A. How Do I Love Thee. Setting for women's chorus
(SSA) and alto soloist with piano. Two part-songs and one song.
EBB231

Gow, George Coleman. "Give Her but a Least Excuse to Love Me."
Part-song for women's voices (SSAA), unacc. RB389

——————. Misconceptions. Part-song for women's voices (SSAA),
unacc. RB245

——————. "You'll Love Me Yet." Part-song for women's voices
(SSAA) with piano. RB389

Lee, E. Markham. The Year's at the Spring. Part-song for women's
chorus (SA) with piano. RB408

Ralston, Frances Marion. Ay! Note That Potter's Wheel. Piano solo
with choral monotone accompaniment (SSAA) and soprano soloist.
RB475

——————. For Note When Evening Shuts. Part-song for women's
chorus (SSAA) with piano. RB475

——————. Grow Old Along with Me. Part-song for women's chorus
(SSAA) with piano. RB475

——————. Not That, Amassing Flowers. Part-song for women's
chorus (SSAA) with piano. RB475

————————. So Take and Use Thy Work. Part-song for two women's choruses (SSAA) (SSAA) with piano. RB475

————————. Yet Gifts Should Prove Their Use. Part-song for women's chorus (SSAA) with piano. RB475

Rossman, Floy Adele. The Year's at the Spring. Part-song for women's chorus (SSAA) with piano. RB433

Smith, David Stanley. Pan. Chorus for women's choir (SSA), soprano soloist, oboe (or flute) obbligato, and piano. EBB52

Stoker, Richard. Here's the Spring Back. Part-song for women's chorus (SSA), unacc. RB231

Warner, H. Waldo. The Cares of Yesterday. Trio for women's chorus (SSA) with keyboard. EBB60

Whitney, Maurice C. Meeting at Night. Part-song for women's chorus (SSA) with piano. RB243

Vocal Music: Male Chorus

Bantock, Granville. Boot and Saddle. Part-song for male chorus (TTBB), unacc. RB43

————————. Give a Rouse. Part-song for male chorus (TTBB), unacc. RB33

————————. The Lost Leader. Part-song for male chorus (TTBB), unacc. RB224

————————. Marching Along. Part-song for male chorus (TTBB), unacc. RB20

————————. Midnight. Part-song for male chorus (TTBBBB), unacc. RB73

————————. O Zeus the King. Part-song for male chorus (TTBB) with short score for keyboard. RB5

————————. Paracelsus. Part-song for male chorus (TTBBBB), unacc. RB283

————————. Song of the Galleys from "Paracelsus." Part-song for male chorus (TTBB), unacc. RB284

Beach, Mrs. H. H. A. The Year's at the Spring. Arranged by Francis Moore. Part-song for male chorus (TTBB) with piano. RB348

Boughton, Rutland. Prospice. Part-song for male chorus (TTBB), unacc. RB456

Farmer, John. Heroes. Song for unison male chorus with piano. RB103 and RB104

Gaul, Harvey B. A Sonnet from the Portuguese. Chorus for male choir (TTBB) with piano. EBB229

Harraden, Ethel. "Over the Sea Our Galleys Went," (Paracelsus). Part-song for male chorus (TTBB) with piano. RB288

Huhn, Bruno. A Meditation. Part-song for male chorus (TTBB) with organ or piano. RB215

Kernochan, Marshall. King Charles. Part-song for male chorus (TTBB) with piano. RB39

Protheroe, Daniel. Ah, Love, but a Day. Arranged by Wayne Howorth. Part-song for male chorus (TTBB) with piano. RB195

——————. Out in the Fields. Part-song for male chorus (TTBB), unacc. EBB58

Stanford, Charles Villiers. Boot, Saddle, to Horse and Away. Song for baritone solo, male chorus (TTBB) with piano. RB58

——————. King Charles. Song for baritone solo, male chorus (TTBB) with piano. RB41

——————. Marching Along. Song for baritone solo, male chorus (TTBB) with piano. RB28

Thomas, D. Vaughan. Prospice. Part-song for male chorus (TTBB), unacc. RB466

Vocal Music: Mixed Chorus

Beach, Mrs. H. H. A. The Year's at the Spring. Part-song for mixed chorus (SATB) with keyboard. RB349

Booth, Guy. Sonnet (Seven) from the Portuguese. Part-song for mixed chorus (SATB), unacc. EBB110

Brahms, Johannes. There's Heaven Above, and Night by Night. Hymn for SATB, unacc. RB213

Bridge, J. Frederick. He Giveth His Beloved Sleep. Meditation for solo soprano, mixed chorus (SATB), and organ (or unacc.). EBB75

Broun, Harry. Comfort. Hymn for SATB, unacc. EBB7

Cain, Noble. How Do I Love Thee. Part-song for mixed chorus (SSAATTBB), unacc. EBB218

——————. Say Thou Lovest Me! Chorus for mixed choir (SSAATTBB), unacc. EBB157

Caldwell, Mary E. Year's at the Spring. Part-song for mixed chorus (SAB) with keyboard. RB361

Cooke, Greville. Oh, to Be in England. Part-song for mixed chorus (SSAATTBB), unacc. RB118

Cowen, Frederic H. He Giveth His Beloved Sleep. Setting for contralto soloist, mixed chorus (SATB), and orchestra. Piano-vocal score. EBB76

Croft, William. O God, Our Help. Hymn for SATB, unacc. RB275

Damrosch, Walter. The Virgin Mary to the Child Jesus. Two motets for mixed chorus (SSAATTBB), unacc. EBB265

Davies, H. Walford. Hervé Riel. Choral setting for baritone solo, mixed chorus (SSAATTBB), and orchestra. Piano-vocal score. RB112

de Lacey, Robert. I Stoop into a Dark Tremendous Sea of Cloud. Anthem for bass and alto soloists, mixed chorus (SATB), and organ. RB285

Ford, D. Rhys. Speak Low to Me, My Savior. Part-song for mixed chorus (SATB) with organ. EBB9

Glarum, L. Stanley. How Do I Love Thee. Part-song for mixed chorus (SATB), unacc. EBB230

Hadley, Henry K. Rabbi Ben Ezra. Part-song for mixed chorus (SATB), unacc. RB471

Hall, William D. Let Down the Bars, O Death. Part-song for mixed chorus (SATB), unacc. EBB36

Harwood, Basil. Love Incarnate. Choral setting for mixed chorus (SSAATTBB), boy sopranos, and organ. RB81

Hathaway, Joseph W. G. Master Hughes of Saxe-Gotha. Choral rhapsody for mixed chorus (SSAATTBB) with piano. RB233

Hattersley, F. Kilvington. Good News from Ghent. Ballad for mixed chorus (SATB) with keyboard. RB129

Lidgey, C. A. Women and Roses. Choral setting for mixed chorus (SATB) with orchestra. Piano-vocal score. RB590

Mueller, Carl F. Grow Old Along with Me. Part-song for mixed chorus [SATBB], unacc. RB473

Perrin, H. C. Pan's Pipes. Ballad for mixed chorus (SATB) and orchestra. Piano-vocal score. EBB50

Protheroe, Daniel. Out in the Fields. Part-song for mixed chorus (SATB) with piano. EBB59

Slater, Gordon. For Life, with All It Yields. Short anthem for mixed chorus (SATB) with organ. RB63

Vaughan Williams, Ralph. Spring. Hymn for SATB, unacc. RB444

—————————. Then Welcome Each Rebuff. Hymn for SATB, unacc.
RB479

Whitney, Maurice C. Meeting at Night. Part-song for mixed chorus
(SATB) with piano. RB242

Wiant, Bliss, editor. Then Welcome Each Rebuff. Hymn for SATB,
unacc. RB480 and RB481

Wilson, Harry Robert. All's Right with the World. Part-song for mixed
chorus (SATB) with piano. RB452

Vocal Music: Children's Chorus

Browning, Robert. O Bell' Andare. Two-part children's chorus [SA],
unacc. RB510, RB511, and RB512

Easson, James. God's in His Heaven. Two-part round, unacc. RB377
and RB378

Ehrmann, Mary B. Pippa's Song. Chorus for unison children's voices
with keyboard. RB379

Hammond, William G. Pippa's Song. Two-part song for children's
chorus, unacc. RB395

Harwood, Basil. Love Incarnate. Choral setting for mixed chorus
(SSAATTBB), boy sopranos, and organ. RB81

Loughridge, Jean M. Pippa's Song. Song for unison children's chorus
with piano. RB412 and RB413

McLeod, Robert. March Them Along. Song for unison boys chorus
with piano. RB26

Martin, Margaret R. The Children's Skipping Dance. Dance for children with flute and keyboard. RB327

—————————. The Dance of the Rats. Dance for children with flute or
piccolo and keyboard. RB328

—————————. The Story. Recitation for reader, children, and keyboard.
RB329

Sarson, H. M. The Year's at the Spring. Part-song for children's
chorus (SS), unacc. RB434

Vocal Music: Unison Chorus

Beringer, Marjorie. The Boy and the Angel. Chant for [unison]
voice[s] with unspecified keyboard (?) instrument. RB16

Caldwell, Mary E. Year's at the Spring. Song for unison chorus with
organ or piano. RB360

Demuth, Norman. Boot and Saddle. Song for unison chorus with piano.
RB46

Dyson, George. Boot, Saddle, to Horse, and Away! Song for unison
chorus with piano. RB48

Easson, James. Boot, Saddle, to Horse and Away. Song for unison
chorus with piano. RB49

Farmer, John. Epilogue, "At the Midnight in the Silence of the Sleep-
time." Song for unison chorus with piano. RB74

—————————. Epilogue [from *Asolando*]. Song for unison chorus with
piano. RB75

Gilchrist, W. W. Pippa's Song. Chorus for unison voices with piano.
RB388

Sarson, May. Cavalier Song. Song for unison voices with keyboard.
RB57.1

Sykes, Harold H. Marching Along. Song for unison choir (with optional descant) with keyboard. RB29

Vocal Music: Cantatas

Ashford, Emma L. Pan Among the Reeds. Cantata with piano. EBB46

Aylwin, Josephine Crew. The Pied Piper of Hamelin. Cantata with
piano. RB307

Boyce, Ethel M. The Lay of the Brown Rosary. Cantata. Piano-vocal
score. EBB33

Boyle, George F. The Pied Piper of Hamelin. Cantata. Piano-vocal
score. RB309

Busch, Carl. Pan's Flute. Cantata with flute and piano. EBB47

Carse, A. von Ahn. The Lay of the Brown Rosary. Cantata. Piano-
vocal score. EBB34

Davies, Walford. The Pied Piper. Chamber cantata. Piano-vocal score.
RB314

Farrington, Frederick W. The Piper of Hamelin. Cantata with flageolet
or flute, piano, and harmonium. Piano-vocal score. RB318

Graham, A. Cyril. The Piper of Hamelin. Cantata. Piano-vocal score.
RB321

Hirsch, Carl. Der Rattenfänger von Hameln. [Cantata] with piano and
organ. RB322

Hudson, Henry. The Pied Piper of Hamelin. Cantata. Piano-vocal
score. RB323

Hurless, Don. The Pied Piper of Hamelin. Cantata. Piano-vocal score.
RB324

Parry, C. Hubert H. The Pied Piper of Hamelin. [Cantata.] Piano-vocal score. RB332

Ralston, Frances Marion. Rabbi Ben Ezra. [Cantata] with piano. RB475

Rathbone, George. The Pied Piper of Hamelin. [Cantata.] Piano-vocal score. RB334

Truman, Ernest. The Pied Piper. Cantata Grotesque. Piano-vocal score.
RB335

Walthew, Richard H. The Pied Piper of Hamelin. [Cantata.] Piano-vocal score. RB337

Wiant, W. R. Exile. Cantata with piano. EBB11

Wodell, Frederick W. A Venetian Night. Cantata with piano. RB165

Wood, Charles. Eden Spirits. Cantata with piano. EBB12

Vocal Music: Oratorios

Ralston, Frances Marion. Saul. Oratorio with pipe organ or piano.
RB491

Vocal Music: Operas and Operettas

Aiken, Walter H. The Pied Piper of Hamelin. Operetta. Piano-vocal score. RB306

Christopher, Carol. The Magic Piper. Operetta. Piano-vocal score.
RB312

Clokey, Joseph W. The Pied Piper of Hamelin. Opera. Piano-vocal score. RB313

Farmer, John. The Pied Piper; or The Rat-Catcher of Hamelin. Opera. Piano-vocal score. RB317

Freer, Eleanor Everest. The Legend of the Piper. [Opera.] Piano-vocal score. RB319

Hageman, Richard. Tragödie in Arezzo (Caponsacchi). Opera. Piano-vocal score. RB486

Klein, Manuel. The Pied Piper. Operatic fantasy. Piano-vocal score. RB325

Neuendorff, Adolf. The Rat-Charmer of Hamelin. Comic opera. Piano-vocal score. RB331

Paulsen, P. Marinus. The Tale of the Pied Piper. Operetta-pageant with keyboard. RB333

Weigl, Karl. Der Rattenfänger von Hameln. [Operetta.] Piano-vocal score. RB338

Vocal Music: Other Dramatic Forms

Brumleu, Ernest. The Pied Piper. Musical play with keyboard. RB310

Martin, Margaret R. The Children's Skipping Dance. Dance for children with flute and keyboard. RB327

——————. The Dance of the Rats. Dance for children with flute or piccolo and keyboard. RB328

——————. The Pied Piper of Hamelin. [Musical play] with flute or piccolo and keyboard. RB327-RB329

Watson, Mary E. Incidental Music to *Pippa's Soliloquy*. Incidental music for speaker, [high] voice, [medium] voice, violin, and harp. RB447

Welch, Jay. Music for Robert Browning's Pippa Passes. Incidental music for oboe, clarinet, harp, soprano, [medium] voice, and [low] voice. RB450

Instrumental Music: Piano

Avison, Charles. "Grand March." March for unspecified keyboard (?) instrument. RB294

——————. March. March for unspecified keyboard (?) instrument. RB295

Bantock, Granville. Amphibian. Piano solo. RB106

——————. Caliban upon Setebos. Piano solo. RB19

——————. Ballade (Childe Roland to the Dark Tower Came). Piano solo. RB61

——————. Gold Hair. Piano solo. RB109

——————. In a Gondola. Piano solo. RB133

——————. Master Hughes of Saxe-Gotha. Piano solo. RB232

——————. Pan and Luna. Piano solo. RB280

——————. Red Cotton Night-Cap Country. Piano solo. RB482

——————. A Serenade at the Villa. Piano solo. RB492

——————. Soliloquy of the Spanish Cloister. Piano solo. RB496

—————. A Toccata of Galuppi's. Piano solo. RB528

Bending, Edwin. In a Gondola. Duet for soprano and tenor with cello or violin obbligato and piano. RB145

Bergh, Arthur. The Pied Piper of Hamelin. Recitation for reader with piano. RB308

Brydson, John C. The Bells of Hamelin. Piano solo. RB311

—————. The Children. Piano solo. RB311

—————. The Mayor and Corporation. Piano solo. RB311

—————. The Pied Piper. Piano solo. RB311

—————. The Pied Piper of Hamelin. Piano suite. RB311

—————. The Rats. Piano solo. RB311

—————. The River Weser. Piano solo. RB311

Bullard, Frederic Field. There's a Woman Like a Dewdrop. Song for high voice, violin, and piano. RB10

Busch, Carl. Pan's Flute. Cantata with flute and piano. EBB47

Caldicott, Alfred J. Unless. Song for [low] voice with violin or cello obbligato and piano. EBB274

—————. Unless. Song for [medium] voice with violin or cello obbligato and piano. EBB275

Caldwell, Mary E. Year's at the Spring. Song for unison chorus with organ or piano. RB360

Church, Frank M. A Passacaglia. Solo for unspecified keyboard (?) instrument. RB300

Clarke, Helen A. One Way of Love. Song for [high] voice with cello obbligato and keyboard. RB276

—————. You'll Love Me Yet. Song for [high] voice with cello and piano. RB365

David, Elizabeth Harbison. Pippa's Song. Song for [medium high] voice with flute, violin, and keyboard. RB373

Davis, Carlyle. Heart's Ease. Piano solo. RB374

—————. The King's Dancer. Piano solo. RB374

—————. Morning at Asolo. Piano solo. RB374

—————. Ottima's Regret. Piano solo. RB374.

—————. Pippa Passes, Four Moods from Browning. Piano suite. RB374

Dillon, Fannie Charles. Saul. Recitation for reader with keyboard. RB488

Dittenhaver, Sarah Louise. Pied Piper's Tune. Piano solo. RB315

Downing, Lulu Jones. A Musical Instrument. Recitation for reader with keyboard. EBB48

Dunhill, Thomas F. The Children Follow. Piano solo. RB316

————. Hamelin Town's in Brunswick. Piano solo. RB316

————. Into the Street. Piano solo. RB316

————. The Mayor Expostulates. Piano solo. RB316

————. The Pied Piper. Piano [suite]. RB316

————. Rats! Piano solo. RB316

————. Ringing the Bells. Piano solo. RB316

Elman, Mischa. In a Gondola. Impromptu for violin and piano. RB150

England, Nick. The All-Loving. Song for baritone, reader, and piano. RB80

Farrington, Frederick W. The Piper of Hamelin. Cantata with flageolet or flute, piano, and harmonium. Piano-vocal score. RB318

Fergus, Phyllis. Thoughts. Recitation for reader with violin and piano. RB151

Forbes, J. Winchell. Toccata. Solo for unspecified keyboard instrument. RB529

French, Emma Weller. Out in the Fields. Song for soprano or tenor, violin (obbligato), and piano. EBB55

Galuppi, Baldassare. Sonata in A major. Edited and revised by Joseph Henius. Sonata for piano. RB531

————. Sonata in D major. Edited and revised by Joseph Henius. Sonata for piano. RB532

Godard, Benjamin. Pan Pastorale. Piano solo. EBB49

Gow, George Coleman. "Colombe." Piano solo. RB62

————. "Colombe's Birthday," Intermezzo Music. Piano solos. RB62

————. Intermezzo Music to "Colombe's Birthday." Piano solo. RB62

————. "Valence." Piano solo. RB62

————. Wedding March. Piano solo. RB62

Harris, Russell G. "Tears." Setting for [high] voice, violin I and II, flute, oboe, clarinet, bassoon, cymbal, and piano. EBB263

Hirsch, Carl. Der Rattenfänger von Hameln. [Cantata] with piano and organ. RB322

Huhn, Bruno. A Meditation. Part-song for male chorus (TTBB) with organ or piano. RB215

Kramer, A. Walter. At Evening. Piano prelude. RB227

Krug, Arnold. The Pied Piper of Hamelin Pipes and Disappears with the Children in the Mountain. Piano solo. RB326

Mackenzie, A. C. There's a Woman Like a Dewdrop. Song for [high] voice with harp or piano. RB15

Martin, Margaret R. The Children's Skipping Dance. Dance for children with flute and keyboard. RB327

——————. The Dance of the Rats. Dance for children with flute or piccolo and keyboard. RB328

——————. The Story. Recitation for reader, children, and keyboard. RB329

Miller, Lewis. Suite for Pied Piper. Trio for flute, piano, and double bass. Piano-conductor's score. RB330

Moore, Mary Carr. Saul. Setting for reader, violin, cello, and piano. RB489

——————. Suite for Strings and Piano. Suite for string quartet and piano. RB490

Nevin, Ethelbert. The Lark Is on the Wing. Piano solo. RB420

Ralston, Frances Marion. Ay! Note That Potter's Wheel. Piano solo with choral monotone accompaniment (SSAA) and soprano soloist. RB475

——————. Saul. Oratorio with pipe organ or piano. RB491

Raphael, Juliet. A Woman's Last Word. Recitation for reader with keyboard. RB585

Smith, David Stanley. Pan. Chorus for women's choir (SSA), soprano solo, oboe (or flute) obbligato, and piano. EBB52

Spier, La Salle. And You Are Ever by Me. Song for [medium high] voice with string quartet and piano. RB439

——————. But Winter Hastens at Summer's End. Song for [medium high] voice with string quartet and piano. RB439

——————. A Cycle of Six Songs from Pippa Passes. Song cycle for [medium high] voice with string quartet and piano. RB439

—————. Day! Song for [medium high] voice with string quartet and piano. RB439

—————. New-Year's Hymn. Song for [medium high] voice with string quartet and piano. RB439

—————. Oh, What a Drear, Dark Close to My Poor Day! Song for [medium high] voice with string quartet and piano. RB439

—————. Overhead the Tree-tops Meet. Song for [medium high] voice with string quartet and piano. RB439

True, Latham. Abt Vogler. Recitation for reader with piano. RB1

Urban, Heinrich. Der Rattenfänger von Hameln. Fantasy for piano. RB336

Warren, Jeanne. Pippa's Holiday (Danse Grotesque). Piano solo. RB445

White, Grace. Three Descriptions from Browning, no. 1. Violin solo with piano. RB241

—————. Three Descriptions from Browning, no. 2. Violin solo with piano. RB124

—————. Three Descriptions from Browning, no. 3. Violin solo with piano. RB298

Worth, John W. Barcarola. Piano solo. RB166

—————. Gondoliera in Lontanza. Piano solo. RB166

—————. In a Gondola. [Song cycle] for soprano, tenor, reader, and piano. RB166

—————. Oh, Which Were Best to Roam or Rest. Recitation for reader with piano. RB166

—————. Prelude. Piano solo. RB166

—————. Row Home? Must We Row Home. Recitation for reader with piano. RB166

—————. Say after Me, and Try to Say My Very Words. Recitation for reader with piano. RB166

—————. What If the Three. Recitation for reader with piano. RB166

Instrumental Music: Piano (Four Hands)

Geiser, Paul. Der Rattenfänger von Hameln. Piano solo for four hands. RB320

Instrumental Music: Harpsichord and Clavichord

Galuppi, Baldassare. Sei Sonate. Four sonatas and two toccatas for harpsichord. RB530

——————. Sonata in B-flat major. Sonata for harpsichord. RB530

——————. Sonata in C major. Sonata for harpsichord. RB530

——————. Sonata in G major. Sonata for harpsichord. RB530

——————. Toccata in D minor. Toccata for harpsichord. RB530

——————. Toccata in F major. Toccata for harpsichord. RB530

[——————. Toccata] in G major. [Toccata for clavichord.] RB533

Instrumental Music: Organ

Bridge, J. Frederick. He Giveth His Beloved Sleep. Meditation for solo soprano, mixed chorus (SATB), and organ (or unacc.). EBB75

Caldwell, Mary E. Year's at the Spring. Song for unison chorus with organ or piano. RB360

de Lacey, Robert. I Stoop into a Dark Tremendous Sea of Cloud. Anthem for bass and alto solists, mixed chorus (SATB) and organ. RB285

Ford, D. Rhys. Speak Low to Me, My Savior. Part-song for mixed chorus (SATB) with organ. EBB9

Harwood, Basil. Love Incarnate. Choral setting for mixed chorus (SSAATTBB), boy sopranos, and organ. RB81

Hirsch, Carl. Der Rattenfänger von Hameln. [Cantata] with piano and organ. RB322

Huhn, Bruno. A Meditation. Part-song for male chorus (TTBB) with organ or piano. RB215

Ralston, Frances Marion. Saul. Oratorio with pipe organ or piano. RB491

Slater, Gordon. For Life, with All It Yields. Short anthem for mixed chorus (SATB) with organ. RB63

Instrumental Music: Flute

Busch, Carl. Pan's Flute. Cantata with flute and piano. EBB47

David, Elizabeth Harbison. Pippa's Song. Song for [medium high] voice with flute, violin, and keyboard. RB373

Farrington, Frederick W. The Piper of Hamelin. Cantata with flageolet or flute, piano, and harmonium. Piano-vocal score. RB318

Harris, Russell G. "Tears." Setting for [high] voice, violin I and II, flute, oboe, clarinet, bassoon, cymbal, and piano. EBB263

Martin, Margaret R. The Children's Skipping Dance. Dance for children with flute and keyboard. RB327

——————. The Dance of the Rats. Dance for children with flute or piccolo and keyboard. RB328

——————. The Pied Piper of Hamelin. [Musical play] with flute or piccolo and keyboard. RB327-RB329

Miller, Lewis. Suite for Pied Piper. Trio for flute, piano, and double bass. Piano-conductor's score. RB330

Smith, David Stanley. Pan. Chorus for women's choir (SSA), soprano solo, oboe (or flute) obbligato, and piano. EBB52

Instrumental Music: Oboe

Harris, Russell G. "Tears." Setting for [high] voice, violin I and II, flute, oboe, clarinet, bassoon, cymbal, and piano. EBB263

Smith, David Stanley. Pan. Chorus for women's choir (SSA), soprano solo, oboe (or flute) obbligato, and piano. EBB52

Welch, Jay. All Service Ranks the Same with God. Song for soprano, oboe, harp, and clarinet. RB450

——————. [Give Her the Least Excuse to Love Me.] Clarinet solo with oboe and harp. RB450

——————. Give Her the Least Excuse to Love Me. Song for soprano, oboe, clarinet, and harp. RB450

——————. A King Lived Long Ago. Song for soprano with oboe and harp. RB450

——————. Music for Robert Browning's Pippa Passes. Incidental music for oboe, clarinet, harp, soprano, [medium] voice, and [low] voice. RB450

——————. Prelude. Prelude for oboe, clarinet, and harp. RB450

Instrumental Music: Clarinet

Harris, Russell G. "Tears." Setting for [high] voice, violin I and II, flute, oboe, clarinet, bassoon, cymbal, and piano. EBB263

Welch, Jay. All Service Ranks the Same with God. Song for soprano, oboe, harp, and clarinet. RB450

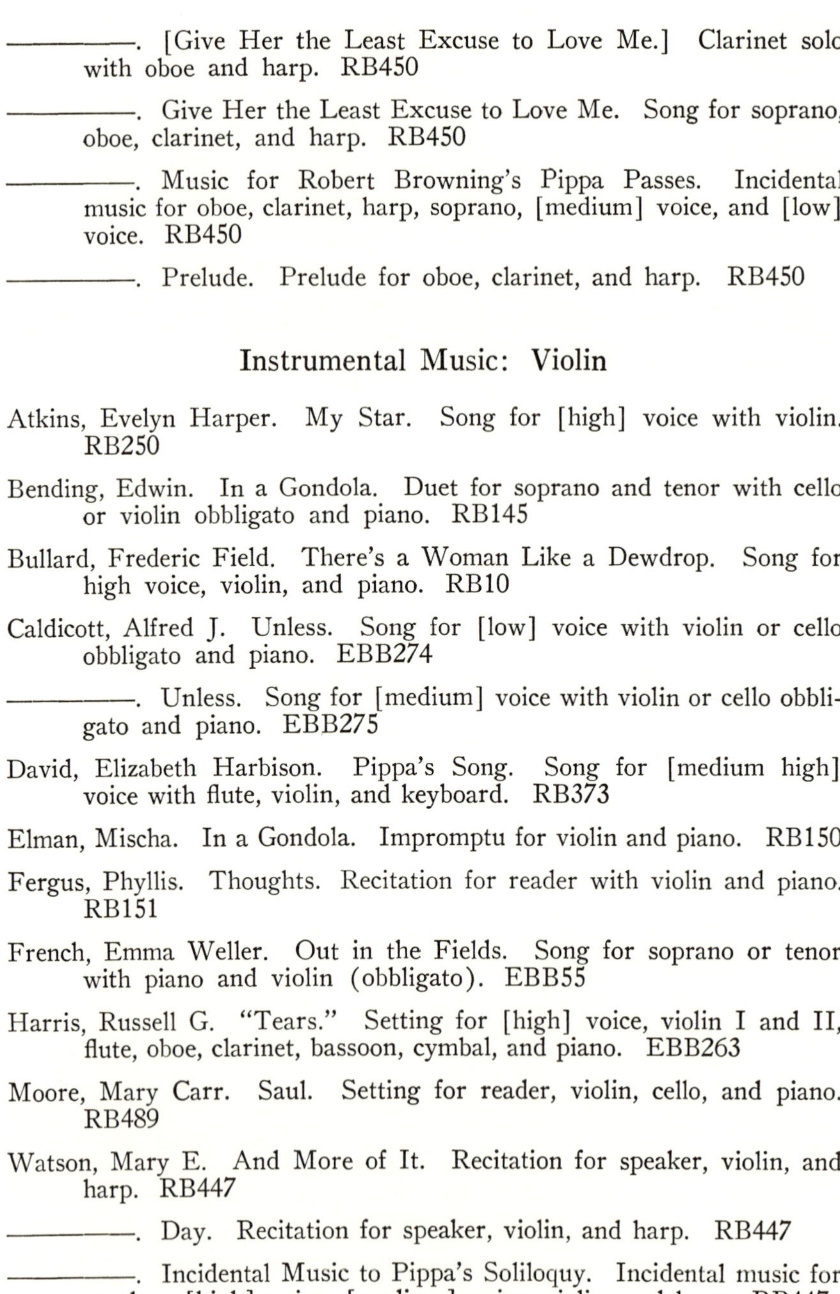

————. [Give Her the Least Excuse to Love Me.] Clarinet solo with oboe and harp. RB450

————. Give Her the Least Excuse to Love Me. Song for soprano, oboe, clarinet, and harp. RB450

————. Music for Robert Browning's Pippa Passes. Incidental music for oboe, clarinet, harp, soprano, [medium] voice, and [low] voice. RB450

————. Prelude. Prelude for oboe, clarinet, and harp. RB450

Instrumental Music: Violin

Atkins, Evelyn Harper. My Star. Song for [high] voice with violin. RB250

Bending, Edwin. In a Gondola. Duet for soprano and tenor with cello or violin obbligato and piano. RB145

Bullard, Frederic Field. There's a Woman Like a Dewdrop. Song for high voice, violin, and piano. RB10

Caldicott, Alfred J. Unless. Song for [low] voice with violin or cello obbligato and piano. EBB274

————. Unless. Song for [medium] voice with violin or cello obbligato and piano. EBB275

David, Elizabeth Harbison. Pippa's Song. Song for [medium high] voice with flute, violin, and keyboard. RB373

Elman, Mischa. In a Gondola. Impromptu for violin and piano. RB150

Fergus, Phyllis. Thoughts. Recitation for reader with violin and piano. RB151

French, Emma Weller. Out in the Fields. Song for soprano or tenor with piano and violin (obbligato). EBB55

Harris, Russell G. "Tears." Setting for [high] voice, violin I and II, flute, oboe, clarinet, bassoon, cymbal, and piano. EBB263

Moore, Mary Carr. Saul. Setting for reader, violin, cello, and piano. RB489

Watson, Mary E. And More of It. Recitation for speaker, violin, and harp. RB447

————. Day. Recitation for speaker, violin, and harp. RB447

————. Incidental Music to Pippa's Soliloquy. Incidental music for speaker, [high] voice, [medium] voice, violin, and harp. RB447

————. Worship Whom Else? Recitation for speaker, violin, and harp. RB447

White, Grace. Three Descriptions from Browning, no. 1. Violin solo with piano. RB241

————. Three Descriptions from Browning, no. 2. Violin solo with piano. RB124

————. Three Descriptions from Browning, no. 3. Violin solo with piano. RB298

Instrumental Music: Cello

Bending, Edwin. In a Gondola. Duet for soprano and tenor with cello or violin obbligato and piano. RB145

Caldicott, Alfred J. Unless. Song for [low] voice with violin or cello obbligato and piano. EBB274

————. Unless. Song for [medium] voice with violin or cello obbligato and piano. EBB275

Clarke, Helen A. One Way of Love. Song for [high] voice with cello obbligato and keyboard. RB276

————. You'll Love Me Yet. Song for [high] voice with cello and piano. RB365

Moore, Mary Carr. Saul. Setting for reader, violin, cello, and piano. RB489

Instrumental Music: Harp

Mackenzie, A. C. There's a Woman Like a Dew-drop. Song for [high] voice with harp or piano. RB15

Watson, Mary E. And More of It. Recitation for speaker, violin, and harp. RB447

————. Day. Recitation for speaker, violin, and harp. RB447

————. Incidental Music to *Pippa's Soliloquy*. Incidental music for speaker, [high] voice, [medium] voice, violin, and harp. RB447

————. Worship Whom Else? Recitation for speaker, violin, and harp. RB447

Welch, Jay. All Service Ranks the Same with God. Song for soprano, oboe, harp, and clarinet. RB450

————. [Give Her the Least Excuse to Love Me.] Clarinet solo with oboe and harp. RB450

————. Give Her the Least Excuse to Love Me. Song for soprano, oboe, clarinet, and harp. RB450

——————. A King Lived Long Ago. Song for soprano with oboe and harp. RB450

——————. Music for Robert Browning's Pippa Passes. Incidental music for oboe, clarinet, harp, soprano, [medium] voice, and [low] voice. RB450

——————. Night Wind. Prelude for harp. RB450

——————. Overhead the Treetops Meet. Song for soprano with harp. RB450

——————. Prelude. Prelude for oboe, clarinet, and harp. RB450

——————. The Year's at the Spring. Song for soprano with harp. RB450

Instrumental Music: Other Solo Instruments

Farrington, Frederick W. The Piper of Hamelin. Cantata with flageolet or flute, piano, and harmonium. Piano-vocal score. RB318

Harris, Russell G. "Tears." Setting for [high] voice, violin I and II, flute, oboe, clarinet, bassoon, cymbal, and piano. EBB263

Komter, Jan Maarten. In a Gondola. Song for [medium] voice with guitar. RB154

Martin, Margaret R. The Dance of the Rats. Dance for children with flute or piccolo and keyboard. RB328

——————. The Pied Piper of Hamelin. [Musical play] with flute or piccolo and keyboard. RB327-RB329

Miller, Lewis. Suite for Pied Piper. Trio for flute, piano, and double bass. Piano-conductor's score. RB330

Instrumental Music: Chamber Music (String Quartet)

Davies, H. Walford. Prospice. Song for baritone with string quartet. RB457

Moore, Mary Carr. Suite for Strings and Piano. Suite for string quartet and piano. RB490

Spier, La Salle. And You Are Ever by Me. Song for [medium high] voice with string quartet and piano. RB439

——————. But Winter Hastens at Summer's End. Song for [medium high] voice with string quartet and piano. RB439

——————. A Cycle of Six Songs from Pippa Passes. Song cycle for [medium high] voice with string quartet and piano. RB439

————————. Day! Song for [medium high] voice with string quartet and piano. RB439

————————. New-Year's Hymn. Song for [medium high] voice with string quartet and piano. RB439

————————. Oh, What a Drear, Dark Close to My Poor Day! Song for [medium high] voice with string quartet and piano. RB439

————————. Overhead the Tree-tops Meet. Song for [medium high] voice with string quartet and piano. RB439

Wellesz, Egon. Du bist da draben im Palast begehrt. Song for soprano and string quartet. EBB98

————————. Ich denk an dich, wie wilder Wien den Baum spriessend umringt. Song for soprano and string quartet. EBB184

————————. Mir scheint, das Angesicht der Welt verging—in einem andern. Song for soprano and string quartet. EBB118

————————. Nur drei jedoch in Gottes ganzem All vernahmen es. Song for soprano and string quartet. EBB90

————————. Sonette der Elisabeth Barret-Browning. Songs for soprano and string quartet. EBB85, EBB90, EBB98, EBB118, and EBB184

————————. Und es geschah mir einst, an Theokrit zu denken. Song for soprano and string quartet. EBB85

Instrumental Music: Chamber Music
(Not Including String Quartet)

Bending, Edwin. In a Gondola. Duet for soprano and tenor with cello or violin obbligato and piano. RB145

Bullard, Frederic Field. There's a Woman Like a Dewdrop. Song for high voice, violin, and piano. RB10

Caldicott, Alfred J. Unless. Song for [low] voice, violin or cello obbligato, and piano. EBB274

————————. Unless. Song for [medium] voice, violin or cello obbligato, and piano. EBB275

Clarke, Helen A. One Way of Love. Song for [high] voice with cello obbligato and keyboard. RB276

————————. You'll Love Me Yet. Song for [high] voice with cello and piano. RB365

David, Elizabeth Harbison. Pippa's Song. Song for [medium high] voice with flute, violin, and keyboard. RB373

England, Nick. The All-Loving. Song for baritone, reader, and piano.
RB80

Fergus, Phyllis. Thoughts. Recitation for reader with violin and piano.
RB151

French, Emma Weller. Out in the Fields. Song for soprano or tenor
with piano and violin obbligato. EBB55

Harris, Russell G. "Tears." Setting for [high] voice with violin I and
II, flute, oboe, clarinet, bassoon, cymbal, and piano. EBB263

Miller, Lewis. Suite for Pied Piper. Trio for flute, piano, and double
bass. Piano-conductor's score. RB330

Moore, Mary Carr. Saul. Setting for reader, violin, cello, and piano.
RB489

Watson, Mary E. And More of It. Recitation for speaker, violin, and
harp. RB447

——————. Day. Recitation for speaker, violin, and harp. RB447

——————. Incidental Music to *Pippa's Soliloquy*. Incidental music for
speaker, [high] voice, [medium] voice, violin, and harp. RB447

——————. Worship Whom Else? Recitation for speaker, violin, and
harp. RB447

Welch, Jay. All Service Ranks the Same with God. Song for soprano,
oboe, harp, and clarinet. RB450

——————. [Give Her the Least Excuse to Love Me.] Clarinet solo
with oboe and harp. RB450

——————. Give Her the Least Excuse to Love Me. Song for soprano,
oboe, clarinet, and harp. RB450

——————. A King Lived Long Ago. Song for soprano with oboe and
harp. RB450

——————. Music for Robert Browning's Pippa Passes. Incidental
music for oboe, clarinet, harp, soprano, [medium] voice, and [low]
voice. RB450

——————. Prelude. Prelude for oboe, clarinet, and harp. RB450

Instrumental Music: Orchestral

Bantock, Granville. Fifine at the Fair. Orchestral drama with a prologue. Miniature score. RB105

Bollinger, Sam'l. Pompilia e Caponsacchi. Overture for orchestra. Conductor's score. RB483

——————. Pompilia e Caponsacchi. Overture for orchestra. Conductor's score with parts. RB484

Cooley, Carlton. "Caponscacchi." Epic poem for orchestra. Conductor's score. RB485

Cowen, Frederic H. He Giveth His Beloved Sleep. Setting for contralto solo, mixed chorus (SATB), and orchestra. Piano-vocal score. EBB76

Davies, H. Walford. Hervé Riel. Choral setting for baritone solo, mixed chorus (SSAATTBB), and orchestra. Piano-vocal score. RB112

Ives, Charles E. Robert Browning Overture. Overture for orchestra. Study score. RB487

Lewis, Leo Rich. Symphonic Prelude to Robert Browning's Tragedy, a Blot in the 'Scutcheon. Symphonic prelude for orchestra. Full score. RB14

Lidgey, C. A. Women and Roses. Choral setting for mixed chorus (SATB) with orchestra. Piano-vocal score. RB590

Perrin, H. C. Pan's Pipes. Ballad for mixed chorus (SATB) and orchestra. Piano-vocal score. EBB50

Saminsky, Lazare. Venezia. [Symphonic poem] for orchestra. Conductor's score. RB157

Somervell, Arthur. Among the Rocks. Song for contralto with orchestra. Piano-vocal score. RB205

——————. By the Fireside. Song for contralto with orchestra. Piano-vocal score. RB201

——————. In the Doorway. Song for contralto with orchestra. Piano-vocal score. RB203

——————. James Lee's Wife. Song cycle for contralto and orchestra. Piano-vocal score. RB198, RB201, and RB203-RB205

——————. James Lee's Wife Speaks at the Window. Song for contralto with orchestra. Piano-vocal score. RB198

——————. On the Cliff. Song for contralto with orchestra. Piano-vocal score. RB204

Wiant, W. R. Prelude to Exile. Ballet-prelude for orchestra. Piano-conductor's score. EBB11.1

Recitations

Bergh, Arthur. The Pied Piper of Hamelin. Recitation for reader with piano. RB308

VII

Biographical Data of Composers

Key to Abbreviations and Symbol

ABL   Armstrong Browning Library

EBB   Elizabeth Barrett Browning

RB   Robert Browning

?   A question mark preceding a composer's name indicates that there is insufficient information available to know conclusively if he is the composer of the Browning music listed in this catalog. Several composers of the same name may be listed where any one of them could be the composer of the specific music listed herein.

The Royal College of Music and the Royal Academy of Music refer to those in London unless stated otherwise.

For the complete description and explanation of this chapter, read page 7 of Chapter I.

Ackert, Bernard G. (1918-   ). Between 1945 and 1949, Ackert attended the Baylor University School of Music. He played in the Baylor Symphony Orchestra and was assistant teacher of double bass. In 1951 he was double bass player in the San Antonio Symphony and music director in the Baptist Temple.[1]

Aiken, Walter H.

Aldrich, Leslie

Alsop, Marion

Anglia. *See* Galsworthy, Ada

Armes, Nancy

---

[1]Records, Baylor University, School of Music; and Willa Lee Clements Moore, "The Baylor University Collection of the Musical Settings of the Poetry of Robert Browning" (unpublished M.M. thesis, Baylor University, 1951), p. 136 (hereafter cited as "Baylor Collection").

Arnott, A. Davidson (1870-1910). Arnott was a Scottish composer born
in Glasgow. Among his compositions are *Young Lochinvar* and *The
Ballad of Carmilhan.*[2]

Ashford, Emma L.

Atkins, Evelyn Harper

Atkins, Sir Ivor Algernon (1869-1953). Born in Wales, Atkins is known
as an English organist, conductor, and composer. About 1902 he
began conducting important orchestral novelties, one being Richard
Strauss's *Tod und Verklärung.* Because of his active participation in
the resumption of festivals after World War I, he was knighted. One
of his best known works is *Hymn of Faith* for soli, chorus, and orchestra. Other compositions include festival works, church music,
and songs. He collaborated with Sir Edward Elgar on what is now
the standard edition of Johann Sebastian Bach's *St. Matthew's Pas-
sion.*[3]

Austin, Frederic (1872-1952). Austin was an English composer and baritone singer who began his music studies with his mother and uncle.
He was a church organist during the first part of his career and then
taught harmony at the Liverpool College of Music. After studying
singing with Charles Lunn he made a successful debut in 1902. Austin
sang contemporary music and did much to encourage English composers. His success as a singer "tended to overshadow his work as
a composer, but here too he did serious and consistent work." Among
his compositions are the *Spring* rhapsody for orchestra, the symphonic
poem *Isabella,* a Symphony in E major, the choral work *Pervigilium
Veneris*, chamber music, songs, and incidental music. Austin wrote
one of the longer songs in the ABL Collection. *Home-Thoughts from
Abroad* is written in impressionistic style. Its melodic line rises and
falls with such regularity that it almost negates the climax at the end
of the song. In the accompaniment are three-against-two relationships, parallel fourths and fifths, "horn fifths," and frequent time
changes, often in several consecutive measures.[4]

Austin, Torrington

Avison, Charles (1709-1770). Avison was an English organist, composer,
and writer on music; he also played the harpsichord, violin, and flute,
and advertised as a teacher of the German flute. In 1752 he pub-

---

[2]Albert E. Wier, ed., *The Macmillan Encyclopedia of Music and Musicians* (New
York: The Macmillan Company, 1938), p. 71 (hereafter cited as *Macmillan Encyclopedia.*)

[3]*Ibid.*, p. 77; Moore, "Baylor Collection," p. 137; and Oscar Thompson, ed., *The
International Cyclopedia of Music and Musicians* (9th ed. by Robert Sabin, ed.; New
York: Dodd, Mead & Company, 1964), p. 92 (hereafter cited as *Cyclopedia*, 9th ed.).

[4]*Grove's Dictionary of Music and Musicians*, ed. by Eric Blom (5th ed.; New
York: St. Martin's Press, Inc., 1955), I, 267 (hereafter cited as *Grove's Dictionary*,
5th ed.); Robert A. Reid, "An Analysis of Selected Solo Songs Set to Poems of
Robert Browning, As Found in the Armstrong Browning Library of Baylor University" (unpublished M.M. thesis, Baylor University, 1970), p. 47 (hereafter cited
as "Analysis of Songs"); and Thompson, *Cyclopedia* (9th ed.), p. 96.

lished the literary work by which he is best known, "An Essay on Musical Expression." "It contains some judicious reflections on the art, and throughout the work we find the highest encomiums of [Benedetto] Marcello and [Francesco] Geminiani, frequently to the detriment of [George Frederick] Handel. . . . The whole book is remarkable for its freedom from the accepted views of the time." During 1753 an answer to Avison's essay was published and in reply Avison published his "Essay," which is the first serious attempt at music criticism by an English writer. His best music is found in the fifty concertos for full orchestra of stringed instruments which have been favorably compared with the concertos of Thomas A. Arne and William Boyce. Avison also wrote chamber music, choral works, and collaborated to write an oratorio.[5]

Aylwin, Josephine Crew. In 1938 Aylwin was known as a contemporary American composer, among whose works was an excellent setting of RB's *The Pied Piper of Hamelin*.[6]

Ayres, Harold

Bantock, Sir Granville (1868-1946). Bantock is the most often found composer in the ABL Collection, and the majority of his music is of fine quality. There are forty-two solo songs (thirteen from a song cycle), nine choral works, eleven piano pieces, and one orchestral piece. Bantock studied for the Indian Civil Service before deciding to pursue his musical career at the Royal Academy of Music, where he won the Macfarren Scholarship. He was founder and editor of *The New Quarterly Music Review* (1893-1896), conductor of choral and orchestral music, and a pioneer in premiering music of his contemporaries. He taught at Birmingham Midland Institute and succeeded Sir Edward Elgar as music professor at Birmingham University. In 1930 Bantock was knighted for his musical accomplishments. The work which brought him his first fame was his setting of Edward Fitzgerald's translation of *Omar Kháyyám* for solo voices, chorus, and orchestra (1909). Bantock's music reflects this interest in the Orient (e.g., *Lyrics from Ferishtah's Fancies*) and also an interest in Celtic cultures, although the music is set in the Western tradition. Bantock believed in the programmatic significance of musical images, as can be seen from the titles of most of his works, which are related to literature, mythology, or legend. A prolific composer, Bantock wrote operas, ballets, incidental music, choral works with orchestra, works for unaccompanied women's chorus, works for children's chorus, orchestral works, works for brass band, works for cello and orchestra, works for solo voice and orchestra, recitations with orchestra, chamber music, violin sonatas, piano solos, songs, and others.[7]

---

[5]*Grove's Dictionary* (5th ed.), I, 275; and Thompson, *Cyclopedia* (9th ed.), p. 96.
[6]Wier, *Macmillan Encyclopedia*, p. 86.
[7]*Grove's Dictionary* (5th ed.), I, 404-16; Reid, "Analysis of Songs," pp. 33-34; Thompson, *Cyclopedia* (9th ed.), pp. 137-38; and Oscar Thompson, ed., *The International Cyclopedia of Music and Musicians* (7th ed. rev. by Nicolas Slonimsky, ed.; New York: Dodd, Mead & Company, 1956), pp. 120-21 (hereafter cited as *Cyclopedia*, 7th ed.).

Barbour, Florence Newell (1867-1946). Barbour was an American pianist and composer. Among her compositions are songs, piano pieces, anthems, choruses for women's voices, and works for strings and piano.[8]

Barlow, Emily

Barnett, Alice (1866-   ). Barnett studied composition with Felix Borowski and Rudolf Ganz in Chicago. In 1916 her setting of Clinton Scollard's *Serenade* won her special attention and merit. With her cycle of eight poems based on RB's *In a Gondola,* she added dramatic power to her lyric talents. Although written as a song cycle, each song from *In a Gondola* was published separately. The style is basically Romantic but tempered with elements of Impressionism. In this song cycle Barnett displays her lyrical ability in developing the shape of a melodic line. The mood created is one of a relaxed and natural melodic flow. She makes little use of chromaticism.[9]

Bateman, Alice

Bates, Anna Craig

Beach, Amy Marcy (Cheney). *See* Beach, Mrs. Henry Harris Aubrey

Beach, Mrs. Henry Harris Aubrey (1867-1944). Amy Marcy (Cheney) Beach was a pianist and one of the first women American composers. Although she had little formal training, her compositions were many and varied. She wrote songs, choral works, church music, violin pieces, piano pieces, chamber music, orchestral works, and a concerto for piano. Beach's music is conservative and rather academic in structure. She set much Browning poetry to music and it was received well by Browning lovers.[10]

Beach, John Parsons (1877-1953). Not thought to be related to the above Mrs. H. H. A. Beach, John Beach was educated in his native country at the New England Conservatory. Later he studied in Paris. He is one of the first American modernists. Teaching piano and composition at the Minneapolis Northwestern Conservatory and at the University of Minnesota, Beach spent several summers in Asolo, Italy, where he came under the influence of the Brownings. The first Browning Pilgrimage Party to tour Europe for the purpose of visiting places which RB had frequented arrived July 26, 1926 in Asolo, which is the setting for RB's poem, *Pippa Passes.* While there, the Browning Pilgrimage was received by Mr. and Mrs. John Beach in their villa which RB had wanted to buy and name *Pippa's Tower.* After RB's death, the son Robert Wiedemann Barrett Browning purchased this same villa (*La Torricello Sotto Castello*). Later it was

---

[8]Thompson, *Cyclopedia* (9th ed.), p. 145.

[9]Reid, "Analysis of Songs," pp. 68-69; *Baker's Biographical Dictionary of Musicians* (5th ed. rev. by Nicolas Slonimsky; New York: G. Schirmer, 1958), p. 89; and John Tasker Howard, *Our American Music* (3rd ed. rev. and enl. by James Lyons; New York: Thomas Y. Crowell Company, 1954), p. 563.

[10]*Baker's Biographical Dictionary of Musicians* (5th ed.), p. 104; and Reid, "Analysis of Songs," pp. 26-27.

acquired by John Beach, who, in 1926, entertained the Browning Pilgrimage Party by playing the introduction to his opera *Pippa's Holiday.*[11]

Beckett, Bessie D.

Bedford, Mrs. Herbert. *See* Lehmann, Liza

?Beecher, Carl Milton (1883-   ). Beecher was an American composer born in La Fayette, Illinois. Among his works are piano pieces, chamber music, and songs.[12]

Behrend, Arthur H. (1853-   ). Behrend is known as a German composer, who was a prolific and successful song writer. His song, *Daddy,* achieved great popularity.[13]

Bending, Edwin

Beningfield, Ethel

?Bennett, Howard Gordon (1894-   ). Bennett is a musicologist who studied at Harvard, the University of Berlin, and the University of Munich. He also studied composition with Rubin Goldmark and piano with Clarence Adler and Franz Schmidt. Later he taught at Denison University, Vassar College, and the University of Vermont.[14]

Berdahl, Arthur C.

Bergh, Arthur (1882-   ). Bergh is an American violinist, conductor, and composer. He was educated in the United States and later became violinist in the New York Symphony. In addition to his teaching post at the New York Institute of Music, Bergh was recording director for Emerson and Columbia phonograph companies, director of radio advertising agencies, and a lecturer on American music. He has written instrumental works, symphonic choral works, an opera, operettas, songs, anthems, violin pieces, piano pieces, and works for band.[15]

Beringer, Marjorie

Beta

Bickford, Zahr Myron

Black, Mrs. Kate Gilmore

Blair, William

Bliss, James Arthur (1891-   ). Bliss is an English composer who was educated at Rugby, Pembroke College, Cambridge, and the Royal

---

[11]Reid, "Analysis of Songs," p. 27; Thompson, *Cyclopedia* (9th ed.), p. 166; and Ola Jones Nisbet, *Browning's Pippa Passes* (Charlotte, N.C.: Presbyterian Standard Publishing Co., 1929), pp. 22-30.

[12]Wier, *Macmillan Encyclopedia,* p. 143.

[13]*Ibid.,* p. 147.

[14]*Who Is Who in Music* (Chicago: Lee Stern Press, 1941), p. 46.

[15]Moore, "Baylor Collection," p. 141; Thompson, *Cyclopedia* (9th ed.), p. 198; and Wier, *Macmillan Encyclopedia,* p. 162.

College of Music. He is married and has one daughter. About 1940 he was teaching at the Royal College of Music. Among his compositions are symphonies, concertos, incidental music, and songs.[16]

Bliss, Philip Paul, Jr. (1872-1933). An American composer and organist, Bliss was also a music educator. Although he studied for the ministry, he received musical training at Princeton and at Philadelphia (with Hugh Archibald Clarke and [Richard] Zeckwer). In Paris he studied with Alexandre Guilmant and Jules Émile Frédéric Massenet. Afterwards he became music editor for the John Church Company in Cincinnati (1904-1911), the Willis Music Company (1911), and the Theodore Presser Company. Bliss has written operettas; church music; songs; solo pieces for organ, violin, and cello; and educational works.[17]

Blumenthal, Jacob (1829-1908). A German pianist and composer, Blumenthal was educated in Hamburg, Vienna, and Paris (Conservatory). He served as pianist to Queen Victoria and was a successful teacher. Among his compositions are piano pieces, works for violin and cello, and songs.[18]

Bode, Alice M.

Bollinger, Samuel (1871-1941). Bollinger was an American composer and music educator. He was a student and instructor at the Royal Conservatory in Leipzig. In addition to his activities as an organist, Bollinger was the organizer and founder of the Bollinger Conservatory at Fort Smith, Arkansas and the Bollinger Piano School at St. Louis. His compositions include orchestral works, pieces for violin, piano pieces, organ pieces, and songs.[19]

Bond, Carrie (Jacobs) (1862-1946). Bond was an American song composer and publisher of her own songs. In 1887 she married Frank L. Bond, a doctor of medicine. One of her most popular songs was *I Love You Truly*. In addition to her songs, she wrote several books.[20]

Booth, Guy

Borton, Alice (fl. late nineteenth century). Borton was an English composer best known for her *Andante and Rondo* for piano and orchestra. She has written several songs and many solo pieces for piano.[21]

---

[16]Adolph Robbins, "Composers Who Have Set Browning's Poetry to Music" (typewritten, undocumented biographical data, Armstrong Browning Library, Vertical File, 1940), pp. 20-21 (hereafter cited as "Composers Who Set Browning's Poetry"); on the title page is written "Copied from practically illegible manuscript, June, 1940;" I could not find the original manuscript; no author's name is given on the title page, but in ink inside the back cover is written "Adolph Robbins, English 101—Sec. 140, 1:40 class."

[17]*Baker's Biographical Dictionary of Musicians* (5th ed.), p. 163; Moore, "Baylor Collection," pp. 141-42; and Thompson, *Cyclopedia* (9th ed.), p. 233.

[18]Thompson, *Cyclopedia* (9th ed.), p. 241.

[19]*Ibid.*, p. 248; and Letter, Edward Eugene and Sarajane Briscoe to Andrew Joseph Armstrong, Feb. 22, 1949, Armstrong Browning Library, Music Correspondence.

[20]Thompson, *Cyclopedia* (9th ed.), p. 249.

[21]Wier, *Macmillan Encyclopedia,* p. 214.

Boughton, Rutland (1878-   ). During his lifetime, Boughton was a prominent English composer. He studied at the Royal College of Music and later taught at the Birmingham Midland Institute. At Glastonbury he formed a theater for the production of music-dramas based on the Arthurian legends; this exact plan did not materialize but an active company was formed. Although Boughton composed choral works, chamber music, and songs, the bulk of his music is for the stage.[22]

Boyce, Ethel Mary (1863-   ). Boyce was an English composer and a pupil of Walter Macfarren. The winner of various prizes and scholarships, she has written choral works, cantatas, orchestral music, violin pieces, piano works, and songs.[23]

Boyle, George Frederick (1886-1948). Boyle was an Australian-American pianist and composer. He studied with [Ferruccio] Busoni in Berlin and later taught in the United States (Peabody Conservatory in Baltimore, Curtis Institute in Philadelphia, Juilliard, and the Philadelphia Musical Academy). Boyle has composed several orchestral works, chamber music, two cantatas, and songs.[24]

Boys, Reginald S.

Brahe, May Hanna. In the discussion of melody in *The Oxford Companion to Music* a melody by Brahe is used as an example to illustrate the point that a familiar tune which imitates or suggests another tune which has already been popular will more likely succeed. Brahe's song, *I Passed by Your Window,* which was quite popular in the early 1920s was based on a popular organ voluntary from the preceding quarter of a century, [Antoine Edouard] Batiste's *Andante.*[25]

Brahms, Johannes (1833-1897). Brahms is one of the greatest composers in the history of music. A German pianist, he was also a proficient player of the violin and cello. He is a master of Classical form and structure in the Romantic style and his music is usually diatonic in melody and harmony and varied in cross rhythms. His songs encompass a wide range of moods and idealize the folksong style. Brahms wrote in all forms except theater, i.e., opera and ballet.[26]

Branscombe, Gena (1881-   ). Branscombe was born in Canada but lived in the United States. She studied composition with Felix Borowski and Englebert Humperdinck and piano with Rudolf Ganz in addition to her studies at New York University and the Institute of

---

[22]Moore, "Baylor Collection," p. 142; Thompson, *Cyclopedia* (9th ed.), p. 261; and *Grove's Dictionary of Music and Musicians,* ed. by H. C. Colles (3rd ed.; New York: The Macmillan Company, 1937), I, 429-30 (hereafter cited as *Grove's Dictionary,* 3rd ed.).

[23]Wier, *Macmillan Encyclopedia,* p. 223.

[24]*Baker's Biographical Dictionary of Musicians* (5th ed.), pp. 194-95; Moore, "Baylor Collection," pp. 142-43; and Thompson, *Cyclopedia* (9th ed.), p. 266.

[25]Percy A. Scholes, *The Oxford Companion to Music* (9th ed. rev.; London: Oxford University Press, 1956), p. 628.

[26]Thompson, *Cyclopedia* (9th ed.), pp. 268-75.

Musical Art.   Later she organized the Branscombe Choral Society and composed orchestral works, chamber music, and choral works. About her song, *What Are We Two* from *In a Gondola* in the ABL Collection, Reid stresses the lyric and singable quality of the melodic line, but says that the strength of the piece lies in its accompaniment.[27]

Bridge, Sir John Frederick (1844-1924).   Bridge was an English organist, composer, and conductor.   After studying at Oxford he became associated with Westminster Abbey (1875-1918), in which capacity he composed *He Giveth His Beloved Sleep* for RB's funeral.   In addition to writing books about music, Bridge composed anthems, cantatas, oratorios, and services.[28]

Brooke, Carol Kelley.   Brooke's compositions were published in the Hathaway catalog and later sold back to her.   She wrote eight songs with the help of Mr. Hathaway, who was a composer and author.[29]

Broun, Harry

Browning, Elizabeth Barrett (1806-1861).   EBB was an English poetess more famous than her husband during her lifetime.   Her musical training was evidently attempted, but with little success for she neglected her studies in this field.   At the residence at Hope End the family had an organ which was played by members of the family although no reference could be found where EBB played it.   A piano was moved to the home in London after the Barrett family had been there for three years, but the musical person was EBB's sister, Henrietta.   EBB's father gave her an Aeolian Harp for her window at the 50 Wimpole Street house and she enjoyed listening to music, especially later after her marriage.   RB often played the piano or organ for her, but she told him that she could not play in return for him. I could find nothing to indicate that she ever studied composition or learned to play any other instrument.[30]

Browning, Robert (1812-1889).   The English poet, RB, was also a studied musician.   His mother first introduced him to music by playing the piano.   An early recollection of his was of his mother playing the once popular *Grand March* in C major of Charles Avison.   Seventy years later he reprinted this simple march from an old manuscript at the end of *Parleyings . . . with Charles Avison*.   John Relfe taught RB piano and theory, which studies aided him to compose songs and fugues, and to consider writing an opera.   RB could play the organ and often he improvised at the piano for close friends.   An active appreciator of music, he was friends with Joseph Joachim and Clara Schumann.[31]

27*Ibid.*, p. 278; *Baker's Biographical Dictionary of Musicians* (5th ed.), p. 203; and Reid, "Analysis of Songs," p. 36.

28Thompson, *Cyclopedia* (9th ed.), p. 284.

29I could find no information about the Hathaway catalog or Mr. Hathaway; Robbins, "Composers Who Set Browning's Poetry," p. 32.

30Dorothy Hewlett, *Elizabeth Barrett Browning* (London: Cassell and Company Ltd., 1953), pp. 8, 10, 61, 91, 92, 211, 215.

31W. Hall Griffin, *The Life of Robert Browning*, completed and ed. by Harry Christopher Minchin, ed. (London: Methuen & Co. Ltd., 1910), pp. 15-16.

Bruguiere, E. A.

Brumleu, Ernest

Brydson, John Callis (1900-   ). Brydson is an Englishman and a
teacher, writer, and composer. He has held positions as an organist
and as choirmaster. Among his compositions are a piano concerto,
an organ sonata, a suite based on *The Pied Piper of Hamelin,* anthems, part-songs, and organ arrangements. He has published several
books about music including one on music appreciation, another on
composition, and one on harmony. He has also contributed articles
to music journals.[32]

Bryson, Robert Ernest (1867-1942). The Scotsman, Ernest Bryson, was
a tradesman by vocation and a composer only by hobby. Nonetheless,
he wrote works for orchestra including two symphonies, the first premiering in London (1908) under the baton of Sir Granville Bantock.
In addition to his orchestral works, Bryson wrote choral music, chamber music, songs, and one opera. Reid considers Bryson's song, *So,
the Year's Done With,* one of the best musical representations of text
in the entire ABL Collection. Written toward the end of his productive period, the song is written in a Romantic vein with many
seventh and ninth chords.[33]

Bullard, Frederic Field (1864-1904). Bullard was an American teacher
and composer. His study began in chemistry but changed to music.
In Munich he studied composition with Joseph Gabriel Rheinberger.
Later he returned to Boston and taught composition himself. He was
music critic for *Time and the Hour.* Bullard has composed songs,
choruses for male voices, and church music.[34]

Busch, Carl (1862-1943). Busch was a Danish-American composer and
conductor. He studied law at the University of Copenhagen and
studied music with private teachers. Later he founded the Kansas
City Symphony Orchestra. His compositions include orchestral
works, chamber music, cantatas, choruses, anthems, songs, and violin
pieces.[35]

Cain, Noble (1896-   ). Cain is an American composer, organist, conductor, and lecturer. His musical training included study at the University of Chicago, the American Conservatory of Music, and Lawrence College, in addition to which was study with Raphael Navas in
Madrid and Allen [Hervey] Spencer in Chicago. Cain has been
guest choral conductor in several places and has been quite active in

---

[32]*Who's Who in Music and Musicians International Directory,* ed. by Peter Townend, managing ed., and David Simmons, ed. (4th ed.; London: Burke's Peerage Limited, 1962), p. 29 (hereafter cited as *Who's Who International*).
[33]Reid, "Analysis of Songs," p. 45; Thompson, *Cyclopedia* (7th ed.), p. 250; and
Thompson, *Cyclopedia* (9th ed.), p. 298.
[34]*Baker's Biographical Dictionary of Musicians* (5th ed.), p. 226; Moore, "Baylor
Collection," p. 144; and Thompson, *Cyclopedia* (9th ed.), p. 303.
[35]Thompson, *Cyclopedia* (9th ed.), p. 307.

this field. Compositions by Cain include choral works, anthems, an oratorio, hymn settings, and several arrangements of folk songs.[36]

Caldicott, Alfred James (1842-1897). Caldicott was an English organist, conductor, composer, and teacher. At the Leipzig Conservatory, he studied with [Ignaz] Moscheles. He also attended Cambridge University. Later Caldicott taught and became director at the Royal College of Music. He composed cantatas, operettas, glees, songs, and part-songs.[37]

Caldwell, Mary Elizabeth (1909-   ). Caldwell is an American composer, conductor, and organist. She was educated at the University of California and studied music with Benjamin Moore. At the Munich Conservatory she studied with Richard Schrey and at Juilliard with Bernard Wagenaar. She has been active as an organist and choir director in churches. Caldwell founded the Youth Opera Program for Pasadena Junior League (California) and directed the Youth Concert Series. Since 1948 she has been the organist and director of the children's choir at San Marino Community Church (California). She is a member of the American Guild of Organists, the Choral Conductors Guild, the American Music Center, and the American Society of Composers, Authors and Publishers. Her compositions include church music and two operas.[38]

Cambridge, W. A. Pickard. *See* Pickard-Cambridge, W. A.

Cantor, Otto

Caraccioli, Luigi (1849-1887). An Italian composer and voice teacher, Caraccioli studied singing in Naples. He became Director of Singing at Dublin Royal Irish Academy of Music. Operas and songs are the main forms of compositions with which he is associated.[39]

Carse, Adam (1878-   ). Carse is known primarily as an English composer and writer on music. He studied in Germany and at the Royal Academy of Music in London. He taught at Winchester College and the Royal Academy of Music. In addition to writing books about music, Carse has written educational music, works for string orchestra, works for solo voice with orchestra, works for violin and orchestra, a dramatic cantata, part-songs, violin pieces, songs, and piano studies.[40]

Carter, Ernest (1866-1953). Carter was an American organist and composer who studied in Berlin and the United States (including work

---

[36]*The Ascap Biographical Dictionary of Composers, Authors and Publishers,* ed. by David McNamara (New York: Thomas Y. Crowell Company, 1948), p. 54 (hereafter cited as *Ascap Biographical Dictionary,* 1948).

[37]Thompson, *Cyclopedia* (9th ed.), p. 326.

[38]*The Ascap Biographical Dictionary of Composers, Authors and Publishers,* comp. and ed. by The Lynn Farnol Group, Inc. (New York: The American Society of Composers, Authors and Publishers, 1966), p. 101 (hereafter cited as *Ascap Biographical Dictionary,* 1966).

[39]Thompson, *Cyclopedia* (9th ed.), p. 338.

[40]*Ibid.,* p. 344.

at Princeton University and Columbia University). He taught in California, at Princeton, and in Berlin. Aside from editing college song books, among them the *Princeton Song Book,* Carter composed stage works, orchestral pieces, chamber music, anthems, male quartets, and songs (*The Lord's Prayer* being one of the most popular).[41]

Carter, Esther May

Caruthers, Julia Lois. Caruthers directed the Caruthers School of Piano in Chicago. She was a pianist and teacher. In 1940 her address was the Fine Arts Building in Chicago.[42]

Castelnuovo-Tedesco, Mario (1895-   ). Castelnuovo-Tedesco is an important Italian composer. At the Cherubini Royal Institute of Music, he studied composition with Ildebrando Pizzetti and piano with Del Valle. His works have been performed by Arturo Toscanini, Jascha Heifetz, and Gregor Piatigorsky. He has been strongly influenced by great poetry, especially Shakespeare, old Hebrew music, and the hills of his native Tuscany. Castelnuovo-Tedesco left Italy for America when his country allied itself with Nazi Germany by instituting its own anti-Semitic program. In November, 1939 he appeared as soloist in the premier of his *Second Concerto for Piano and Orchestra.* Castelnuovo-Tedesco has composed film music, piano pieces, ballets, chamber music, choral music, orchestral music (numerous concertos), songs, and song cycles.[43]

Chanter, Arthur

Christopher, Carol

Church, Frank M. Born in Ohio, Church is known as an organist and pianist. He attended the New England Conservatory, Oberlin Conservatory, and the American Conservatory. Among his teachers were [Henry Morton] Dunham, George W. Andrews, Frank Van Dusen, Alexandre Guilmant, Charles Widor, and Swayne. Church has presented recitals throughout the United States; from 1921 to 1922 he was Director of Music at Baylor University, and in 1941 he was on the faculty of Athens College. In addition to the passacaglia in the ABL Collection, Church has written *Passacaglias* [*sic*] *Melody* in A for violin, sacred songs, and waltzes.[44]

Clark, Ruth Kinney (1893-   ). Clark was born in California and married Amos Edwin Clark. She has a son and a daughter. Educated at San Jose State College, College of Pacific Conservatory, Worcester Conservatory of Music, and the Los Angeles Conservatory, Clark became a music educator. She taught at San Jose State College, the Teachers State College, in public schools in Los Gatos, California, and in private schools for handicapped children in Los Angeles. She

---

[41]*Ibid,* p. 347.
[42]Robbins, "Composers Who Set Browning's Poetry," p. 38.
[43]David Ewen, comp. and ed., *American Composers Today* (New York: The H. W. Wilson Company, 1949), pp. 51-52.
[44]*Who Is Who in Music,* p. 66.

served as organist and choir director for various churches, helped to organize oratorio societies in Handford and Ventura (California), and set up scholarships at Occidental College and Pepperdine College. Clark has received several awards and honors, among which are the Honored Teacher of California Award (1961), the Los Angeles City Council Citation (1961), and the Apple of Gold Award from the International Senior League. She is a member of the National League of American Pen Women, the World Affairs Council, the American Guild of Organists, the Women's Ruskin Art, and the Los Angeles Browning Societies. Clark has written a song collection, piano pieces, and songs. She has recorded on tape *Bible Stories Children Love* (for blind children), and is the author of *The Teacher's Prayer*. Her address is 340 South Norton Avenue, Los Angeles, California 90005.[45]

Clarke, Helen Archibald (fl. 1889-1926). Clarke was the daughter of Jane M. Clarke and the composer Hugh Archibald Clarke, who taught at the University of Pennsylvania. A graduate of the University of Pennsylvania, Miss Clarke was an amateur composer of songs and piano music and a lecturer on poetry, drama, and mythology. Along with Charlotte Porter, she co-edited *The Poems of Robert Browning; Robert Browning's Complete Poetical Works; Mrs. Browning's Complete Works;* and *Poet-Lore, "A Monthly Magazine Devoted to Shakespeare, Browning and the Comparative Study of Literature"* (1889-1925). She was the author of *Browning's England, Browning's Italy,* and *Browning and His Century.* Clarke was an honorary member of the Boston Browning Society and a member of the New York Browning Society. She was president of The Boston Centre [*sic*] American Music Society Club, was one of the founders of the American Music Society, and was vice-president of the American Poetry Association and of the Poetry Society of London.[46]

Clarke, Henry Leland (1907-   ). Not believed to be related to Helen Archibald Clarke, Henry Leland Clarke is an American author on music and a composer. His musical training included piano lessons with Ruth Olive Roberts, violin and organ lessons at the Thornton Academy, and composition with Nadia Boulanger and Gustav Holst. Other teachers were Otto Luening and Hans Weisse. He attended Harvard and Columbia University and was the recipient of several fellowships and grants. He held positions with the New York Public Library Music Division, Bennington College, Westminster Choir College (Chairman of the Graduate Faculty), Vassar College, and the University of California at Los Angeles. Clarke has also been Chairman

---

[45]*Who's Who of American Women* (5th ed.; Chicago: The A. N. Marquis Company, Incorporated, 1968-1969), p. 230.

[46]By 1894 the title page of *Poet-Lore* read *Poet-Lore, "A Monthly Magazine of Letters Devoted to the Appreciation of the Poets and to Comparative Literature;"* in each of the first four annual volumes of *Poet-Lore* was a setting of an RB text by Clarke; Wier, *Macmillan Encyclopedia,* p. 344; Janice Jones, "Browning and Music" (unpublished M.A. thesis, Baylor University, 1930), pp. 141-43; and *Who Was Who in America* (Chicago: The A. N. Marquis Company, 1943), I, 226.

of the Southern California Chapter of the American Musicological Society. He has written several articles for music journals in addition to composing a chamber opera, choral works, pieces for solo instruments with piano, pieces for solo voice and various instruments, and songs.[47]

Clarke, Hugh Archibald (1839-1927). Father of Helen Archibald Clarke, Hugh A. Clarke was a Canadian-born organist and professor of music at the University of Pennsylvania. He was educated at Knox College and the University of Pennsylvania. Clarke was director of the male chorus, "The Abt," for many years. Aside from his compositions for piano, songs, and incidental music for plays, Clarke published textbooks on harmony, counterpoint, organ, and piano.[48]

Clarke, Reginald

Clarke, Robert Coningsby (1879-1934). Clarke was an English song composer. A pupil of Sir John Frederick Bridge at Westminster Abbey, he became organist at Oxford. He composed many popular ballads and piano pieces.[49]

Clokey, Joseph Waddell (1890-   ). An American composer and organist, Clokey studied at Miami University and the Cincinnati Conservatory of Music. He taught theory at Miami University and later became professor of organ at Pomona College in Claremont, California. Clokey has written several operettas, cantatas, and other sacred music, as well as songs, part-songs, and works for organ and voice.[50]

Coleridge-Taylor, Samuel (1875-1912). Coleridge-Taylor was an Englishman of African Negro descent. An accomplished violinist and composer, he attended the Royal Academy of Music where he later taught violin. Although he conducted the London Handel Society, he was more devoted to his teaching and composing at Croydon. Much of his music is characterized with the folksong element, particularly the Negro. Coleridge-Taylor has written several works for soloists, chorus, and orchestra; orchestral music; violin pieces; piano pieces; and chamber music.[51]

Colvin, (Otis) Herbert, Jr. (1923-   ). Born in Arkansas, Colvin studied chemistry and math before pursuing his music education. He attended Baylor University (Bachelor of Music, piano), the University of Colorado in Boulder (Master of Music, music literature), Eastman School of Music (Doctor of Philosophy, theory), and spent

---

[47]*Grove's Dictionary* (5th ed.), II, 330-31; and Wier, *Macmillan Encyclopedia,* p. 344.

[48]Moore, "Baylor Collection," p. 145; and John Denison Champlin, Jr., ed., *Cyclopedia of Music and Musicians,* critically ed. by William Foster Apthorp (New York: Charles Scribner's Sons, 1888), I, 328-29.

[49]*Baker's Biographical Dictionary of Musicians* (5th ed.), p. 298.

[50]*Ibid.,* p. 303; Moore, "Baylor Collection," p. 146; and Thompson, *Cyclopedia* (9th ed.), p. 414.

[51]Moore, "Baylor Collection," p. 146; Thompson, *Cyclopedia* (9th ed.), pp. 420-21; and Wier, *Macmillan Encyclopedia,* pp. 356-57.

one summer at Juilliard. In addition to his work as a minister of music and teacher of piano, music literature, and theory, Colvin has given both piano and organ recitals, and has been soloist with orchestras. He has also accompanied various artists (Jean Madeira, Virginia MacWatters, Zvi Seitlin). In addition to the articles he has written for music journals, Colvin has composed organ preludes, organ pieces, a hymn tune, and has edited some choral works of William Billings.[52]

Cooke, Greville

Cooley, Carlton (1898-   ). Cooley was born in New Jersey and is known as a violinist, violist, and composer. He studied with Frederick Hahn and C[amille] W. Zeckwer at the Philadelphia Musical Academy and with Percy Goetschius at the Institute of Musical Art. He was principal violist with the Cleveland Symphony and won the Stowkowsky medal for his violin playing. The Cleveland Symphony premiered *Caponsacchi,* his orchestral poem in 1934. According to Denoe Leedy, the Cleveland *Press* music editor, *Caponsacchi* was written during the summer of 1933. Cooley based his epic poem not so much on RB's poem as on the play based upon it by Arthur Goodrich and Rose Amelia Palmer. The orchestral poem sketches in music some of the episodes from the Goodrich and Palmer play. Leedy criticizes Cooley's work for being too sectional from the standpoint of its dramatic continuity and for the uneven inspiration of the themes; however, Leedy says the chief attraction is the orchestra which " 'sounds' to perfection."[53]

Coombs, Charles Whitney (1859-1940). Coombs was an American organist and composer, who studied at Stuttgart, Dresden, and New York (Syracuse University). In 1922 he was awarded the honorary Doctor of Music degree by Syracuse University. He composed much church music, including a cantata, canticles, and anthems, but he wrote a number of songs also.[54]

Cowen, Sir Frederic Hymen (1852-1935). Born in Jamaica, Cowen was brought to England when he was four years old. He began studying music immediately and published a waltz when he was six. Among his teachers were Henry Russell, [John] Goss, [Julius] Benedict, [Ignaz] Moscheles, [Ernst Friedrich Edward] Richter, and [Carl Heinrich Carsten] Reinecke. Cowen was a composer, concert pianist, and conductor. He composed orchestral works, chamber music, operas, oratorios, cantatas, choral works, and songs.[55]

Cowley, Elsie M.

---

[52]Biographical data sheet compiled by Colvin.

[53]Review, Cleveland *Press,* Dec. 29, 1933; Program, Cleveland Symphony, Dec., 1933; Moore, "Baylor Collection," p. 147; and Wier, *Macmillan Encyclopedia,* p. 375.

[54]*Baker's Biographical Dictionary of Musicians* (5th ed.), p. 316; Moore, "Baylor Collection," pp. 147-48; and Thompson, *Cyclopedia* (9th ed.), p. 438.

[55]David Ewen, comp. and ed., *Composers of Today* (2nd ed.; New York: The H. W. Wilson Company, 1936), pp. 56-57.

Craddock, Reginald W.

Cripps, A. Redgrave

Croft, William (1678-1727). Croft was an English composer and organist. He was one of the collaborators for the collections of *Ayres for
the Harpsichord or Spinnet* and was a member of the Chapel Royal.
From the post of organist of St. Anne, Soho, Croft became organist of
the Chapel Royal and later succeeded John Blow as organist for Westminster Abbey. At this time he was also made Master of the Children
and Composer to the Chapel Royal. Croft wrote much of his best
music in these posts, especially the two volumes of Anthems and the
Burial Service which is often used at ceremonial funerals. He has
written odes and anthems, songs, sonatas for flute and for violin, and
hymns. Croft is buried in Westminster Abbey.[56]

Crumpler, Mary Frances

Curtis, Natalie (1875-1921). Curtis was an American writer and lecturer.
She studied piano with Arthur Friedheim at the National Conservatory in New York, with Ferruccio Busoni in Berlin, Auguste Alfred
Giraudet in Paris, [William] Wolf in Bonn, and Julius Kniese at the
Bayreuth Wagner-Schule. Later she married Paul Burlin and became interested in the North American Indian and Negro. She not
only wrote books and lectured about the American Indian, but she
also collected much of their music. Curtis composed songs and
choruses.[57]

Damrosch, Walter Johannes (1862-1950). Damrosch was a United States
citizen (naturalized) known mainly as a conductor and composer. He
was a pupil of his father and later of Hans von Bülow and attended
Columbia University and Princeton University. Damrosch organized
and toured the Damrosch Opera Company, reorganized the United
States Army bands, and was a pioneer in improving symphonic appreciation. His only book is his autobiography and his compositions
include operas, choral works, chamber music, and songs.[58]

Dansie, Redgewell. No information could be found about this composer,
but his setting of the *Cavalier Tunes* is one of the finest in the ABL
Collection. All three songs are lively and robust and are written in
modified strophic two-part song form. For baritone, they are worth-
while concert material.[59]

David, Elizabeth Harbison

Davidson, Frank

Davies, Sir Henry Walford (1869-1941). Davies was an English organist
and composer. After attending the Royal College of Music, he taught

---

[56]Thompson, *Cyclopedia* (9th ed.), p. 470.
[57]*Ibid.*, p. 475; Moore, "Baylor Collection," p. 148; and Wier, *Macmillan Ency-*
clopedia, p. 404.
[58]Thompson, *Cyclopedia* (9th ed.), p. 484.
[59]Reid, "Analysis of Songs," p. 52.

at the University of Wales as well as the Royal College of Music and became Master of the King's Musick, during which time he wrote the coronation service book for George VI. In addition to these posts Davies was also Director to the Royal Air Force. He has composed orchestral works, choral music, chamber music, church music, part-songs, and songs.[60]

Davis, Blevins

Davis, John Carlyle. Davis was born in Cincinnati and is known primarily as a composer. He attended Harvard, the University of Cincinnati, and Cincinnati College of Music, where he was a Gold Medal piano pupil. A member of American Society of Composers, Authors, and Publishers, Davis has written songs and piano works and has also made transcriptions. Among his publishers are Schirmer, John Church Company, Theodore Presser, Oliver Ditson, Willis, Boosey and Company, and B. F. Wood.[61]

Dawson, William Levi (1898-   ). Dawson is an American Negro composer. Born in Alabama, he studied composition and orchestration at Washington College in Topeka, Kansas. Later he studied theory and composition with Carl Busch at Homer Institute of Fine Arts in Kansas City. Dawson then went to Chicago where he studied composition at the American Conservatory of Music. He was music director in Topeka and in Kansas City and was first trombonist in the Chicago Civic Orchestra for three years. Since 1931 he has been director of the School of Music at Tuskegee Institute and director of the Tuskegee Choir. Among his compositions are two orchestral works, choral works, and chamber music.[62]

De Francesco, Louis E. (1888-   ). De Francesco is an Italian composer and conductor. Educated at the Conservatory of Naples, where he received the Diploma of Maestro, he has been active in America conducting light operas and film music. De Francesco has composed songs and many film scores, two of which are *Six Hours to Live* and *State Fair*.[63]

De Koven, Henry Louis Reginald (1859-1920). De Koven was an American composer of light operas. His training included study at St. John's College in Oxford and in Stuttgart, Frankfort, Florence, Vienna, and Paris with Clément Philibert Léo Delibes. A music critic as well as conductor, De Koven organized the Philharmonic Orchestra of Washington, D.C. He possessed an adept melodic ability with a particularly keen scoring talent. Aside from operas, De Koven composed songs, piano pieces, a piano sonata, an orchestral suite, and ballets.[64]

---

[60]*Grove's Dictionary* (3rd ed.), II, 21-23; Moore, "Baylor Collection," pp. 148-49; and Thompson, *Cyclopedia* (9th ed.), pp. 492-93.
[61]*Who Is Who in Music*, p. 75.
[62]Thompson, *Cyclopedia* (9th ed.), p. 494.
[63]*Ascap Biographical Dictionary* (1966), p. 162.
[64]*Baker's Biographical Dictionary of Musicians* (5th ed.), pp. 362-63; Moore, "Baylor Collection," pp. 149-50; and Thompson, *Cyclopedia* (9th ed.), p. 513.

De Lacey, Robert. On the front cover of the music which is in the ABL Collection is written that Robert de Lacy [*sic*] was organist and choir master of the Smith Place Religious Society in London.

Dello Joio, Norman (1913-   ). Dello Joio was born in New York, the descendant of a long line of Italian musicians. His father Casimiro Dello Joio, a composer and organist, was his first teacher; and his godfather Pietro Yon taught him to play the organ when he was fifteen. Dello Joio continued his education at the Institute of Musical Art in New York and in 1939 received a fellowship to do graduate work at Juilliard, where he was a composition pupil of Bernard Wagenaar. Later he studied at Yale with Paul Hindemith, who was the decisive influence in his musical development. Hindemith taught Dello Joio to discipline himself and to develop his many ideas into durable forms. Hindemith encouraged him to freely display his natural lyricism and to be himself. Dello Joio also studied at the Berkshire Music Center. In 1944 and 1945 he was awarded Guggenheim Fellowships and in 1946 received a $1,000 grant from the American Academy of Arts and Letters. He has also been given the Elizabeth Sprague Coolidge Award and the Town Hall Award. Dello Joio was musical director for Eugene Loring's Dance Players from 1941 to 1943. From 1945 to 1950 he was a composition teacher at Sarah Lawrence College and from 1958 to 1962 at the Mannes College of Music. Dello Joio has lectured widely in colleges and has written for musical journals. His best music is a combination of spontaneity, firm structure, and classic ease. A prolific and versatile composer, Dello Joio has written orchestral works, operas, dance music, concertos, television scores, choral music, incidental music, film scores, chamber music, piano works, and songs.[65]

del Riego, Teresa (1876-   ). Del Riego is credited with helping to improve the quality of English song writing, especially the ballad type, which was being replaced with songs of a less sentimental type by men such as Sir Hubert Parry and Sir Charles Villiers Stanford. Del Riego, who became Mrs. Teresa Ledbetter, composed sentimental ballads and religious songs primarily.[66]

Demuth, Norman (1898-   ). An Englishman whose fame lies mainly in the fields of composition and conducting is Demuth, who studied at Windsor (St. George's), at Repton, and at the Royal Academy of Music, where he later taught. His compositions include works for orchestra, chamber music, piano pieces, songs, part-songs, and military band pieces.[67]

de Sousa, Leon

---

[65]Thompson, *Cyclopedia* (9th ed.), pp. 521-23; and Bernard Taylor, ed., *Songs in English, Nineteen Contemporary Settings by American and English Composers* (New York: Carl Fischer, Inc., 1970), p. 3.

[66]*Grove's Dictionary* (5th ed.), VII, 954-55; Reid, "Analysis of Songs," p. 31; and Thompson, *Cyclopedia* (9th ed.), p. 525.

[67]Thompson, *Cyclopedia* (9th ed.), p. 526.

Dichmont, William.   No biographical data was found for Dichmont. His song cycle, *A Woman's Last Word,* is compiled of three songs which are basically Romantic in style, although the second song suggests Impressionistic writing with its sequential diminished seventh chords. Taken as a whole, the cycle is dramatic and in good taste and requires a fine singer to portray the mood.[68]

Dickinson, Clarence (1873-   ).   Educated at Miami University, Northwestern University and studying in Paris and in Berlin (with [Heinrich] Reimann), Dickinson is an American organist. His accomplishments include directing the Chicago Cosmopolitan School of Music, founding the Music Art Society and the American Guild of Organists, and teaching at the Union Theological Seminary. Dickinson has composed songs, anthems, organ music, and has edited collections of church music.[69]

Dillon, Fannie Charles (1881-1947).   Dillon was an American composer and pianist. She studied at Pomona College in Claremont, California, in Berlin with Hugo Kaun and Leopold Godowsky, and in New York with Rubin Goldmark. Later Dillon taught at Pomona College and in the Los Angeles high schools. Among her compositions are orchestral works, piano pieces, songs, chamber music, and church music.[70]

Dittenhaver, Sarah Louise (1901-   ).   Dittenhaver is an American composer, author, pianist, and teacher. Educated at the Cosmopolitan Conservatory in Chicago and Oberlin Conservatory, she has been active in several music organizations including the American Society for Composers, Authors, and Publishers. Dittenhaver has composed songs, anthems, and piano works.[71]

Dougherty, Celius (1902-   ).   Dougherty is an American composer and pianist who studied at the University of Minnesota, Juilliard, and with Rubin Goldmark and Josef Lhevinne. He has written many piano works, songs, and chamber music.[72]

Downing, Lulu Jones.   Born in Indiana, Downing is a pianist and composer. She received musical training in Indiana, Chicago, and New York and has presented concerts of her own works. Downing is a member of several music clubs and has composed songs and piano works.[73]

Drakeford, Louis

Duncan, William Edmondstoune (1866-1920).   Duncan was born in England and was a student of Sir Hubert Parry, Sir Charles Villiers Stanford, and Sir George Macfarren. After attending the Royal College

---

[68]Reid, "Analysis of Songs," p. 75.

[69]Thompson, *Cyclopedia* (9th ed.), p. 541.

[70]*Ibid.,* p. 810; *Baker's Biographical Dictionary of Musicians* (5th ed.), p. 383; and Moore, "Baylor Collection," pp. 150-51.

[71]*Ascap Biographical Dictionary* (1966), p. 177.

[72]*Ibid.,* p. 182.

[73]*Who Is Who in Music,* p. 82.

of Music on a scholarship, he became a music critic and taught at the Oldham College of Music. Duncan has written two books about music and has composed music for chorus and orchestra, works for soprano and orchestra, an opera, a string trio, and songs.[74]

Dunhill, Thomas Frederick (1877-1946). Dunhill was an English composer, teacher, and author. He studied at the Royal College of Music and afterward taught piano at Eton College. From there he went to the Royal College of Music as professor of harmony and counterpoint; he was also on the faculty of the University of London. Among his published books are *Chamber Music, Sullivan's Comic Operas,* and another analyzing Mozart's string quartets. Dunhill wrote chamber music mostly, but he also composed orchestral works, children's cantatas, and operettas.[75]

Dyson, George (1883-   ). Dyson is an English composer, teacher, and organist. Educated at Oxford and at the Royal Academy of Music, where he received several scholarships for organ and composition, including the Mendelssohn prize, he later taught in public schools and eventually became director of the Royal College of Music. Dyson has equal compositional facility in classical forms and in modern devices. Among his works are chamber music, orchestral music, piano pieces, songs, choral works, and church music.[76]

Easson, James (1895-   ). Easson was born and educated in Scotland, where he was active as a music educator and organist. Among his compositions are *String Arrangements of Scottish Lore,* orchestral works, songs, school music, and madrigals.[77]

Ehrmann, Mary Bartholomew (1862-1939). Ehrmann was born in Cincinnati, where she later graduated from the Bartholomew English and Classical School. In 1893 she married Dr. George Bigler Ehrmann and had three sons and a daughter. Besides writing several books of songs for children, Ehrmann wrote a book of short poems named *The Lure of Miami* (1933).[78]

Elgar, Sir Edward (1857-1934). Elgar was an English composer, who was self-taught for the most part, although he did receive training from his father. A teacher at Birmingham University and Master of the King's Music, Elgar was the first English composer to succeed in symphonic writing. He composed orchestral works, concertos, choral works, chamber music, violin pieces, songs, organ music, duets, a band piece, and transcriptions.[79]

---

[74]*Baker's Biographical Dictionary of Musicians* (5th ed.), p. 408; Jones, "Browning and Music," pp. 144-45; and Thompson, *Cyclopedia* (9th ed.), p. 569.

[75]*Grove's Dictionary* (3rd ed.), II, 109-10; Moore, "Baylor Collection," p. 151; and Thompson, *Cyclopedia* (9th ed.), p. 569.

[76]Moore, "Baylor Collection," pp. 151-52; Thompson, *Cyclopedia* (9th ed.), p. 580; and Arthur Eaglefield Hull, ed., *A Dictionary of Modern Music and Musicians* (New York: E. P. Dutton & Co., 1924), p. 132.

[77]*Who's Who International,* p. 64.

[78]*Who Was Who in America,* I, 363.

[79]Thompson, *Cyclopedia* (9th ed.), pp. 595-97.

Ellingham, Harry

Elman, Mischa (1891-   ). The Russian-American violinist, Elman, studied at the St. Petersburg Conservatory after his teacher, Leopold Auer, obtained permission from the Tsar (1902) to suspend the regulation preventing Jews from entering the Imperial Conservatory. A pupil of César Antonovich Cui, Elman became one of the world's leading violinists and was noted particularly for his extensive repertoire. He has published several arrangements for violin as well as some of his own pieces, a light opera, and some songs.[80]

England, Nicholas M., Jr. (1923-   ). England is a native of Texas and was a theory teacher at Baylor University, where he received his Bachelor of Music degree (composition, 1947) and Master of Music degree (composition, 1949). He has also studied with Paul Hindemith at Yale University. He is presently with the Walt Disney California Institute of Art. He has written two film scores, two music dramas, orchestral works, choral works, and chamber music.[81]

Farley, Roland (1892-1932). Farley was born in Aspen, Colorado and at the age of five was totally blind. He studied piano with Jos[eph] Gahm and violin with Hans Albert. At twenty he went to the Royal Conservatory of Leipzig where he studied piano with Jos[eph] Pembauer and theory with Gustave Schreck. Later Farley studied in Berlin with Ernest Hutcheson. In addition to arranging some quartets, he has written songs and choral works.[82]

Farmer, John (1836-1901). Farmer was an English musician who was educated at the Leipzig Conservatory and who later studied with Andreas Späth at Saxe Coburg. He taught at Zurich and at the Harrod School and served as examiner for the Society of Arts in addition to teaching at Balliol.[83]

Farrington, Frederick W.

Fergus, Phyllis. Born in Chicago, Fergus attended Smith College and the American Conservatory of Music. She studied composition with Adolf Weidig, violin with Albert Dietz, and piano with Regina Watson. Fergus is a composer and teacher and is active in several music clubs. Among her compositions are songs and works for ensemble, chorus, and piano. She has also written three books (*Story Poems, Dramatic Readings,* and *Religious Readings*).[84]

Fisher, Charles R. In a letter from E. C. Watt of A. Weekes & Co. Ltd. to Andrew Joseph Armstrong dated June 29, 1933, Watt writes that

---

[80]*Ibid.,* p. 599; *Baker's Biographical Dictionary of Musicians* (5th ed.), pp. 434-35; Jones, "Browning and Music," p. 145; Moore, "Baylor Collection," p. 152; and Waldo Selden Pratt, ed., *The New Encyclopedia of Music and Musicians* (New York: The Macmillan Company, 1924), p. 334.

[81]Personal interview between Moore and England July, 1951, Moore, "Baylor Collection," pp. 153-54; and Records, Baylor University, School of Music.

[82]*Ascap Biographical Dictionary* (1948), p. 109.

[83]*Grove's Dictionary* (5th ed.), III, 31-32; Jones, "Browning and Music," p. 145.

[84]*Who Is Who in Music* (1941), p. 92.

they have no idea as to the whereabouts of Charles R. Fisher. "When last we heard of him, some years ago, he was in Nova Scotia."[85]

Fisher, William Arms (1861-1948). Fisher was an American editor and composer, who studied in New York, London, and with Horatio Parker and Antonin Dvorák. He taught at the New York National Conservatory of Music and was editor and publishing manager, later becoming vice president, of the Oliver Ditson Company. In addition to the books he wrote about music, Fisher composed songs, pieces for violin and piano, part-songs, anthems, carols, arranged Negro spirituals, and edited many songs.[86]

Floyd, Alfred Ernest (1877-   ). Floyd is an English organist, conductor, and composer who was active in the musical life of Australia from 1915 to 1947, particularly in choral music. He has been in great demand as an adjudicator, lecturer, journalist and music appreciation teacher. Floyd has composed much church music, part-songs for school and adult choirs, and many organ works.[87]

Foote, David

Forbes, J. Winchell

Ford, D. Rhys

Forrester, James Cliffe (1860-1941). Forrester was an English composer, educated at the National Training School and at the studios of Sir Frederick Bridge. He was conductor of the Ealing Choral Society and wrote the book, *Anthems Ancient and Modern*. Forrester has written anthems, part-songs, cantatas, songs, chamber music, and pieces for piano, and for violin.[88]

Forster, Beatrice. On the front cover of the music in the ABL Collection is written "Beatrice Forster Sep. 2nd, 1902."

Francesco, Louis E. de. *See* De Francesco, Louis E.

Freer, Eleanor Everest (1864-1942). Freer was an American composer. She founded the American Opera Society of Chicago and was an honorary member of many music clubs, especially in Chicago. She has written operas, operettas, vocal trios and quartets, piano pieces, and songs.[89]

French, Emma Weller

Frey, Adolf (1865-1938). Frey was a German pianist and a pupil of Clara Schumann, Immanuel Gottlob Friedrich Faiszt, and Johannes Brahms. From 1887 to 1893 he was musician to Prince Alexander

---

85Charles R. Fisher folder, Armstrong Browning Library, Music Correspondence.
86Thompson, *Cyclopedia* (9th ed.), p. 659.
87*Grove's Dictionary* (5th ed.), III, 164-65.
88Thompson, *Cyclopedia* (9th ed.), p. 729.
89*Ibid.*, p. 747; *ibid.* (4th ed. rev. and enl. by Nicolas Slonimsky, ed.; 1946), p. 628 (hereafter cited as *Cyclopedia*, 4th ed.); and Moore, "Baylor Collection," p. 154.

Friedrich of Hesse. He then came to Syracuse University where he later was head of the piano department for forty years. In 1935 he founded the Frey School of Music in Watertown, New York, which he directed until his death.[90]

Fuller, Caroline M.

Gabert, Abel

Gabriel, Mary Ann Virginia (1825-1877). Gabriel was an English pianist and composer. She studied piano with [Johann Peter] Pixis, Dohler, and Sigismond Thalberg, and composition with Wilhelm Bernhard Molique. Much of her libretti was written by her husband, George E. March. Among her compositions are three cantatas, five operettas, piano pieces, and songs.[91]

Galsworthy, Ada

Galsworthy, Mrs. John. *See* Galsworthy, Ada

Galuppi, Baldassare (1706-1785). Galuppi was an Italian composer and a pupil of Antonio Lotti. He was an accomplished player and composer of music for the harpsichord. Galuppi held posts at St. Marks, St. Petersburg (Catherine II), and the Venice Conservatorio del Incurabili. His 112 operas and twenty oratorios are now obsolete. Galuppi also composed cantatas, sacred music, and harpsichord sonatas.[92]

Ganz, Rudolf (1877-   ). Born in Switzerland, Ganz became an American citizen. He was a successful pianist and conductor, who began his musical training with his uncle Carl Eschmann and later attended the Zurich Conservatory, and continued his studies in Lausanne, Straussburg, Berlin, and the United States (Grinnell College, Eastman, De Paul University, and Cincinnati Conservatory). Ganz was head of the piano department at the Chicago Musical College and in 1921 was conductor of the St. Louis Symphony Orchestra. He promoted the music of little known composers such as Claude Debussy, Vincent d'Indy, Maurice Ravel, and Béla Bartók. He has written a symphony, choruses for male voices, songs, and piano pieces.[93]

Gaul, Harvey Bartlett (1881-1945). Gaul was an American organist and composer. He studied organ with Alexandre Guilmant, Abel Decaux, and Charles Widor at the Schola Cantorum in Paris. Gaul was music critic for the Cleveland *News*, a teacher at the Pittsburgh Carnegie Institute of Technology, and was conductor for several musical socie-

---

[90]*Baker's Biographical Dictionary of Musicians* (5th ed.), p. 512; Moore, "Baylor Collection," p. 154; and Thompson, *Cyclopedia* (9th ed.), p. 749.

[91]*Grove's Dictionary* (3rd ed.), II, 331; Moore, "Baylor Collection," p. 155; and Thompson, *Cyclopedia* (9th ed.), p. 761.

[92]*Baker's Biographical Dictionary of Musicians* (5th ed.), pp. 532-33; Moore, "Baylor Collection," p. 155; and Thompson, *Cyclopedia* (9th ed.), p. 768.

[93]Hull, *Dictionary of Modern Music and Musicians*, p. 174; Moore, "Baylor Collection," pp. 155-56; and Thompson, *Cyclopedia* (9th ed.), pp. 769-70.

ties. He has composed orchestral works, chamber music, organ pieces, operettas, and anthems.[94]

Geisler, Paul (1856-1919). Geisler was a German composer and conductor. In addition to conducting at Leipzig and Bremen, he served as the director of the Conservatory at Posen. Among his compositions are operas, symphonic poems, cantatas, songs, and piano works. Most of his music is unpublished.[95]

Gelrud, Paul. The piece of music in the ABL Collection which Gelrud composed was written in Ithaca, New York.

Gilberte, Hallett (1875-1945). Gilberte was an American song composer and singer who studied with John Orth, C. Bärmann, and Ethelbert Nevin. Aside from songs, Gilberte wrote several choral works, and pieces for piano and violin.[96]

Gilchrist, William Wallace (1846-1916). Gilchrist was an American choral director and composer. He was a pupil of Hugh Archibald Clarke at the University of Pennsylvania, and, except for teaching in Cincinnati from 1872 to 1873 he lived in Philadelphia, where he was active in the music circles and where he taught singing (Philadelphia Music Academy). Among his works are orchestral music, songs, church music, chamber music, and cantatas.[97]

Giorza, Paolo (1838-1914). Giorza was an Italian teacher and composer of ballets and one opera.[98]

Glarum, L. Stanley (1908-   ). Glarum is an American composer, conductor, and educator. Educated at Olaf College and the University of Washington, he was a high school teacher and supervisor for five years and was an accompanist and arranger for radio and concerts for ten years. During World War II he was a chaplain's assistant. In 1947 he joined the music faculty at Lewis and Clark College and has been chairman of the music department since 1959. Glarum has been a church organist and choirmaster since 1934. He has written several sacred songs.[99]

Goatley, Alma

Godard, Benjamin Louis Paul (1849-1895). A French composer, Godard studied violin with Hammer and entered the Paris Conservatory in 1863. He was the co-winner, with Th[éodore] Dubois of the Prix de la Ville de Paris for *Le Tasse,* a dramatic symphony with soloists

---

[94]Thompson, *Cyclopedia* (9th ed.), p. 776.

[95]*Ibid.,* p. 780; *Grove's Dictionary* (3rd ed.), II, 362; and Moore, "Baylor Collection," p. 156.

[96]*Baker's Biographical Dictionary of Musicians* (5th ed.), p. 562; Moore, "Baylor Collection," p. 156; and Thompson, *Cyclopedia* (9th ed.), p. 793.

[97]Moore, "Baylor Collection," p. 157; Thompson, *Cyclopedia* (9th ed.), p. 793; and Wier, *Macmillan Encyclopedia,* p. 670.

[98]Thompson, *Cyclopedia* (9th ed.), p. 796.

[99]*Ascap Biographical Dictionary* (1966), p. 263.

and chorus. Among the several operas he wrote is *Jocelyn* which contains the familiar *Berceuse.* Other compositions are chamber music, piano pieces, songs, and orchestral works. Superficiality of style and hasty workmanship have resulted in little survival of his music.[100]

Goldsworthy, William Arthur (1878-   ). Goldsworthy was born in England and came to the United States in 1887. He is a composer, conductor, and organist. A pupil of Samuel Prowse Warren and Charles Jolley, Goldsworthy served as church organist and director at St. Ann's, St. Andrews, and St. Marks-in-the-Bouwerie. He is a member of the American Guild of Organists and of the American Society of Composers, Authors and Publishers. In addition to the series of [Johann Sebastian] Bach *Cantatas* he edited, Goldsworthy has composed works for organ, an opera, an oratorio, and a music drama.[101]

Goodeve, Mrs. Arthur (fl. nineteenth century). As a composer, Goodeve wrote many songs and ballads that were extremely popular. *Fiddle and I* was still sung widely in 1938.[102]

Gow, George Coleman (1860-1938). Gow was an American music educator, who graduated from Brown University and Newton Theological Seminary in addition to which he studied in Berlin. Later he taught at Smith College in Northhampton, Massachusetts and at Vassar College. Among his compositions are songs, duets, part-songs, an organ sonata, and choral music. Gow is the author of the theory books, *Structure of Music,* and *Lessons in Theory and Harmony.*[103]

Grace, Harvey (1874-1944). Grace was an English organist, music critic, and writer. He edited the London *Musical Times* and helped to spread its influence. Aside from writing several books, articles, and essays about music, Grace composed choral music and organ works.[104]

Gracey, William Adolphe

Graham, A. Cyril

Gregory, Eleanor C.

Hadley, Henry Kimball (1871-1937). Hadley was an outstanding American composer and conductor. He attended the New England Conservatory, Tufts College, and studied in Vienna with Eusebius Mandyczewski. Hadley wrote programmatically and even though he avoided the unresolved dissonances of the then avante garde, he used somewhat advanced harmonies in an impressionistic vein and often employed exotic colors when the subject matter demanded it. An

---

[100]Thompson, *Cyclopedia* (9th ed.), p. 809.
[101]*Ascap Biographical Dictionary* (1966), p. 272.
[102]Wier, *Macmillan Encyclopedia,* p. 693.
[103]*Baker's Biographical Dictionary of Musicians* (5th ed.), p. 596; Moore, "Baylor Collection," pp. 157-58; and Thompson, *Cyclopedia* (9th ed.), p. 822.
[104]*Grove's Dictionary* (3rd ed.), II, 428; Moore, "Baylor Collection," p. 158; and Thompson, *Cyclopedia* (9th ed.), p. 823.

active member of the National Association for American Composers, Authors and Publishers, he contributed much to the growth of American music. Hadley composed theater music (opera, masque, comic opera), orchestral music, choruses, and chamber music.[105]

Hageman, Richard (1882-   ).   Hageman is a Dutch-American composer and conductor, who studied at the Amsterdam Conservatory, where his father was director, and later at the Brussels Conservatory. Among the important conducting posts he has held are those at the Amsterdam Royal Opera House, Metropolitan Opera, Chicago Opera, Los Angeles Opera, and orchestras in San Francisco, Pittsburgh, and Philadelphia.   Hageman has been head of the voice department and vice-president of the Chicago Musical College.   His compositions include film music, songs, and operas.[106]

Hall, William D.

Halley, Margaret A.

Hammer, Marie von (fl. nineteenth century).   Von Hammer was an American composer whose music includes a *Romanza* for piano and cello and songs.[107]

Hammond, William G. (1874-1945).   Best known for his songs, Hammond was an American, who served as the organist at the Dutch Reformed Church in Brooklyn from 1914 to 1945.[108]

Harraden, Ethel (fl. 1938).   Active as a contemporary English composer in 1938, Harraden's opera *The Taboo* was successfully produced at the Trafalgar Square Theater in London, where it was favorably received by the critics.   Another important work is her operetta *His Last Chance*.   She has also written instrumental music.[109]

Harris, Russell G.

Harrison, Julius (1885-   ).   Harrison is an English conductor and composer.   Upon completing his studies with Sir Granville Bantock at the Birmingham Midland Institute, he held conducting posts at the Beecham Opera Company, the Scottish Symphony Orchestra, the British National Opera Company, the Handel Society, and the Hastings Corporation.   Harrison has written two operas, orchestral works, a cantata, chamber music, songs, piano pieces, organ music, and sacred music.[110]

Hartmann, Arthur Martinus (1881-1956).   The Hungarian-American, Hartmann, was a child-prodigy on the violin, who toured at the age of

---

[105]*Baker's Biographical Dictionary of Musicians* (5th ed.), pp. 635-66; Reid, "Analysis of Songs," p. 33; and Thompson, *Cyclopedia* (9th ed.), pp. 865-66.

[106]Moore, "Baylor Collection," pp. 159-60; and Thompson, *Cyclopedia* (9th ed.), p. 868.

[107]Wier, *Macmillan Encyclopedia*, p. 752.

[108]*Ascap Biographical Dictionary* (1966), p. 307.

[109]Wier, *Macmillan Encyclopedia*, p. 768.

[110]*Baker's Biographical Dictionary of Musicians* (5th ed.), p. 660; Moore, "Baylor Collection," p. 160; and Thompson, *Cyclopedia* (9th ed.), pp. 898-99.

twelve playing much of the modern violin repertoire. In Philadelphia he studied with Van Gelder, Charles Loeffler, and H. Norris. He played in recitals with Claude Debussy. Hartmann transcribed previously written music in addition to composing original violin pieces, orchestral works, a string quartet, and songs. His essay on Johann Sebastian Bach's *Chaconne* [in D minor] has been translated into fourteen languages. He discovered and edited six sonatas of Felice de Giardini.[111]

Hartog, Cécile S.

Harts, Harry Lawson

Harwood, Basil (1859-1949). An English organist and composer, Harwood attended Oxford and the Leipzig Conservatory. He edited the *Oxford Hymn Book* and composed many organ works, a cantata, songs, and church music.[112]

Hathaway, Joseph W. G.

Hattersley, F. Kilvington

Hawley, Charles Beach (1858-1915). Hawley was an American singer, organist, and song composer. After studying with Dudley Buck, he helped to organize the Metropolitan Conservatory. Hawley has also composed part-songs for male voices.[113]

Hervey, Augusta E.

Herz, Maria (1878-   ). Herz is a German composer whose musical training included study with M[ax] Pauer (piano), [August von] Othegraven (theory), and H[ermann] H[ans] Wetzler (theory). She composed a piano concerto, a string quartet, and songs with various accompaniments. In addition Herz edited [Johann Sebastian] Bach's *Giacona* for string quartet.[114]

Hill, Mildred J. (1859-1916). Hill was an American composer, pianist, and author. A church organist, a concert pianist, and an authority on Negro spirituals, Hill studied with her father and Calvin Cady and Adolph Weidig. She is the author of *Song Stories for the Kindergarten and Primary School.* Two of her songs are *Good Morning to All* and *Happy Birthday to You.*[115]

Hinkle, Daisy

Hirsch, Karl (1858-1918). The Bavarian composer, Hirsch, conducted choirs throughout Europe. His music includes works for chorus, cantatas, and songs.[116]

---

[111]*Baker's Biographical Dictionary of Musicians* (5th ed.), pp. 662-63; Moore, "Baylor Collection," pp. 160-61; and Thompson, *Cyclopedia* (9th ed.), p. 901.

[112]*Grove's Dictionary* (3rd ed.), II, 553; Moore, "Baylor Collection," p. 161; and Thompson, *Cyclopedia* (9th ed.), p. 903.

[113]Thompson, *Cyclopedia* (9th ed.), p. 909.

[114]Wier, *Macmillan Encyclopedia*, p. 811.

[115]*Ascap Biographical Dictionary* (1966), p. 335.

[116]Thompson, *Cyclopedia* (9th ed.), pp. 956-57.

Hoberg, Margaret

Hollander, Benno (1853-1942). Hollander was a Dutch violinist who studied at the Paris Conservatoire, training with Camille Saint Saëns. After serving as concertmaster with the German Opera, he returned to London and taught at the Guildhall School of Music. Hollander composed violin concertos, orchestral works, violin pieces, chamber music, and piano pieces.[117]

Hollins, Dorothea (fl. 1938). Hollins was a contemporary English composer in 1938, whose compositions included a violin sonata.[118]

Homer, Sidney (1864-1953). Between 1899 and 1915, Homer produced about 100 of America's best songs, even compared with the works of Charles Griffes, John Alden Carpenter, and Charles Martin Loeffler. During this period he composed songs almost to the exclusion of instrumental music. The bulk of these songs were written while he was teaching harmony and counterpoint privately in Boston. About great literature Homer has said it is "angular, stiff, heavy, long-worded, stretched beyond the musical phrase, interrupted with parentheses. I should be ashamed to tell how many big things I started. I loved them but they didn't love music. . . . Unless a song makes itself the game is up. All the King's horses and all the King's men. . . . Much of my life has been wasted in vain attempts." Homer's songs often appear in concerts. An American, he studied in Boston and Germany and later lectured on symphonies and Wagnerian operas.[119]

Hopkins, Franklin (1879-   ). Hopkins is an American composer and writer on music. He was a pupil of Walter Spalding and John Knowles Paine. Later he helped to popularize the New York Plectrum Orchestra. Hopkins has composed hymns, anthems, and songs.[120]

Hopkins, Joseph P.

Howe, Julia Ward (1819-1910). Although she is known for her activities as the American suffragist and for writing *The Battle Hymn of the Republic,* Howe was also active in prison reform, wrote poetry, lectured, worked for world peace, and was a philanthropist.[121]

Hudson, Henry

---

[117]*Ibid.,* p. 995.

[118]Wier, *Macmillan Encyclopedia,* p. 834.

[119]S. Homer, *My Wife and I* (New York, 1909), p. 120 as quoted in James Husst Hall, *The Art Song* (Norman: University of Oklahoma Press, 1953), pp. 269-70; Thompson, *Cyclopedia* (9th ed.), p. 1000; and Denis Stevens, ed., *A History of Song* (New York: W. W. Norton & Company, Inc., 1960), p. 430.

[120]Wier, *Macmillan Encyclopedia,* p. 839.

[121]*The New Century Cyclopedia of Names,* ed. by Clarence L. Barnhart with the assistance of William D. Halsey (New York: Appleton-Century-Crofts, Inc., 1954), II, 2064-65; and *Webster's New Collegiate Dictionary* (Springfield, Mass.: G. & C. Merriam Co., Publishers, 1959), p. 1030.

Hughes, Rupert (1872-1956). Hughes was an American novelist, composer, and music critic. He studied in Cleveland, New York, and
London. As a composer, Hughes experimented with dissonances
which were then considered advanced. Among his compositions are
piano pieces, songs, and a dramatic monologue for baritone and piano.
Hughes has written several books about music and musicians as well
as short stories, novels, and works for motion pictures; he also edited
Thirty Songs by American Composers. In addition to these activities
Hughes has produced films.[122]

Huhn, Bruno (1871-1950). Huhn was an English-born American pianist,
composer, voice teacher, and self-taught organist. He taught conducting and was a member of many musical organizations, including the
American Society of Composers, Authors and Publishers. Huhn
helped to found and conduct the Forest Hills Choral Society and
other musical societies. His compositions include choral works, anthems, part-songs, organ music, piano pieces, and songs.[123]

Hullah, John Pyke (1812-1884). Hullah, an English composer and organist, was quite active as a music educator. He formed his own
Singing School for Schoolmasters at Exeter Hall and was professor
of singing at King's College, Bedford College, and Queen's College.
He also conducted the Royal Academy of Music Concerts, played the
organ for the Charterhouse School, and served as Inspector of Training Schools. Edinburgh University conferred the honorary Doctor
of Literature degree upon him. Hullah has written books and essays
about music and has edited collections of vocal music (including
psalms and hymns). He has composed operas, anthems, motets,
choruses, part-songs, and songs.[124]

Hurless, Don

Iles, Edward

Inches, Charles

Ives, Charles (1874-1954). Many believe that Ives is the greatest American composer that has lived. He was undoubtedly the most original
and inventive composer during his productive period. Ives studied
with his father and attended Yale. Although he was a composer and
an organist, he was the head of his own successful insurance business.
Ives did not seek to have his music performed and he did not listen
to other music for fear it would contaminate his own compositions.
One of the most prolific composers, Ives wrote works for orchestra,
songs, choral music, chamber music, and piano music.[125]

---

[122]*Baker's Biographical Dictionary of Musicians* (5th ed.), p. 746; Moore, "Baylor
Collection," p. 162; and Thompson, *Cyclopedia* (9th ed.), p. 1016.
[123]*Baker's Biographical Dictionary of Musicians* (5th ed.), p. 747; Moore, "Baylor
Collection," pp. 162-63; Reid, "Analysis of Songs," p. 40; and Thompson, *Cyclopedia*
(9th ed.), p. 1016.
[124]*Grove's Dictionary* (3rd ed.), II, 678-79; Moore, "Baylor Collection," pp. 163-
64; and Thompson, *Cyclopedia* (9th ed.), pp. 1016-17.
[125]Thompson, *Cyclopedia* (9th ed.), p. 1049.

Jervis-Read, Harold Vincent (1883-   ). Born in England, Jervis-Read was a professor of composition at the Royal Academy of Music. He has written choral works; songs; and a concerto for two violins, piano, and string orchestra.[126]

Johnson, F. Arthur (1874-   ). Johnson is an American composer, organist, pianist, and teacher. A student of [Hermann] Scholtz in Dresden and of Robert Teichmueller in Leipzig, he attended the Leipzig Conservatory and did further study in Zuoz, Switzerland. He taught piano and theory and was the Director of Music at Texas Christian University (Fort Worth) and at Baylor University.[127]

Johnson, Leslie

Johnson, Noel

Johnstone, Harry

Jordan, Jules (1850-1927). Jordan was an American concert and oratorio tenor singer, who studied in Boston, London, and Paris. He portrayed Faust in the first performance of Hector Berlioz's *Damnation of Faust* in New York (1880). Jordan was also a composer and choral conductor. Brown Univeristy conferred the honorary Doctor of Music upon him. He has composed operas, cantatas, anthems, choral and orchestral works, and songs.[128]

Jowett, Albert

Kaiser, Charles Alfred (1872-   ). Kaiser is a Belgian composer, born in Brussels. He studied with [Anton] Bruckner, J[osef] Förster, and with private teachers in Prague. Around 1940 he was living in London. Among his compositions are five operas, an operetta, a ballet, a symphony, a piano concerto, three serenades for strings, and two piano trios.[129]

Kellie, Lawrence (1862-1932). Educated at the Royal Academy of Music, Kellie was an English singer and song composer.[130]

Kernochan, Marshall Rutgers (1880-1955). Kernochan was born in New York and was a pupil of Iwan Knorr at Frankfort and of Percy Goetschius at the New York Institute of Musical Art. He lived in Massachusetts as a composer and wrote a cantata, choral works, and songs.[131]

Klein, Bruno Oscar (1858-1911). After studying with his father, Klein attended the Munich Conservatory. He was a German pianist, or-

---

[126]*Baker's Biographical Dictionary of Musicians* (5th ed.), p. 782; and Moore, "Baylor Collection," p. 164.

[127]F. Arthur Johnson, credential card, Armstrong Browning Library, Music Correspondence; and Wier, *Macmillan Encyclopedia*, p. 906.

[128]Moore, "Baylor Collection," pp. 164-65; Thompson, *Cyclopedia* (4th ed.), p. 912; and Thompson, *Cyclopedia* (9th ed.), p. 1086.

[129]Robbins, "Composers Who Set Browning's Poetry," p. 83.

[130]Thompson, *Cyclopedia* (9th ed.), p. 1103.

[131]*Ibid.,* p. 1106; and Jones, "Browning and Music," p. 149.

ganist, and composer whose posts included teaching at the New York National Conservatory. He wrote an opera, Masses, motets, songs, orchestral music, works for solo instruments and orchestra, chamber music, and piano pieces.[132]

Klein, Manuel (1876-1919). Born in England, Klein was an American composer and conductor. He studied in London and New York and later was music director and composer for many of the productions at the Hippodrome in New York. In 1915 he returned to London where he held a similar position at the Gaiety Theatre. Klein has written orchestral works and musical productions such as *The Pied Piper,* an operatic fantasy.[133]

Kobbé, Gustav (1857-1918). Kobbé was an American music critic who studied at Columbia University, Columbia University Law School, in Wiesbaden, and in New York with private teachers. He was music critic for several New York papers and was editor of the *Musical Review.* Kobbé wrote several books and magazine articles about music and also wrote one novel, *Signora, A Child of the Opera House.*[134]

Komter, Jan Maarten

Koven, Reginald De. *See* De Koven, Reginald

Kramer, Arthur Walter (1890-   ). Kramer has been active in several areas of music. American born, he attended the New York College of the City and became a composer, editor, and author. He was music critic for *Musical America* and several newspapers, was co-founder of the Society for the Publication of American Music, and was managing director and vice president of Galaxy Music Corporation. He also composed over 300 works, including orchestral music, choral music, piano pieces, organ pieces, chamber music, violin pieces, and songs. Kramer was an active supporter of American music. The setting in the ABL Collection, *The Patriot,* was dedicated to the American tenor Evan Williams, whose recitation of the poem had encouraged Kramer to write the song. In the foreword to the music Kramer says that the song is not a "patriotic" one and that he purposely waited until after World War I to finish it so that it would avoid comparison with "those wretched concoctions that were ground out by the hundreds in those days." The song is entirely through-composed and the melody has no discernible repetitions of lines. Much of it is in the recitative, declamatory style and, as Reid points out, Kramer must be admired more for the fact that he set the entire poem (111 measures) than for the quality of the work.[135]

---

[132]Thompson, *Cyclopedia* (9th ed.), p. 1117.

[133]*Ibid.,* p. 1118; Moore, "Baylor Collection," p. 165; and Wier, *Macmillan Encyclopedia,* p. 953.

[134]*Baker's Biographical Dictionary of Musicians* (5th ed.), p. 845; Moore, "Baylor Collection," p. 165; and Thompson, *Cyclopedia* (9th ed.), p. 1122.

[135]Reid, "Analysis of Songs," pp. 47-48; and Thompson, *Cyclopedia* (9th ed.), pp. 1136-37.

Krug, Arnold (1849-1904). Krug was a German conductor, teacher, and composer. He first studied with his father, Diederich Krug, and later with [Cornelius] Gurlitt and [Carl Heinrich Carsten] Reinecke. Among his compositions are several large orchestral pieces, a violin concerto, and chamber music.[136]

Krull, Fritz

Lacey, Robert De. *See* De Lacey, Robert

Lee, Ernest Markham (1874-1956). Lee was an English organist and composer. A graduate of Emmanuel College, he became professor of organ at the London Guildhall School of Music and established a series of chamber music concerts at Woodford Green. Lee was the author of several books, in addition to his compositions which include songs, piano music, anthems and other music for church services.[137]

Lehmann, Liza (1862-1918). Elizabeth Nina Mary Fredericks or Liza Lehmann was English by birth but was reared in an intellectual and artistic climate in Germany, France, and Italy. A concert singer, Lehmann married an English painter, Herbert Bedford; she was one of the first successful women composers in England and the United States. In 1913 she taught singing at the London Guildhall School of Music. Her best known work is the song cycle, *In a Persian Garden,* and it was this form for which she created an interest in England. The song in the ABL Collection, *A Lover's Quarrel,* is noteworthy because of the careful and artistic way that the wide melodic leaps (two sevenths and one twelfth) are handled.[138]

Lewando, Ralph (1891-   ). An American violinist and teacher, Lewando studied at the Vienna Conservatory and was a violin pupil of [Ottokar] Sevcik and [Leopold] Auer. He was music editor of the Pittsburgh *Press,* founder of the Brahms Trio, and a composer of works for the violin and piano, songs and chamber music.[139]

Lewis, Ella V.

Lewis, Leo Rich (1865-1945). Lewis was an American composer, teacher, and author. He studied at Tufts College, Harvard, and the Munich Akademie der Tonkunst. His name is usually associated with his books about music and about education, although he wrote many songs, a cantata, an operetta, and orchestral music. Lewis's song in the ABL Collection, *A King Lived Long Ago,* is 146 measures long and is vocally taxing with its range of a-g^2, but nonetheless is effective.[140]

---

[136]Wier, *Macmillan Encyclopedia,* p. 990.

[137]*Baker's Biographical Dictionary of Musicians* (5th ed.), p. 166; and Thompson, *Cyclopedia* (9th ed.), p. 1178.

[138]*Baker's Biographical Dictionary of Musicians* (5th ed.), p. 931; Moore, "Baylor Collection," p. 167; Reid, "Analysis of Songs," p. 26; Stevens, *History of Song,* p. 157; and Wier, *Macmillan Encyclopedia,* p. 1035.

[139]Thompson, *Cyclopedia* (9th ed.), p. 1195.

[140]*Ibid.,* pp. 1195-96; and Reid, "Analysis of Songs," p. 56.

Liddle, Samuel (1868-   ). Liddle was an English pianist and song writer, who attended the Royal College of Music.[141]

Lidgey, C. A.

Lippé, Edouard

Löhr, Hermann Frederic. Born in England, Löhr was a pupil at the Royal Academy of Music where he won the Charles Lucas Medal. He is a song composer primarily.[142]

Loomis, Harvey Worthington (1865-1930). The American composer, Loomis, studied at the Brooklyn Polytechnic Institute and with Antonin Dvorák at the New York National Conservatory. He wrote essays for periodicals and lectured on Indian music, plus he composed operas, musical pantomimes, children's pieces, school choruses, chamber music, piano pieces, incidental music, and songs.[143]

Loughridge, Jean M.

Lynes, Frank (1858-1913). Lynes was an American organist, conductor, and composer. After studying at the New England Conservatory and the Leipzig Conservatory, he lived in Boston where he held several positions as church organist and conducted the "Cantabrigia Choral Class." Lynes has written pedagogical works as well as piano pieces, songs, anthems, and chamber music.[144]

McDaniel, William J. (1918-   ). Born in Jellico, Tennessee, McDaniel spent most of his childhood in Glasgow, Kentucky. He received a Bachelor of Science degree from Western Kentucky State University and a Master of Arts degree from George Peabody College for Teachers. He also attended Indiana University and the University of Denver. McDaniel was on the music faculty at Wayland Baptist College in Plainview, Texas and was Chairman of the Music Department for the Missouri Baptist College in Poplar Bluff and is presently Chairman of the Music Department of Southern Baptist College in Walnut Ridge, Arkansas. He is married and has two sons. Among his compositions are three orchestral works, a ballet, two chamber operas, songs, a song cycle, choral music (including one spoken choral work), a piano sonata, a harpsichord sonatina, a band piece, and chamber music for woodwind instruments. His style of composition is primarily the quartal system with the flow of the music determining the form.[145]

Mc. Hardy, James M. P.

McLeod, Robert

---

[141]Thompson, *Cyclopedia* (9th ed.), p. 1207.

[142]Wier, *Macmillan Encyclopedia*, p. 1071.

[143]*Ibid.*, p. 1075; Moore, "Baylor Collection," p. 168; and Thompson, *Cyclopedia* (9th ed.), p. 1231.

[144]*Baker's Biographical Dictionary of Musicians* (5th ed.), p. 997; Moore, "Baylor Collection," p. 169; and Thompson, *Cyclopedia* (9th ed.), p. 1242.

[145]Biographical data sheet compiled by McDaniel.

MacKenzie, Sir Alexander Campbell (1847-1935). MacKenzie was reared in a musical Scottish family, studied music in Germany, and taught at the Sonderhausen Conservatory and the Royal Academy of Music. He was also a successful concert violinist and the recipient of many honorary degrees of music. His best music is Romantic in style and strongly imaginative. MacKenzie handled Scottish themes, whether musical or poetical, quite naturally. The song which is in the ABL Collection, *One Who Never Turned His Back,* is unique because of its style of composition and media of presentation. It is included in *King Albert's Book* as one of the tributes to the Belgian King and his people following World War I. The song is an excellent example of text painting; it "sounds like background music that might have been used for newsreels during World War I." Other music by MacKenzie includes operas, operettas, incidental music, oratorios, cantatas, orchestral music, works for solo instrument and orchestra, chamber music, anthems, pieces for violin and piano, part-songs, and songs.[146]

MacLean, Alick (Alexander Morvaren) (1872-1936). MacLean was an English composer and conductor. He received the Moody-Manners prize for his opera *Petruccio* in 1895. Four years later he became musical director to Charles Wyndham at the Scarborough Spa Company and from 1915 to 1923 he directed the Queen's Hall Light Opera. His compositions are primarily operas.[147]

Macmillan, Sir Ernest Campbell (1893-   ). Macmillan was a Canadian organist, conductor, and composer who was educated at the University of Toronto, Oxford, the University of British Columbia, Edinburgh, and in Paris and in Bayreuth. A Fellow of the Royal College of Organists, he held posts at the Toronto Conservatory of Music, the University of Toronto, and was president of the Canadian College of Organists. Aside from textbooks, and settings of French-Canadian folk songs, Macmillan wrote for chorus and orchestra, chamber groups, and the solo voice.[148]

Macmillen, Francis (1885-   ). Macmillen is an American violinist who was highly successful. He studied at the Chicago College of Music, in Berlin with Joseph Joachim, at the Brussels Conservatory, and in Petrograd. After his debut with the New York Symphony in 1906, Macmillen toured extensively until 1929 when he began teaching at the Conservatory of Music in Ithaca. He has also taught and concertized in Europe as well as composing violin music.[149]

---

[146]Reid, "Analysis of Songs," pp. 56-57; *Grove's Dictionary* (5th ed.), V, 473-78; and Thompson, *Cyclopedia* (9th ed.), p. 1254.

[147]*Grove's Dictionary* (3rd ed.), III, 273; Moore, "Baylor Collection," pp. 169-70; and Thompson, *Cyclopedia* (9th ed.), p. 1254.

[148]Thompson, *Cyclopedia* (9th ed.), p. 1255.

[149]*Baker's Biographical Dictionary of Musicians* (5th ed.), p. 1005; Moore, "Baylor Collection," p. 170; and Thompson, *Cyclopedia* (9th ed.), p. 1255.

Madsen, Dora L. At the bottom of the first page of music in *Rabbi Ben Ezra,* from the ABL Collection, is written "Mrs. J. Chester Madsen, 1267 Crystal Ave., Salt Lake City, Ut." The letter I mailed to this address was returned marked "address unknown" and "no longer at this address."

Madsen, Mrs. J. Chester. *See* Madsen, Dora L.

Mallinson, Albert (1870-1946). Mallinson was an English organist and composer, who studied at St. Chad's Church in Leeds and with William Creser. In 1903 he toured Denmark and Germany with his wife, the Danish singer Anna Steinhauer, who introduced his own songs. From Denmark he toured successfully throughout the world. Beginning in 1926 Mallinson taught singing in Rome and was an examiner at the Trinity College of Music. He has written chamber music and over 300 songs in German, English, and Danish.[150]

Mana-Zucca (Augusta Zuckerman) (1890-   ). Mana-Zucca is an American pianist, composer, and singer. As a child she made her piano debut with the New York Symphony and was hailed as a prodigy. In 1914 she sang her debut as a soprano in London. She successfully sang light opera in New York. Later she became a composer remembered for her song, *I Love Life.* Mana-Zucca has been an active interpreter of her own piano works and songs. Since 1940 she has lived in Miami.[151]

Manney, Charles Fonteyn (1872-1951). Manney was an American conductor and composer. He studied with William Arms Fisher in New York and with [John] Wallace Goodrich and Percy Goetschius in Boston. He was music editor for Oliver Ditson Company and conductor for several choirs and for the Footlight Orchestra. Among his compositions are an opera, three cantatas, songs, and piano pieces.[152]

Markham, Robert (June 27, 1898-   ). Markham was born in Beeville, Texas and is an organist and organ-builder and organ teacher. In 1924 he received the Bachelor's Degree from Baylor University and in 1942 the honorary Doctor of Music degree from Boguslawski College of Music in Chicago. For three years Markham studied in New York at the Institute of Musical Art (later Juilliard) and with private teachers. He studied pipe organ at Columbia University in the summers of 1935 and 1937. Markham began teaching piano at Baylor in 1919 as an assistant instructor. From 1939 to 1945 he taught piano and organ. He was head of the organ department from 1946 until his retirement in 1972. Markham wrote music reviews for the Waco, Texas newspapers from 1941 to 1952 in addition to his teaching activities.[153]

---

[150]Moore, "Baylor Collection," pp. 170-71; Thompson, *Cyclopedia* (9th ed.), p. 1276; and Wier, *Macmillan Encyclopedia,* p. 1111.

[151]*Baker's Biographical Dictionary of Musicians* (5th ed.), pp. 1018-19; Moore, "Baylor Collection," p. 171; Reid, "Analysis of Songs," p. 36; and Thompson, *Cyclopedia* (9th ed.), p. 1276.

[152]Thompson, *Cyclopedia* (4th ed.), p. 1087; and Thompson, *Cyclopedia* (9th ed.), p. 1279.

[153]Biographical data sheet compiled by Markham.

Martin, Margaret R.

Marzials, Théodor (1850-   ). Marzials was a Belgian baritone and
    song writer. After studying in London with Lawson, in Paris and in
    Milan, he became superintendent of the music department of the
    British Museum. By singing his own songs, Marzials was able to
    introduce and popularize them.[154]

Mason, Mrs. Alexander O.

Mayer, Max (1859-1931). Mayer was a German pianist and composer.
    In Hamburg he studied with Levin and Ludwig Siegfried Meinardus,
    in Stuttgart with Dionys Pruckner and Seyfriz, and in Weimar with
    Franz Liszt. Later he became a professor of piano at the Royal Col-
    lege of Music. Often Mayer played in chamber music concerts and
    as an accompanist for his own songs.[155]

Metcalf, C. S.

Metcalf, John W. (1856-   ). Metcalf was an American pianist, teacher,
    and composer. He studied with [Carl Heinrich Carsten] Reinecke,
    [Salomon] Jodassohn, and [Bruno] Zwintscher. Included in his
    compositions are many piano pieces and songs.[156]

Metcalfe, W.

Millar, A. F.

Miller, Anne Stratton

Miller, Karl (1871-   ). Miller was born in Philadelphia, where he
    was an organist and director of music in the school for the blind. He
    was a piano student of B[runo] O[scar] Klein. In 1903 the Amer-
    ican Guild of Organists awarded Miller the prize for writing the
    best organ composition. He gave many organ recitals and composed
    organ works, songs, and church music.[157]

Miller, Lewis

Mills, Edward (1849-   ). Mills was an English organist, teacher, and
    author. He studied at St. Jolius College, Oxford, and with Arthur
    Sullivan (harmony) and Sir Frederick Bridge. In 1885 Mills mar-
    ried Florence Crofts. In addition to his church music, Mills has writ-
    ten several books, among which are *Training College Music Course,
    A Degree Exercise,* and *Ladies Voices.*[158]

Mokrejs, John (1875-   ). Mokrejs is an American pianist, composer,
    and teacher. Born in Cedar Rapids, Iowa, he was educated at the
    American Conservatory of Music in Chicago and at Columbia Uni-

---

154Wier, *Macmillan Encyclopedia,* p. 1133.
    155*Baker's Biographical Dictionary of Musicians* (5th ed.), p. 1053; and Moore,
"Baylor Collection," p. 172.
    156Wier, *Macmillan Encyclopedia,* p. 1171.
    157Robbins, "Composers Who Set Browning's Poetry," p. 101.
    158*Ibid.,* p. 102.

versity. He has composed operas, pageants, melodramas, songs, and piano pieces, but he is best known for his teaching pieces for the piano and his text books for theory and counterpoint. The song in the ABL Collection, *You'll Love Me Yet,* is written in Romantic style. Worth noting is the use of a chain phrase in the last nine measures to expand the form and emphasize the repeated text.[159]

Molineux, Marie Ada (April 19, 1857-1936). Born in Castroville, California, Molineux moved to Boston in 1858. In 1926 she had never been farther west than Chicago. Molineux's mother was Henrietta Molineux, her grandparents were James [Mctt.] K. M. and Sarah Molineux. Apparently Molineux's mother and father separated and Molineux's mother returned to her maiden name as did the daughter, Marie Ada. The ABL owns a small photograph of Marie Ada Molineux when she was approximately five years old and also a life-size portrait of her when she was elderly. She was known primarily for her efforts in Browning scholarship. She was an active member of the Boston Browning Society, being one of the charter members, and later wrote its history. She held three degrees from Boston University, one of which was the Doctor of Philosophy. Most of her time was spent in Boston and in Lynn, Massachusetts. She wrote several books concerning RB in addition to articles for periodicals. For many years her *A Phrase Book from the Poetic and Dramatic Works of Robert Browning* was a standard reference tool. In Asolo, Italy, Molineux was the guest of RB's sister, Sarianna Browning, and son, Robert Wiedemann Barrett Browning. She was a member of the Browning Pilgrimages led by Andrew Joseph Armstrong in 1926 and 1927. To the ABL Molineux has given many rare books from her personal library, numerous pamphlets and newspaper clippings, sheet music, and various other items, such as a lock of RB's hair. Aside from her Browning activities, Molineux worked for the board of health in Massachusetts, was in charge of the pathological laboratory in a Lynn hospital during World War I, was assistant to the head of the bacteriological department at Massachusetts Institute of Technology, and was on the staff of a Boston weekly newspaper. She was also a collector of Japanese art.[160]

Moore, Mary Carr (1873-1957). Moore was an American composer. A pupil of E. Dewhurst, J[ohn Harraden] Pratt, H[enry Bickford] Pasmore, and Mariner-Campbell, she taught at the Tulare [*sic*] School of Music, Seattle Conservatory, Chapman College, and Olga Steeb Piano School. Moore received the David Bispham award for her opera *Narcissa.* She was often a guest conductor for California

---

[159]Reid, "Analysis of Songs," p. 55; and *Who Is Who in Music,* p. 168.
[160]Article, Baylor University *Lariat,* Jan. 19, 1929 and March 13, 1930; Article, Boston *Republican,* July 26, 1924; Article, Lynn, Massachusetts *Daily Evening Item,* Dec. 21, 1929; Article, New Orleans *Times-Picayune,* [Dec., 1929 or Jan., 1930]; and Marie Ada Molineux, card with photograph, Armstrong Browning Library, Picture Collection.

orchestras. Among her compositions are operettas, operas, songs, and piano pieces.[161]

Mozart, Wolfgang Amadeus (1756-1791). Mozart is one of the greatest composers in the history of music. Born in Austria, he began his study of music with his father and by the time he was six years old had established himself as a prodigy on the piano. The very essence of his style is Classical because of its graceful elegance and keen adherence to structure and form. Mozart's insight into human nature is seen best in his operas, most of which are standard repertoire for any opera company. He wrote extensively and superbly in all forms.[162]

Mueller, Carl F. (1892-   ). Mueller is an American composer, organist and conductor. His education includes study at Elmhurst College, Strassberger Conservatory, and Westminster Choir College where he worked with John Finley Williamson. Active as a church organist and director, Mueller has also served as minister of music (First Presbyterian Church of Red Bank, New Jersey) and as choral director for Montclair State College and as minister of the Choir College. He has composed much choral music.[163]

Needham, Alicia Adelaide (1875-   ). Needham is an English composer who studied at the Royal Academy of Music. For six successive years she won the song-competition prize at the Irish Music Festival. She has published more than 600 songs.[164]

Neidlinger, William Harold (1863-1924). Neidlinger was an American organist, composer, and teacher. He was a pupil of Dudley Buck and C[arl Christian] Müller in New York and E[dward George] Dannreuther in London. Aside from his activities as an organist, Neidlinger directed choral societies and taught singing in Paris, London, and Chicago. Devoted to the study of child psychology, he established a school for sub-normal children in New Jersey. Most of his compositions are children's songs.[165]

Neuendorff, Adolf (1843-1897). Neuendorff was a German-American conductor and composer as well as a concert violinist and pianist. He has written orchestral works, comic operas, cantatas, choruses, and songs.[166]

Nevin, Ethelbert Woodbridge (1862-1901). Nevin was an American composer and pianist who studied piano with Von der Heide and William Guenther in Pittsburgh and with Franz Boehme in Dresden. Some of his other teachers included Stephen Austen Pearce, Benjamin Johnson Lang, and Stephen Albert Emery. Later he graduated

---

[161]Thompson, *Cyclopedia* (9th ed.), p. 1380; and Wier, *Macmillan Encyclopedia*, p. 1210.

[162]Thompson, *Cyclopedia* (9th ed.), pp. 1391-1406.

[163]*Ascap Biographical Dictionary* (1966), p. 528.

[164]Wier, *Macmillan Encyclopedia*, p. 1291.

[165]*Ibid.*, p. 1293; Moore, "Baylor Collection," p. 173; and Thompson, *Cyclopedia* (9th ed.), p. 1454.

[166]Thompson, *Cyclopedia* (9th ed.), p. 1458.

from the Klindworth School in Berlin with high honors. This resulted in further study with Hans von Bülow and Carl Bial. Nevin's compositions are "confined almost entirely to songs and short piano pieces, which have a graceful lyric vein, and a feeling for melody which is sometimes oversentimental, but often finely expressing the gentler moods, amorous, gay and introspective." He has also written a few pieces for violin and piano and some for organ.[167]

Nicholson, Alfred

Nicholson, May E.

Nisbet, Ola (Jones) (-1929). *See* p. xi

Norén, Helmer

Oldroyd, George (1886-1951). Oldroyd was an English organist and composer. After studying with Arthur Eaglefield-Hull, J. Rasch, and F[rank Thomas] Arnold, he became a professor at London University. The author of several books about music, Oldroyd was primarily a church music composer, but he did write for organ and for solo voice.[168]

Olds, William Benjamin (1874-1948). Olds was an American conductor and educator, who studied at Beloit College, the Oberlin Conservatory, and at the American Conservatory, where his teacher was O[scar] Seagle. He taught voice at Grinnell College, Illinois College, and the James Millikin University. In 1923 he became dean of the music school at Redland University in California. His compositions include works for orchestra, choral pieces, and songs.[169]

Ormerod, Helen J.

Ormsby, George F.

Parker, Phyllis Norman

Parker, Willetta (1850-   ). Parker, born in England, was a concert violinist. She was a professor and concertmaster of the London Philharmonic Society and also conductor of the Civil Service Orchestra and the Colet Orchestra Society.[170]

Parry, Sir Charles Hubert Hastings (1848-1918). Educated at Eton and Oxford, Parry was an outstanding student and received several honorary degrees. He was an English composer and author and taught at the Royal College of Music, London University, and Oxford. From 1894 until his death he was director of the Royal College of Music. Parry has composed choral works, orchestral works, incidental music, an opera, oratorios, motets, chamber music, organ works, piano music, violin pieces, works for solo voice and orchestra, and songs.[171]

---

[167]*Ibid.*, pp. 1460-61.

[168]*Ibid.*, p. 1493; *Baker's Biographical Dictionary of Musicians* (5th ed.), p. 1181; and Moore, "Baylor Collection," p. 174.

[169]*Ascap Biographical Dictionary* (1966), p. 549; Moore, "Baylor Collection," pp. 174-75; and Reid, "Analysis of Songs," p. 37.

[170]Robbins, "Composers Who Set Browning's Poetry," p. 110.

[171]Champlin, *Cyclopedia of Music and Musicians* (1890), III, 85-86; and Thompson, *Cyclopedia* (9th ed.), pp. 1587-88.

Pascal, Florian (1847-1923). Pascal's real name was Joseph Williams. He was an English composer and head of the Joseph Williams Limited Publishing house. Most of his compositions were for chamber groups.[172]

Pascal, Julian

Passailaigue, Mary Flournoy (1908-   ). Mrs. Passailaigue was born in Columbus, Georgia, where she is presently living. She is an artist rather than a musician, and her training was not in the field of music. Among her teachers was Wayman Adams, who has painted five of the portraits in the ABL. She has written several songs.[173]

Patterson, Janie Alexander

Patton, Arthur

Paulsen, P. Marinus. Born in Denmark, Paulsen is a contemporary Danish-American conductor. He studied at the Sherwood Music School in Chicago, at the Chicago Musical College, with [Alexander] Raab, [Bernhard] Listemann, and [Felix] Borowski in Chicago, and with [Johan Severin] Svendsen in Copenhagen. At the age of sixteen Paulsen made his debut as violinist in Chicago. He has been active as a conductor in Chicago and was made head of the violin and orchestra department at Sherwood Music School. Among his compositions are a symphonic poem and cantatas.[174]

Pease, Alfred H[umphries] (1838-1882). Pease was an American concert pianist and composer, who studied with [Theodor] Kullak and [Hans Guido Freidherr] von Bülow. Theodore Thomas has performed an orchestral piece of his.[175]

Peel, Gerald Graham (1877-1937). Peel was an Englishman who studied with Ernest Walker. He wrote songs and song cycles.[176]

Perrin, Harry Crane (1865-1953). Educated at Dublin Trinity College, Perrin was a Fellow in the Royal College of Organists and was director of the Montreal McGill University Conservatorium. He composed orchestral works, cantatas, songs, and church music.[177]

Philp, Elizabeth (1827-1885). Philp was an English singer, teacher, and composer. A pupil of [Salvatore] Marchesi, she wrote a book about singing and composed songs and ballads.[178]

Pickard-Cambridge, W. A.

Pierce, Allie Coleman

Ponssen, Mary Eleanor

---

[172]Thompson, *Cyclopedia* (9th ed.), p. 1590.
[173]Biographical data sheet compiled by Passailaigue.
[174]Thompson, *Cyclopedia* (7th ed.), p. 1374.
[175]Wier, *Macmillan Encyclopedia*, p. 1390.
[176]Thompson, *Cyclopedia* (9th ed.), p. 1602.
[177]*Ibid.*, p. 1611.
[178]*Ibid.*, p. 1622.

Protheroe, Daniel (1866-1934). Protheroe was a Welsh choral conductor
    and composer. He was educated at Normal College in Swansea,
    Wales, and at Toronto University and the New York Grand Con-
    servatory. He was active in forming choral societies and taught at
    Sherwood Music School. Protheroe compiled a Hymnal for the Welsh
    Presbyterian Church and liturgical music for the Scottish Rite. He
    is the author of courses about choral conducting and harmony. He
    has composed orchestral works, chamber music, church music, choral
    works with orchestra, and songs.[179]

Ralston, Fanny Marion (1875-   ). Ralston is an American composer,
    pianist, and teacher who studied at the New England Conservatory
    in Boston. In 1896 she gave a recital in St. Louis of her own compo-
    sitions. She has written songs and piano pieces.[180]

Raphael, Juliet

Rathbone, George (1874-   ). Rathbone was an English pianist and an
    organist at Carmel Priory Church. A pupil at the Royal College of
    Music, he has composed several cantatas for children, anthems, part-
    songs, and songs.[181]

Raymond, Ralph

Read, Harold Vincent Jervis. *See* Jervis-Read, Harold Vincent

Reed, (Rev.) C. H.

Reinagle, Caroline (Orger) (1818-1892). Reinagle married into a musical
    family, her husband Alexander Robert Reinagle being the nephew of
    the early American composer, Alexander Reinagle. She was an Eng-
    lish pianist and teacher and composer of piano works, a concerto,
    chamber music, and songs.[182]

Renaud, Emiliano

Rhodes, Harold (1889-   ). Rhodes is an English organist and com-
    poser. He has given piano recitals and conducted different amateur
    choral and orchestral groups. While attending the Royal College of
    Music in London he won a scholarship for his organ playing and
    later for composition. Rhodes studied with [Walter] Parratt and at-
    tended London University. He has written many songs, part-songs,
    anthems, an orchestral rhapsody, and a sonata for cello and piano.[183]

Riego, Teresa del. *See* del Riego, Teresa

Robbins, Reginald Chauncey

<hr>

[179]*Ibid.*, pp. 1698-99.
[180]Wier, *Macmillan Encyclopedia*, p. 1503.
[181]Moore, "Baylor Collection," p. 176; and Thompson, *Cyclopedia* (4th ed.), p.
1498.
[182]*Grove's Dictionary* (3rd ed.), IV, 359; Moore, "Baylor Collection," pp. 176-77;
and Reid, "Analysis of Songs," p. 32.
[183]*Grove's Dictionary* (5th ed.), VII, 149.

Robyn, Alfred George (1860-1935). Robyn was an American organist. He succeeded his father as organist at St. John's Church in St. Louis, where he worked for many years. Robyn also accompanied and composed light operas, a symphony, a piano concerto, orchestral works, piano pieces, oratorios, and songs.[184]

Rogers, Clara Kathleen Barnett (1844-1931). Rogers was born in England, the daughter of John Barnett who was the "father of English opera." Her father was her first teacher and later she studied piano with Ignaz Moscheles at the Leipzig Conservatory and singing in Italy. Rogers was a successful opera singer in England and Europe, after which she taught singing in Boston at the New England Conservatory. She wrote four books about singing and diction and composed songs and violin pieces.[185]

Rogers, James Hotchkiss (1857-1940). Born in Connecticut, Rogers studied music in Chicago, Berlin, Paris, and Iowa. He taught in Iowa and later moved to Cleveland where he was church organist, conductor, and music critic (Cleveland *Plain Dealer*). Rogers composed cantatas, anthems, part-songs, organ pieces, piano music, and songs.[186]

Rohrer, Mildred

Rorem, Ned (1923-   ). The American composer, Rorem, studied in Chicago. He was a scholarship winner at the Curtis Institute in Philadelphia and a student at the Berkshire Music Center, Juilliard (where he was a pupil of Bernard Wagenaar), and a private student of Aaron Copland and Virgil Thomson. Among his honors are the Gershwin Memorial Award, the Lili Boulanger Award, a Fulbright Fellowship, and a Guggenheim Fellowship. Rorem's music is written in the style of the modern French school, especially Maurice Ravel, although in a style very definitely his own. His music has the French school's formal clarity, harmonic elegance, and rhythmic wit, but also American idioms and rhythms, even jazz. Rorem is basically a lyrical composer and has written many songs. His compositions are fluent, charming, and clever, and have attracted a wide public. Among his works are two operas, orchestral works, choral music, chamber music, works for piano and for organ, and works for solo voice.[187]

Rossman, Floy Adele

Rowley, Alec (1892-1958). Rowley was an English composer, organist, and pianist. He studied at the Royal Academy of Music. Aside from

---

[184]Moore, "Baylor Collection," p. 177; Thompson, *Cyclopedia* (4th ed.), p. 1561; and Thompson, *Cyclopedia* (9th ed.), p. 1815.

[185]*Baker's Biographical Dictionary of Musicians* (5th ed.), p. 1359; Moore, "Baylor Collection," p. 177; Thompson, *Cyclopedia* (7th ed.), p. 1565; and Thompson, *Cyclopedia* (9th ed.), p. 1820.

[186]Moore, "Baylor Collection," p. 178; Thompson, *Cyclopedia* (4th ed.), p. 1565; and Thompson, *Cyclopedia* (9th ed.), p. 1820.

[187]Thompson, *Cyclopedia* (9th ed.), p. 1828.

the pedagogic works for children, he composed a ballet, a suite for orchestra, cantatas, chamber music, violin pieces, piano pieces, organ works, choral music, and songs.[188]

Roy, William (1928-1958). Roy was an American composer and pianist. In addition to attending the Hollywood Professional School, he studied music with Arthur Laage, Joseph Achron, Edward Kilenyi, Eada Rubinstein, and Rina Larson. As a child, Roy acted in films and later composed and played for Julius Monk night club revues. He has composed a Broadway stage score (*Maggie*) and songs, including *How Do I Love Thee.*[189]

Royle, Popplewell

Ryan, Margaret

Saar, Louis Victor (1868-1937). Saar was a Dutch-American composer and teacher. He was a student of Johannes Brahms and of the Strasbourg University and the Munich Royal Academy of Music. He was head of the theory and composition department at the Cincinnati College of Music. He also taught in New York at the National Conservatory and the College of Music and at the Chicago Musical College. Saar was an opera accompanist with the Metropolitan Opera in New York and served as music critic for several publications. In addition to these activities, he also gave piano recitals. Saar has composed orchestral works, choral music, chamber music, piano pieces, violin music, and songs.[190]

Sabin, Wallace Arthur (1869-1937). An English organist, Sabin received his musical training at Banbury and at Oxford. He was a Fellow of the Royal College of Organists and directed several musical societies. Sabin composed incidental music, church music, and part-songs for male voices.[191]

Saminsky, Lazare (1882-1959). Educated at the Moscow Conservatory and Petrograd Conservatory, Saminsky was a Russian composer, conductor, and author. Among his achievements is the founding of the League of Composers. He has written orchestral works, chamber music, choral music, piano pieces, songs, and stage works.[192]

Sarson, H. M.

Sarson, May

Schaefer, Harold Herman (Hal) (1925-   ). Schaefer is an American composer, pianist, and arranger. He was educated at the High School

---

188*Ibid.,* p. 1845; *Baker's Biographical Dictionary of Musicians* (5th ed.), p. 1381; and Moore, "Baylor Collection," p. 178.
189*Ascap Biographical Dictionary* (1966), p. 627.
190Hull, *Dictionary of Modern Music and Musicians,* p. 430; Moore, "Baylor Collection," p. 179; and Thompson, *Cyclopedia* (9th ed.), p. 1860.
191Thompson, *Cyclopedia* (9th ed.), pp. 1860-61.
192*Ibid.,* p. 1877; Ewen, *American Composers Today,* pp. 211-12; and Moore, "Baylor Collection," p. 179.

of Music and Art and studied with Mario Castelnuovo-Tedesco and Henry Brant. Schaefer has been the pianist in various orchestras including those of Lee Castle, Ina Ray Hutton, Boyd Raeburn, and Harry James. He has accompanied several singers among whom is Peggy Lee. From 1948 to 1955 he was an arranger and vocal coach for Twentieth Century-Fox Studios. He has also conducted and arranged for U[nited] A[rtists] Records. Among his compositions are the film background score for *The Money Trap,* songs, and instrumental works.[193]

Schlesinger, Sebastian Benson (1837-1917). Schlesinger was born in Germany, but came to the United States when he was thirteen and studied with Otto Dresel in Boston. As a talented amateur composer, Schlesinger's music was praised by eminent musicians. He has written more than 120 songs and many piano works.[194]

Schmidt, Louis

Schuyler, Georgiana (fl. nineteenth century). Schuyler was primarily an American song composer.[195]

Sears, Marie. *See* Hammer, Marie von

Shapleigh, Bertram (1871-1940). Shapleigh was an American composer, who was originally educated for the medical profession. Later he attended the New England Conservatory. Shapleigh lectured on Oriental music and on art and was also active as a musical adviser for Breitkopf and Härtel. He edited *The Concert Program Exchange* and wrote poetry. Among Shapleigh's compositions are orchestral works, operas, choral music, songs, pieces for violin with piano, for cello with piano, and for solo piano.[196]

Sharpe, Cedric (1891-   ). Sharpe was an English cellist with the London Symphony and String Quartet. He attended the Royal College of Music where he was a scholarship recipient. Most of his compositions are for chamber groups.[197]

Shillington, Mary

?Simon, Eric (1907-   ). Born in Vienna, Eric Simon is a conductor and clarinetist. After attending the State Academy in Vienna, he made his American debut at the Coolidge Festival in Washington (1940). Simon has played with several chamber music groups in America and Europe. He was on the editorial staff of *Anbruch* in 1931 and the following year he founded the Vienna Concert Orchestra. Simon is the former clarinetist with the Moscow Philharmonic Orchestra

---

[193]*Ascap Biographical Dictionary* (1966), pp. 644-45.
[194]Wier, *Macmillan Encyclopedia,* p. 1668.
[195]*Ibid.,* p. 1699.
[196]*Baker's Biographical Dictionary of Musicians,* ed. by Paul Pisk (4th ed.; New York: G. Schirmer. Inc., 1940), p. 1013; Moore, "Baylor Collection," p. 180; and Thompson, *Cyclopedia* (9th ed.), p. 2005.
[197]*Grove's Dictionary* (3rd ed.), IV, 738; Moore, "Baylor Collection," p. 180; and Thompson, *Cyclopedia* (9th ed.), p. 2005.

and is presently Associate Conductor of New Friends of Music Orchestra in New York, where he now resides.[198]

?Simón, Eric (1908-   ). Simón was born in Germany, but is known as an Uruguayan conductor. He attended the State Conservatory of Würzburg for his musical training, but he also graduated in medicine. He has been active in Latin-American music since 1933. In 1951 he toured extensively in Europe.[199]

?Simon, Ernst (1850-1916). Simon was a German composer and teacher who wrote orchestral music, piano pieces, and humorous songs.[200]

Slater, Gordon Archbold (1896-   ). Slater is an English organist, conductor, and composer, who studied privately and at York Minster. His specialties include adjudicating and lecturing. He has composed organ music, songs, church music, anthems, and hymn tunes.[201]

Smith, David Stanley (1877-1949). Studying at Yale University, where he later taught, Smith was a pupil of Horatio Parker. He was an American composer, teacher, conductor, and organist. Smith's compositions show a consistent regard for form and structure and are free of sentimentality. This is particularly obvious in his four symphonies. Smith has composed orchestral works, chamber orchestra works, choral music, chamber music, piano pieces, a song cycle, and an opera.[202]

Smith, Leo (1881-   ). Born in England, Smith is a Canadian cellist, composer, and teacher. He has also written about music. After attending the Royal Manchester College of Music, Smith taught at the Toronto Conservatory of Music and the University of Toronto. He has composed two string quartets, pieces for cello, for violin, for piano, school songs, and songs.[203]

Smith, Lewis Worthington

Somervell, Sir Arthur (1863-1937). Somervell was a pupil of Sir Charles Villiers Stanford at Cambridge and attended the Berlin Hochschule for composition and afterward studied with Sir Hubert Parry at the Royal College of Music, where he later taught. Somervell was music inspector to the Board of Education. He was a prolific composer of large works as well as choral works, chamber music, children's operettas, piano pieces, songs, and several song cycles. Somervell's style of composition is early Romantic in the vein of the great German song writers such as Johannes Brahms and Franz Schubert.[204]

---

[198]*Who Is Who in Music,* p. 209.
[199]*Grove's Dictionary* (5th ed.), VII, 796.
[200]Wier, *Macmillan Encyclopedia,* p. 1740.
[201]*Who's Who International,* p. 194.
[202]Thompson, *Cyclopedia* (9th ed.), p. 2047.
[203]*Ibid.,* p. 2048; Jones, "Browning and Music," p. 155; and *International Who's Who in Music and Musical Gazetteer,* ed. by César Saerchinger (New York: Current Literature Publishing Company, 1918), p. 598.
[204]*Baker's Biographical Dictionary of Musicians* (5th ed.), pp. 1535-36; Reid, "Analysis of Songs," pp. 70-73; Stevens, *History of Song,* p. 158; and Thompson, *Cyclopedia* (9th ed.), p. 2054.

Sousa, Leon de. *See* de Sousa, Leon

Spencer, Fannie Morris (nineteenth century). Spencer was born in New York and is known primarily as a composer of anthems, hymns, and songs.[205]

Spier, La Salle (fl. 1938). Spier is an American composer and pianist. A native and resident of Washington, D.C., he studied under Rafael Joseffy in New York and Richard Burmeister in Berlin. Spier has appeared with the Berlin Philharmonic Orchestra and the Lenox, Rich, and National Quartets. He is a member of the Composers' Club of Washington. Hans Kindler, conducting the National Symphony Orchestra in Washington, D.C., presented the world premier of Spier's *Impressions of the Bowery.* Other compositions are works for voice, piano, chamber-music instruments, and orchestra.[206]

Stanford, Sir Charles Villiers (1852-1924). Stanford was an Irish composer, conductor, and teacher, educated at Queen's College in Cambridge, at Trinity College, and in Leipzig and Berlin. He held several important conducting posts in England and was on the staff at the Cambridge Royal College of Music. He was knighted in 1901 and three years later became the first Englishman in the Berlin Academy of Arts. He is the author of numerous books, some of which are *History of Music, Pages from an Unwritten Diary,* and *Musical Composition.* Stanford has composed operas, incidental music to plays, orchestral works, chamber music, instrumental works, and songs.[207]

Stebbins, George Waring (1869-1930). Stebbins was born in New York and educated in Brooklyn, Paris, and London. He helped to found the American Guild of Organists and was a teacher of singing at the New York Teachers' Training Institute. Stebbins married the former Caroline T. Worth of Brooklyn. He was active in New York musical societies and composed pieces for organ, anthems, choruses, and songs.[208]

Stephens, Ward (1869-1940). A pupil of Johannes Brahms, Stephens was an American composer, conductor, organist, and pianist. He conducted both opera and symphonic orchestras. Stephens composed religious and secular songs primarily.[209]

Sternberg, Daniel Arie (1913-   ). Born in Poland, Sternberg was an honor graduate in conducting and piano at the Vienna State Academy. For six years he studied composition with Karl Weigl in addition to which he studied law at the Vienna State Academy. Sternberg has

---

[205]Wier, *Macmillan Encyclopedia,* p. 1772.

[206]*Ibid.,* p. 1773; Biographical fly-leaf of reviews, Armstrong Browning Library, Music Correspondence.

[207]Thompson, *Cyclopedia* (9th ed.), pp. 2092-93.

[208]*Ibid.,* p. 2098; *Baker's Biographical Dictionary of Musicians* (5th ed.), p. 1559; and Jones, "Browning and Music," p. 156.

[209]*Ascap Biographical Dictionary* (1966), p. 705; and Reid, "Analysis of Songs," p. 38.

appeared in concert as a pianist and as orchestral conductor in Europe and the United States (especially in the field of opera). He is now Dean of the Baylor University School of Music and Conductor of the Waco Symphony. In 1948 his *Concert Overture* won the Harold Abrahm Award and was played by the Dallas Symphony. His style of composition is Romantic, is based on traditional harmony, and does not employ experimentation. He has published church music and chamber music. The setting in the ABL Collection, *Pippa's Song,* opens with an eight-measure introduction for the piano. The song is marked "lively and exuberant" *alla breve.* The lilting melody equals the mood of the accompaniment, which is characterized by skips of fifths and sixths.[210]

Stewart, Humphrey John (1856-1932). Stewart was an Englishman who was organist for several San Francisco churches. He was the official organist for the Panama Exposition in 1915 at San Diego where he continued to play for years. He was educated with private teachers in London and received the Doctor of Music degree from the University of the Pacific. Stewart was co-founder of the American Guild of Organists and was also active in other musical organizations. He composed oratorios, an opera, incidental music, orchestral works, songs, choruses, Masses, piano pieces, organ music, and violin works.[211]

Stisted, Maria E. H.

Stoker, Richard

Stothart, Herbert (1885-1949). Stothart was an American composer, conductor, and pianist. He attended Milwaukee Teachers College and the University of Wisconsin in addition to further study in Europe. Afterward he taught in the Milwaukee public schools and at the University of Wisconsin. He composed the scores for many Broadway stage musicals and conducted and wrote songs for Metro-Goldwyn-Mayer films. Eventually Stothart became the general music director for MGM for whom he wrote background music, for such films as *The Good Earth, Romeo and Juliet, Mutiny on the Bounty, Mrs. Miniver,* and *The Picture of Dorian Gray.* He has collaborated with such musicians as Oscar Hammerstein, II, Vincent Youmans, and George Gershwin. Among his compositions are songs, a musical pageant, and a cantata.[212]

?Stratton, George (Robert) (1897-1954). Stratton was an English violinist and teacher. He was concertmaster of the London Symphony and founder of the Stratton Quartet. Stratton and Alan Frank wrote the book, *The Playing of Chamber Music.*[213]

---

[210]Personal interview between S. East and Sternberg, March, 1972; Moore, "Baylor Collection," pp. 181-82; and Reid, "Analysis of Songs," p. 25.

[211]*Baker's Biographical Dictionary of Musicians* (5th ed.), p. 1571; Moore, "Baylor Collection," p. 182; and Thompson, *Cyclopedia* (9th ed.), pp. 2108-09.

[212]*Ascap Biographical Dictionary* (1966), p. 712.

[213]*Baker's Biographical Dictionary of Musicians* (5th ed.), p. 1581; Reid, "Analysis of Songs," p. 43; and Thompson, *Cyclopedia* (9th ed.), pp. 2123-24.

Surinach, Carlos (1915-   ). Surinach is a Spanish composer and conductor, who was educated at the Barcelona Musical Conservatory, the Cologne Hochschule, and the Berlin Preussische Akademie der Künste. He is a successful conductor and his music is characterized with a Spanish flavor, harmonic boldness, slashing rhythms, and vivid orchestral colors. He has written dance music, orchestral works, a wind symphony, works for mixed chorus and percussion, works for voice and orchestra, small orchestral works, chamber music, songs, piano works, guitar pieces, works for accordion, and transcriptions.[214]

Sykes, Harold H.

Taylor, Samuel Coleridge. *See* Coleridge-Taylor, Samuel

Tedaldi, F.

Tedesco, Mario Castelnuovo. *See* Castelnuovo-Tedesco, Mario

Thayer, Arthur Wilder (1857-1934). Thayer was an American composer and conductor. He was a public school music superintendent and conducted several Massachusetts choral societies. Thayer belonged to the Harvard Musical Association and composed songs, part-songs, church music, and piano pieces.[215]

Thomas, Adelaide Louise (fl. nineteenth century). Thomas was an English composer and writer on music. Her compositions include church music and *The Royal Road to Pianoforte Playing*.[216]

Thomas, David Vaughan (1873-1934). Thomas was an Irish composer, who was educated at Llandovery College and Oxford Exeter College. He taught in several schools and colleges and was music inspector under the Central Welsh Board. He has written cantatas; works for solo voice with orchestra; works for voice, harp, and strings; part-songs; songs; and anthems.[217]

Threlkeld, Beulah

Toye, John Francis (1883-   ). Toye is an Englishman known primarily for his music criticism. He was a pupil of Sidney Peine Waddington and Edward Joseph Dent. Toye was critic for several London periodicals, including the London *Daily Telegraph*. He has written a number of books, among them *Verdi* and *Rossini* and he has composed some music.[218]

Treharne, Bryceson (1879-1948). Treharne was a Welsh teacher, composer, and editor, who attended the Royal College of Music under the Erard scholarship. Later he taught at the University of Wales, the University of Adelaide in Australia, and the McGill University in

---

[214]Thompson, *Cyclopedia* (9th ed.), p. 2152.
[215]*Ibid.*, pp. 2205-06; *ibid.* (4th ed.), p. 1882; and Moore, "Baylor Collection," p. 182.
[216]Wier, *Macmillan Encyclopedia*, p. 1855.
[217]Thompson, *Cyclopedia* (9th ed.), p. 2210.
[218]*Ibid.*, p. 2244; Hull, *Dictionary of Modern Music and Musicians*, p. 499; and Moore, "Baylor Collection," p. 183.

Montreal. While in a concentration camp near Berlin in 1914, Treharne wrote almost 200 songs and some orchestral works. In 1928 he became music editor for the Boston Music Company and Willis Music Company. Treharne composed incidental music for plays, operas, and cantatas for women's voices.[219]

Troup, Emily Josephine (-1912). Troup was an English composer of piano pieces, violin music, vocal trios, and songs.[220]

True, Latham (1873-   ). True was born in Maine and studied at Toronto College and the University of Toronto. In 1943 he wrote to Andrew Joseph Armstrong that he received his Doctor of Music forty years earlier. He was a church organist, ensemble pianist, conductor, teacher, and composer of songs and anthems. He was Musical Director of the New York Ger[man] Conservatory and an associate [professor] at the Royal College of Organists in London. True was a Fellow in the American Guild of Organists and was the organist and president of the Kotzchmar Club of Portland. He and his wife retired to 2277 Bryant Street, Palo Alto, California, about 1938. Reid found that most of the seven songs in the ABL are filled with trite musical ideas. He singled out *The Moth's Kiss and the Bee's Kiss* for the nice lyric quality of its vocal line.[221]

Truman, Ernest (1869-   ). Truman is an English organist and composer who was the city organist at Town Hall in Sydney, Australia. Among his compositions are a magnificat for soloists, chorus, and orchestra; a cantata grotesque; chamber music; songs; and organ music.[222]

Urban, Heinrich (1837-1901). Urban was a German violinist, music critic, teacher, and composer. His teachers included [Hubert] Ries, [Ferdinand?] Laub, and Hellman. In 1881 Urban became a teacher at Kullack's Conservatory in Berlin. Among his pupils were Arthur Bird, [Ignace Jan] Paderewski, and [Traugott] Ochs.[223]

Vaille, Clara Hinman

Vannah, Kate (-1933). Vannah was an American composer who studied with [Johann] E[rnst] Perabo. She composed church music, piano works, operettas, and songs.[224]

Vaughan Williams, Ralph (1872-1958). Vaughan Williams was an English composer, conductor, and organist. He received his musical training at Cambridge Trinity College, the Royal College of Music, the

---

[219]*Baker's Biographical Dictionary of Musicians* (5th ed.), p. 1664; Moore, "Baylor Collection," p. 183; and Thompson, *Cyclopedia* (9th ed.), p. 2248.
[220]Wier, *Macmillan Encyclopedia*, p. 1888.
[221]Reid, "Analysis of Songs," p. 48; Robbins, "Composers Who Set Browning's Poetry," p. 136; Letters, True to Andrew Joseph Armstrong, Feb. 18, Feb. 28, March 18, March 30, 1943, Armstrong Browning Library, Music Correspondence.
[222]Wier, *Macmillan Encyclopedia*, p. 1889.
[223]Thompson, *Cyclopedia* (7th ed.), p. 1944.
[224]Wier, *Macmillan Encyclopedia*, p. 1922.

Berlin Akademie der Künste, and with Maurice Ravel. Vaughan Williams collected and studied old English country folk tunes and incorporated his well-learned material into his music, which resulted in a distinctive "English" style. Other elements found in his music are modal counterpoint, Tudor madrigals and church music flavor, and, in his later works, speech-song like elements, and strident and harsh dissonances. He has written much music, among which are stage works, orchestral works, choral music, chamber music, songs, song cycles, hymns, organ music, and piano pieces.[225]

Versel, Louis

Vogler, Georg Joseph (1749-1814). Vogler, or Abt Vogler, was a German composer, theorist, and the teacher of Aloysia Weber and Giacomo Meyerbeer. He was educated at the Jesuits' College and studied law at Bamberg; he also studied in Padua and in Bologna (with [Giovanni Battista] Martini). Vogler founded several musical societies and schools and was the inventor of a portable organ called the "orchestrion." Aside from his many theoretical writings, he composed operas, cantatas, choruses, church music, chamber music, and piano concertos.[226]

Von Hammer, Marie. *See* Hammer, Marie von

Von Woyrsch, Felix. *See* Woyrsch, Felix von

Walthew, Richard Henry (1872-1951). Walthew was an English composer who studied at the Guildhall School of Music and at the Royal College of Music where he worked with Sir Hubert Parry. He later taught at Queen's College and was conductor of the University College Music Society and was director of the opera class at the Guildhall School of Music. Walthew wrote *The Development of Chamber Music* and composed orchestral works, chamber music, operettas, cantatas, songs, pieces for violin with orchestra, and a piano concerto.[227]

Warburg, Frederic S.

Ware, Harriet (1877-   ). Ware is an American composer, who studied at the Minnesota Pillsbury Academy, in New York with William Mason, and in Paris and Berlin. She composed a piano concerto, a cantata, a tone poem, a work for voice and piano (or orchestra), a song cycle, songs, and piano pieces.[228]

Warner, H. Waldo (1874-1945). Warner was an English violist and composer. He attended the Guildhall School of Music and studied violin with Alfred Gibbon and composition with R. O. Morgan. He was the recipient of an associateship and a gold medal and was made professor. Warner played viola in the London String Quartet and

---

[225]Thompson, *Cyclopedia* (9th ed.), pp. 2293-95.
[226]*Ibid.*, p. 2329.
[227]*Ibid.*, p. 2358; *Grove's Dictionary* (3rd ed.), V, 622; and Moore, "Baylor Collection," p. 184.
[228]Thompson, *Cyclopedia* (9th ed.), p. 2361.

was first violist in the New Symphony and in the Royal Philharmonic Orchestra. Among his compositions are piano trios, string quartets, an opera, pieces for violin with piano, violin sonatas, viola sonatas, cello pieces, three orchestral suites, songs, and part-songs.[229]

Warren, Jeanne

Watson, Mary E. (fl. 1927). At the request of Ola Jones Nisbet, Watson composed music for a presentation of *Pippa Passes* that was to be given by the Kansas City Browning Society in 1927. The play was postponed, but the music was purchased from Watson and given to Nisbet to be placed in her publication of the acting edition of *Pippa Passes*.[230]

Weems, Mrs. J. Eddie

Weigl, Karl (1881-1949). Weigl was an Austrian teacher, composer, and conductor. He was a pupil of Alexander von Zemlinsky and Guido Adler at Vienna University, and he received the Doctor of Philosophy degree from the Vienna Conservatory. Under Gustav Mahler, Weigl was the solo repetitor at the Hofoper and later taught at the Neues Wiener Konservatorium. Among the honors he has received are the Beethoven prize, the Philadelphia Mendelssohn prize, and the City of Vienna award for his compositions. Weigl has composed four symphonies, orchestral works, a piano concerto for the left hand, a violin concerto, chamber music, songs, choruses, piano pieces, and organ works.[231]

Welch, Jay

Wellesz, Egon (1885-   ). A specialist in Byzantine music, Wellesz is an Austrian-born composer and music scholar. He studied musical science and history with Guido Adler at Vienna University, harmony with Carl Frühling, counterpoint with Arnold Schönberg, and composition with Bruno Walter. Wellesz has taught music history at the Neues Konservatorium, at Vienna University, and at Oxford University. He was on the editorial board and contributed to the *New Oxford History of Music*. Wellesz has written operas, ballets, chamber music, choral music, symphonic works, and songs. He has published numerous articles about music.[232]

White, Grace

White, Maude Válerie (1855-1937). White studied at the Royal Academy of Music and in Vienna. She was the first woman to be elected a Mendelssohn Scholar (1879) and one of the first women to establish herself as a composer in England. Born in France, White was primarily a song writer.[233]

---

[229]*Ibid.*, p. 2362.

[230]Nisbet, *Browning's Pippa Passes*, p. 12.

[231]*Baker's Biographical Dictionary of Musicians* (5th ed.), p. 1769; Moore, "Baylor Collection," pp. 184-85; and Thompson, *Cyclopedia* (9th ed.), pp. 2383-84.

[232]Thompson, *Cyclopedia* (9th ed.), pp. 2389-90.

[233]*Ibid.*, p. 2397; *ibid.* (4th ed.), p. 2048; *Baker's Biographical Dictionary of Musicians* (5th ed.), p. 1787; and Reid, "Analysis of Songs," p. 29.

Whitmer, Thomas Carl (1873-   ). Born in Pennsylvania, Whitmer is
a composer of orchestral works, choral music, chamber music, piano
music, organ pieces, songs, and anthems. Some of his teachers were
William Wallace Gilchrist, Charles H. Jarvis, and Samuel Prowse
Warren. Whitmer taught at Stephens College in Missouri, Pennsylvania College for Women in Pittsburgh, and the Pittsburgh Musical
Institute. He also served as a church organist and wrote several
articles for different musical journals in addition to writing two
books.[234]

Whitney, Maurice C. (1909-   ). Whitney is an American composer,
conductor, oboist, pianist, and educator. His education includes study
at Ithaca College, New York University, Teachers College at Columbia University, Westminster Choir School, and the New England
Conservatory. He has arranged music for dance and theater orchestras, has been the oboist for the Cornell and Columbia College Symphonies, and has been the piano soloist for several symphony orchestras. Whitney was the conductor of the Glen Falls Oratorio Society
and Operetta Club of New York. He has been active as organist and
choir director in several churches. From 1932 to 1944 he was director of the music department of public schools in Hudson Falls, New
York, and since 1944 he has been at Glen Falls. Whitney has taught
summer sessions at the University of Iowa, the University of Colorado, and has taught music camps at Laurel, Connecticut and Ernest
Williams New York State. He has been guest conductor throughout
the United States. He is the vice president and executive board
member of the New York State School Music Association and has
been president of the Eastern Division of Music Educators National
Conference and since 1963 has been president of the New York State
School Music Association. He is on the board of editors of the *Music
Educators Journal*. Whitney is the author of two books in addition
to his compositions for chamber musicians, for band, for solo instruments, and for chorus.[235]

Wiant, William Robert (1902-   ). Wiant was born in West Virginia
and has made his home there for most of his life. He studied percussion, conducting, and composition and was a student at Carnegie Institute of Technology (now Carnegie-Mellon Institute) for three years.
Among his teachers were Sergie Koussevitzky, Leo Schrade, and Paul
Hindemith. Wiant has been conductor for the Moundsville Civic
Orchestra and Chorus, the Huntington (West Virginia) Symphony,
and the Charleston (West Virginia) Orchestra. He is currently the
choirmaster of the Sacred Heart Catholic Church and the Charleston
Light Opera Guild. In 1971 he was elected to honorary membership
in Music Masters of America for outstanding contribution to music
in his community. Wiant has composed church music, songs, organ

---

234*Baker's Biographical Dictionary of Musicians* (5th ed.), p. 1790; Moore, "Baylor Collection," p. 185; and Thompson, *Cyclopedia* (9th ed.), p. 2399.
235*Ascap Biographical Dictionary* (1966), p. 788.

works, violin solos, pieces for light orchestra, ballets, and parade marches.[236]

Wickins, Florence

Willan, Healey (1880-   ). Willan is a Canadian-born composer, educator, and organist. He studied at the University of Toronto and later held a post there. Willan has also taught at the Toronto Conservatory and founded the Tudor Singers. Willan is an authority on plainchant and is a Fellow Royal College of Organists. He has composed cantatas, anthems, motets, part-songs, songs, and organ pieces.[237]

Wilson, Alec

Wilson, Harry Robert (1901-   ). Wilson is an American composer, author, conductor, and educator. He was educated at Manhattan (Kansas) State College, at Columbia University, and at Juilliard where he studied with Rubin Goldmark and Albert Stoessel. From 1921 to 1926 Wilson was a singer and conductor in Wichita, Kansas. Later he was director of public school music in Eureka, Kansas and in Hastings-on-Hudson, New York. From 1932 to 1937 he was in charge of music for New College, Columbia University. Since 1937 he has been professor of music education at Teachers College in Columbia University and since 1958 chairman of the music education department. He has been guest conductor and lecturer throughout the United States. He has written several books on high school music and choral music. His compositions include choral music and an oratorio.[238]

Wodell, Frederick William (1859-1938). Born in England, Wodell was a conductor of the People's Choral Union in Boston and a voice teacher. In addition to the two books he wrote, Wodell composed a cantata, an opera, anthems, part-songs, and songs.[239]

Wood, Charles (1866-1926). Wood was an Irish composer and teacher, who was a pupil of Sir Frederick Bridge, and Sir Charles Villiers Stanford. He attended Cambridge and the Royal College of Music, where he later taught. Leeds awarded him an honorary Doctor of Law degree. Wood composed orchestral music, works for chorus and orchestra, chamber music, choral works, songs, and part-songs.[240]

Wooley, C.

Worth, John W. (fl. 1912). Two substantial compositions in the ABL Collection are by Worth: *Twelve Songs by Browning,* a manuscript, and *In a Gondola,* a song cycle published by H. W. Gray in 1912.

---

[236]Biographical data sheet compiled by Wiant.
[237]Thompson, *Cyclopedia* (9th ed.), p. 2405.
[238]*Ascap Biographical Dictionary* (1966), p. 794.
[239]Thompson, *Cyclopedia* (9th ed.), p. 2414; Moore, "Baylor Collection," p. 186; and Wier, *Macmillan Encyclopedia,* p. 2027.
[240]Thompson, *Cyclopedia* (9th ed.), p. 2424.

From these Reid only finds one worth noting, *Evelyn Hope* from *Twelve Songs by Browning*. As a beautiful example of Romantic song, *Evelyn Hope* creates a mood of grief and bewilderment by the way in which Worth weaves the melody and harmony. The result is one of reverence for the untimely death of "beautiful" Evelyn Hope. In 1924 Worth was an organist in New York City. He gave several pieces of his music based on Browning poetry to the ABL.[241]

Woyrsch, Felix von (1860-1944). Von Woyrsch was born in Austrian Silesia and became a conductor and organist. He taught music at the Prussian Academy and composed religious music primarily. The song cycle in the ABL Collection, *Rattenfänger Lieder,* uses occasional expressionistic and impressionistic devices, but is more neo-classical in style. It emphasizes block structure, rigid tonal relationships, and form rather than content. Reid found it to be tedious and boring halfway through the work. Von Woyrsch has published German folk songs and has composed three operas, five symphonies, choral works with orchestra, chamber music, and choruses.[242]

Young, Dalhousie (1866-1921). Young was born in India, but studied in England. A pupil of Theodor Leschetizky and [Ignaz Jan] Paderewski, he became a concert pianist. Many of his songs and chamber music were somewhat popular; he also composed orchestral works and a cantata.[243]

Zucca, Mana. *See* Mana-Zucca

Zuckerman, Augusta. *See* Mana-Zucca

---

[241]Reid, "Analysis of Songs," p. 56; News release from Andrew Joseph Armstrong to the Baylor *Lariat* dated "10/7/24," Armstrong Browning Library, Music Correspondence.

[242]Reid, "Analysis of Songs," p. 74; *Baker's Biographical Dictionary of Musicians* (5th ed.), p. 1824; Moore, "Baylor Collection," p. 186; and Thompson, *Cyclopedia* (7th ed.), p. 2074.

[243]Hull, *Dictionary of Modern Music and Musicians,* p. 539; Moore, "Baylor Collection," p. 186; Reid, "Analysis of Songs," pp. 64-68; and Wier, *Macmillan Encyclopedia,* p. 2047.

VIII

Desiderata

Key to Abbreviations

ABL   Armstrong Browning Library

BNP   Broughton, Leslie Nathan; Northup, Clark Sutherland; Pearsall, Robert, compilers. *Robert Browning: A Bibliography, 1830-1950.* Ithaca: Cornell University Press, 1953

E1   a number preceded by the letter "E" refers to the setting which is listed in BNP

EBB   Elizabeth Barrett Browning

RB   Robert Browning

For the complete description and explanation of this chapter, read page 7 of Chapter I.

Aldrich, L. Paean. New York: W. W. Gray Co., 1918. BNP. E62

Andrews. Song cycle (from letters of RB to EBB).

Austin, (Miss). The Cares of Yesterday.

——————. I Have More Than a Friend. Los Angeles Browning Society Program. April, 1917.

Bainton, Edgar L. A Musical Instrument. Part-song. Galaxy Music Corp.

Bantock, Granville. Boot and Saddle. From Orpheus, no. 322. London: Novello & Co., 1898. BNP. E38

——————. Boot and Saddle. From Tonic Sol-Fa Series, no. 1411. London: Novello & Co., [1905]. BNP. E38

——————. Fifine at the Fair. Orchestral drama with a prologue for orchestra. Full score. London: Novello & Co., 1912. BNP. E72

——————. Five Songs from Dramatic Lyrics: The Guardian Angel, Home-Thoughts, In a Year, My Star, Now. London: Swan & Co., 1920. BNP. E76, E80, E115, E166, E181

——————. Give a Rouse. Four-part song for men's voices. From Tonic Sol-Fa Series, no. 1520. London: Novello & Co., [1907]. BNP. E28

—————. A Grammarian's Funeral. From Three Choruses for Male Voices. Oxford Choral Songs, no. 615. London: Oxford U. Press, 1930. BNP. E75

—————. The Lost Leader. Part-song for male voices. From Choruses for Men's Voices. London: Breitkopf & Härtel, 1913. BNP. E147

—————. Lyric Poem. Piano solo. Belwin-Mills Publishing Corp.

—————. Marching Along. From Novello Tonic Sol-Fa Series, no. 1756. London: Novello & Co., 1907. BNP. E18.1

—————. Marching Along. Published singly. London: Novello & Co., 1898. BNP. E18.1

—————. Red Cotton [Night-Cap Country]. Piano solo. Boston: B. F. Wood Music Co., 1935. BNP. E342

—————. Through the Metidja. Key of C. Full orchestral score. London: Boosey & Co., 1912. BNP. E375

Barlow, Emily. Entreaty. Key of E-flat. London: J. B. Cramer & Co., 1907. BNP. E403

Beach, Mrs. H. H. A. Ah, Love, but a Day! Vocal duet. From Three Browning Songs. Boston: Arthur P. Schmidt, 1900. BNP. E122

—————. My Star. Los Angeles Browning Society Program. Feb., 1918.

—————. The Year's at [the Spring]. Duet with violin obbligato. Boston: A. P. Schmidt, 1900. BNP. E243

—————. The Year's at [the Spring]. Duet with violin obbligato. Boston: A. P. Schmidt, 1909. BNP. E243

—————. The Year's at [the Spring]. Duet with violin obbligato. Boston: A. P. Schmidt, 1919. BNP. E243

—————. The Year's at [the Spring]. Duet with violin obbligato. London and New York: Boosey & Co., 1900. BNP. E243

—————. The Year's at [the Spring]. Duet with violin obbligato. London and New York. Boosey & Co., 1904. BNP. E243

—————. The Year's at [the Spring]. Four-part song. Boston: A. P. Schmidt, 1909. BNP. E243

—————. The Year's at [the Spring]. Four-part song. Boston: A. P. Schmidt, 1919. BNP. E243

—————. The Year's at [the Spring]. Four-part song. London and New York: Boosey & Co., 1900. BNP. E243

—————. The Year's at [the Spring]. Four-part song. London and New York: Boosey & Co., 1904. BNP. E243

——————. The Year's at [the Spring]. Four-part song for women's voices. From Three Browning Songs. Boston: A. P. Schmidt, 1900. BNP. E243

Beach, John. Pippa's Holiday. Opera. New York: G. Schirmer, Inc., 1940.

Bending, Edwin. The Boy and the Angel. London Browning Society Program. June 27, 1884. British Museum.

——————. In a Gondola. Duet for mezzo soprano or contralto and baritone with cello or violin obbligato. London: Purcell & Co., 1886. BNP. E99

——————. In a Gondola. Duet for mezzo soprano or contralto and baritone with cello or violin obbligato. London: Purcell & Co., 1890. BNP. E99

Berger, Jean. A Song of Seasons. Choral setting for mixed chorus, melodica, and percussion. Boulder, Colorado: J. Sheppard Music Press, 1968.

Blanchard, Mrs. Maude Conway. I Have More Than a Friend. San Francisco Browning Society. March 6, 1904.

[——————.] My True.

——————. Out of My Own Great Woe. San Francisco Browning Society. March 6, 1904.

——————. Thy Face. Boston Browning Society Program. April 18, 1911.

Borton, Alice. Be Love, Your Light. From Ferishtah's Fancies. London Browning Society. Feb. 10, 1885.

——————. Man I Am and Man Would Be, Love. From Ferishtah's Fancies. London Browning Society. 1885.

Boyle, G. F. The Pied Piper. Cantata for soli (contralto, tenor, baritone), chorus, and orchestra. London: Chappell & Co., 1911. BNP. E204

Brahe, May H. The Year's at [the Spring]. Key of E-flat. From Two Songs. London: Enoch & Sons, 1915. BNP. E248

Branscombe, Gena. Serenade: I Send My Heart Up to Thee. Key of F. For soprano or tenor voice. Boston and New York: Arthur P. Schmidt Co., 1905. BNP. E100

——————. Serenade: I Send My Heart Up to Thee. Key of F. For soprano or tenor voice. From Four Songs. Newton Center, Mass.: Wa-Wan Press, 1905. BNP. E100

——————. What Are We Two? From Four Songs. Newton Center, Mass.: Wa-Wan Press, 1905. BNP. E101

Bruguire, Emil. Love Me Sweet with All My Heart. San Francisco Browning Society. Sept. 12, 1903 and March 6, 1904.

Brumleu, E. The Pied Piper. A one-act play for children. New York: Dutton, 1913. BNP. E207

Bryson, E. So, the Year's Done With. For low voice. London: Oxford University Press, 1927. BNP. E59

[C.] W. The Moth's First Kiss. Baylor *Bulletin,* Browning Series V.

Cain, Noble. The Year's at the Spring. Part-song for mixed chorus (soprano, alto, bass).

Caruthers, Julia L. Pippa's Spring Song. From *Music* (Dec., 1901). BNP. E250

Chanter, Arthur. There's a Woman Like a Dewdrop. Key of E-flat. For alto or baritone. New York: G. Schirmer, 1890. BNP. E10

————. There's a Woman Like a Dewdrop. Key of F. For mezzo soprano. New York: G. Schirmer, 1890. BNP. E10

————. There's a Woman Like a Dewdrop. Key of G. For soprano or tenor. New York: G. Schirmer, 1890. BNP. E10

Clarke, Helen A. Ask Not One Least Word of Praise. For medium voice. From *Poet-Lore* (May, 1881). BNP. E237

————. My Star. Philadelphia: Poet-Lore Co., n.d. BNP. E167

————. Round Us the Wild Creatures. New York: Carl Fischer, n.d. BNP. E57

————. You'll Love Me Yet. For voice, cello and piano. New York: Carl Fischer. BNP. E251

Cohen, Robert. Meeting at Night, op. 13. For soprano and piano. Robert Cohen c1964.

Coleridge-Taylor, Samuel. Death and Life. New York Browning Society. April 9, 1919.

Coombs, Charles Whitney. I Send My Heart Up to Thee. Twentieth-Century Club; Corsicana, Texas; Feb. 14, 1924. Historical and Literary Club; Lufkin, Texas; Feb. 4, 1926. Athenean Club; Amarillo, Texas; Feb. 19, 1931.

Cripps, A. R. The Year's at [the Spring]. Key of B-flat. London: Novello & Co., 1909. BNP. E253

Dalhousie, J. Y. Pippa's Song. London: Boosey & Co., 1904. BNP. E255

David, Kington. The Year's at the Spring, no. 2. From *Oddments.*

Davies, H. W. Hervé Riel. Cantata. London: Novello & Co., [1912]. BNP. E78

De Koven, Reginald. In a Gondola. Los Angeles Browning Society. Nov. 20, 1912.

Del Riego, Teresa. All's Right [with the World]. From *Music Pictures, a Series of Songs*. London: Chappell & Co., 1906. BNP. E257

——————. All's Right [with the World]. From the Portrait Series of Teresa Del Riego Album. London: Chappell & Co., 1914. BNP. E257

Dickinson, Clarence. How Do I Love Thee. Manuscript. Letter. Feb. 26, 1935. ABL. Music Correspondence.

——————. One Way of Love. New York Browning Society; Nov. 20, 1912. Manuscript; Letter; Feb. 26, 1935; ABL; Music Correspondence.

Downing, Lulu J. Apparitions. From Three Songs. Chicago: Music Art Shop, [1909]. BNP. E384

——————. My Star. From Three Songs by Lulu J. Downing. Chicago: Music Art Shop, 1910. BNP. E168

Echols, Dot. Inclusions. Letter. Nov. 1, 1925. ABL. Music Correspondence.

Fergus, Phyllis. Thoughts. From In a Gondola. Chicago: Clayton F. Summy Co., 1916. BNP. E103

Fitz, Adeline Frances. A King Lived Long Ago. Boston Browning Society. April 3, 1911.

Forrester, J. C. Devotion. Key of F. From Songs. London: London Music Pub. Co., n.d. BNP. E351

Freer, Eleanor E. The Legend of the Piper. Operetta. Boston: C. C. Birchard & Co., 1921. BNP. E214

——————. The Year's at [the Spring]. Chicago: Music Library of Chicago, 1938. BNP. E261

Fuller, Caroline. Give Her but a Least Excuse to Love Me. New York Browning Society. May 12, 1909.

Gabriel, Virginia. At the Window. Key of D. Philadelphia: Trumper, [188-]. BNP. E127

——————. At the Window. Key of G minor. Philadelphia: Trumper, [188-]. BNP. E127

Galsworthy, Ada. In the Doorway. For high voice and piano. From Two Songs by Mrs. Galsworthy with words by Robert Browning. London: Weekes & Co., [1907]. BNP. E128

Geisler, P. Der Rattenfaenger von Hameln. Symphonische Dichtung. Pianoforte zu vier Händen. Leipzig: E. F. Steinacker, n.d. BNP. E215

Gilbert, H. P. You'll Love Me Yet. New York Browning Society. Dec., 1917.

Goatley, Alma. Now That April's [T]here. For soprano or tenor voices. From Two Songs with pianoforte accompaniment. London: Schott & Co., 1917. BNP. E84

Gordon, Cyril A. The Pied Piper. Manchester: Heyward of Deansgate, 1916.

[Gore, Walter. Confessional. Ballet. Music by Sibelius.]

Gow, G. C. The Year's at [the Spring]. Published separately. Boston: G. Schirmer, Boston Music Co., 1892. BNP. E266

Grace, H. The Year's at [the Spring]. Song for mezzo soprano. London: Richards & Co., 1912. BNP. E267

Graham, A. C. The Piper. A tenor solo for a chorus (soprano I and II, alto), tenor solo, and orchestra. New York: H. W. Gray Co., 1916. BNP. E217

Grainer, Ron. "Robert and Elizabeth" or "The Barretts and Mr. Browning." Musical.

Greenhill, J. A Lover's Quarrel. Performed June 20, 1882 at University College, London Browning Society. *Poet-Lore,* I, 431 (1889).

Guchaninow. She Was Thine.

————. Tears. Los Angeles Browning Society. Dec., 1916.

Haden, Arthur C. Evelyn Hope. London Browning Society. Oct. 31, 1890.

Hageman, R. Tragödie in Arezzo (Caponsacchi). New York: Theatre Program Corp., 1931. BNP. E343

————. Tragödie in Arezzo (Caponsacchi). New York: Theatre Program Corp., 1936. BNP. E343

Hadley, H. K. Rabbi Ben Ezra. From the Lowell [Laurel?] Song Book. Boston: C. C. Birchard & Co., 1927. BNP. E338

————. There's a Woman. Boston: Arthur P. Schmidt, 1898. BNP. E11

————. You'll Love Me Yet. For medium voice. From Five Songs. Boston: Oliver Ditson Co., 1900. BNP. E269

Halley, Margaret A. To Perfect the Summer. From Two Songs. London, Edinburgh, and elsewhere: Paterson, Sons, & Co., 1907. BNP. E401

————. The Year's at [the Spring]. Key of C. From Two Songs by Frances Mary Butts and Margaret A. Halley. Edinburgh and London: Paterson & Co., 1910. BNP. E270

————. The Year's at [the Spring]. Key of D-flat. From Two Songs by Frances Mary Butts and Margaret A. Halley. Edinburgh and London: Paterson & Co., 1910. BNP. E270

Hammond, W. G. Pippa's Song. From Miscellaneous Songs in One, Two, or Three Parts. New York: Silver, Burdett & Co., 1915. BNP. E271

Harraden, Ethel. The Lost Leader. London Browning Society. June 27, 1884. *Poet-Lore,* I, 431 (1889).

Hartog, Cecile S. The Year's at [the Spring]. Key of A-flat. From English Songs, Second Series. Boston: O. Ditson Co., n.d. BNP. E272

Harvey, Grace. The Year's at [the Spring]. Song for mezzo soprano. London: Richards & Co., 1912. BNP. E273

Hattersley, F. K. How They Brought [the Good News from Ghent]. Choral Ballad. String parts. London: Novello & Co., 1905. BNP. E92

——————. You'll Love Me Yet. London: H. W. Gray, n.d. BNP. E274

Hausmein, Rosalie. Such a Starved Bank of Moss. San Francisco Browning Society. Oct. 13, 1916.

Hawke, E. L. [Songs for] Pippa Passes. Production of Mrs. Eve Acton-Bond. Letter. Feb. 19, 1935. ABL. Music Correspondence.

Hinkle, Daisy. Home-Thoughts from Abroad. For mezzo soprano. New York: Schirmer, n.d. BNP. E85

Hollins, Dorothea. Boot and Saddle. From Four Songs. London: Novello, Ewer, & Co., 1892. BNP. E45

Homer, Sidney. Sleep. New York Browning Society. Dec. 8, 1909.

Hopkins, Joseph M. Go from Me.

——————. If Thou Must Love Me.

Hudson, H. The Pied Piper. A cantata for ladies' voices in two parts, with soli for mezzo soprano and contralto. Tonic Sol-Fa Edition. London: J. Williams, 1914. BNP. E219

Hughes, Rupert. A Gondolier's Song. Key of A. Chicago: Lyon & Healey, 1892. BNP. E105

Inches, C. Summum Bonum. From Two Songs. Edinburgh: R. W. Pentland, 1908. BNP. E367

——————. Summum Bonum. Published alone. Edinburgh: R. W. Pentland, 1908. BNP. E367

Jervis-Read, H. V. My Mistress. From Two Ecstasies. London: Edwin Ashdown, n.d. BNP. E354

Jones, Abbie Errish. If I Were Thou.

Keep, Charles H. Rabbi Ben Ezra.

Kernochan, Marshall Rutgers. King Charles. Song for voice with piano. Revised edition. New York: Galaxy Music Corporation, 1933. G.M.613.

Land, B. J. He Giveth His Beloved Sleep. Boston Browning Society. Jan. 28, 1890.

Lawson, Malcolm. All June I Bound the Rose in Sheaves. London Browning Society, n.d. *Poet-Lore,* I, 431 (1889).

——————. Is She Not Pure Gold. London Browning Society. June 29, 1883. *Poet-Lore,* I, 431 (1889).

——————. My Mistress. London Browning Society. June 29, 1883.

——————. Nay, but You Who Do Not Love Her. *Poet-Lore,* I, 431 (1889). London Browning Society, n.d.

——————. One Way of Love. London Browning Society. June 29, 1883. *Poet-Lore,* I, 431 (1889).

——————. You'll Love Me Yet. London Browning Society. June 29, 1883. *Poet-Lore,* I, 431 (1889).

Lehmann, Liza. Incident of the French Camp. New York: Chappell & Co., 1909. BNP. E120

Leith, (Miss) L. von der. Third Verse of Epilogue Asolando. Los Angeles Browning Society. March, 1917.

Levey, Sivori. The Boy and the Angel. Narrative opera. Journal of the "Robert Browning Guild," I, 1, 2.

——————. The Pied Piper of Hamelin. Incidental music. Journal of the "Robert Browning Guild," I, 1, 2.

Lewis, Mrs. Leo. Grow Old Along with Me. Boston Browning Society. March 17, 1914.

Lidgey, C. A. Women and Roses. A choral setting of Robert Browning's poem with accompaniment for orchestra. Second edition. London: Pitt & Hatzfeld, 1891. BNP. E417

Loomis, H. W. Morning Song. Key of E. Newton Center, Mass.: Wa-Wan Press, 1902. BNP. E286

Loughridge, Jean. Pippa's Song. Published separately. Boston: O. Ditson. BNP. E287

Mackenzie, A. C. Serenade from A Blot [in the 'Scutcheon]. London: Novello, Ewer & Co., 1885. BNP. E13

——————. There's a Woman. Key of D. London: H. W. Gray Co., n.d. BNP. E14

Marshall, Mrs. Julian. On the First of the Feast of the Feasts. From *Dramatis Personae* . . . Epilogue. Boston Browning Society. Oct. 31, 1890.

Marzials, Theo. Give Her but a Least Excuse. London: Boosey & Co., 1886. BNP. E289

——————. Pippa Passes. London: Boosey & Co., 1886.

Matthews, Richard H. The Pied Piper. Cantata for tenor and bass soloists, chorus, and orchestra. London, New York: Ewer & Co.

Mokrejs, J. You'll Love Me Yet. Key of E-flat. New York: The Author, 1907. BNP. E292

Moor, C. W. [Two songs based on lyrics by EBB]. W. H. Gray Company. Letter; Oct. 22, 1934; ABL; Music Correspondence.

Neidlinger, W. H. Thy Face. Key of A-flat. For baritone or mezzo-soprano. From Two Songs. Cincinnati: G. B. Jennings. BNP. E392

Nessler, Victor. The Pied Piper of Hamelin. Opera. 1879.

Nevin, E. The Wedding Morn. Key of G. For high voice with piano accompaniment. New York: G. Schirmer, [1909]. BNP. E295

——————. The Wedding Morn. Key of G-flat. For high voice with piano accompaniment. New York: G. Schirmer, [1909]. BNP. E295

Oldroyd, G. Tresses. New York: G. Ricordi, 1924. BNP. E355

——————. Tresses. New York: Galaxy Music Corp., 1924. BNP. E355

Orth, John. On Horseback. Boston Browning Society. May 7, 1924.

Parry, Charles Hubert Hastings. I Believe It from Browning's Saul. For bass and organ. London, 1912.

——————. The Pied Piper. For tenor and bass soli, chorus, and orchestra. London: Novello & Co., 1905. BNP. E224

——————. The Pied Piper. For tenor and bass soli, chorus, and orchestra. London: Novello & Co., 1924. BNP. E224

——————. The Pied Piper. For tenor and bass soli, chorus, and orchestra. Piano score with string parts. London: Novello & Co., 1905. BNP. E224

——————. The Pied Piper. For tenor and bass soli, chorus, and orchestra. Separate chorus parts. London: Novello & Co., 1906. BNP. E224

——————. The Pied Piper. For tenor and bass soli, chorus, and orchestra. Tonic Sol-Fa notation. London: Novello & Co., 1906. BNP. E224

——————. Saul. Anthem for solo voice with organ. *Fellowship* (May 15, 1912).

Pascal, J. Ah, Love, but a Day. Key of D. For medium voice. Boston: Oliver Ditson Co., 1901. BNP. E134

Ralston, Frances Marion. A King Lived Long Ago. Pasadena Browning Club. May 8, 1924.

Rathbone, G. The Pied Piper. For soprano solo and chorus. London: Novello & Co., 1920. BNP. E228

——————. The Pied Piper. For soprano solo and chorus. Tonic Sol-Fa edition. London: Novello & Co., 1924. BNP. E228

Reed, Frank L. Daybreak. From Pippa Passes. New York Browning Society. Jan. 13, 1915.

Rogers, Clara Kathleen. Prospice. Twentieth-Century Club; Corsicana, Texas; Jan. 17, 1924. Athenean Club; Amarillo, Texas; May 7, 1931.

——————. Thy Face. Los Angeles Browning Society. Nov., 1916.

——————. A Woman's Last Word. Key of C. London: Novello & Co., 1919. BNP. E415

——————. The Year's at [the Spring]. Boston: A. P. Schmidt, 1882. BNP. E304

Rogers, James H. Give a Rouse. Los Angeles Browning Society. Feb., 191[7].

Romelli. At Parting.

Ross, Gertrude. Paracelsus. Los Angeles Browning Society. Letter; May 17, 1933; ABL; Music Correspondence.

Salter, Mary Turner. To the Souls of Fire. New York Browning Society. Jan. 28, 1927.

Schmidt, L. All's Right [with the World]. Key of D-flat. New York: William Maxwell Music Co., 1907. BNP. E307

Schuyler, Georgina. Give Her but a Least Excuse to Love Me. Pasadena Browning Club. May 8, 1924.

——————. The Page Sings to the Queen. For mezzo soprano. From Songs from . . . English and American Poets. New York: G. Schirmer, 1882. BNP. E308

——————. This Is a Spray. For mezzo soprano. From Songs from English and American Poets. New York: G. Schirmer, 1882. BNP. E165

Scott. The Unforeseen. New York Browning Society. May 13, 1925.

Shapleigh, B. Oh to Be in England. From Three English Songs for Contralto or Baritone. Leipzig: Breitkopf und Härtel, 1907. BNP. E86

Sharpe, C. The Year's at [the Spring]. Boston: Boston Music Co.
BNP. E309

Shenk, Louis. Robert Browning. Words by Flora Warren Brown.

Shillington, Mary. Apparitions. New York: E. Schubert[h], 1902.
BNP. E397

Sibelius, Jean. Confessional. Music for ballet by Walter Gore.

Smith, A. A. How Do I Love Thee. Newark: Savoy Music Co., c1962.

Somervell, Arthur. James Lee's Wife. For contralto solo and orchestra.
Song cycle selected from the poem, etc. London: Boosey & Co.,
1907. BNP. E137

Spencer, Frederick. All's Blue. From "At the 'Mermaid.'" San Francisco Browning Society. Oct. 13, 1916.

Spier, L. A Cycle of Songs from Pippa Passes. New York: Carl
Fischer, 1940. BNP. E311

Staat. Round Us the Wild Creatures. New York Browning Society.
May 15, 1940.

Stahleschmidt, Arthur Edward. How Do I Love Thee. Letter. July 15,
1940. ABL. Music Correspondence.

Stratton, G. R. Boot, Saddle, [to Horse, and Away]. For medium
voice. London: Murdoch, Murdoch & Co., 1929. BNP. E50

A Supplication for Love. From Old British Hymnal. Based on words
by EBB. H. W. Gray Co.

Thayer, A. W. Nay, but You. From Three Songs. Boston: H. B.
Stevens Co., 1893. BNP. E357

Thomas, Adelaide L. Prospice. [Sussex]: Brighton, Scientific Training School for Pianists, [1910]. BNP. E333

Thomas, Edith Lovell, adaptor and harmonizer. The Year's at the Spring.
Carol. Edith Lovell Thomas c1962.

Toye, F. Nay, but You [Who Do Not Love Her]. From Songs. London: Elkins & Co., n.d. BNP. E358

True, L. Abt Vogler. For high voice and piano. Accompanied reading.
From Browning Songs. Portland, [Maine]: Cressey & Allen, 1932.

——————. Give Her but the Least Excuse to Love Me. Portland,
[Maine]: Cressey & Allen, 1943. BNP. E313

——————. Prospice. For high voice and piano. From Browning
Songs. Portland, [Maine]: Cressey & Allen, 1932. BNP. E335

Vogler, Le Abbe [George Johann]. The Echo.

Walthew, R. H.   The Pied Piper.   For tenor and bass soli, chorus, and orchestra.   London: Novello & Co., 1893.   BNP.   E231

The Ways of Love.   New York Browning Society.   Nov. 20, 1912.

White, Grace.   Home Thoughts from Abroad.   For violin and piano. From Three Descriptions from Browning.   New York: G. Schirmer, 1919.   BNP.   E87

—————.   Meeting at Night.   For violin and piano.   From Three Descriptions from Browning.   New York: G. Schirmer, 1919.   BNP. E160

—————.   Parting at Morning.   For violin and piano.   From Three Descriptions from Browning.   New York: G. Schirmer, 1919. BNP.   E196

White, Maude Valerie.   In Memoriam.

[Wiant, Bliss, editor].   Then Welcome Each Rebuff.   From Christian Fellowship Hymns.   Peiping, [China]: Yenching University, 1931. BNP.   E336

Wickins, Florence.   Oh to Be in England.   Duet for mezzo soprano and baritone.   London: J. B. Cramer & Co.   BNP.   E89

Wilson, A.   Oh to Be in England.   Brighton and Hove, Lyon and Hall, 1908.   BNP.   E90

Worth, J. W.   Evelyn Hope.   Key of C.   New York: G. M. Schirmer, n.d.   BNP.   E69

—————.   Pisgah Sights.   New York Browning Society.   Nov. 11, 1914.

Bibliography

Books

Apel, Willi. *Harvard Dictionary of Music.* 2nd edition, revised and enlarged. Cambridge: The Bellknap Press of Harvard University Press, 1969.

The Ascap Biographical Dictionary of Composers, Authors and Publishers. Compiled and edited by The Lynn Farnol Group, Inc. New York: The American Society of Composers, Authors and Publishers, 1966.

The Ascap Biographical Dictionary of Composers, Authors and Publishers. Edited by David McNamara. New York: Thomas Y. Crowell Company, 1948.

Baker's Biographical Dictionary of Musicians. 4th edition by Paul Pisk. New York: G. Schirmer, Inc., 1940.

Baker's Biographical Dictionary of Musicians. 5th edition revised by Nicolas Slonimsky. New York: G. Schirmer, 1958.

Bernhardt, William F., editor. *Granger's Index to Poetry.* 5th edition, revised and enlarged. Morningside Heights, New York: Columbia University Press, 1962.

Bowlin, William R., compiler and editor. *A Book of Living Poems.* Chicago: Albert Whitman & Company, 1934.

Broughton, Leslie Nathan; Northup, Clark Sutherland; and Pearsall, Robert, compilers. *Robert Browning: A Bibliography, 1830-1950.* Ithaca: Cornell University Press, 1953.

Browning, Elizabeth Barrett. *Last Poems.* London: Chapman and Hall, 1862.

__________. *Poems.* 4th edition. London: Chapman & Hall, 1856. I-III.

Browning, Robert. *Asolando: Fancies and Facts.* London: Smith, Elder, & Co., 1894.

__________. *The Poetical Works of Robert Browning.* London: Smith, Elder, & Co., 1889. I-XVI.

Champlin, Jr., John Denison, editor. *Cyclopedia of Music and Musicians.* Critically edited by William Foster Apthorp. New York: Charles Scribner's Sons, 1888 and 1890. I and III.

Ewen, David, compiler and editor. *American Composers Today.* New York: The H. W. Wilson Company, 1949.

——————. *Composers of Today.* 2nd edition. New York: The H. W. Wilson Company, 1936.

Felleman, Hazel, compiler. *The Best Loved Poems of the American People.* Garden City: Garden City Publishing Co., 1936.

Griffin, W. Hall. *The Life of Robert Browning.* Completed and edited by Harry Christopher Minchin, editor. London: Methuen & Co. Ltd., 1910.

Grove's Dictionary of Music and Musicians. Edited by Eric Blom. 5th edition. New York: St. Martin's Press, Inc., 1955. I-III, V, VIII.

Grove's Dictionary of Music and Musicians. Edited by H. C. Colles. 3rd edition. New York: The Macmillan Company, 1937. I-V.

Hall, James Husst. *The Art Song.* Norman: University of Oklahoma Press, 1953.

Hewlett, Dorothy. *Elizabeth Barrett Browning.* London: Cassell and Company Ltd., 1953.

Howard, John Tasker. *Our American Music.* 3rd edition, revised and enlarged by James Lyons. New York: Thomas Y. Crowell Company, 1954.

Hull, Arthur Eaglefield, editor. *A Dictionary of Modern Music and Musicians.* New York: E. P. Dutton & Co., 1924.

International Who's Who in Music and Musical Gazetteer. Edited by César Saerchinger. New York: Current Literature Publishing Company, 1918.

Kenyon, Frederic G., editor. *New Poems by Robert Browning and Elizabeth Barrett Browning.* London: Smith, Elder, & Co., 1914.

The Letters of Robert Browning and Elizabeth Barrett Barrett. Reprint of the 2 volume Smith, Elder & Co. 1899 edition in one volume. London: John Murray, 1923.

Miller, Betty. *Robert Browning, a Portrait.* New York: Charles Scribner's Sons, 1953.

The New Century Cyclopedia of Names. Edited by Clarence L. Barnhart with the assistance of William D. Halsey. New York: Appleton-Century-Crofts, Inc., 1954. II.

Nisbet, Ola Jones, editor. *Browning's Pippa Passes.* Charlotte, N. C.: Presbyterian Standard Publishing Co., 1929.

Pratt, Waldo Selden, editor. *The New Encyclopedia of Music and Musicians.* New York: The Macmillan Company, 1924.

Scholes, Percy A. *The Oxford Companion to Music.* 9th edition, revised. London: Oxford University Press, 1956.

Stevens, Denis, editor. *A History of Song.* New York: W. W. Norton & Company, Inc., 1960.

Taylor, Bernard, editor. *Songs in English, Nineteen Contemporary Settings by American and English Composers.* New York: Carl Fischer, Inc., 1970.

Thompson, Oscar, editor. *The International Cyclopedia of Music and Musicians.* 4th edition, revised and enlarged by Nicolas Slonimsky, editor. New York: Dodd, Mead & Company, 1946.

——————. *The International Cyclopedia of Music and Musicians.* 7th edition, revised by Nicolas Slonimsky, editor. New York: Dodd, Mead & Company, 1956.

——————. *The International Cyclopedia of Music and Musicians.* 9th edition by Robert Sabin, editor. New York: Dodd, Mead & Company, 1964.

Webster's New Collegiate Dictionary. Springfield, Mass.: G. & C. Merriam Co., Publishers, 1959.

Who Is Who in Music. Chicago: Lee Stern Press, 1941.

Who Was Who in America. Chicago: The A. N. Marquis Company, 1943. I.

Who's Who. Edited by Albert Nelson Marquis. Chicago: A. N. Marquis & Company, 1914. VIII.

Who's Who in Music and Musicians International Directory. Edited by Peter Townend, managing editor, and David Simmons, editor. 4th edition. London: Burke's Peerage Limited, 1962.

Who's Who of American Women. 5th edition. Chicago: The A. N. Marquis Company, Incorporated, 1968-1969.

Wier, Albert E., editor. *The Macmillan Encyclopedia of Music and Musicians.* New York: The Macmillan Company, 1938.

Newspapers and Periodicals

Baylor University *Lariat.* Article, January 19, 1929.

Baylor University *Lariat.* Article, March 13, 1930.

Boston *Republican.* Article, July 26, 1924.

Cleveland *Press.* Review, December 29, 1933.

Lynn, Massachusetts *Daily Evening Item.* Article, December 21, 1929.

New Orleans *Times-Picayune*. Article, [December —, 1929 or January —, 1930].

Roberts, W. Wright. "Music in Browning." *Music & Letters,* XVII, 3 (July, 1936), 237-48.

Unpublished Materials

Armstrong Browning Library. Music Correspondence.

Armstrong Browning Library. Picture Collection.

Baylor University. School of Music. Records.

Cleveland Symphony. Program, December, 1933.

Colvin, Jr., (Otis) Herbert. Biographical data sheet.

Jones, Janice. "Browning and Music." Unpublished M.A. thesis, Baylor University, 1930.

McDaniel, William J. Biographical data sheet.

Markham, Robert A. Biographical data sheet.

Moore, Willa Lee Clements. "The Baylor University Collection of the Musical Settings of the Poetry of Robert Browning." Unpublished M.M. thesis, Baylor University, 1951.

Passailaigue, Mary Flournoy. Biographical data sheet.

Reid, Robert A. "An Analysis of Selected Solo Songs Set to Poems of Robert Browning, As Found in the Armstrong-Browning Library of Baylor University." Unpublished M.M. thesis, Baylor University, 1970.

Robbins, Adolph. "Composers Who Have Set Browning's Poetry to Music." Undocumented biographical data, 1940. Armstrong Browning Library. Vertical File. (Typewritten.)

Wiant, William Robert. Biographical data sheet.